The Politics of Global Regulation

The Politics of Global Regulation

Edited by
Walter Mattli and Ngaire Woods

PRINCETON UNIVERSITY PRESS

PRINCETON AND OXFORD

Copyright © 2009 by Princeton University Press

Requests for permission to reproduce material from this work should be sent to
Permissions, Princeton University Press

Published by Princeton University Press, 41 William Street,
Princeton, New Jersey 08540

In the United Kingdom: Princeton University Press, 6 Oxford Street,
Woodstock, Oxfordshire OX20 1TW

All Rights Reserved

Library of Congress Cataloging-in-Publication Data

The politics of global regulation / Edited by Walter Mattli and Ngaire Woods.
p.   cm.
Includes bibliographical references and index.
ISBN 978-0-691-13960-9 (hardcover : alk. paper)
ISBN 978-0-691-13961-6 (pbk. : alk. paper)
1. Foreign trade regulation. 2. International trade. 3. International economic
integration. I. Mattli, Walter. II. Woods, Ngaire.
K3943.P65 2009
343′.087—dc22
2008035344

British Library Cataloging-in-Publication Data is available

This book has been composed in Sabon

Printed on acid-free paper. ∞

press.princeton.edu

Printed in the United States of America

10   9   8   7   6   5   4   3   2   1

Contents

CHAPTER EIGHT
Economic Integration and Global Governance:
Why So Little Supranationalism?

Figures and Tables

Introduction

Walter Mattli and Ngaire Woods

JUST AS OUR PROJECT on the Politics of Global Regulation was nearing its conclusion, a global financial crisis erupted. It began with the rapid increase of defaults in subprime mortgages in the United States and a few other countries and quickly spread across highly intertwined financial markets, affecting millions of people. What went wrong? Who is to blame?

Broadly speaking, two related factors explain the latest global financial fiasco: inadequate regulation that generated a mismatch between private reward and public risk; and failure of regulators to comply with their supervisory duties.

Global banking regulation has been inadequate. Banks have long lobbied against more robust regulation, and they have been successful. The existing rules—the Basel II capital adequacy framework—allow large banks to use their own models for risk assessment in determining the minimum amount of regulatory capital to buffer against unexpected losses. The result has been rules that create a perverse incentive to underestimate credit risk; banks were tempted to be overoptimistic about their risk exposure in order to minimize required regulatory capital and maximize return on equity.

Regulatory oversight has also been inadequate. Regulators have taken a highly relaxed attitude toward oversight. They bought into the banks' arguments that complex derivative instruments improve risk management and distribution as well as enhance market efficiency and resilience. They outsourced critical regulatory functions to private-sector credit rating agencies. However, whereas in the past, rating agencies sold their assessments of financial instruments to investors, they now were being paid handsomely by the very banks whose securitized products they were rating, posing a serious conflict of interest.

The fallout of the financial crisis is staggering and still unfolding. While governments pour public money into shoring up the banking system, they and their regulators—under tremendous public pressure—are also compiling long lists of measures they pledge to implement to fix the global financial regulatory system. These measures include constraints on complex securitized financing through the adoption of global standards for valuation and disclosure, deeper capital cushions and enhanced supervision of investment banks and other nonbanking institutions, changes in the operation of rating agencies, and enhanced internationally coordinated scrutiny of global banks and brokerages.

Financial institutions are likely to fight tooth and nail against the adoption of most of these proposals. What then would it take to translate the aspiration for a more effective global regulatory regime into reality in finance and beyond? This is precisely the kind of question that this book seeks to address.

The first chapter sets out a framework for analyzing whether changes in global regulation are likely to occur and with what impact. Walter Mattli and Ngaire Woods contrast regulatory change that benefits narrow vested interests (as a result of "capture" by those whose actions the regulation is supposed to control) with regulatory change that achieves wider public purposes (common interest regulation). They then probe the conditions under which a global regulatory outcome is more likely to favor broad as opposed to narrow interests and vice versa. They highlight the institutional context within which regulation takes place. The more open, accessible, transparent, and accountable the process, the less prone it will be to capture. That said, while some rules are formulated in open and transparent negotiations, the implementation of the rules may subsequently be delegated to far less open, transparent, or accountable agencies, heightening the risks of capture.

Mattli and Woods argue that common interest regulation cannot be assured even in a formally open institutional context unless so-called demand-side conditions are satisfied. First is information. Without proper information on deficiencies and biases of the regulatory status quo, negatively affected constituencies will have no motivation to demand change. Disasters or demonstrations of failure can reveal to the public the negative externalities of no or poor regulation, triggering a demand for better regulation. But actual change will require at least two other conditions to be in place, one relating to (converging) interests of key actors and the other to ideas.

Change is a protracted battle pitting potential winners and losers and fought over multiple stages as the detail of regulation is negotiated, then implemented, monitored, and enforced. Change requires the sustained support of "entrepreneurs" offering technical expertise, financial resources, and an organizational platform if it is to succeed. Entrepreneurs know how to capitalize on a crisis or failure; they may be public officials, nongovernmental groups, or private-sector actors. The latter group has often been ignored. Yet private-sector actors may become powerful entrepreneurs for regulatory change if they are suffering from existing regulation either as corporate consumers of poorly regulated services or products; as newcomers to an industry whose regulation has been captured by established firms; as firms at risk from the negative publicity and fallout from an industry disaster; or from the fact that other firms with whom they must compete are not on a level playing field.

Entrepreneurs will be most successful in changing regulation where they can form a broad coalition against defenders of the regulatory status quo. To this end, a shared set of new ideas about how to regulate will often be crucial. When a disaster or failure triggers change, it also undermines the legitimacy of the ideas that supported the old order, opening up space for a battle over competing alternative ideas. Successful change is made more likely where new ideas provide a way to regulate that both offers a common ground to a coalition of entrepreneurs pressing for change and fits well with not-discredited existing institutions.

Chapter 2 develops the theoretical framework offered in the first chapter in three important ways. First, Kenneth Abbott and Duncan Snidal more systematically elaborate the five stages of the regulatory process: agenda-setting, negotiation, implementation, monitoring, and enforcement (ANIME). Their more detailed depiction of the regulatory process permits them to proceed to a second important contribution. They systematize the different competencies required for institutions effectively to discharge each of the five tasks. For example, whereas representativeness is vital at the negotiation stage, independence and operational capacity are more important for effective monitoring and enforcement. A third important way in which Abbott and Snidal take forward the analysis is through their exploration of a new emerging trend in transnational regulation which they describe as "regulatory standard-setting" (RSS). The process they describe involves combinations of firms, states, and nongovernmental organizations acting together as partners to promulgate norms or voluntary standards. They argue that these processes are emerging precisely because the different competencies of states, firms, and NGOs are required at each stage of the regulatory process. They draw their argument together in a "governance triangle" which depicts the variations across different RSS schemes that emerge as a result of different combinations of states, firms, and NGOs. Their interest in RSS stems from the observation that there is dramatically less regulatory control over transnational production than over domestic production, even as transnational production increases. One major issue they consider is whether RSS schemes, and the larger context in which they operate, can serve broad societal interests rather than being captured by particular interests. They find that states retain the authority to indirectly shape RSS processes involving firms and NGOs to ensure socially desirable outcomes. The likely effectiveness of such arrangements is probed further in chapter 5, which examines six cases of such new regulatory arrangements.

Chapter 3 presents the first of several case studies that illuminate the ways particular actors shape regulatory outcomes through their engagement at different stages of the regulatory process, their access to information, their capacity to lobby, their ideas for reform, and the institutional setting within which they participate. Eric Helleiner examines two international initiatives that have brought the restructuring of sovereign debts owed to private foreign creditors under new forms of regulation. Since 2003, almost all new international bond issues have come to include collective-action clauses, and an international code of conduct to govern sovereign bond restructuring episodes has been endorsed by the leading representatives of private creditors and public authorities in both emerging market and creditor countries. The process of regulatory change was initiated by the international financial crises of the mid- to late 1990s which demonstrated very publicly the costs associated with the old bailout model of handling sovereign debt crises. U.S. officials, key sovereign debtors, and lead private creditor groups then acted as "entrepreneurs" pressing the case for the new regulatory initiatives, particularly after the 2001 Argentine crisis demonstrated the costs of the absence of regulation in the post-bailout world. They succeeded in mobilizing a powerful pro-change coalition of private creditor interests, sovereign debtors, and financial officials in creditor states who were driven by a range of normative, distributional, and strategic motivations. The result was a regulatory standard-setting scheme akin to that described by Abbott and Snidal in chapter 2. At its core are voluntary principles agreed upon by a small group of partners from both the private and the public sectors. The theoretical framework of this book highlights that the likely weakness of the scheme lies in the limited and nontransparent procedures for implementation and enforcement which make it vulnerable to capture unless two sets of conditions emerge: first, that the procedures are opened up to public scrutiny; and second, that in the face of a crisis (such as that which began in 2007), a powerful and sustained demand for effective implementation and enforcement emerges, drawing together powerful actors, reinforced by a set of ideas that present an alternative to the previous regulation.

In chapter 4, Kathryn Sikkink analyzes the emergence of a new regulatory model in the treatment of human rights violations. In the period after the Second World War, the regulation of human rights was dominated by a state accountability model. In other words, states agreed on self-restraining rules among themselves through international treaties and the like. However, the enforcement of these rules was very weak. More recently, a new regulatory model of individual legal criminal accountability for human rights violations has emerged. Catalyzing the new, more effective regulation were the manifest failures of the old model such as in the Balkans and Rwanda. Human rights activists joined with like-minded states in pushing the new idea of individual criminal accountability, borrowed from the domestic criminal system. This change is too recent to measure its impact with any certainty, but the dramatic increase in human rights trials in the world and their geographical spread suggest that the individual criminal accountability model will not be easily reversed. The theoretical framework of the book highlights several conditions likely to affect this prognosis. First, as Sikkink points out, the new regulatory model has emerged in countries with a participatory and open institutional context. Second, the demand for human rights regulation has been pushed by a coalition of actors including some of those who supported the previous "impunity" model. However, the emergence of a new alternative set of ideas about restorative justice is now drawing some of those supporters away, creating a competing model of regulation which could harness key actors in the coalition that successfully promulgated the rise of individual criminal responsibility.

In chapter 6, Sam Barrows examines the dramatic changes that have taken place in global shipping regulation since the 1970s, including the passage of dozens of international conventions in shipping and the creation in many countries of effective monitoring and enforcement mechanisms. The catalyst for better regulation has been a series of maritime disasters that highlighted increasing risks as tankers become larger, faster, and more numerous. In 1967, the *Torrey Canyon* ran aground, causing the largest pollution incident ever recorded. Subsequent disasters, such as the sinking of the *Herald of Free Enterprise* and the grounding of the *Amoco Cadiz*, have spurred further refinements to regulation. In the wake of each disaster, a powerful pro-change coalition of public entrepreneurs, including influential environmental NGOs and well-resourced private-sector entrepreneurs (most notably insurance companies and classification societies), have pushed for better regulation. Even shipowners who benefited from little regulation reversed themselves when they realized that stringent new global standards and strict domestic-level enforcement in some regions would disadvantage them unless the standards became global (and therefore equally constrained all of their competition). That said, global regulatory effectiveness will depend upon "flag states" and "port states" enforcing the rules. The theoretical framework of the book highlights that this will depend upon both the institutional context in these countries and the sustained demand for regulatory change. As Barrows notes, in many developing countries, demand factors are weak as is the institutional context, limiting the likely effectiveness of global shipping regulation.

In chapter 5, David Vogel explores cases of the type of regulation conceptualized by Abbott and Snidal in chapter 2. In contrast to global shipping regulation, which is a state-centered system of rule-making, implementation, and enforcement, Vogel examines the emergence of "civil regulation" or transnational business governance associated with corporate social responsibility. He highlights that civil regulation has emerged because states have failed to regulate nationally or internationally issues of public concern such as labor and human rights, animal protection, or environmental standards. This failure has led policy entrepreneurs (NGOs often supported by some national governments and international organizations) to persuade firms to forge their own collectively self-restraining rules. The entrepreneurs have effectively challenged the idea behind previously existing regulatory arrangements; the idea that it is legitimate for corporations to be concerned purely with their private business has been replaced with the view that corporations have social responsibilities. This has created a highly visible and increasingly legitimate dimension of global economic governance, shifting the boundaries of what is considered "appropriate'" behavior for firms, NGOs, and states. That said, inadequate mechanisms of enforcement and accountability mean that the impact of civil regulation is both limited and uneven. Put in terms of the theoretical framework of the book, civil regulation lacks sufficient economic and political "demand" for more responsible global corporate conduct on the part of both firms and governments.

Shifting the focus from the demand side of global regulation to the institutional context within which regulatory processes take place, in chapter 7 Judith Goldstein and Richard Steinberg examine rule-making in international trade. Their study explores the shift away from rule-setting through a negotiated legislative process in the General Agreement on Tariffs and Trade/World Trade Organization (GATT/WTO) associated with trade rounds. They argue that over the last fifteen years trade regulation has moved to a judicial process. The catalyst for this shift has been the failure of the trade talks and the new institutional context of the dispute settlement mechanism in the WTO. The failure of trade talks, including the current impasse in the Doha Round, has resulted from a regulatory system that permitted powerful protectionist interests to form in industrialized countries and into which developing nations, often speaking as a bloc, have exacerbated disjunctures in U.S. and European preferences on trade policy. The failure of the ministerial negotiating process has opened up space for public-sector entrepreneurs—the Appellate Body—to push for regulatory change. This shift is assisted by the fact that the same divisions that have undermined trade talks have made it increasingly difficult for the membership to provide a check on judicial lawmaking. Furthermore, the use of a robust dispute settlement mechanism has made public information about the costs of protectionism and has passed the burden of these costs on to exporters who may now face retaliatory actions in their main markets. The result pits the traditional coalition of national lawmakers and industries seeking protection against a new coalition of the Appellate Body judges, exporters, and other public and nongovernmental entrepreneurs who seek to use the more robust dispute settlement mechanism. Taken together, these developments suggest that we are entering a period of "judicial liberalization" at the WTO, led by the Appellate Body. This regulatory shift from the legislative to the judicial has increased the efficiency of the organization and enhanced open trade by freeing member states from capture by entrenched domestic interests. The argument underscores the influence of institutional context on global regulation, specifically by providing incentives and a forum within which reformers can demand more effective regulation.

In the final chapter of the book, Miles Kahler and David Lake reflect more broadly on the institutional context of global regulation, assessing the implications of emerging forms of global governance for the politics of global regulation. Existing economic models of international governance, they argue, would lead us to expect increasing supranationalism in global regulation as states pool decision-making powers and delegate implementation and enforcement. Yet this has not occurred in the past quarter-century. First, this is because two other modes of international governance exist: hierarchy, in which states transfer regulatory authority to dominant states for certain limited purposes, and networks, in which states, private actors, or both share regulatory authority through coordinated and repeated interaction. Hierarchies and networks serve as functional substitutes for supranational delegation to international institutions. This leads to a second reason why there is less supranationalism than predicted by economic models. The range of institutional contexts (supranationalism, hierarchy, and networks) creates a politics of its own. Actors will seek to influence which institutional form is chosen so as to advance their interests, which may be narrow, rent-seeking interests or broader, "public interest" rationales. The different institutional forms vary in their impact on distributional conflicts, the distribution of preferences, and the pattern of governance at the national level. Framed in this way, it becomes apparent that informal networks (or purely national governance) will be preferred by secure, concentrated interests who enjoy regulatory capture at the national level. Supranationalism does not appear to offer any inherent bias for or against regulatory capture relative to hierarchies or networks. Hierarchy will reflect politically powerful interests in the dominant state.

In conclusion, the editors of this book would like to acknowledge generous financial support without which the project would have been impossible. Support for the project was provided through the Global Economic Governance Programme at University College, Oxford University, for which thanks go both to the College and to the John T. and Catherine D. MacArthur Foundation and the International Development Research Centre. Walter Mattli also gratefully acknowledges the support of the British Academy which granted him a Research Leave Fellowship. He also thanks St. John's College of Oxford University for research and financial support. This was a genuinely collaborative project, and the patience and active engagement of all the authors made it immensely fruitful. We are indebted to many other colleagues for their support, comments, and contributions to the project including Guy Goodwin-Gill, Andrew Hurrell, Vijay Joshi, Dan Kelemen, Robert Mabro, Kalypso Nicolaidis, Louis Pauly, Beth Simmons, David Victor, Jennifer Welsh, Mark Zacher, and the excellent work of Chuck Myers and his team at Princeton University Press.

The Politics of Global Regulation

CHAPTER ONE

In Whose Benefit? Explaining Regulatory Change in Global Politics

Walter Mattli and Ngaire Woods

FEW TOPICS ARE as central and of consequence to the lives and well-being of individuals as regulation, broadly defined as the organization and control of economic, political, and social activities by means of making, implementing, monitoring, and enforcing of rules. Regulation is increasingly global as elements of the regulatory process have migrated to international or transnational actors in areas as diverse as trade, finance, the environment, and human rights. This trend has triggered a fierce debate among economists about the impact of global regulation. On one side, Joseph Stiglitz argues that the rules of the game have been set largely by advanced industrial countries, and in particular by special interests within these countries. "[N]ot surprisingly, they have shaped globalization to further their own interests. They have not sought to create a fair set of rules, let alone a set of rules that would promote the well-being of those in the poorest countries of the world."[1] He adds darkly, "[t]hose who benefit from the current system will resist change, and they are very powerful."[2]

A different view proposes that global regulation helps to break down inefficient and discriminatory domestic regulatory schemes as well as old-fashioned value systems subservient to the interests of corrupt national elites. As Jagdish Bhagwati put it, "[Anti-globalization] protesters do not adequately appreciate that, as has been documented by numerous development economists who have studied both the working of controls and the rise of corruption in developing countries, far too many bureaucrats

For helpful comments, we thank Ken Abbott, Sam Barrows, Morten Broberg, Tim Büthe, Paul Craig, Deborah Davenport, Rodney Bruce Hall, Eric Helleiner, Vijay Joshi, Miles Kahler, David Lake, Kate MacDonald, Kalypso Nicolaidis, Lou Pauley, Kathryn Sikkink, Duncan Snidal, Richard Steinberg, Jennifer Tobin, David Vogel, and two anonymous reviewers.

[1] Joseph Stiglitz, *Making Globalization Work: The Next Steps to Global Justice* (London: Penguin Books, 2006), 3; see also Joseph Stiglitz, *Globalization and Its Discontents* (New York: Norton, 2002).

[2] Stiglitz, *Making Globalization Work*, 13.

impose senseless restrictions just to collect bribes or to exercise power. Letting markets function is therefore often an egalitarian allocation mechanism."[3] This more optimistic view assumes that global regulation is less susceptible to capture; technocrats at the international level can get on and do their job without having to bother about rent-seekers. This theme is echoed by some international legal scholars who argue that governments risk becoming "prisoners of the sirene-like pressures of organized interest groups unless they follow the wisdom of Ulysses (when his boat approached the island of the Sirens) and tie their hands to the mast of international guarantees."[4] In short, the key difference between the critics and optimists is that whereas the former argue that global regulation intensifies the capture problem, the latter view it as an effective remedy.

Given the prominence of these debates, it is surprising that no sustained attempt has been undertaken in the field of international relations (IR) to take stock of the broad picture of the politics of global regulation by systematically tackling questions such as: What major global regulatory changes have taken place in key issue-areas over the past few decades and what drove these changes? What institutional forums are selected for regulatory activities and what explains these choices? How is compliance monitored and enforced? Who are the winners and losers of global regulation and why? What explains variation across issue-areas?[5] Although economists and political scientists have explored similar questions at a national level, few have attempted to address them at the global level.

We distinguish global regulation from domestic regulation in terms of where the regulatory activity takes place. Recognizing that regulation is a process comprising several stages (including agenda-setting, negotiation, implementation, monitoring, and enforcement),[6] we emphasize that

[3] Jagdish Bhagwati, *In Defense of Globalization* (Oxford: Oxford University Press, 2004); see also Martin Wolf, *Why Globalization Works* (New Haven, CT: Yale University Press, 2004).

[4] Ernst-Ulrich Petersmann, "The Transformation of the World Trading System through the 1994 Agreement Establishing the World Trade Organization," *European Journal of International Law* 6 (1995), 161–221.

[5] These questions differ markedly from the focus on the implications to state sovereignty that have dominated analyses of the globalization of regulation; see Philip Cerny, "Globalization and the Erosion of Democracy," *European Journal of Political Research* 36, no. 1 (August 1999), 1–26; Susan Strange, *The Retreat of the State: The Diffusion of Power in the World Economy* (Cambridge: Cambridge University Press, 1996); Rodney Hall and Thomas Biersteker, eds., *The Emergence of Private Authority in Global Governance* (Cambridge: Cambridge University Press, 2002); Saskia Sassen, "Territory and Territoriality in the Global Economy," *International Sociology* 15, no. 2 (2000), 372–393.

[6] In their study in this project, Abbott and Snidal use the acronym ANIME to refer to these stages: Kenneth Abbott and Duncan Snidal, "The Governance Triangle: Regulatory Standards Institutions and the Shadow of the State," this volume.

global regulation does not necessarily imply a shift of the whole regulatory process to the global level. In some instances, formal negotiations are moved beyond the borders of the state where public and private actors cooperate in the setting of rules, while the other stages of regulation remain at the national level. For example, human rights standards have been negotiated internationally but their enforcement is taking place nationally. As documented by Kathryn Sikkink, some 88 percent of human rights trials have taken place in the domestic legal system of the country where the crime was committed, and only 4 percent of cases have been prosecuted in international tribunals.[7] A central point of our study is that a thorough assessment of the effectiveness of any piece of global regulation necessitates an examination of the politics at each stage of the regulatory process: what actors are in or out at key junctures, why, and with what distributional consequences?

Global regulation also differs from national regulation in the nature of rules being set. National regulation is primarily about hard rules, that is, laws made, implemented, and enforced by governments. By contrast, much of global regulation has traditionally been soft law, that is, voluntary standards, best practices, and their like.[8] Differences in the detail and quality of regulation at the global level may reflect differences in the way regulation is created and subsequently implemented. Soft law is often created by public-private or purely private networks to which no rule-making authority has been delegated.[9] Some such forums are small, secretive, and closed, whereas others are large, transparent, and inclusive. Over the last decade or so, governments have increasingly endorsed soft law issued by various forums, thereby hardening it and giving it real bite. Assessing global regulation thus also requires an analysis of the broader institutional context in which rules are produced and enforced.

We seek to fill some of the gap in the international relations literature by developing an analytical framework capable of assessing major regulatory changes at the global level. We illustrate the framework's central propositions with examples from a wide range of areas of global regulation.

---

[7] Kathryn Sikkink, "From State Responsibility to Individual Criminal Accountability: A New Regulatory Model for Core Human Rights Violations," this volume.

[8] Kenneth Abbott and Duncan Snidal, "Hard and Soft Law in International Governance," *International Organization* 54 (2000), 421–56; Walter Mattli, "The Politics and Economics of International Institutional Standards Setting: An Introduction," *Journal of European Public Policy* 8, no. 3 (June 2001), 328—344; Dieter Kerwer, "Rules that Many Use: Standards and Global Regulation," *Governance* 18, no. 4 (October 2005), 611–632.

[9] Claire Cutler, Virginia Haufler, and Tony Porter, *Private Authority and International Affairs* (Albany, NY: SUNY Press, 1999); Philipp Pattberg, "The Institutionalization of Private Governance: How Business and Nonprofit Organizations Agree on Transnational Rules," *Governance* 18, no. 4 (October 2005), 589–610.

Briefly summarized, our account of global regulatory change contrasts outcomes that do little more than entrench narrow interests (regulatory capture) and those that fulfill broader public purposes (common interest regulation). The theoretical framework we develop to explain shifts toward one or the other outcome focuses on the demand for regulation and how it is affected by varying institutional contexts. The institutions within which regulation takes place vary widely in openness and commitment to proper due process. Regulatory institutions that supply participatory mechanisms that are fair, transparent, accessible, and open (case of "extensive" institutional supply) are more likely to produce common interest regulation. That said, these are difficult conditions to fulfill in global politics. Even when extensive participatory mechanisms are in place, common interest regulation is not assured unless key demand-side conditions are satisfied; these can be summarized as "information, interests, and ideas."

First among demand-side factors is information. Without information on deficiencies and biases of the regulatory status quo, negatively affected constituencies will have no motivation to demand change. Disasters or demonstrations of failure can reveal to the public the negative externalities of no or poor regulation, triggering a demand for better regulation. But actual change will require at least two other conditions to be in place, one relating to (converging) interests of key actors and the other to ideas. Change is a protracted battle, pitting potential winners and losers and fought over multiple stages as the detail of regulation is negotiated, then implemented, monitored, and enforced. Change requires the sustained support of "entrepreneurs" offering technical expertise, financial resources, and an organizational platform if it is to succeed. Entrepreneurs know how to capitalize on a crisis or failure; they may be public officials, nongovernmental groups, or private-sector actors. The latter group has often been ignored. Yet private-sector actors may become powerful entrepreneurs for regulatory change if they are suffering from existing regulation either as corporate consumers of poorly regulated services or products; as newcomers to an industry whose regulation has been captured by established firms; as firms at risk from the negative publicity and fallout from an industry disaster; or from the fact that other firms with whom they must compete are not on a level playing field.

Entrepreneurs will be most successful in changing regulation where they can form a broad coalition against defenders of the status quo. To this end, a shared set of new ideas about how to regulate will often be crucial. When a disaster or failure triggers change, it also undermines the legitimacy of the ideas that supported the old order, opening up space for a battle over competing alternative ideas. Successful change is made more likely where new ideas provide a way to regulate that both offers a common ground to a coalition of entrepreneurs pressing for change and fits well with not-discredited existing institutions.

The main propositions that derive from our framework can be summarized as follows (see figure 1.1 on page 16): An intersection of limited institutional supply of global due process and weak demand for change because of suppressed information about the social cost of poor regulation or failure of other demand-side conditions will favor sustained regulatory capture. The emergence of broad societal demand for change in a context of extensive institutional supply will produce common interest regulation. Broad demand for change that has been shut out because of closed regulatory forums (i.e., limited institutional demand) may take to the street or engage in naming and shaming or other "pinprick" strategies in an effort to obtain regulatory concessions and compromises from capture actors. Finally, extensive institutional supply that is not met by broad demand because of failings on the demand side will also favor narrow interests rather than broader ones—the "haves" at the expense of the "have-nots." The result is de facto capture even though the institutional context may have been designed with the objective of serving the common interest.

BUILDING ON EXISTING EXPLANATIONS OF GLOBAL REGULATION

In considering the politics of global regulation, the wide-ranging analysis of the impact of globalization on business regulation offered by John Braithwaite and Peter Drahos is an important early contribution, influenced primarily by approaches and methods in sociology and anthropology.[10] More closely anchored in the field of international political economy, two other recent contributions stand out, one by Beth Simmons and the other by Daniel Drezner.

The work by Braithwaite and Drahos is remarkable not only for its many detailed and informative case studies, but also for its rich and wide-ranging conceptual discussions. Using examples from history and some five hundred interviews, Braithwaite and Drahos trace the complex ways in which contests involving multiple and sometimes conflicting principles (including transparency, reciprocity, rule compliance, and national sovereignty), various public and private actors, and diverse "mechanisms" (in-

---

[10] John Braithwaite and Peter Drahos, *Global Business Regulation* (Cambridge: Cambridge University Press, 2000). Another recent contribution, rooted in sociological institutionalism, is Marie-Laure Djelic and Kerstin Sahlin-Andersson, eds., *Transnational Governance: Institutional Dynamics of Regulation* (Cambridge: Cambridge University Press, 2006).

cluding coercion, rewards, and modeling) have produced very uneven outcomes in global regulation. While globalization has "ratcheted up" regulation concerning the environment, safety, and financial security, it has "ratcheted down" most economic regulation, with the powerful exception of intellectual property. Braithwaite and Drahos conclude that frequently globalization of regulation is a story of domination: "The global lawmakers today are the men who run the largest corporations, the U.S. and the EC."[11] However, they also provide many episodes where regulation has been successfully strengthened to protect communities from the abuse of corporate power, or where successful deregulation has reduced corporate monopoly power. Although the eclecticism of their approach is highly suggestive, Braithwaite and Drahos present in the end a rather unwieldy framework for analysis. It accommodates all possible influences on global regulation and excludes none. Our approach, by contrast, is anchored in the political economy tradition and seeks to bring some parsimony to explaining global regulation.

Simmons focuses more specifically on why particular modes of regulation are taken up by financial regulators in different countries. She examines regulation in four areas: capital adequacy, accounting, anti–money laundering, and information sharing among securities regulators.[12] Her analytical framework focuses on the strategic interaction between a hegemonic "regulatory innovator" and the rest of the world. The hegemon in finance is argued to be the United States; it is in a position unilaterally to change the context for financial markets worldwide. Regulators in other countries can choose to emulate new U.S. regulation or diverge.[13] If divergence is costly to the United States, in other words, it is a source of negative externality for the United States, then the hegemon will mobilize political pressure to coerce foreign regulators to fall in line with U.S. rules. Specifically, when the sources of externalities are distinct or the externality is divisible, the United States will target its pressure through unilateral action or bilateral agreement. When the source of externality is uncertain or shifting and thus not easy to target, the United States will create and back multilateral institutions to exert overt political pressure on diverging

[11] Braithwaite and Drahos, 629.

[12] Beth Simmons, "International Politics of Harmonization: The Case of Capital Market Regulation," *International Organization* 55 (Summer 2001), 589–620.

[13] If new hegemonic regulation renders nonconforming jurisdiction relatively costly or risky sites for conducting business, a logical competitive move for a regulator is to emulate hegemonic regulation to maintain or attract business. In the contrary case where new hegemonic regulation renders a nonconforming jurisdiction a more attractive site for business, the regulator of such jurisdiction may choose to diverge. Simmons, "International Politics of Harmonization," 596.

jurisdictions.[14] The Simmons account departs from the traditional "liberal functionalist formulations" of global cooperation. "There is nothing . . . Pareto-improving [in the account] . . . Regulators elsewhere may not even have been consulted or have participated in any meaningful way in decisions that fundamentally alter their regulatory landscape. Smaller financial centers may have to adjust decisions made by the U.S. to avoid worse outcomes, but many have preferred no innovation by the dominant center to begin with."[15]

Simmons's analysis is a highly valuable contribution to the study of global regulation. Nevertheless, it suffers from three limitations: First, as Simmons readily concedes, "[F]ew . . . areas of international activity [other than finance] are so profoundly dominated by only one or two countries." If finance is unlike most other areas and thus unrepresentative, we would expect the insights derived from studying regulation in this area to be of limited generalizability. Second, Simmons offers a theory not of the emergence but of the *diffusion* of a given regulatory model. "The framework . . . takes U.S. regulatory innovation itself as . . . exogenous."[16] In other words, the framework explains when and how U.S. financial regulation travels across jurisdictions; it does not explain the domestic political process by which such regulation comes about or changes in the first place. Finally, the impetus for global harmonization is assumed to be regulatory innovation in a dominant state—an assumption common in the literature on regulatory diffusion.[17] However, transnational regulation may emerge as the collective response by key actors—public or private—to a transnational problem or crisis.[18]

---

[14] When no externality is felt, the United States remains indifferent about whether the rest of the world follows its regulation.

[15] Simmons, "International Politics of Harmonization," 600.

[16] Ibid., 595.

[17] See, for example, Beth Simmons, Frank Dobbin, and Geoffrey Garrett, "Introduction: The International Diffusion of Liberalism," *International Organization* 60 (Fall 2006), 781–810; Duane Swank, "Tax Policy in an Era of Internationalization: Explaining the Spread of Neoliberalism," *International Organization* 60 (Fall 2006), 847–882; and Chang Kil Lee and David Strang, "The International Diffusion of Public-Sector Downsizing: Network Emulation and Theory-Driven Learning," *International Organization* 60 (Fall 2006), 883–909; see also David Levi-Faur and Jacint Jordana, *The Rise of Regulatory Capitalism: The Global Diffusion of a New Order*, special issue of the Annals of the American Academy of Political and Social Science, vol. 598 (March 2005).

[18] To paraphrase Lee and Strang, while in epidemiology the disease rather than the remedy is infectious, in the diffusion literature the reverse seems true (Lee and Strang, "The International Diffusion of Public-Sector Downsizing," 892). However, the "disease" may be global and transnational regulation may be a response by many to a systemic risk or crisis.

A third major contribution to the study of global regulation is recent work by Daniel Drezner.[19] Drezner proposes a theory of transnational regulatory processes and outcomes and tests the theory on cases from a wide range of issue-areas, including the Internet, international finance, genetically modified organisms, intellectual property rights, and pharmaceuticals. Similarly to Simmons, Drezner posits that (1) great powers (mainly the United States and the European Union) are the key actors forging the rules of the global economy;[20] (2) great powers coerce others into compliance when necessary; and (3) governments' "ideal points" are their "own pre-existing national regulatory framework[s]"—frameworks that developed in response to domestic problems and predate globalization.[21] Who shapes the preferences of great power governments? Drezner explains: "[I]t is the groups that face the greatest barriers to market exit or internal adjustment—in other words, the least globalized elements of domestic politics—who exert a stronger influence on government preferences. These actors, by exercising their political voice, raise the adjustment costs to governments of regulatory coordination."[22] Drezner thus hypothesizes that regulatory coordination is less likely when the regulation directly affects mature or nontradable economic sectors—sectors expected to generate the highest level of adjustment costs. "Even as globalization increases gross benefits, the costs relative to other sectors or factors of production remain relatively high. Coordination is therefore a less likely outcome."[23] His case studies shed corroborating light on the theory proposed.

Nevertheless, as a general framework of global regulation, the theory has certain limitations—limitations that our framework tackles head on. By positing that governments are only responsive to (or captured by) businesses that stand to lose from global regulation, the approach overlooks the role of corporate and other actors who stand to gain from global regulatory coordination. Groups disadvantaged by the regulatory status quo will not necessarily sit quietly. They may threaten to exit a jurisdiction opposed to change in order to amplify their voice in domestic regulatory politics, or they may build powerful coalitions of pro-change groups to lobby governments; such mobilization may succeed or fail. In other

---

[19] Daniel Drezner, *All Politics Is Global: Explaining International Regulatory Regimes* (Princeton, NJ: Princeton University Press, 2007).

[20] Drezner writes: "The key variable affecting global regulatory outcomes is the distribution of interests among the great powers. A great power concert is a necessary and sufficient condition for effective global governance over any transnational issue" (ibid., 5); he defines power in terms of relative size and diversity of a country's internal market.

[21] Ibid., 40.

[22] Ibid., xii–xiii.

[23] Ibid., 54.

words, the theory proposed by Drezner does not consider the economic and social consequences of capture. It thus fails to ponder (1) the conditions under which the consequences of capture become politicized, triggering a process of regulatory change; and (2) the conditions under which such process is likely to succeed or fail. Finally, the view that "most regulatory issues start out as domestic problems before globalization makes them international issues" underplays the fact that a good deal of transnational regulation is motivated by uniquely transnational problems; and that transnational institutional structures may offer privileged access to some actors, biasing global regulatory outcomes in ways difficult to comprehend from a purely domestic perspective.

Our analytical framework seeks to contribute to the fledgling IR literature on transnational regulation by focusing in particular on the conditions under which regulatory capture is likely to occur in global regulation. To this end, we draw on insights from the rich and stimulating theoretical debates on domestic regulation and regulatory change of the 1970s and 1980s. In these debates, two views clashed—the "public interest" theory and the capture view of regulation.

Public interest theory of regulation takes a benevolent view of regulators: they are rational, trustworthy, disinterested, and public-spirited experts who produce rules that ensure general economic efficiency and maximum welfare for society. These rules pre-empt or remedy a variety of market failures and welfarist problems.[24] The regulation of monopolies, for example, seeks to harness the benefits of scale economies and to counter the tendency of monopolies to raise prices and lower output. The reason for regulating externalities (or spillovers) is that the price of a product may not reflect the true cost to society of producing that good; regulation thus forces producers to internalize spillover costs. Regulation may also be needed to protect consumers against predatory pricing and other forms of anti-competitive behavior. Where consumers possess inadequate information about the safety and quality of products, regulatory

[24] See Stephen Breyer, *Regulation and Its Reform* (Cambridge, MA: Harvard University Press, 1982), especially 15–35; Robert Baldwin and Martin Cave, *Understanding Regulation: Theory, Strategy and Practice* (Oxford: Oxford University Press, 1999), chap. 2; Anthony Ogus, *Regulation: Legal Form and Economic Theory* (Oxford: Oxford University Press, 1994), chap. 3; Alfred Kahn, *The Economics of Regulation: Principles and Institutions* (Cambridge, MA: MIT Press, 1988); James Landis, *The Administrative Process* (New Haven, CT: Yale University Press, 1938); and Robert Cushman, *The Independent Regulatory Commissions* (New York: Oxford University Press, 1941). Baldwin and Cave note that public interest theory of regulation may complement "functionalist" accounts of regulatory origins and developments insofar as functionalism sees regulation as largely driven by the nature of the task at hand (as identified in terms of public needs and interests) rather than by private, individual, or self-interests (Baldwin and Cave, *Understanding Regulation*, 19).

intervention may facilitate informed consumer choice. Finally, although the attainment of economic efficiency remains a central objective, regulators may also be concerned with social justice and equitable distribution of welfare within society.

Capture (or special interest) theorists of regulation dismiss the public interest approach as politically naïve and thus wrong both analytically and empirically. These theorists take the view that far from being public-spirited and disinterested, politicians are narrowly self-interested and venal, selling regulatory policy to the highest special-interest bidder able to sway votes, either directly or through campaign contributions. Patronage and other forms of bribe are also valued by politicians. The result is regulatory capture, that is, de facto control of the state and its regulatory agencies by the "regulated" interests, enabling these interests to transfer wealth to themselves at the expense of society.[25] In George Stigler's influential formulation, "every industry or occupation that has enough political power to utilize the state will seek to control entry . . . and retard the rate of growth of new firms."[26] By erecting political barriers to entry, airline companies, truck operators, broadcasters, doctors, lawyers, and other protected industry groups and professions end up pocketing supernormal profits at the expense of society. Stigler explains the lack of effective opposition or resistance by society to such wealth transfers with reference to the *high cost* the average voter faces *of acquiring information* about the merits of various regulatory proposals and their distributional implications. As a result, the voter "will know little about most matters before the legislature."[27]

James Wilson complements Stigler's explanation in helpful ways. Drawing on Mancur Olson's theory of collective action,[28] he argues that

[25] See George Stigler, "The Theory of Economic Regulation," *Bell Journal of Economics and Management Science* (Spring 1971), 137–146; reprinted in Kurt Leube and Thomas Moore, eds., *The Essence of Stigler* (Stanford, CA: Hoover Press, 1986), 243–264; Sam Peltzman, "Toward a More General Theory of Regulation?" *Journal of Law and Economics* 19 (August 1976), 211–240; Gary Becker, "A Theory of Competition among Pressure Groups for Political Influence," *Quarterly Journal of Economics* 98 (August 1983), 371–400; Richard Posner, "Theories of Economic Regulation," *The Bell Journal of Economics and Management Science* 5, no. 2 (1974), 335–358; Robert Tollison, "Rent Seeking: A Survey," *Kyklos* 35 (1982), 576–602. An influential older publication is Marver Bernstein, *Regulating Business by Independent Commission* (Princeton, NJ: Princeton University Press, 1955); see also Theodore Lowi, *The End of Liberalism* (New York: Norton, 1969), chapters 3–4; and Murray Edelman, *The Symbolic Uses of Politics* (Urbana: University of Illinois Press, 1964).

[26] Stigler, "The Theory of Economic Regulation," 246.

[27] Ibid., 253.

[28] Mancur Olson, *The Logic of Collective Action* (Cambridge, MA: Harvard University Press, 1961).

the distributional consequences of regulatory proposals affect the incentives to engage in collective action and form lobbying organizations. "When the benefits of a prospective policy are concentrated but the costs widely distributed, client politics is likely to result. Some small easily organized group will benefit and thus has a powerful incentive to organize and lobby; the costs of the benefit are distributed at a low per capita rate over a large number of people, and hence they have little incentive to organize in opposition—if, indeed, they even hear of the policy."[29] However, when both costs and benefits are narrowly concentrated, small but politically powerful groups with conflicting regulatory preferences are likely to face each other in competitive lobbying—a scenario Wilson labels "interest-group politics." The outcome is difficult to predict in this case since it will depend on factors other than the ratios of relative concentration and stakes.[30]

Wilson deserves credit for pushing the debate on domestic regulation beyond the question of whether the "public interest" school or the capture camp got it "right" to a reflection on the conditions under which rent-seeking interest groups are most and least likely to end up with favorable regulation. Again, his explanation of regulatory outcomes turns primarily on the different combinations of relative concentration and dispersion of the costs and benefits of regulation. We further develop this insight in our analytical framework by considering how the costs and benefits to different groups change at different stages of the global regulatory process.

Institutions have also attracted the focus of scholars seeking to explain variation in regulatory outcomes at the national level. For example, representative democracy is said to be more vulnerable to capture than direct democracy because its legislative committees can be dominated by a small number of members who may all be in the pocket of organized interests. Others have argued that the level of government at which regulation operates may matter too, with strongly centralized national regulatory structures more likely to be captured by well-funded lobby groups than decentralized and plural structures.[31] On the other hand, the strength and

[29] James Wilson, "The Politics of Regulation," in James Wilson, ed., *The Politics of Regulation* (New York: Basic Books, 1980), 357–394, 369.

[30] Wilson distinguishes two additional scenarios: "Majoritarian politics" emerges when both costs and benefits are widely distributed. In this case, "[a]ll or most of society expects to gain; all or most of society expects to pay. Interest groups have little incentive to form" (Ibid., 367). Finally, "entrepreneurial politics" describes a situation where the proposed regulation confers general benefits at a cost to be borne chiefly by a small segment of society.

[31] The theoretical case for decentralization is made by William Bratton and Joseph McCary, "The New Economics of Jurisdictional Competition: Devolutionary Federalism in a Second-Best World," *Georgetown Law Journal* (November 1997), but note the competing

independence of the bureaucracy can make a difference. Indeed, some have put forth the view that strong states endowed with central professional bureaucracies run by technocratic elites will be less permeable to lobbying pressure than weak states.[32]

Few of these arguments have systematically been transposed to the global level. We argue that they offer important insights into how institutions and actors with competing interests may shape global regulation. Building on these insights, this study develops an analytical framework of the politics of global regulation capable of explaining different outcomes ranging from pure capture regulation to common interest regulation. Changes in the values of our explanatory variables account for moves between various regulatory outcomes.

AN ANALYTICAL FRAMEWORK: INSTITUTIONAL SUPPLY- AND DEMAND-SIDE CONDITIONS

We begin the presentation of our analytical framework by defining capture and public (or common) interest. Capture is the control of the regulatory process by those whom it is supposed to regulate or by a narrow subset of those affected by regulation, with the consequence that regulatory outcomes favor the narrow "few" at the expense of society as a whole. More specifically, the result of capture is either absence of regulation where rules would have imposed costs on or eliminated privileges from capture groups; regulation that is inadequate to safeguard broad societal preferences; regulation that on paper meets these preferences but is not enforceable or enforced; or, finally, regulation that eliminates present and future competition for capture groups, thereby maximizing their rents. It follows, for example, that change from capture in the direction of public interest need not mean more regulation. If capture regulation undermines competition to the benefit of the powerful few, then change

empirical evidence against decentralization presented by Susan Rose-Ackerman, *Corruption and Government: Causes, Consequences, and Reform* (Cambridge: Cambridge University Press, 1999).

[32] Peter Evans, *Embedded Autonomy: States and Industrial Transformation* (Princeton, NJ: Princeton University Press, 1995); Peter Katzenstein, ed., *Between Power and Plenty: Foreign Economic Policies of Advanced Industrialized States* (Madison: University of Wisconsin Press, 1978); see also Max Weber, *Economy and Society*, vol. 1, edited by Guenther Roth and Claus Wittich (Berkeley: University of California Press, 1978); John Olsen, "Maybe It Is Time to Rediscover Bureaucracy," *Journal of Public Administration Research and Theory* 16, no. 1 (2006), 1–24; and for a contrasting approach, Patrick Dunleavy, *Democracy, Bureaucracy and Public Choice: Economic Explanations in Political Science* (New York: Harvester Wheatsheaf, 1991).

may mean less regulation (or deregulation). However, if capture results in inadequate safeguards, then change is likely to mean a deeper and more extensive regulatory regime.

The definition of public interest is more difficult. The concept has been widely used by politicians and in scholarly writings, but no generally agreed meaning has emerged.[33] Three broad schools of thought can be identified.[34] The "idealist" school holds that the public interest consists of the course of action that is best for society as a whole according to some absolute standard of values. "Public opinion need not be consulted, though it should be educated to understand the wisdom of the policies arrived at."[35] The "rejectionist" school denies that the concept of public interest has any meaning or validity. There can be no public interest because there is no public or community; only individuals and special-interest groups exist with heterogeneous preferences over regulatory means and ends.[36] Finally, the "proceduralist" school associates public interest with the regulatory process itself, provided certain standards of due process are observed.[37] That is, regulation is said to be in the public interest

[33] See, for example, Pendleton Herring, *Public Administration and the Public Interest* (New York: McGraw-Hill Books, 1936); Glendon Schubert, *The Public Interest* (Glencoe, IL: The Free Press, 1960); Carl Friedrich, ed., *Nomos V: The Public Interest* (New York: Atherton Press, 1962); Arthur Bentley, *The Process of Government* (Cambridge, MA: Belknap Press of Harvard University Press, 1967, first published by Chicago: University of Chicago Press in 1908); Virginia Held, *The Public Interest and Individual Rights* (New York: Basic Books, 1970); David Truman, *The Governmental Process: Political Interests and Public Opinion* (New York: Alfred Knopf, 1971, first published in 1951); Frank Sorauf, "The Public Interest Reconsidered," *Journal of Politics* 19 (November 1957), 616–639; Anthony Downs, "The Public Interest: Its Meaning in a Democracy," *Social Research* 29 (Spring 1962), 1–36; J. A. Gunn, "Jeremy Bentham and the Public Interest," *Canadian Journal of Political Science* 1 (December 1968), 398–413; Michael Marmon, "Administrative Policy Formation and the Public Interest," *Public Administration Review* 29 (September/ October 1969), 484–491; Clarke Cochrane, "Political Science and 'The Public Interest'," *Journal of Politics* 36 (May 1974), 327–355; Mike Feintuck, *'The Public Interest' in Regulation* (New York: Oxford University Press, 2004).

[34] Numerous typologies of such schools have been proposed in the literature. The three schools mentioned in this section overlap with most typologies.

[35] Downs, "The Public Interest," 11; see also discussion of this school in Schubert, *The Public Interest*.

[36] See Bentley, *The Process of Government*; Truman, *The Governmental Process*; Glendon Schubert, "'The Public Interest' in Administrative Decision-Making," *American Political Science Review* 51 (June 1957), 346–368; Schubert, "The Theory of 'The Public Interest' in Judicial Decision-Making," *Midwest Journal of Political Science* 2 (February 1958); Frank Sorauf, "The Conceptual Muddle," in Friedrich, *Nomos V: The Public Interest*, 183–190.

[37] Herring, *Public Administration and Public Interest*; Harmon, *Administrative Policy Formation and the Public Interest*; Emmette Redford, *Democracy in the Administrative State* (New York: Oxford University Press, 1969); see also Richard Stewart, "The Reformation of American Administrative Law," *Harvard Law Review* 88 (1975), 1667–1813; and

if it is arrived at through a deliberative process that allows everyone likely to be affected by it to have a voice in its formation. Individuals and groups will accept outcomes as being in the public interest as long as they feel that existing procedures of consultation and involvement offer them a fair chance to put their views across and influence regulation in their own favor, even if they are not always successful.[38] Proper due process mechanisms are said to produce regulation most likely to benefit most in society.[39]

A particularly common understanding of public interest within the idealist school is the one used in welfare economics, upholding economic efficiency as its main benchmark value. Welfare economists do not problematize the state, that is, they assume that state institutions supply regulation reliably remedying market deficiencies. Unlike welfare economists, proceduralists accept that the institutional context in which regulation is produced can vary and fail to foster public interest regulation. Again, an inclusive forum offering proper due process is said to promote the public interest, whereas a closed and exclusive forum favors capture. In other words, proceduralists suggest that the institutional context in which regulation is produced be carefully examined to assess the extent to which the public interest may be satisfied in regulation. We fully accept this suggestion—for the institutional context in which global regulation is produced has become tremendously complex and varied as the relative significance of the state and state-based institutions in international rule-making has been weakened over the last two decades by the rapid rise of a diverse group of non-state regulatory agents. As noted by Kenneth Abbott and Duncan Snidal: "The state is far from the only game in town, and may no longer be the most important game in town."[40] Similarly, Miles Kahler and David Lake note that traditional supranationalism is

---

Daniel Esty, "Good Governance at the Supranational Scale: Globalizing Administrative Law," *Yale Law Journal* 115 (May 2006), 1490–1562. The "proceduralist" label is suggested by Cochrane, "Political Science and 'The Public Interest'," 342.

[38] Procedural fairness and justice is a major theme in the book by Tom Tyler, *Why People Obey the Law* (New Haven, CT: Yale University Press, 1990). In social choice language, the Arrow problem says that there is no necessary public interest. However, a set of legitimate procedures can lead to structurally induced "public interest" seen as acceptable by all. (We thank Duncan Snidal for this formulation.)

[39] The challenge is to design mechanisms that optimize the gains from wide societal participation without losing the capacity to make decisions in an efficient and representative manner. See Esty, "Good Governance at the Supranational Scale: Globalizing Administrative Law," 1521; and Jerry Mashaw, "Reinventing Government and Regulatory Reform: Studies in the Neglect and Abuse of Administrative Law," *University of Pittsburgh Law Review* 57 (1996), 405–441.

[40] Abbott and Snidal, "The Governance Triangle: Regulatory Standards Institutions and the Shadow of the State," this volume.

not the only form of global governance. In fact, "throughout the global economy, [it] . . . plays a less central role than many believe."[41] Networks and hierarchies are often effective alternatives to supranationalism. The studies in this book offer a rich canvas of global institutional variety on the supply side.

In sum, we agree with proceduralists that any conclusion about regulation requires a careful assessment of the relative inclusiveness, openness, transparency, fairness, and accessibility of regulatory institutions. However, we sharply part with proceduralists in one important respect. We argue that supply of proper due process mechanisms is not enough to ensure common interest regulation.[42] Just as welfare economists are naïve in assuming that state intervention is easy, cheap, and effective, proceduralists are naïve in assuming that the very existence of proper due process institutions translates into common interest regulation. Proper institutional supply needs to be met by robust societal demand (from the public and private sectors alike) for common interest regulation to emerge. Such demand is not necessarily forthcoming. In Downs's words, "[M]ost people are almost totally uninformed about most public issues."[43] They may be too busy eking out a living to pay attention to issues that nonetheless will affect them; they may lack technical expertise to comprehend the complexity of regulatory proposals; or they simply may not have adequate resources or suffer from collective-action problems to "activate" due process mechanisms and sustain an interest in an issue throughout the often lengthy regulatory process. In the absence of broad societal demand, industry and other concentrated groups targeted for regulation may be the most frequent users of due process channels—because of their organizational capacity, resources, and expertise—and thus may succeed in influencing the fine details of regulation to benefit themselves.[44]

---

[41] Miles Kahler and David Lake, "Economic Integration and Global Governance: Why So Little Supranationalism?" this volume.

[42] A similar point was made earlier in Walter Mattli and Tim Büthe, "Global Private Governance," in Benedict Kingsbury, Nico Krisch, Richard Stewart, and Jonathan Wiener, eds., The Emergence of Global Administrative Law, special issue of Law and Contemporary Problems 68 (Summer/Autumn 2005), 225–262, especially 226–227. Not one public exists but multiple publics or groups. We thus prefer to use the term common rather than (single) public interest.

[43] Downs, "The Public Interest," 12; see also Susanne Lohmann, "An Information Rationale for the Power of Special Interests," American Political Science Review 92 (December 1998), 809–827.

[44] Martin Shapiro has similarly argued that administrative law maximizing transparency and participation has the paradoxical effect of maximizing transparency and participation for "the interested" (typically interest groups) and minimizing them for "the disinterested" (typically the average citizen). Shapiro provides as an example the EU comitology process and writes: "While virtually every interest group finds a place on the committees, European citizens are generally unaware that the committees even exist." Martin Shapiro, "Adminis-

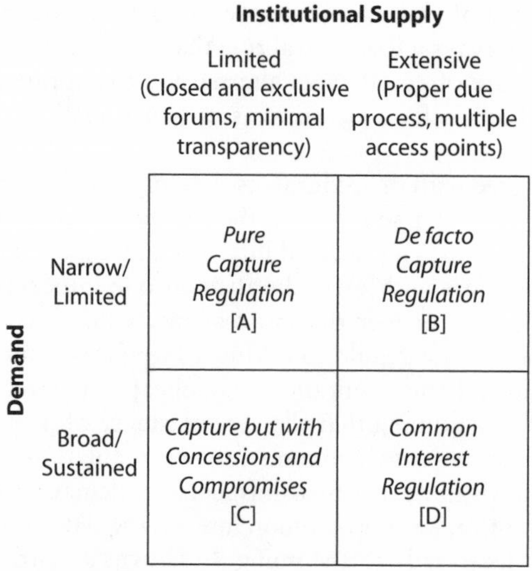

Institutional Supply

	Limited (Closed and exclusive forums, minimal transparency)	Extensive (Proper due process, multiple access points)
Narrow/ Limited	Pure Capture Regulation [A]	De facto Capture Regulation [B]
Broad/ Sustained	Capture but with Concessions and Compromises [C]	Common Interest Regulation [D]

Demand (vertical axis label)

Figure 1.1. Regulatory outcomes

In short, stark asymmetries in information, financial resources, and technical expertise among groups nationally and internationally create conditions conducive to regulatory capture even in an institutional context offering extensive formal due process and access, thus privileging narrower interests (the "haves") at the expense of broader interests (the "have-nots"). The outcome is de facto capture regulation even though the institutional context may have been designed with the objective of promoting the common interest (B in figure 1.1).

The outcome is also one of capture, of course, in the classic case of limited institutional supply and narrow demand. The "haves" will be in charge of the regulatory process from the agenda-setting stage on and need not fear interference by any other groups, since the forums of regulation are exclusive and regulatory schemes are shrouded in secrecy (A in figure 1.1).

We further argue that the emergence of broad societal demand for change is a function of the diffusion of information about the social cost of the regulatory status quo via glaring inadequacies and failures (demonstration effects) and the ability of those opposed to the status quo to forge

trative Law Unbounded: Reflections on Government and Governance," *Indiana Journal of Global Legal Studies* 8 (2001), 369–377, 373. See also Mathew McCubbins, Roger Noll, and Barry Weingast, "Administrative Procedures as Instruments of Political Control," *Journal of Law, Economics, and Organization* 3 (Fall 1987), 243–277, especially 262.

powerful and lasting pro-change alliances. Public and private entrepreneurs play key roles in mobilizing opposition, and ideas may offer the necessary frames for pro-change interests and glue for coalitions.

In short, broad and sustained demand that intersects with extensive institutional supply produces common interest regulation (D in figure 1.1). However, broad demand for change shut out because of closed regulatory forums may take to the street or engage in naming and shaming and other pinprick strategies in an effort to obtain regulatory concession and compromises from capture actors (C in figure 1). The following subsection discusses global institutional supply in greater detail. It is followed by an analysis and illustrations of demand-side conditions.

Institutional Supply

The institutional context of regulation describes the locus where rules are drafted, implemented, monitored, and enforced. As summarized in figure 1.1, the institutional context in which these regulatory processes take place can be relatively extensive or limited. An extensive institutional context signifies open forums, proper due process, multiple access points, and oversight mechanisms. A limited institutional context indicates that the few regulatory forums are club-like, that is, exclusive, closed, and secretive. In some instances, the drafting of regulation takes place in an open forum, the implementation is delegated to a more exclusive and secretive agency, while the enforcement is left decentralized or unspecified.[45]

Rule-making traditionally has been undertaken in international governmental organizations (IGOs), such as the UN, IMF, or the WTO. More recently, a strikingly wide range of non-state organizations have gained prominence as rule-makers. They include private-sector standard-setters, such as the International Organization for Standardization (ISO), the International Accounting Standards Board (IASB), and the International Electro-technical Commission (IEC), as well as trade unions, such as the International Textile Workers Association, and global trade associations for coffee, chemicals, mining, apparel, toys, and cacao.[46] This extension of rule-making to more specialized non-state actors reflect what Abbott and Snidal explain as follows: "While the state traditionally has

---

[45] See, for example, the case of Collective Action Clauses in Helleiner, "Filling a Hole in Global Financial Governance? The Politics of Regulating Sovereign Debt Restructuring," this volume.

[46] See David Vogel, "The Private Regulation of Global Corporate Conduct," this volume; and Abbott and Snidal, "The Governance Triangle: Regulatory Standards Institutions and the Shadow of the State," this volume.

been seen as the appropriate overseer of domestic business activity, the scale and structure of contemporary global production challenge the capacity of even highly developed states to regulate activities that extend beyond their borders."[47]

Several international organizations—public or private—have been adopting mechanisms to improve access to rule-making deliberations through provision for greater participation and transparency, often in response to general criticisms about their lack of legitimacy. Examples include the adoption and extension of notice-and-comment procedures, such as by the ISO, IASB, IEC, Basel Committee, and OECD. These actions have not always been followed through with an equal opening-up to scrutiny of the implementation and enforcement functions of these organizations.

As regards the implementation of rules, some international organizations have opened up their operations and invited collaboration with others. Many organizations have sought to improve transparency by maintaining Web sites containing abundant material on internal decision making. For example, the World Bank, IMF, and WTO have each widened public access to deliberations and internal documents, and have sought to include consultation processes as part of their strategies of implementation. Some organizations have taken steps to involve a wider range of NGOs in their regulatory processes, as is the case of the Codex Alimentarius Commission.[48]

Finally, with regard to enforcement and accountability, new oversight mechanisms in international organizations have also been created. For example, the World Bank Inspection Panel was established to improve compliance of World Bank staff with internal directives and to offer individuals and groups a forum in which to challenge compliance of the World Bank with its project-related policies.[49] In the United Nations, an Office

---

[47] Abbott and Snidal, "The Governance Triangle: Regulatory Standards Institutions and the Shadow of the State," this volume. See also Mattli and Büthe, "Global Private Governance."

[48] The examples are drawn, in part, from Benedict Kingsbury, Nico Krisch, and Richard Stewart, "The Emergence of Global Administrative Law," *Law and Contemporary Problems*, 15–61; see also Steve Suppan, *Consumers International's Decision-Making in the Global Market*, Codex Briefing Paper (2004) at http://www.tradeobservatory.org/library.cfm?RefID=36988, accessed on February 6, 2007.

[49] See Dana Clark, Jonathan Fox, and Kay Treakle, eds., *Demanding Accountability: Civil-Society Claims and the World Bank Inspection Panel* (Lanham, MD: Rowman & Littlefield, 2003); and Gudmundur Alfredsson and Rolf Ring, eds., *The Inspection Panel of the World Bank: A Different Complaints Procedure* (Boston, MA: Brill Academic Publishers, 2000). See also Benedict Kingsbury, Nico Krisch, and Richard Stewart, "The Emergence of Global Administrative Law," in B. Kingsbury, N. Krisch, R. Steward, and J. Wiener, eds., special issue of *Law and Contemporary Problems*, 31–34.

of Internal Oversight Services (OIOS) was established in 1994 to add "value by providing worldwide audit, investigation, inspection, programme monitoring, evaluation and consulting services to the UN Secretariat and a wide range of UN operational funds, programmes and tribunals."[50] It is worth emphasizing that these post-facto accountability exercises permit public groups to question the institution's adherence to its own rules (in the case of the Inspection Panel) or to question the institution's success in terms of its own goals (in the UN), but these innovations do not permit the public to question the rules, nor can they lead to requirements for alternative actions to be taken.

These developments in opening up global regulatory processes to wider participation and scrutiny have led a group of leading international legal experts to conclude: "[T]he overall picture is of widespread and growing commitment both to principles of transparency, participation, reasoned decision and review in global governance;"[51] therefore, "the separation between prevailing models of domestic and international regulation has been eroding faster in practice than it has in . . . theory."[52]

This assessment strikes us as overly optimistic for four reasons. First, the new opening-up of international regulatory agencies is often confined to the rule-making process and accountability but not necessarily to implementation and enforcement. The scope for reducing vulnerability to capture is therefore limited. Second, although traditional international organizations may well be relatively transparent and open to political scrutiny, as noted above, they are by no means the only loci of global regulation. Kahler and Lake persuasively argue that alternative institutional structures, most notably regulatory networks that have been enjoying a comeback after being supplanted by international organizations in the wake of World War II, tend not to be transparent and open. Network governance is based on shared or pooled authority and repeated, enduring, and reciprocal relationships among like-minded actors in different national jurisdictions. Kahler and Lake write that "networked gover-

---

[50] See http://www.un.org/Depts/oios/.

[51] Benedict Kingsbury, Nico Krisch, Richard Stewart, and Jonathan Wiener, "Foreword: Global Governance as Administration—National and Translational Approaches to Global Administrative Law," *Law and Contemporary Problems* 68 (Summer/Autumn 2005), 4. The authors define "global administrative law" as "comprising the mechanisms, principles, practices, and supporting social understandings that promote or otherwise affect the accountability of global administrative bodies, in particular by ensuring they meet adequate standards of transparency, participation, reasoned decision, and legality, and by providing effective review of the rules and decisions they make," 17. See also Esty, "Good Governance at the Supranational Scale: Global Administrative Law."

[52] Kingsbury, Krisch, Stewart, and Wiener, "Foreword: Global Governance as Administration—National and Translational Approaches to Global Administrative Law," 3.

nance, despite its many benefits and its recent fashionable status, is the likeliest to incorporate capture by narrower economic interests. Its very strengths . . . can easily be transformed into barriers to wider participation, legal accountability, and public scrutiny."[53] In short, the existence of alternative forms of governance implies that capture at the global level may be more pervasive than what an analysis based only on traditional supranationalism may suggest.

Third, and relatedly, many global non-state regulatory forums clearly are and remain exclusive and secretive, serving as effective vehicles of capture. Eric Helleiner offers a nice illustration. In 2002, the powerful Washington-based Institute of International Finance (IIF), whose members are major international banks, developed an international code of conduct for debt restructuring that preempted an ambitious IMF proposal for an international bankruptcy mechanism backed by some debtor countries and NGOs, "shift[ing] the terms of the international debate on bond restructuring mechanisms onto terms that were more friendly to private creditor interest."[54]

The problem posed by closed processes for rule-making, implementation, and enforcement is compounded at the global level by the lack of an overarching sovereign but constitutionally constrained authority that oversees regulators on behalf of the people. In national systems, regulators are held to account by the legislative, public auditors and inspectors, independent review boards, whistle-blowers, and the courts. In global regulation, such oversight remains rare.[55] This makes the openness of regulatory processes from rule-making through to enforcement yet more important for effective global regulation.

Last but not least, while we agree with international legal scholars that several major global regulators have changed their organizational structure to conform to fundamental principles of administrative law, we caution against jumping to conclusions. As noted above, it would be naïve to think that the supply of global institutional mechanisms of due process automatically generates extensive demand of the use of these mechanisms. Such supply is a necessary but not sufficient condition for common interest regulation, as indicated in figure 1.1. Demand-side conditions must also be satisfied. The following subsection turns to a discussion of these conditions.

[53] Kahler and Lake, "Economic Integration and Global Governance: Why So Little Supranationalism?" this volume.

[54] Helleiner, "Filling a Hole in Global Financial Governance? The Politics of Regulating Sovereign Debt Restructuring," this volume.

[55] Ruth Grant and Robert Keohane, "Accountability and Abuses of Power in World Politics," *American Political Science Review* 99 (2005), 29–43.

Demand-side Conditions: Information + Interests + Ideas

The price of "activating" institutional due process mechanisms (where they exist) is often too high to generate wide societal demand because of asymmetries in the distribution of information about regulatory proposals, technical expertise, and financial as well as organizational resources. At the global level, these difficulties may be particularly acute for the following reasons. First, international processes of regulation are further removed from the public gaze than national ones, rendering it more difficult and costly to collect information about regulatory proposals, the details of negotiations, or possible shortcomings in implementation, monitoring, and enforcement of regulation. Timely information is of the essence in global regulation for it confers a "first-mover advantage" upon a group, that is, it gives the group a big say at critical junctures of the regulatory process. Groups receiving information later find themselves in a much weaker position effectively to influence regulatory outcomes.[56] Second, the requisite expertise and financial as well as organizational capacity to participate meaningfully in global regulation are not evenly distributed across countries or transnational non-state actors, rendering broad and sustained participation by all those potentially affected by regulation difficult.[57]

In short, as summarized in figure 1.1, if only a few have access to information and the capacity to use it, the resulting demand for regulatory change will favor the "haves" at the expense of the "have-nots"—regardless of whether the institutional supply of due process mechanisms is extensive or limited.

What then are the demand-side conditions under which a wider range of societal groups is likely to be willing and able effectively to partake in global regulation? In other words, what explains a change in demand from narrow and limited to broad and sustained (see figure 1.1)? First, groups need a motivation to act for change. We argue that such motivation is provided by the diffusion of *information* about the social cost of capture, that is, demonstration effects. Second, pro-change groups must succeed in building broad alliances in which public or private entrepreneurs play a critical role. Such entrepreneurs may enable pro-change forces to coalesce around a convergence of *interests* or driven by particular sets of *ideas* to remain actively involved in the lengthy process of regulatory change. For the sake of presentational simplicity, we discuss these analytical factors in order—even though some may coincide and interact in practice, as we shall note.

[56] See, for example, Walter Mattli and Tim Büthe, "Setting International Standards: Technological Rationality or Primacy of Power?" *World Politics* 53 (2003), 1–43.
[57] See Mattli and Büthe, "Global Private Governance."

DEMONSTRATION EFFECTS: DIFFUSION OF INFORMATION

Demonstration effects can trigger—but not sustain—the process of regulatory change. As emphasized by Stigler and Downs, high information cost constitutes for many a high hurdle to reaching cognizance of the social damage of capture. However, the information cost may fall precipitously in the face of a major crisis, disaster, or scandal that reveals or demonstrates the "egregious" or "shocking" extent of failings, abuse, or incompetence of regulators. The free mass media, ever so eager to report on the *extra*-ordinary on which it thrives, and the ever more accessible World Wide Web, will diffuse previously unknown facts of influence-peddling, dereliction of duty, and social cost to a dismayed general public and thus create a first demand-side condition for regulatory change. It follows that where disasters or failures are not broadly revealed or occur in countries or regions where the general public is not politically empowered, they are unlikely to trigger processes of regulatory change.

Several examples illustrate the importance of demonstration effects as triggers of regulatory processes. Outcomes in each process varied significantly: sometimes regulation was effective and sometimes it was not, as will be explained later.

In December 1984, some forty tons of poisonous gas leaked from a Union Carbide pesticide plant in the city of Bhopal, India, killing at least 3,800 people and affecting hundreds of thousands of others, many of whom later died of gas-related illnesses like lung cancer, kidney failure, and liver disease.[58] Bhopal soon created a media storm and was described by *US Today* and *Time* magazines as the world's worst industrial disaster.[59] It emerged that cost-cutting resulting in faulty equipment (the alarm on the tank that overheated had not worked for four years) and an inadequate safety regime all played a part in the accident. The regulatory response, however, was weak in the end. In 1989, the chemical industry established a voluntary code called "Responsible Care."[60] The efficacy of the code is highly disputed. Critics argue that it was planned as a public relations exercise aimed at reassuring the public and minimizing the risk of adverse legislation or direct regulation. Scholars who have examined

---

[58] Ramana Dhara and Rosaline Dhara, "The Union Carbide Disaster in Bhopal: A Review of Health Effects," *Archives of Environmental Health* 57, no. 5 (September/October 2002), 391–404. The casualty figure is from the Union Carbide Web site: www.bhopal.com/chrono.htm.

[59] "India's Disaster," *Time*, December 17, 1984; Nirmala George, "Thousands Commemorate Bhopal Industrial Disaster," *USA Today*, March 12, 2004.

[60] Joseph Rees, "Development of Communitarian Regulation in the Chemical Industry," *Law and Policy* 19, no. 4 (1997), 477–528.

the impact of the code on corporate behavior describe it as weak and of little restraining effect.[61]

Another incident whose exposure sparked calls for regulation was the thalidomide disaster, described in the early 1960s by *Time* magazine as "the greatest prescription disaster in medical history."[62] Thalidomide, the product of a German pharmaceutical company, was sold mainly as a prescription drug to pregnant women to combat morning sickness and help them sleep. Scientists in the company had tested thalidomide for toxicity on animals and found the substance neither to kill the animals nor to have any other effect; on humans, however, a sedative effect was detected. Without further or subsequent independent tests, the product was marketed and sold between 1957 and 1961 as a "perfectly safe hypnotic drug" in forty-six countries.[63] An estimated 8,000 to 12,000 infants of mothers who had taken thalidomide early in pregnancy were born with stunted limbs or other defects, including deafness, blindness, and damage to the nervous system and vital organs. Of these, only about 5,000 survived beyond childhood.[64]

This disaster caused a lasting media storm that contributed to fundamentally altering the regulatory landscape of the pharmaceutical industry in the developed world and beyond. Many countries adopted legislation similar to the U.S. Federal Food, Drug and Cosmetic Act of 1938, requiring safety and efficacy testing of drugs before they could be marketed.[65] The thalidomide tragedy also spurred drug regulation at the European and international levels.[66]

[61] Andrew King and Michael Lenox, "Industry Self-regulation without Sanctions: The Chemical Industry's Responsible Care Program," *Academy of Management Journal* 43, no. 4 (2000), 698–716.

[62] "The Thalidomide Disaster," *Time*, Friday, August 10, 1962.

[63] See Henning Sjöström and Robert Nilsson, *Thalidomide and the Power of the Drug Companies* (Hammondsworth: Penguin, 1972).

[64] See Trent Stephens and Rock Brynner, *Dark Remedy: The Impact of Thalidomide and Its Revival as a Vital Medicine* (Cambridge, MA: Perseus Publishing, 2001).

[65] Revealingly, the passage of the 1938 Federal Food, Drug and Cosmetic Act was itself motivated by a national disaster—the 1937 Elixir Sulfanilamide scandal that cost the lives of 105 people, many of them children being treated for sore throats or ear infections. The Elixir contained a deadly poison normally used as an antifreeze. Prior to the 1938 Act, no laws existed requiring safety studies on new drugs; the U.S. pharmaceutical industry had long opposed costly safety requirements. See Paul Wax, "Elixirs, Diluents, and the Passage of the 1938 Federal Food, Drug and Cosmetic Act," *History of Medicine* 122, no. 6 (1995), 456–461; "Taste of Raspberries, Taste of Death: The 1937 Elixir Sulfanilamide Incident," *FDA Consumer Magazine* (June 1981) at www.fda.gov/oc/history/elixir.html; see also John Braithwaite, *Corporate Crime in the Pharmaceutical Industry* (London: Routledge & Kegan Paul, 1984).

[66] See EEC (Council) Directives 65/65/EEC, 75/318/EEC, and 75/319/EEC.

Perhaps the most dramatic modern case of large-scale negative externality due to inadequate regulation (despite known risks) is the Chernobyl nuclear power plant disaster. On April 26, 1986, a massive explosion in one of the reactors at the plant threw 50 million curies of radioactive isotopes into the atmosphere—500 times the amount released by the atomic bomb in Hiroshima. A flawed reactor design, lax safety standards, and a faulty inspection regime were key contributing factors of the disaster.[67] Several nuclear accidents had occurred in the Soviet Union in the 1970s and 1980s but were covered up.[68] Corruption, incompetence, secrecy, and oppression offered no incentive for broad-based demand for change to form and for the system to correct itself. More disasters were bound to happen. Chernobyl, however, was of unprecedented scale, making it difficult to hide. Its plume of radioactive fallout drifted over parts of the western Soviet Union, Eastern and Western Europe, Scandinavia, the United Kingdom, Ireland, and eastern North America. Large areas of Ukraine, Belarus, and Russia were particularly badly contaminated, necessitating the evacuation and resettlement of over 336,000 people. Of the estimated 6.6 million highly exposed persons, about 9,000 may die from some form of cancer.[69]

Chernobyl had a powerful mobilizing effect on the people in most western democracies, halting the expansion of the nuclear industry in several countries. In Italy, for example, a 1988 referendum effectively shut down nuclear power plants and stopped further development of nuclear technology. This was followed in Switzerland by a ten-year moratorium on issuing nuclear power plant licenses.[70] As further discussed below, Chernobyl also led to the establishment in 1989 of the World Association of

[67] A concise summary of causes is offered by Luis Lederman (Acting Head of the Safety Assessment Section in the IAEA Department of Nuclear Safety), "Nuclear Safety Aspects," *IAEA* 38, no. 3 (1996).

[68] See Grigori Medvedev, *No Breathing Room: The Aftermath of Chernobyl* (New York: Basic Books, 1993); see also Alla Yaroshinskaya, *Chernobyl: The Forbidden Truth* (Lincoln: University of Nebraska Press, 1995).

[69] The estimates of likely deaths vary widely; some are as high as 70,000. For an excellent source of information on Chernobyl, see "IAEA Report—In Focus: Chernobyl" at www.iaea.org/NewsCenter/Focus/Chernobyl, accessed January 16, 2007; see also the WHO Chernobyl report entitled Health Effects of the Chernobyl Accident and Special Health Care Programmes at www.who.int/ionizing-radiation/chernobyl/who_chernobyl_report_2006pdf; and Chris Busby and Alexey Yablokov, eds., *Chernobyl: 20 Years On* (Aberystwyth: Green Audit Press, 2006).

[70] OECD, *Public Participation in Nuclear Decision-Making* (Paris: OECD, 1993). Braithwaite and Drahos note: "This is one area where, in the battle between diffuse public interests and the concentrated interest of the industry association, the latter is losing . . . In no other area of regulation does the direct sovereignty of citizens have so much influence over specific regulatory decisions." See Braithwaite and Drahos, *Global Business Regulation* (Cambridge: Cambridge University Press, 2000), 309.

Nuclear Operators (WANO), which is credited with having significantly improved nuclear plant safety standards worldwide.

In sum, a first factor facilitating a move away from capture regulation in the direction of common interest regulation is the strength of demonstration effects, that is, the extent to which the negative consequences of capture are revealed to the wider public. Such strength crucially depends on the ease with which information about costs diffuses throughout society. In the Soviet Union, nuclear accidents preceding Chernobyl had been kept secret: state control of information inhibited effective change. By contrast, the Bhopal disaster occurred in a country with a thriving free press; it created media storms nationally and beyond, and triggered a process of regulatory change—albeit in the end resulting in a minimalist regulatory instrument of questionable efficacy.

The critical importance of demonstration effects as triggers of regulatory processes is further illustrated by several studies in this book. The study by Helleiner shows that a move toward regulating sovereign debt restructuring was initiated by the international financial crises of the mid- to late 1990s, which demonstrated very publicly the cost associated with the bailout model of handling sovereign debt crises. Bailouts served private creditors' interests and imposed considerable costs on others, including taxpayers in creditor countries, and seemed to do little to discourage further crises. The $50 billion bailout of Mexico, in particular, symbolized in a "visible and dramatic way how international financial policy-making had been increasingly captured by the interests of private creditors."[71]

Similarly, Sikkink writes that the discovery of concentration camps in the heart of Europe fifty years after World War II as well as the ineffectiveness of the international response to the genocide in Rwanda in 1994 offered deeply disturbing demonstrations of the failure of the existing regulatory regime to prevent major human rights violations. This regime was a classic case of capture that protected state officials from any individual legal accountability. Its dramatic failures mobilized action in favor of a regulatory approach based on individual criminal accountability.[72]

Samuel Barrows notes that the passage of dozens of international conventions in shipping and the creation in many countries of effective monitoring and enforcement mechanisms are traceable to a series of recent maritime disasters that generated broad public and political outcry. Major shipowners had long lobbied against stringent maritime regulation, fearing high costs of compliance and much diminished profits. The scale of the

---

[71] Helleiner, "Filling a Hole in Global Financial Governance? The Politics of Regulating Sovereign Debt Restructuring," this volume.

[72] Sikkink, "From State Responsibility to Individual Criminal Accountability: A New Regulatory Model for Core Human Rights Violations," this volume.

negative externalities generated by major disasters, however, had grown dramatically with the expansion in the size of tankers and the rapid increase in the number of ships, triggering a process of regulatory change.[73]

Finally, the study by David Vogel shows how the development of private regulation governing corporate conduct ("civil" regulation) has been directly related to policy failures associated with globalization as evidenced, for example, by unsustainable forestry practices, business investments that support corrupt governments, and natural resource developments that adversely affect human rights and environmental quality. These failures often stem from the political influence of global firms that have captured existing regulatory arrangements and effectively oppose governmental proposals to expand regulation to cover their global operations.[74]

INTERESTS: ACTORS AND ALLIANCES

Demonstration effects reveal the cost of capture to society, thereby creating a demand by the general public for remedial regulation. The greater the scale and scope of the externality, the broader and more insistent the demand for change. Public outrage or discontent, however, rarely suffices for effective new regulation. Effective change is a lengthy and arduous process of many stages involving agenda-setting, negotiations, implementation, monitoring, and enforcement of new regulation.[75] Each stage offers a new opportunity for potential losers to decelerate, distort, weaken, or otherwise undermine the process of regulatory change if not watched and checked by countervailing forces. During this intricate process, the public is at a distinct disadvantage relative to concentrated groups with a preference for the regulatory status quo: its resources are generally modest, knowledge about often technical and arcane regulatory issues is limited, and size typically too large to easily overcome the collective-action problem. In addition, the public suffers from attention deficit. As Downs pointed out, "[The] public attention rarely remains sharply focused upon any one . . . issue for very long—even if it involves a continuing problem of crucial importance to society. Instead, a systematic 'issue-attention cycle' seems strongly to influence public attitudes and behaviour concerning most key . . . problems. Each of these problems suddenly leaps into prominence, remains there for a short time, and then—though still largely

---

[73] Samuel Barrows, "Racing to the Top . . . At Last: The Regulation of Safety in Shipping," this volume.

[74] Vogel, "The Private Regulation of Global Corporate Conduct," this volume.

[75] Abbott and Snidal, "The Governance Triangle: Regulatory Standards Institutions and the Shadow of the State," this volume.

unresolved—gradually fades from the center of public attention."[76] It is precisely during moments of fading public attention that well-resourced special-interest groups with great stakes in the regulatory status quo will quietly seek to regain the upper hand in the process. When "the cameras go away" these groups may, for example, seek to influence the day-to-day technical decisions of the implementing agency to benefit themselves after regulation has been adopted.

It follows that the public needs resourceful, expert, well-organized, and committed allies at each stage of the regulatory process to ensure that defenders of the status quo do not succeed in distorting or hijacking the process of change. The broader the coalition of groups with a vested interest in change, the more sweeping, durable, and effective the new rules. In the absence of such a coalition, change will be elusive, as illustrated by the following example.

During the late 1960s and early 1970s, criticism built up about the activities of multinational corporations (MNCs) in the Third World. They were accused of abusing market power, engaging in predatory pricing and other restrictive business practices, rigging transfer prices to evade taxes, violating labor rights, bribing officials to obtain concessions, and engaging in numerous other forms of extortion and exploitation.[77] A specific focus for the critics arose in the wake of the 1973 overthrow of the Chilean president, Salvador Allende, who had threatened to nationalize the American ITT Corporation. The events in Chile heightened a growing climate of public outrage which prompted the UN and OECD to establish a series of committees of eminent persons to study the effects of MNCs and issue codes regulating their conduct. MNCs were implacable in their opposition to such codes or any other form of business regulation and persistently lobbied their governments to disband the various committees. In the end, no mechanism for complaints against abuse of power by MNCs was established, and the few codes and guidelines adopted had no legal force whatsoever. "[I]t was a classic case of . . . diffuse interests such as consumers getting symbolic rewards (like a platitudinous set of guidelines) and concentrated interests (MNCs) getting tangible rewards (non-enforcement, business as usual, Pinochet replacing Allende)."[78]

---

[76] Anthony Downs, "Up and Down With Ecology—The "Issue-Attention Cycle," *Public Interest* 28 (Summer 2001), 38.

[77] Richard Barnett and Ronald Mueller, *Global Reach: The Power of the Multinational Corporations* (New York: Simon & Schuster, 1974); S. Litvac and T. Maule, "The Multinational Firm and Conflicting National Interests," *Journal of World Trade* 3 (1969), 309–316; Seymore Rubin, "Multinational Enterprises and National Sovereignty: A Skeptic's Analysis," *Law and Policy in International Business* 3, no. 1 (1971), 1–41.

[78] Braithwaite and Drahos, *Global Business Regulation*, 193; and Edelman, *The Symbolic Uses of Politics*.

The general point is that publics will need support from concentrated groups with real resources, power, and expertise to bring about effective regulatory change. Such allies can be nongovernmental, public-sector, or private-sector "entrepreneurs" of change. They are entrepreneurs because they know how to mobilize public sentiment by capitalizing on a crisis or failure. The entrepreneur seeks to sustain public attention by providing information at key junctures of the regulatory process. Crucially, the entrepreneur involves himself or herself to the best of his or her abilities in the process of change, offering counsel, logistics, financial and technical expertise, or otherwise empowering poorly resourced societal groups adversely affected by the regulatory status quo. The motives of the entrepreneur need not be altruistic; they can be perfectly self-interested.

Nongovernmental Entrepreneurs of Regulatory Change. Wilson, a keen observer of the U.S. regulatory scene, noted in the late 1970s: "[A]n important organizational change has occurred that has altered the normal advantage enjoyed by [special interests] . . . —the emergence of 'watchdog' or 'public interest' associations that have devised ways of maintaining themselves without having to recruit or organize the people who will be affected by a policy."[79] He attributed the emergence of these groups to a reduction in the cost of obtaining effective access to the political process. He also pointed out that "public interest" lobbies had been successful in attracting funding via the Ford foundation and similar sponsors and the use of computerized direct-mail fund-raiser.[80]

A similar trend is observable at the transnational level. International NGOs and various other civil society groups have been mushrooming over the last twenty years. Their activities have been facilitated by the Internet revolution that dramatically reduced communication and information costs. Increasingly, non-state actors engage in networks and coalitions jointly to highlight common concerns. Some NGOs go further, playing a prominent oversight role by creating their own global monitoring schemes or feeding into or coopting existing oversight structures, as illustrated in Sikkink's project study in which she notes: "[H]uman rights NGOs and networks have been the most important sources of timely information in the process of human rights regulation. Even when international organizations and domestic and international courts became more deeply involved in the process of human rights regulation, NGOs often provided the original sources of information about human rights viola-

---

[79] Wilson, "The Politics of Regulation," 369. See also Michael Pertschuk, *Revolt against Regulation: The Rise and Pause of the Consumer Movement* (Berkeley: University of California Press, 1982), 5–45.

[80] Wilson, "The Politics of Regulation," 385.

tions used by these actors. To the degree that effective oversight requires costly information, these non-profit NGOs have often taken on the burden and the cost of providing this information."[81]

The main problem with nongovernmental entrepreneurs, however, remains that their resources frequently do not match their ambitions or needs and are insignificant compared to the means at the disposal of industry groups. Equally, they lack the formal authority of public officials. While they are often effective in attracting attention to a cause, they seldom have the resources, expertise, or authority to influence the implementation and enforcement of regulation. For example, the ineffective regulatory response to the Bhopal disaster may be attributed, in part, to the weakness of the alliance demanding change to follow through after the glare of publicity had died down. The alliance comprised mainly NGOs, such as Greenpeace, Amnesty International, and the Sierra Club—organizations with limited budgets and crowded agendas.

In his analysis of civil regulation, Vogel sums up the limits of NGOs as entrepreneurs, noting that although they have been relatively effective in demonstrating failures and mobilizing support to create new regulatory mechanisms, their lack of sufficient resources often prevents them from "persuad[ing] significant numbers of firms to adhere to [these mechanisms] or . . . developing effective monitoring and enforcement mechanisms that . . . change and challenge the regulatory status quo."[82] We would add that there are strong incentives for NGOs to focus their attention on the first phase of regulation—agenda-setting. The immediate benefits to NGOs of mobilizing campaigns are likely to be high: media attention brings them funding, new members, and public support. By contrast, engagement in the detailed elaboration of regulations or closely monitoring their enforcement is more time-consuming, more resource-intensive, and less easily effective or noticed.

Public Officials as Entrepreneurs of Regulatory Change. Public officials are a second important category of entrepreneurs of regulatory change. In contrast to NGOs, some public officials have the resources, expertise, and authority with which to affect regulation beyond the agenda-setting phase, shaping implementation and enforcement. For ex-

---

[81] Sikkink, "From State Responsibility to Individual Criminal Accountability: A New Regulatory Model for Core Human Rights Violations," this volume; Margaret Keck and Kathryn Sikkink, *Activists Beyond Borders: Advocacy Networks in International Politics* (Ithaca, NY: Cornell University Press, 1998); and David Held, Anthony McGrew, David Goldblatt, and Jonathan Perraton, *Global Transformations* (Stanford, CA: Stanford University Press, 1999). See also chapters by Abbott and Snidal, Barrows, Helleiner, and Vogel, this volume.

[82] Vogel, "The Private Regulation of Global Corporate Conduct," this volume.

ample, judges are one group of public officials who have often been effective defenders of the interests of weaker societal groups against capture actors.[83] In the United States, for example, state and federal courts have made it rather easy to challenge decisions by regulatory agencies through liberalizing the rules governing standing.[84] Courts have insisted on public participation in the decision-making process of regulatory agencies and also have demanded high levels of transparency; specifically, regulators are enjoined to demonstrate that they have not only invited but also taken into account public inputs.[85] More recently, courts have asked that agency decisions implementing *global* regulation must be subject to the same administrative law procedures and review on the same basis as purely domestic agency action.[86]

At the international level, judicial review is now quite robust within the EU and WTO. The European Court of Justice (ECJ) offers a particularly striking case of public entrepreneurship at the implementation and enforcement stages. In the years following the signing of the Treaty of Rome which established the European Economic Community, small concentrated groups opposed to integration managed to successfully lobby na-

---

[83] We mentioned courts in the discussion of institutional supply of oversight mechanisms. In that section, courts are passive actors. Courts can also be activist, in which case we classify them as public entrepreneurs. Laffont and Tirole offer a similar distinction; they write: "We are here taking a passive view of the role of courts. That is, they act on hard information transmitted by various parties (i.e., whistle-blowers, including consumers, mass media, discontented or idealistic civil servants, etc.) and content themselves with correcting deviations from what is specified in the constitution . . . Courts may exert a more activist role and act on the basis of soft information. They then have discretionary power and compete with the executive and legislative branches in filling in unforeseen contingencies" (Jean-Jacques Laffont and Jean Tirole, "The Politics of Government Decision Making: Regulatory Institutions," *Journal of Law, Economics, and Organization* 6 (Spring 1990), 1–31, 5. The question of why some judges or public officials more generally become activists as opposed to servants to capture forces is deep and highly relevant but beyond the scope of this study.

[84] Wilson, "The Politics of Regulation," 385–386; McCubbins, Noll, and Weingast, "Administrative Procedures as Instruments of Political Control," 272.

[85] Martin Shapiro, "'Deliberative', 'Independent' Technocracy v. Democratic Politics: Will the Globe Echo the EU?" *Law and Contemporary Problems* 68 (Summer/Autumn 2005), 356; see also Richard Stewart, "The Reformation of American Administrative Law," *Harvard Law Review* (1975), 1667; and Cass Sunstein, "Factions, Self-Interest, and the APA: Four Lessons Since 1946," *Virginia Law Review* 72 (1986), 271–296. In addition, legal doctrinal developments since the 1980s, in conjunction with new civil procedures, have made class actions, multi-districting, and consolidation possible. This has allowed groups concerned, for example, with the health risks of tobacco to launch salvos of lawsuits against tobacco companies and contribute to changing tobacco from a virtually unregulated drug to one whose advertising is banned and consumption in public places prohibited (Braithwaite and Drahos, *Global Business Regulation*, 374).

[86] See Richard Stewart, "US Administrative Law: A Model for Global Administrative Law?" *Law and Contemporary Problems* 68 (2005), 63–108, 79.

tional governments for nontariff barriers and other trade protectionist measures, thereby robbing European consumers of significant economic benefits promised in the Treaty. All governments were complicit in trade violations; thus, none had an incentive to sue another member-state government for fear of tit-for-tat retaliation.

The judges on the ECJ could seemingly do little since only member-states and the Commission had a right to bring cases to them, and very few cases were brought despite a growing number of violations. However, the judges waged a vigorous information campaign about a previously obscure provision in the Treaty, namely Article 177, which authorizes the Court to issue "preliminary rulings" on any question involving the interpretation of Community law arising in the national courts. In particular, the Article 177 procedure provided a framework for links between the Court and individual litigants, their lawyers, and lower national courts, enabling them to challenge national regulation incompatible with the Treaty. Through this Court-built alliance, the judges successfully transferred a large portion of the business of interpreting and applying Community law away from the immediate province of captive member-state governments.[87]

A further example in the arena of trade is given by Judith Goldstein and Richard Steinberg, who trace the way members of the Appellate Body of the WTO Dispute Settlement Mechanism have used their discretion to open up the dispute process as well as to shape trade rules. These public officials have opened up the dispute process by allowing amicus curiae briefs submitted by non-state actors, as well as by permitting private lawyers to represent governments in oral proceedings despite U.S. and EU opposition. They have shaped trade rules by interpreting ambiguities in formal agreements such as in widening the territorial area over which states can claim action to conserve exhaustible natural resources (the Shrimp-Turtle case).[88]

Judicial activism also plays a key role in the study by Sikkink. Individual judges, such as Judge Garzon in Spain, have become powerful drivers of greater regulation of human rights and in particular of more enforcement, notably by offering new judicial avenues to the victims of human rights abuses. Sikkink notes: "The inclusion of litigants . . . in the pro-change alliance multiplies by hundreds the number of potential actors

[87] See Anne-Marie Burley and Walter Mattli, "Europe Before the Court: A Political Theory of Legal Integration," *International Organization* 47 (1993), 44–76; and Walter Mattli and Anne-Marie Slaughter, "Revisiting the European Court of Justice," *International Organization* 52 (1998), 177–209.

[88] Judith Goldstein and Richard Steinberg, "Regulatory Shift: The Rise of Judicial Liberalization at the WTO," this volume.

who could intervene in core human rights issues."[89] Other public entrepreneurs have also made fundamental contributions toward improving the effectiveness of the human rights regime. The drafting of the statute of the International Criminal Court (the ICC), for example, was the product of a transgovernmental network of foreign ministry lawyers from a core group of like-minded countries, including Canada, Argentina, Sweden, Norway, and Holland.

In sum, public officials are vested with formal authority to ensure that regulation is implemented and enforced. This includes officials ranging from legislators and bureaucrats to experts in specialized agencies and judges. Although public officials often are subject to capture, we have argued that where public officials use their authority to ensure that regulation is applied to meet broader societal interests, they become key actors in coalitions of entrepreneurs of regulatory change.[90]

Private-Sector Entrepreneurs of Regulatory Change. Finally, although often ignored, specific private-sector (or corporate) actors may also be a crucial group of entrepreneurs of regulatory change. Their expertise, resources, and interests make them particularly important in negotiations over the details of regulation (where often they have more expertise than government officials), and in the implementation and enforcement of regulation. But do they have an incentive? Here we explore why some corporate actors may diverge in their assessment of the desirability and suitability of the regulatory status quo.

We propose four categories of corporate entrepreneurs who may have an economic incentive to organize and lobby against capture regulation and to join alliances fighting for regulatory change.

1. *Corporate consumers* are firms that suffer the consequences of capture as purchasers of goods and services. They may turn against regulated producers for the same reasons individual consumers do, namely excessive prices or faulty products. Corporate consumers tend to be concentrated and highly influential—unlike mass consumers. They will have an incentive to oppose capture regulation when the proportion of the product of a regulated (i.e., sheltered) industry bought by these users increases,

[89] Sikkink, "From State Responsibility to Individual Criminal Accountability: A New Regulatory Model for Core Human Rights Violations," this volume.

[90] For more examples and discussion, see Abbott and Snidal, "The Governance Triangle: Regulatory Standards Institutions and the Shadow of the State," this volume; see also Abraham Newman, "Building Transnational Civil Liberties: Transgovernmental Entrepreneurs and the European Data Privacy Directive," *International Organization* 62, no. 1 (2008), 103–130.

perhaps in conjunction with a profit squeeze or technological development.[91] For example, financial sector firms came to rely increasingly on advanced telecommunication services for trading during the 1970s and 1980s. The prices of these services were regulated and high, resulting in quickly growing operational costs for corporate users. Unsurprisingly, these users decided to fight the rigid price structure for IT services and to push energetically for deregulation in national telecommunication industries, along with other major users of computerized communications. The greatest push and quickest deregulation response occurred in the United States, United Kingdom, and Japan—countries with the largest capital markets.[92]

2. *Corporate newcomers* are actors who enter the business scene after capture regulation has been negotiated. Such regulation is frequently meant to allow established firms to control entry and retard growth of new firms. Technological advances, however, may spawn new competitors who, alongside consumer groups, will oppose the regulation. In communications, for example, the advent of the silicon chips, microwave towers, and satellites allowed new firms, such as MCI, to challenge the incumbent monopolist, AT&T, whose business was built on buried-cable technology. The new firms became powerful lobbyists for deregulation domestically and internationally.[93]

3. *Corporations at risk* comprise a third and prominent type of corporate actors who can be particularly effective in promoting regulatory change. These are actors who come to support change because their economic viability or survival depends on new regulatory models. Survival may be at stake as a result of a significant increase in the scale and risk of negative consequences deriving from the regulatory status quo. Such increase, in turn, may be due to revolutionary changes in production, information, and telecommunication technologies or fundamental institutional or legal changes (e.g., introduction of new accountability mechanisms or changes in liability rules).

Consider the following example: In the pre-Chernobyl era, vendors of nuclear plants strove to satisfy no more than minimum national safety regulation. This mind-set was fundamentally altered by the Chernobyl disaster. Besieged, the nuclear power industry jettisoned its traditional hardware-oriented minimum standards approach and replaced it with a

[91] Christopher Hood, *Explaining Economic Policy Reversals* (Buckingham: Open University Press, 1994), 31.

[92] Jill Hills, *Deregulating Telecoms: Competition and Control in the United States, Japan, and Britain* (London: Pinter, 1986).

[93] Martha Derthick and Paul Quirk, *The Politics of Deregulation*, 174–206.

commitment to full transparency and continuous safety improvement. The reason was plain: the industry could not afford a second Chernobyl; it had become a "global community of fate"[94] where an attitude of "not my brother's keeper" had been replaced by "everything my brother does is going to affect me."[95] As a result, nuclear operators worldwide established the World Association of Nuclear Operators (WANO) in 1989 to "maximize the safety and reliability of the operation of nuclear power plants by exchanging information and encouraging communication, comparison and emulation among its members."[96] The organization is credited with having built up the capacity of less sophisticated operators to implement and comply with demanding new industry safety standards via technical support and exchange programs. In addition, WANO publishes annually updated performance indicators of the industry in the areas of nuclear plant safety, reliability, and personnel safety.[97] Such transparency and proactive self-regulatory stance are the industries' best bet for survival and constitute a stark contrast with its pre-Chernobyl approach.[98]

Insurers offer another example of "corporations at risk." They have an intrinsic interest in reducing the risk of having to pay for catastrophic loss of life and similar events resulting from capture regulation. As such risks increase, insurers will push for and help to enforce stricter safety standards. Global regulatory improvements in the safety of sea transport, for example, were from time immemorial "not [driven by] concern for the lives of sailors, slaves, or emigrants, but concern for the security of maritime investment."[99] More recently, most insurers would not offer services to shippers who did not comply with strict safety regulation; and shippers unable to present insurance certificates cannot enter most ports of the world.[100] The Barrows study compellingly illustrates how insurers have

[94] Braithwaite and Drahos, *Global Business Regulation*, 319; see also Joseph Rees, *Hostages of Each Other: The Transformation of Nuclear Safety Since Three Mile Island* (Chicago: University of Chicago Press, 1994).

[95] Rees, *Hostages of Each Other*, 45.

[96] See www.wano.org.uk.

[97] The data are posted on its Web site.

[98] See Kiran Verma, Barry M. Mitnick, Alfred A. Marcus, "Making Incentive Systems Work: Incentive Regulation in the Nuclear Power Industry," *Journal of Public Administration Research and Theory* 9, no. 3 (July 1999), 395–436.

[99] Braithwaite and Drahos, *Global Business Regulation*, 436.

[100] Jack Plano, *International Approaches to the Problems of Marine Pollution*, Institute for the Study of International Organization Monograph Series, no. 7 (Sussex: University of Sussex, 1972). At the domestic level, insurers have similarly been key promoters of regulatory change. For example, in alliance with consumer groups, they have ensured the success of campaigns for compulsory airbag installation in motor vehicles; and they assisted effective tobacco regulation, for example, by threatening to withdraw insurance coverage from companies that failed to protect workers and the public from passive smoking.

become "corporations at risk" as the explosion in the size of tankers and the rapid increase in the number of ships increased their exposure to the point where maritime disasters endanger their very survival.[101]

Other examples of "corporations at risk" are presented by Vogel, who focuses particularly on global firms that market to consumers.[102] If such firms become associated with a disaster, scandal, or failure, anti-corporate campaigners are likely to target them, taking advantage of the firms' vulnerability to threats to their public reputation and the value of their brands. As a result, many such highly visible firms have forged alliances with NGOs, producing civil regulation judged to be relatively effective.

4. *Corporate levelers of the playing field* are corporate actors who—faced with more stringent and costly regulation than competitors elsewhere—will support societal groups lobbying for more stringent regulation on a wider scale. If they have to abide by the rules, so should others.

For example, European corporate actors, already subject to an EU regulation requiring Eco-Management and Auditing Scheme (EMAS) standards on public disclosure of the results of company policies to achieve continuous environmental improvement,[103] forged an alliance with the international green movement to force U.S. and Asian businesses to abide by the same demanding rules. Together they succeeded in writing key features of the European regulation into global standards issued by the International Organization for Standardization (ISO).[104] Similarly, German corporate actors teamed up with environmental groups in the late 1980s to lobby for a pan-European regulation curbing nitrogen oxide emissions which cause acid rain, a move opposed by corporate groups in France, Italy, and the United Kingdom. This initiative can be explained, in part, with reference to a 1983 German regulation requiring cars to have catalytic converters. A European regulation would level the playing field and open a vast market to German manufacturers of converters and related technologies such as fuel injection.[105]

---

[101] Barrows, "Racing to the Top . . . At Last: The Regulation of Safety in Shipping," this volume. For a discussion of the role of insurers in global environmental regulation, see Deborah Saunders Davenport, *Global Environmental Negotiations and US Interests* (New York: Palgrave Macmillan, 2006), 201–202.

[102] Vogel, "The Private Regulation of Global Corporate Conduct," this volume.

[103] EU Directive 1836/93; see also Kelly Kollman and Aseem Prakash, "Green By Choice? Cross-National Variations in Firms' Responses to EMS-Based Environmental Regimes," *World Politics* 53 (April 2001), 399–430.

[104] Braithwaite and Drahos, *Global Business Regulation,* 265–266 and 281.

[105] Marc Levy, "European Acid Rain: The Power of Tote-Board Diplomacy," in Peter Haas, Robert Keohane, and Marc Levy, eds., *Institutions for the Earth: Sources of Effective International Environmental Protection* (Cambridge, MA: MIT Press, 1993), 95; Braithwaite and Drahos, *Global Business Regulation,* 265. For more examples of the "level playing field" logic, see Elizabeth DeSombre, "Baptists and Bootleggers for the Environment: The Origins of United States Unilateral Sanctions," *Journal of Environment and Develop-*

Global firms targeted by NGO activists may similarly turn into corporate levelers of the playing field. The adoption of higher social or environmental standards in response to activist pressure will raise the firms' costs. They thus have an incentive to work toward industry-wide regulation, seeking to get their competitors to adopt similar standards to create a more level playing field.[106]

In sum, there are at least four categories of private-sector actors who may become entrepreneurs of regulatory change. Endowed with specialist expertise that is often greater than that of governments with formal authority over regulation, such private-sector entrepreneurs are crucial actors in coalitions that can ensure regulatory change in the direction of broader public rather than narrower private interest.

IDEAS

We have argued that crises, failures, and public outrage can bring together alliances of entrepreneurs to put pressure on those who have captured regulation. The resulting pressures may well "constrain" the agents of capture but will not necessarily change their preferences. This makes the regulatory process vulnerable to back-sliding: as soon as the pressure diminishes, the agents of capture will return to life as usual. A shift in ideas or the emergence of a new set of ideas, however, may have a particularly powerful effect on change if it can offer a new mind-set to former capture actors, reshaping their preferences and redefining their understanding of what regulatory arrangements are best for them. Such a change in mind-set can permit a shift toward a more public interest basis for regulation. Put simply, when some capture actors can no longer rationalize or justify their policies or actions in the old terms, they seek new ideas to frame their actions.

As argued above, where disasters, scandals, and the like come to public attention, they can trigger a process of regulatory change. Accidents and disasters not only shake public confidence in the managers, politicians, and regulators at fault, they may also shake the ideas, values, or ideologies that underpin the status quo, destroying the legitimacy of the old way of framing regulation. For example, in international human rights, the legitimacy of the state accountability model for enforcing rights weakened considerably after revelations that it was failing and resulting in impunity. This discredited the individuals or governments who were charged with

---

ment 4 (1995), 53–75; David Vogel, *Trading Up: Consumer and Environmental Regulation in a Global Economy* (Cambridge, MA: Harvard University Press, 1995); and David Vogel and Robert Kagan, eds., *Dynamics of Regulatory Change: How Globalization Affects National Regulatory Policies* (Berkeley: University of California Press, 2004).

[106] See chapters by Abbott and Snidal, Barrows, and Vogel.

prosecuting within the old regulatory framework. It also broke the coherence of the model itself, producing space for a new set of values and beliefs to emerge.[107] Similarly, the values of major decision-makers were reordered when the IMF-led bailout model for dealing with financial crises failed in the late 1990s. For example, moral hazard became ranked as a much higher concern and one which the old model could not adequately deal with.[108]

The failure of the old set of ideas in each case opened up space for new ideas to emerge. A battle is usually triggered among competing alternative ideas. For example, in the international human rights example above, the alternatives to the discredited "impunity" model were either restorative justice or retributive justice. With regard to the financial crises example, the alternatives to the discredited "bailouts" included either a statutory mechanism or a market-based one.

In each case, competing ideas provided alternatives among which entrepreneurs could chose—including for strategic or consequential reasons rather than value or ideational reasons. For example, in financial regulation, the choice by bankers (previously hostile to further regulation) to back Collective Action Clauses was made in part to avert a statutory mechanism for resolving financial crises.[109] In the human rights example, some of those who backed a restorative justice mechanism did so to avert criminal liability.[110] Although the motivation for change can be strategic or instrumental—as these examples suggest, by taking up and supporting regulation backed by a new set of ideas, actors propel themselves into a new politics replete with new drivers and constraints, making it more difficult to slide back to old justifications (such as for non-regulation), and creating the scope for broadening and deepening a coalition supporting change.

Crucially, ideas do not just provide choices for individual entrepreneurs; they also provide a basis for the formation of coalitions among entrepreneurs pressing for regulatory change. To quote Goldstein and Keohane, ideas "may serve as coalitional glue to facilitate the cohesion of particular groups."[111] A coalition of entrepreneurs may not share the

---

[107] Sikkink, "From State Responsibility to Individual Criminal Accountability: A New Regulatory Model for Core Human Rights Violations," this volume.

[108] Helleiner, "Filling a Hole in Global Financial Governance? The Politics of Regulating Sovereign Debt Restructuring," this volume.

[109] Ibid.

[110] Sikkink, "From State Responsibility to Individual Criminal Accountability."

[111] Goldstein and Keohane, *Ideas and Foreign Policy*, 12. Put more formally in terms of the folk theorem, because almost all games with repeated play have multiple equilibria, the ideas held by players are often the key to a game's outcome. Ibid., 17.

same interest, but may well join forces where a particular set of ideas creates a common ground for them.

In other words, faced with competing new regulatory solutions, coalitions comprising public, private, and non-state actors will form around the solution that best meets their interests. This does not imply that solutions perfectly "fit" the interests of each member of the coalition. It is precisely because they do not—because they are a loose fit—that ideas can create common ground capable of drawing together a coalition. However, the consequence may be that the emerging new regulatory regime is more constraining than initially thought by some. For example, for some companies embracing self-regulatory codes, the resulting constraints have been sharper and more severe than initially expected--as investors, insurers, auditors, and consumers have joined activists in holding the companies to account.[112]

In sum, on the demand side of our account of regulatory change, ideas can make a difference because after a crisis or disaster, some actors may have to reframe their regulatory preferences. This can involve choosing a new set of ideas which can catalyze broader, deeper coalitions for change, and stronger constraints than initially envisaged, making any backsliding on regulatory change even more difficult.

Ideas also affect the institutional setting within which regulation takes place. The following scenarios are worth considering. The first effect concerns the way ideas embedded in institutions affect human actions. As sociologists of institutions March and Olsen remind us, ideas can embed particular approaches in institutions by framing the sense of appropriateness that officials use to choose among possible actions.[113] These embedded ideas about what is appropriate (or not) guide actors when their interests are unclear, or when it is unclear to them how best to pursue specific interests. For example, where institutionally embedded framing ideas favor innovation or risk-taking, they may affect choice beyond what demand-side factors do and thus further limit backsliding on regulatory change.

Ideas can also have an effect on the nature of regulatory discourse and thus the de facto openness and participatory nature of regulatory institutions. The narrower and more technical the regulatory discussions thought necessary or appropriate by regulators and those they regulate to tackle a problem, the less likely they will be subject to broad scrutiny.

---

[112] David Graham and Ngaire Woods, "Making Corporate Self-Regulation Effective in Developing Countries," in Dana Brown and Ngaire Woods, eds., *Making Global Self-Regulation Effective in Developing Countries* (Oxford: Oxford University Press, 2007).

[113] James March and Johan Olsen, *Rediscovering Institutions: The Organizational Basis of Politics* (New York: Free Press, 1989).

This may favor capture since the language and concepts used by regulators and those they regulate are less accessible or understood by the public, hence information is harder to interpret, and coalitions for change are less likely to form. De facto, the institutional setting becomes more closed. However, when the ideas underpinning the industry and its regulators are demonstrated to fail, the paradigm must change for both regulators and the regulated.

Finally, while ideas may shape pro-change coalitions as well as institutional practices, institutions, in turn, may influence the outcome of battles of ideas triggered by a regulatory crisis. A new regulatory idea that "fits" with already existing but not-discredited institutional mechanisms (for implementing and enforcing regulation, for example) may well prevail over rival ideas that necessitate the creation of costly new institutions for these ideas to work. For example, "restorative justice" in the human rights case would have demanded whole new structures and tribunals. By contrast, retributive justice ideas in the human rights case fit with existing laws and precedents embodied in national criminal justice procedures. This made regulatory change easier. Likewise in the financial crisis case, collective-action clauses were familiar practice in London bond markets, whereas a statutory mechanism demanded the creation of a new independent institution that could adjudicate among creditors' claims.

In sum, the set of ideas most likely to triumph after a crisis is not only that which best expresses the interests of powerful entrepreneurs and permits a coalition to form, but that which fits most easily into existing and not discredited institutions and mechanisms, representing the smallest step into the unknown.

DEMAND IN INSTITUTIONAL CONTEXT

As discussed at the outset, demand always operates in a specific institutional context. The openness of governments, the effectiveness of a bureaucracy, the robustness of the rule of law, the structure of regulatory institutions and oversight, as well as political culture each condition the impact of demand on regulation. As already argued, at the global level, the institutional context is more complex: there is no unitary regulator with a coercive fiat.[114] The global institutional arena is a patchwork of different contexts. This explains variations in the impact of global regulation and demonstrates the extent to which the relative success of demand

---

[114] Jonathan Baert Wiener, "Global Environmental Regulation: Instrument Choice in Legal Context," *Yale Law Journal* 108, no. 4 (January 1999), 677–800.

in bringing about regulatory change is conditioned by what we called "institutional supply."

The project studies offer several fascinating illustrations of the interplay between demand and supply which are consistent with the propositions summarized in figure 1.1. Let us mention four.

Helleiner describes how the initial ambitious proposal for a formal Sovereign Debt Restructuring Mechanism (SDRM) ended up being replaced by a much weaker solution, namely Collective Action Clauses (CAC) and a voluntary code of conduct for debt restructuring. The groups demanding far-reaching changes quickly faced staunch opposition, especially from the private creditor community. On the institutional supply side, the initial SDRM debate took place in quite an inclusive context involving "access points" not just for governmental actors but also for the private sector and not-for-profit groups in various international forums involving IMF and governmental officials. "But when consensus could not be reached . . . the negotiations . . . took place in a very different institutional context . . . [T]he process [became] dominated by private negotiations between a small self-select informal 'club' of sovereign debtors and representatives of the private creditor interests. These contexts left each process closed to the wide range of actors who had contributed to the SDRM debate and more vulnerable to capture by the very group—wealthier sovereign debtors and private creditors—who had historically been most wary of the construction of international rules in this area."[115]

Sikkink's study on human rights finds that several institutional features affect the ability of victims and their NGO allies to successfully pursue lawsuits. First, democratic countries with rule-of-law systems that are at least minimally fair, transparent, accessible, and open are more likely to hold human rights trials. Not surprisingly, Latin America, the region experiencing the most significant wave of transition to democracy, is also the region with the largest number of trials. Second, institutional features of the legal system also matter. Civil law systems with provisions for private prosecution in criminal cases give victims and their allies more access to domestic courts than common law systems or civil law systems without provisions for private prosecutions. "Judicial institutions where the government controls access to criminal prosecution will be more open to capture than judicial institutions where private citizens have some ability to

---

[115] Helleiner, "Filling a Hole in Global Financial Governance? The Politics of Regulating Sovereign Debt Restructuring," this volume. A similar narrowing of participation to private actors is traced by Jayne Godfrey and Ian Langfield-Smith in respect of Australia's adoption of global accounting standards: "Regulatory Capture in the Globalisation of Accounting Standards," *Environment and Planning* 37 (Autumn 2005), 1975–1993.

initiate criminal trials."[116] Third, regional institutions also make a difference. Latin America, with its high density of Inter-American human rights norms and institutions, has a more propitious legal context for human rights activism than Asia or the Middle East with no such institutions. On the demand side, Sikkink finds that the level of severity of human rights violations affects the decision to use trials. Countries with more severe violations are more likely to use trials than those with less severe violations. This fits with the argument that scale and scope of negative externalities associated with the regulatory status quo influence the demand for change. Finally, countries that have negotiated or pacted transitions to democracy are less likely to use trials than those that have society-led transitions forcing authoritarian regimes out of power. This is consistent with the proposition that the relative power of the pro-change alliance vis-à-vis capture groups determines outcomes. "[I]n pacted transition, the military used their power to ensure their continued capture of regulation."[117]

The study by Vogel shows that civil regulation is weak in some areas because of lack of forceful demand, often in conjunction with flimsy institutional supply. Pro-change coalitions can be weak for three reasons. First, most consumers buy products on the basis of price, convenience, and quality—not on whether the goods were produced "responsibly"— and thus may not be keen on joining pro-change alliances. Second, civil society in many developing countries is weak; further, repressive regimes will prevent such societies from developing and defending their own social, political, and environmental interests vis-à-vis the ruling elite and industry groups. Third, private-sector entrepreneurs may be rare. Few firms are willing to mobilize in favor of Corporate Social Responsibility (CSR) simply because the financial benefits of CSR remain for the most part either modest or elusive. "As long as more 'responsible' global firms do not enjoy consistently stronger financial performance than their less responsible competitors—and to date they do not—the incentives of firms to invest substantial resources into complying with civil regulation will remain limited."[118] Further, the growing economic prominence of global firms based in non-western countries, who face fewer domestic pressures from activist groups, has exacerbated the competitive challenge faced by more "responsible" western firms. Last but not least, the weakness or absence of institutional mechanisms of monitoring and enforcement remains the Achilles' heel of much civil regulation. In the areas where civil

---

[116] Sikkink, "From State Responsibility to Individual Criminal Accountability: A New Regulatory Model for Core Human Rights Violations," this volume.

[117] Ibid.

[118] Vogel, "The Private Regulation of Global Corporate Conduct," this volume.

regulation is effective, it "is in large measure due to the fact that . . . [it was] embedded in voluntary agreements between or among governments with both private and public enforcement mechanisms complementing one another."[119]

The study by Barrows, finally, provides an example of rapidly increasing regulatory effectiveness in global shipping. Indeed, since the 1970s, dozens of international conventions have been drafted and enhanced by working monitoring and enforcement mechanisms. On the demand side, large-scale maritime disasters have mobilized a powerful pro-change coalition of public entrepreneurs, such as influential environmental NGOs and well-resourced private-sector entrepreneurs, most notably insurance companies and classification societies. Owners of large ships in developed countries have also joined the pro-change coalition in an attempt to ensure that the cost of regulation is shared equally within the global industry. The resulting broad and sustained demand for regulatory change has been operating in an "extensive" institutional context, favoring common interest regulation. Specifically, beginning in the 1960s, the development of more accessible participatory mechanisms at the supranational level, notably in the International Maritime Organization and the International Labour Organization, have played a major role in enabling broad-based negotiations. These mechanisms ensured that the views of seafarers, civilians using sea transport, and the populations in many coastal states, as well as various NGOs and other pro-change groups were taken into consideration. These actors have become active participants not only during the agenda-setting and negotiation stages but also in the later stages of the regulatory process, thus ensuring a dramatic improvement in safety regulation in shipping. Some pockets of regulatory laxity persist, however. Barrows explains them also in terms of demand and supply factors. The regulatory regimes in developing countries with failing legal systems and lacking democratic tradition tend to be captured by shipowners with no interest in international shipping conventions. Unsurprisingly, enforcement of these conventions in these countries is practically nonexistent.

CONCLUSION

When accidents such as Bhopal and Chernobyl occur, or global challenges arise such as climate change or financial stability in the wake of crises like the recent U.S. subprime mortgage crisis, how do we know whether a new set of regulations will be adopted, how robustly it will be implemented and enforced, and in whose benefit? The answer lies in the politics that

---

[119] Ibid.

plays out at each stage of the regulatory process. At the core of our framework are demand- and supply-side factors that explain varying regulatory outcomes.

We have derived the demand side from national-level theories of regulatory capture, highlighting "information" as a key factor. Going further, we have developed an analytical framework to deal with the reality that when the glare of adverse publicity about a crisis recedes, powerful and well-resourced defenders of the regulatory status quo might quietly take over the details of change in regulation, creating convenient loopholes and weakening the capacity and resolve of regulators. We have identified conditions under which coalitions of nongovernmental, public-sector, and private-sector entrepreneurs may emerge, rendering such backsliding less likely. In particular, we have developed categories of private-sector entrepreneurs who could have an incentive to push against regulatory capture and whose resources and expertise would permit a longer-term and more effective pressure for adequate implementation and enforcement. Finally, ideas form the third element of the demand side of regulatory change. New ideas are required to inform on how to regulate in novel ways. They also provide a new common ground or glue to hold together a broader coalition of entrepreneurs.

Supply-side factors are equally crucial in our model. By this we mean the institutional context within which the demand for regulatory change is formed, implemented, monitored, and enforced. It is no surprise that those who wish to capture regulation will prefer institutions that they control, in which few competing interests can participate, and to which little public access exists. And this may be easy to achieve in global regulation. In some areas, institutions have been reformed to permit a more timely and informed participation by those representing broader interests. But in many areas of global regulation this is not the case. Global regulation is at great risk of capture. In part this risk is due to institutional constraints—the lack of transparency, due process, and mechanisms of accountability at the global level. Equally important, however, the risk of capture is due to the weakness and unevenness of demand for robust regulation at the global level, largely because the requisite expertise and financial as well as organizational capacity to participate meaningfully in global regulation are not evenly distributed across affected countries or transnational non-state actors.

The Governance Triangle: Regulatory Standards Institutions and the Shadow of the State

Kenneth W. Abbott and Duncan Snidal

WHO SHOULD REGULATE global production? While the state traditionally has been viewed as the appropriate overseer of domestic business activity, the scale and structure of contemporary global production challenge the capacity of even highly developed states to regulate activities that extend beyond their borders. Many developing states lack even the capacity to regulate domestically. Such difficulties have led to calls for alternative forms of governance: "above" the state, in the form of international regulation,[1] and "below" the state, in the form both of nongovernmental organization (NGO) efforts to challenge state regulation and of business initiatives for self-regulation.

These issues are starkly presented by the emergence—mainly since the 1980s—of a plethora of non-state and public-private governance arrangements focused on setting and implementing standards for global production in the areas of labor rights, human rights, and the environment. Key examples include firms and industry associations that adopt self-regulatory codes; NGOs that promote standards for voluntary adoption by firms; and multi-stakeholder organizations involving different combinations of business, NGO, and (limited) state participation that promulgate and implement codes for member and non-member firms.[2]

We thank Sonya Sceats, who has worked with us on key aspects of this project; Walter Mattli and Ngaire Woods, who have provided important oversight of the project; and all of the participants in this volume for valuable suggestions.

[1] Kahler and Lake note that governments sometimes turn to "above the state" solutions based on hierarchy—assigning regulatory authority to dominant states or their regulatory agencies—rather than supranationalism, typified by formal international organizations. Miles Kahler and David Lake, "Economic Integration and Global Governance: Why So Little Supranationalism?" this volume.

[2] In addition, international organizations are increasingly taking account of private actors in standard-setting, as participants and as targets. For example, the ILO and OECD have adopted soft law standards that address firms directly, rather than working indirectly through member states' domestic regulation.

Because they promulgate voluntary norms, these institutions could be viewed as "standards" bodies, more akin to the International Organization for Standardization (ISO) or Codex Alimentarius Commission than to traditional state "regulatory" agencies. However, because of the nature of the substantive problems that their norms address (which reflect social and environmental externalities rather than demands for technical coordination) and the corresponding importance of monitoring and enforcement (due to the strategic structure of those externalities), we view these institutions as engaging in "regulatory standard-setting" (RSS)[3]—essentially a new form of transnational "regulation."[4,5]

RSS schemes exist not only in large numbers, but in great variety. Many are controlled by a single actor or actor type: for example, a firm or industry association or an NGO. Others are managed by two actor types, including such odd bedfellows as firms and NGOs. Still others are tripartite, from the International Labor Organization (ILO) to more recent, looser collaborations that we introduce below. Certain types of arrangements are especially numerous: company and industry codes number in the hundreds, if not the thousands. Other types are relatively uncommon: few tripartite schemes have been created. These empirical patterns raise important questions about the origin and evolution of RSS schemes.

Can these RSS institutions be effective regulators—both individually and taken together as a regulatory system? One major issue, as Mattli and Woods emphasize in their framework chapter, is whether RSS

[3] Regulatory standards aim to control Pigovian externalities, which typically have a Prisoners' Dilemma structure, rather than network externalities, which typically have a Coordination structure, as discussed in Kenneth W. Abbott and Duncan Snidal, "International 'Standards' and International Governance," *Journal of European Public Policy* 8, no. 3 (2001), 345–370.

[4] RSS falls within the definition of "regulation" adopted in the framework chapter— "the organization and control of economic . . . and social activities by means of making, implementing, monitoring, and enforcing of rules"—even though RSS rules are voluntary. Walter Mattli and Ngaire Woods, "In Whose Benefit? Explaining Regulatory Change in Global Politics," this volume.

[5] Vogel's contribution to this volume provides a complementary analysis of what he labels "private" or "civil" regulation, including more detailed analyses of a few important cases. See David Vogel, "The Private Regulation of Global Corporate Conduct." There is a burgeoning literature on the relation between public and private authority in international governance. Important early works include A. Claire Cutler, Virginia Haufler, and Tony Porter, eds., *Private Authority and International Affairs* (Albany, NY: State University of New York Press, 1999); and Virginia Haufler, *A Private Role for the Private Sector: Industry Self-Regulation in a Global Economy* (Washington, DC: Carnegie Endowment for International Peace, 2000). An important recent work that is critical of private authority from a statist perspective is Daniel Drezner, *All Politics Is Global: Explaining International Regulatory Regimes* (Princeton, NJ: Princeton University Press, 2007). We cite other important work below.

schemes, and the larger institutional context in which they operate, can serve the "public interest" or "common interests" rather than being "captured" by particular interests. In addition, RSS schemes take on significant practical and political challenges in attempting to fill perceived gaps in state and international regulation.

As with any regulation, creating standards is only part of the task. Advocates must first place an issue on the political agenda and galvanize relevant groups to action; once substantive standards have been negotiated, drafted, and promulgated, the institution must promote their implementation within target firms, monitor compliance, and even "enforce" them—or at least promote compliance and respond to noncompliance. We refer to these five tasks (Agenda-setting, Negotiation of standards, Implementation, Monitoring, and Enforcement—ANIME) as the "regulatory process."[6]

To act effectively throughout the regulatory process, an institution needs a suite of "competencies." We identify four essential competencies: *independence, representativeness, expertise*, and *operational capacity*. Independence and representativeness help guarantee the "openness and commitment to proper due process" that Mattli and Woods argue are needed for common interest regulation in a proceduralist understanding.[7] Those competencies are also crucial in meeting the political challenges of RSS, including promoting the adoption and implementation of voluntary standards and mobilizing the public to demand compliance. Expertise and operational capacity are essential to effective action throughout the regulatory process.

In principle, these competencies inhere in well-functioning states at the domestic level; yet even the most developed states lack some competencies essential for transnational regulation.[8] It is difficult if not impossible, moreover, for any non-state actor to provide all the competencies on its own. Thus, the most promising strategy may be collaboration: assembling the needed competencies by bringing together actors of different types.

---

[6] Kenneth W. Abbott and Duncan Snidal, "The International Standards Process: Setting and Applying Global Business Norms," in Peter Nobel, ed., *International Standards and the Law* (Berne: Staempfli Publishers, 2005). We thank Walter Mattli and Ngaire Woods for suggesting that we differentiate the first two stages, which were elided in our earlier analysis.

[7] Mattli and Woods, "In Whose Benefit? Explaining Regulatory Change in Global Politics," this volume.

[8] Even a strong domestic state needs the cooperation of firms—as Lindblom argues with respect to the "privileged position" of business—but the prospects for state regulation at the international level are even further impaired, both because firms have vastly enhanced exit options and because states have diminished capacities for regulation. See Charles E. Lindblom, *Politics and Markets: The World's Political-Economic Systems* (New York: Basic Books, 1977).

Yet while there exist many important multi-stakeholder institutions, far more numerous are single-actor schemes, especially company codes. These manifestly lack crucial competencies, notably independence and representativeness, and may be driven by motives akin to capture rather than by common interests.[9] Thus, while certain RSS institutions are promising transnational regulators, one cannot paint too rosy a picture: all the schemes that have emerged are not optimal, and all the optimal schemes have not emerged.[10]

We focus primarily on a positive analysis of the RSS outcomes we observe—including the prevalence of schemes that lack essential competencies—and the possibilities for increasing their effectiveness and public interest orientation. The variables identified by Mattli and Woods are relevant here. In terms of the demand for regulation, information (including demonstration effects), entrepreneurs, and ideas all play significant roles in the emergence and shaping of RSS. In terms of the institutional context, two features stand out. First, in the transnational arena, entrepreneurs can create RSS institutions and promulgate standards at relatively low cost, especially where such schemes do not challenge the authority of states or intergovernmental organizations (IGOs) but only fill gaps in their coverage. Second, once created, RSS schemes face little if any centralized oversight; RSS thus entails a decentralized process of competition for influence, and sometimes of collaboration, especially among private and public-private actors and institutions. Such a process may promote the public interest, but that is not assured.

Within this flexible and decentralized setting, we explain the emerging patterns of regulatory governance as products of distributive bargaining. Just as in their efforts to capture domestic state regulators, firms, NGOs, and other actors operate in the transnational regulatory space not as neutrals seeking "good governance," but as partisans pursuing their special interests and values with differential power and capabilities. Actors bargain implicitly—through individual actions including the strategic creation of single-actor schemes—and explicitly—over the creation, management, and control of collaborative schemes. In this complex bargaining game, competencies serve as power resources as well as regulatory attributes.

[9] An actor cannot be said to "capture" an institution that it creates and controls, but the motive and effect may be similar.

[10] We use "optimal" to refer to an RSS scheme's contribution to the public interest or common interests, based on the proceduralist understanding adopted in the framework chapter, and to its effectiveness in meeting the political and practical challenges of regulation in a global context. We recognize, however, that "optimality" is an inherently problematic and contested concept.

Finally, we return to the role of the state. The RSS system reflects a nuanced, evolving relationship between states (acting singly and collectively) and transnational regulation. The emergence of the system demonstrates that the simple view of the state as centralized, mandatory regulator is inapplicable in the transnational realm. Yet even as transnational governance forms are evolving, states and IGOs continue to play—or have the potential to play—significant roles. Transnationally, at least, states and IGOs act not through coercion but through leadership, legitimation, and support. These background and entrepreneurial roles can influence the bargaining power of other actors and the openness and transparency of RSS procedures in ways that promote outcomes closer to the public interest.

The first section of this chapter introduces the Governance Triangle, which depicts the transnational regulatory space and a range of RSS institutions in terms of the participation of three key actor groups: States, Firms, and NGOs. We characterize these groups broadly, and assume that actors in each group pursue their own interests and values when they participate in an RSS scheme or bargain implicitly or explicitly for influence. Points on the Triangle represent actual schemes. Their dispersion demonstrates that the three actor groups have created a wide variety of institutional forms; these span most of the regulatory space, but are unevenly distributed. This section also shows how the pattern of regulatory governance has shifted over time, from predominantly domestic state regulation to firm self-regulation and NGO schemes, and finally to multi-actor schemes. These empirical patterns pose important questions: why do we see such diversity and uneven distribution among RSS schemes, and how can we explain the variations in RSS over time?

The second section considers which types of RSS schemes are plausible transnational regulators. By examining the stages of the regulatory process, we identify four competencies that are necessary (but not sufficient) for effective common-interest regulation: independence, representativeness, expertise, and operational capacity. We consider which actor groups possess or can acquire which competencies. We conclude that no single group—and hence no single-actor scheme—possesses all necessary competencies. Collaborative schemes can potentially assemble a satisfactory bundle of competencies, yet single-actor RSS institutions far outnumber collaborative schemes. This poses an even deeper puzzle: why do we see so many suboptimal schemes?

In the third section, we address these questions by analyzing the RSS bargaining game. We emphasize interactions between firms and NGOs, largely setting aside the state because of its limited direct role in bargaining. We argue that actor competencies are power resources, supporting both the "go it alone power" that underwrites unilateral schemes and the "inclusion power" that determines participation and influence in collaborative schemes. Because firms generally have the best unilateral alternatives, the most frequent outcome is self-regulation; this will be socially deficient to the extent firms either pursue their own particular interests or, if they are socially responsible, lack the independence and representativeness needed for effective public interest regulation. In some cases, however, NGOs have sufficient power that bargaining will lead to collaboration, which may improve social outcomes. Yet NGO capacities depend on particular circumstances and may not be sufficient in all economic sectors where regulation is demanded. In any event, NGOs are at best imperfect representatives of common interests.

Finally, the discussion turns to how the background roles of states and IGOs may shift the bargaining balance between firms and NGOs in order to achieve socially preferable outcomes. Entrepreneurial state roles include promulgating and promoting norms for adoption by RSS schemes, convening and facilitating bargaining and participation, and creating transparency and other rules that promote regulatory due process and enhance monitoring and enforcement. The state's ultimate capacity is the threat of direct regulation, which encourages private actors to improve their regulatory performance. The last section offers a brief conclusion: The appropriate extent and form of regulation are normative questions, but states' control of key competencies gives them substantial ability to shape transnational regulatory outcomes.

THE GOVERNANCE TRIANGLE

Mapping RSS Schemes on the Triangle

The Governance Triangle in figure 2.1 provides a systematic depiction of the potential universe and actual variety of RSS institutions.[11] It helps us to examine empirically the emergence and distribution of such schemes, and to analyze theoretically the strengths and weaknesses of different structures. As noted above, we define the Triangle in terms of *direct* participation by States, Firms, and NGOs. The surface of the Triangle represents the transnational regulatory space; for clarity, we divide that space into seven zones that represent the possible combinations of actor participation. The labeled points on the Triangle depict RSS institutions; these are identified in table 2.1.[12]

---

[11] For a related but different depiction of the interrelation of these three actors in regulatory activities using a Venn diagram–like logic, see Stepan Wood, "Voluntary Environmental Codes and Sustainability," in Benjamin J. Richardson and Stepan Wood, eds., *Environmental Law for Sustainability* (Oxford: Hart, 2006), 229–276.

[12] Many NGO, industry, and collaborative RSS institutions were created expressly for the purpose of adopting a set of regulatory standards, so that the institution and its regula-

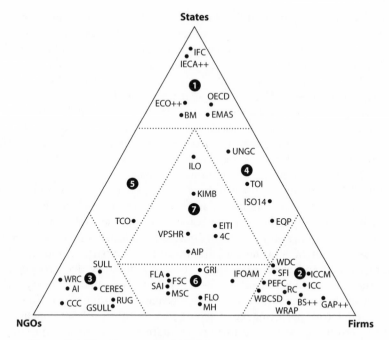

Figure 2.1. The Governance Triangle

The vertex triangles (Zones 1–3) represent situations in which an actor (or set of actors[13]) from a single group adopts and implements regulatory standards largely on its own, with only modest participation, if any, from actors of other types.[14] Zone 1 includes arrangements by which a state, or a group of states in an IGO, sets and applies standards directly to business through national law, IGO rules, soft law or the like. The point labeled OECD in Zone 1, for example, represents the OECD Guidelines for Multinational Enterprises; IECA represents the 1938 Indian Employment of Children Act, an early example of national labor legislation; and ECO represents the 1978 German "Blue Angel" eco-labeling scheme, an

---

tory outcome are tightly intertwined. In the case of preexisting, often larger institutions such as IGOs and states (which may sponsor or participate in multiple RSS schemes), we identify the relevant regulatory outcome in table 2.1.

[13] We only briefly address collective-action and other governance problems presented by the need to organize actors within a given category.

[14] We focus on direct participation in RSS schemes, not indirect impact. Of course, firms, NGOs, and other interest groups often participate in the decision process that underlies states' decisions. Still, the final action, for example, a legislative enactment, is taken by the state alone. Indeed, our ultimate point is that even when the state is not directly involved in RSS schemes, it can nevertheless play an important role in the overall system of regulatory governance.

TABLE 2.1
RSS Schemes on the Governance Triangle

Zone 1	IECA	The Employment of Children Act (India) 1938
	OECD	OECD Guidelines for Multinational Enterprises 1976
	ECO	German Blue Angel eco-label 1978
	BM	WHO Code of Marketing for Breast-milk Substitutes 1981
	EMAS	UK Eco-Management and Audit Scheme 1992
	IFC	World Bank International Finance Corp. Safeguard Policies 1998
Zone 2	GAP	Individual labor rights scheme of Gap Inc. 1992
	BS	The Body Shop's "Trade Not Aid" initiative 1991
	ICC	Int'l Chamber of Commerce Charter for Sustainable Development 1991
	RC	Responsible Care, chemical industry environmental scheme 1987
	WDC	World Diamond Council warranty system for conflict diamonds 2004
	WRAP	Worldwide Responsible Accredited Production, industry labor code 2000
	SFI	Sustainable Forestry Initiative 1994
	PEFC	Programme for the Endorsement of Forest Certification 1999
	WBCSD	World Business Council for Sustainable Development 1992
	ICCM	International Council on Mining and Metals 2001
Zone 3	SULL	Sullivan Principles 1977
	AI	Amnesty International Human Rights Guidelines for Companies 1997
	CCC	Clean Clothes Campaign Code of Labor Practices for apparel 1998
	CERES	CERES Principles on environmental practices and reporting 1989
	RUG	Rugmark labeling scheme to control child labor in carpets 1994
	GSULL	Global Sullivan Principles on economic and social justice 1999
	WRC	Worker Rights Consortium 2000
Zone 4	ISO14	International Organization for Standardization 14001 environmental management standard 1996
	UNGC	United Nations Global Compact 2000
	TOI	Tour Operators Initiative 2000
	EQP	Equator Principles 2003
Zone 5	TCO	TCO Development; office workers' environment standards 1993
Zone 6	IFOAM	International Federation of Organic Agriculture Movements 1972
	FLA	Fair Labor Association; apparel industry scheme 1999
	FLO	Fairtrade Labeling Organization "fair trade" umbrella scheme 1997
	FSC	Forest Stewardship Council certification, labeling scheme 1993
	GRI	Global Reporting Initiative; standards for social, environ. reports 1997
	SAI	Social Accountability Int'l standard for supplier labor practices 1997
	MH	Max Havelaar Fair Trade certification, labeling for coffee 1988
	MSC	Marine Stewardship Council 1997
Zone 7	AIP	Apparel Industry Partnership; Clinton administration initiative convening firms, unions, NGOs, other industry stakeholders 1996–97
	EITI	Extractive Industries Transparency Initiative; UK disclosure scheme for payments by firms, host government expenditures 2002–03
	ILO	International Labor Org. Declaration on Multinational Enterprises 1977
	KIMB	Kimberley Process on conflict diamond trade 2003
	VPSHR	Voluntary Principles on Security and Human Rights (private security forces) 2000
	4C	Common Code for the Coffee Community 2006

early example of voluntary government regulatory programs. The "++" signs after IECA and ECO indicate the many additional domestic laws and programs that could be included in Zone 1.

Zone 2 includes firm and industry self-regulatory schemes. GAP represents the labor code of Gap Inc., BS the social and environmental standards of The Body Shop. These were two early leaders in business self-regulation; corporate social responsibility (CSR) policies have now become standard for (especially large) firms operating internationally. We again use "++" to indicate the many Firm schemes these examples represent. Zone 3 includes codes promulgated and administered by NGOs and NGO coalitions. WRC represents the Worker Rights Consortium, a labor rights scheme targeting the apparel industry created by United Students against Sweatshops and other NGOs.

The quadrilaterals along each side (Zones 4–6) include schemes in which actors from two groups share governance responsibility, with the third playing no more than a minor role. UNGC in Zone 4 represents the UN Global Compact, in which the UN Secretariat and other IGOs collaborate with firms, with limited input from civil society. Finally, the central triangle (Zone 7) includes institutions in which actors of all three types play a vital role. ILO represents the Declaration on Multinational Enterprises and Social Policy of the ILO, with its tripartite structure.

The placement of schemes on the Triangle reflects the "shares" actor types exercise in their governance. Each actor type exercises a 100 percent share in schemes located at its vertex.[15] That share declines in points located farther from its vertex, until at the opposite side of the Triangle the other two actor types share exclusive control. For example, the placement of UNGC reflects approximate shares of {60%, 30%, 10%} for States (acting through the UN), Firms, and NGOs respectively.

The governance shares exercised in an institution depend in part on its formal rules. For example, the ILO constitution requires that national delegations include representatives of governments and of workers' and employers' associations in a fixed proportion; ILO is placed relatively high in Zone 7 because the government proportion is 50 percent. But governance shares also depend on tacit operating norms. For example, if a company code engaged NGOs to monitor compliance, the arrangement would be placed between the Firm and NGO vertices.

The Triangle is a heuristic device designed to structure analysis of widely varying forms of governance. Thus, the boundaries of zones and the placement of points are not intended as precise representations of

---

[15] We have drawn figure 2.1 so that, for all institutions within a vertex triangle, the dominant actor category has a share of two-thirds or more in governance. However, such measurements are only impressionistic and should not be over-interpreted.

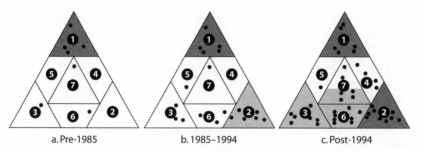

a. Pre-1985   b. 1985–1994   c. Post-1994

Figure 2.2. Evolution of the Governance Triangle

complex arrangements. Exact placement is less important than relative location; in particular, placing a scheme on one side or the other of a zone boundary is a matter of judgment.

As a snapshot of the current regulatory situation, figure 2.1 demonstrates both the large number of RSS schemes and their great diversity: every zone but one includes several schemes, and they occupy substantially different positions within each zone. Yet schemes are not evenly dispersed around the Triangle. If figure 2.1 were a complete mapping, some areas would be densely populated: Zone 1 would include thousands of points representing national laws as well as some interstate instruments; Zone 2 would include thousands of points representing firm and industry codes. Other areas, such as Zone 5 and the upper part of Zone 7, would remain sparse.

When examined over time, the picture is more complex. Throughout history, with a few notable exceptions—from the abolition of the slave trade in the British Empire in 1807 to the establishment of the ILO in 1919 to the enunciation of the Sullivan Principles (SULL in Zone 3) in 1977—concern for transnational RSS has been most notable by its absence. Only in recent decades have a significant array of single-actor schemes and a growing number of collaborative schemes emerged, both within and across actor types. We represent these developments in figures 2.2a–c, which divide the schemes depicted in figure 2.1 into three periods based on the dates of their entry into RSS: those that entered before 1985, those that entered from 1985 to 1994, and those that entered after 1994. In addition, we use shading to highlight the overall density of schemes in particular zones at different points in time—although density should not be confused with effectiveness. While this periodization is somewhat arbitrary, it illuminates the developing cascade and the fundamental shifts in RSS governance.[16]

---

[16] Although we do not have either the universe of cases or a representative sample in a statistical sense, we do include most of the important schemes in Zones 3–7, while in Zones 1 and 2 we use shading to reflect the general trends. We code the dates of schemes from

The pre-1985 period shown in figure 2.2a is notable for its lack of RSS schemes. Two exceptions in Zone 1 are the 1984 WHO Code of Marketing for Breast-Milk Substitutes (BM) and the 1978 German "Blue Angel" eco-label (ECO). We also see schemes organized through the OECD (Zone 1) and ILO (Zone 7) in response to criticisms of the transnational impact of multinational enterprises (MNEs)—and it is noteworthy that both of these IGOs formally incorporate business and labor voices to varying extents. The Sullivan Principles are an historic but somewhat lonely NGO initiative from this period—and here it is revealing that the Reverend Leon Sullivan used his position on the Board of Directors of General Motors as a platform for his efforts. In addition, of course, there was extensive domestic regulation during this period, represented by IECA++ and the dark shading of Zone 1 in figure 2.2a.

Figure 2.2b shows the emergence of a wide range of RSS schemes during the 1985–94 decade. On one hand, we see several NGO efforts—CCC, CERES, and Rugmark (RUG)—to address perceived adverse consequences of global production. On the other hand, we see the beginning of substantial CSR efforts by firms (Gap and Body Shop) and industry associations (ICC and the Responsible Care (RC) program of the global chemical industry).[17] We lightly shade Zone 2 to indicate the emerging

---

their first significant efforts at RSS, not necessarily their inception. For example, CCC was formed in 1990 but we date it from its 1998 "Code of Labor Practices for the Apparel Industry, Including Sportswear." We also do not code subsequent revisions or extensions of regulations by the same scheme (e.g., we include the IFC 1998 Safeguard Policies but not the 2006 Performance Standards), and we do not include subsequent imitator schemes (e.g., we include the first national EMAS, in the UK, from 1992, but not the EU EMAS from 1993). Dating individual schemes precisely is sometimes difficult because, especially in their formative years, institutions often go through organizational changes. For example, EITI has roots in a 1999 Global Witness exposé of secret payments by oil companies to the Angolan government; that report mobilized a set of NGOs to address transparency in the extractive industries; the UK government initiated a voluntary scheme at the 2002 Johannesburg World Summit on Sustainable Development; and only in 2003 did a multi-stakeholder conference adopt the "Statement of Principles and Agreed Actions" that constitute the EITI framework. Such developmental sequences often involve "internal dynamics" whereby schemes change their composition—here moving from NGO-based to NGO/state-based to NGO/state/firm-based—and thus move across the Governance Triangle. Our coding procedures are sufficiently gross-scale that we do not attempt to depict such dynamic transitions, but rather simply locate schemes by their initial effort at international regulation.

[17] Some corporations began minimal self-audits in the early 1970s, but these were primarily focused on environmental and domestic concerns. Pioneering firms at the transnational level include the Body Shop, which became one of the first firms to initiate internationally oriented CSR by sponsoring posters for Greenpeace (1985), creating an Environmental Projects Department which launched a "Save the Whales" campaign in conjunction with Greenpeace (1986), creating a Community Trade Program to source "natural ingredients from disadvantaged communities around the world" (1986), and establishing the Body Shop Foundation in 1990 to fund "human rights and environmental protection groups"

density of Firm schemes. We also see the first multi-stakeholder schemes: in Zone 4 the ISO 14000 standard, a firm-state collaboration; and in Zone 6, Max Havelaar (MH), the first fair trade certification scheme, and the Forest Stewardship Council (FSC), which brings together environmental and human rights activists with timber users and traders. There was a corresponding upsurge in domestic state-sponsored voluntary regulatory programs during this period, including the 1992 UK eco-management and audit scheme (EMAS), but no substantial increase in transnational Zone 1 activity.

The post-1994 period has witnessed even greater RSS activity. The darker shading of Zone 2 in figure 2.2c reflects the continued proliferation of firm schemes. Although a number of firm schemes were initiated before this period, the key point is that since 1994 it has become standard business practice for firms to adopt (or at least claim) some form of CSR and to discuss it regularly in shareholder and other reports.

Of even greater significance are the increased number of NGO schemes in Zone 3 and especially the emergence of collaborative schemes: bilateral schemes typically involving multiple NGOs and multiple firms in Zone 6—including FLA, SAI, GRI, and FLO—and tripartite schemes in the lower half of Zone 7—including VPSHR, AIP, and EITI. We have lightly shaded these areas to indicate the emergence of multi-actor schemes. Thus, it is not only the density of RSS schemes, but also their distribution in the regulatory space defined by the Governance Triangle that has changed over time. Again, there are few new State schemes in this period, with the IFC standards as a notable exception. However, a small number of state-firm alliances such as the Global Compact, Equator Principles (EQP), and Tour Operators Initiative (TOI) do emerge in Zone 4. Zone 5 schemes involving NGOs and States without Firm involvement are even rarer; we include the TCO certification system for computer hardware—created by a labor union confederation, environmental NGO, and government agency—as a sole example.

Figures 2.1 and 2.2a–c pose important and complex puzzles: why are there so many RSS schemes, why have they emerged at different times, and why are they so widely and unevenly dispersed? The analytical approach proposed by Mattli and Woods provides substantial purchase on these issues.

On the demand side, three factors are especially relevant. First, demonstration effects triggered many Triangle schemes and standards. Such

(www.thebodyshopinternational.com). For an overview of the emergence of RSS schemes, see Alice Tepper Marlin and John Tepper Marlin, "A Brief History of Social Reporting," *Business Respect* 51 (March 9, 2003), available at http://www.mallenbaker.net/csr/CSRfiles/page.php?Story_ID=857.

effects included the revelation of adverse consequences from poor or non-existent regulation, such as unsustainable practices in forestry and fishing, adverse human rights impacts of extractive industries, trade in diamonds that financed civil conflicts, and harsh labor practices in apparel, carpets, and agriculture. Dramatic scandals produced especially powerful demonstration effects, often leading to direct institutional responses: the Bhopal crisis (Responsible Care), the *Exxon Valdez* oil spill (CERES, which later established GRI), the execution of Ken Saro-Wiwa in Nigeria (Voluntary Principles on Security and Human Rights), and the Kathy Lee Gifford sweatshop scandal (AIP).

Second, entrepreneurs played prominent roles in the formation of RSS schemes. Norm entrepreneurs, especially northern NGOs, framed and publicized many of these regulatory failures and scandals through exposés and campaigns. Indeed, NGOs have taken the lead in establishing not only Zone 3 schemes, but virtually all the collaborative schemes in Zone 6 and some in Zone 7. NGO campaigns also stimulated many firm- and state-based initiatives. Public entrepreneurs sometimes played leading roles, even outside of Zone 1: Secretary-General Annan in the Global Compact, U.S. Secretary of Labor Reich in the AIP, and UK Prime Minister Blair in EITI. Firms also acted as entrepreneurs, adopting their own codes and programs and promoting sectoral (RC, WRAP, WDC, ICMM) and broader industry initiatives (ICC Business Charter for Sustainable Development). As discussed below, private-sector entrepreneurs included not only "corporations at risk" and "levelers of the playing field,"[18] but also firms seeking to distinguish themselves positively by their social or environmental policies.

Third, ideas have been important for the redefinition of interests, advocacy, and institutional design. Most significant, perhaps, is the concept of CSR, which has been evolving since the early twentieth century.[19] This concept includes the core notion of CSR, reflecting a mix of long-term self-interest and social obligation; understandings of the areas of activity in which CSR should operate; and the concept of responsibility to stakeholders. CSR is especially powerful because of its "fit" with existing institutions: firms themselves. Advocates have pressed CSR on firms even as parallel ideas about the possibility and appropriateness of non-state governance have supported the growth of NGO and collaborative schemes. Finally, states, firms, and NGOs have each developed new understandings of workable regulatory techniques, such as external audits,

[18] Mattli and Woods, "In Whose Benefit? Explaining Regulatory Change in Global Politics," this volume.

[19] See CSRQuest, "CR Theoretical Background," http://www.csrquest.net/default.aspx?articleID=13126&heading= .

auditor accreditation, social and environmental reporting, and social and environmental labels.

As to the institutional context, "no unitary regulator with a coercive fiat" can make and enforce transnational regulatory decisions.[20] Instead, the two contextual features identified above have shaped transnational regulatory responses. First, the low cost of institutional creation has enabled entrepreneurs within and across the NGO, Firm, and State actor groups to respond to social demand by establishing new RSS schemes and promulgating new regulatory standards that further their interests and values. In sectors such as forestry and labor rights, this has led to the proliferation of multiple schemes, controlled by actors and coalitions from different groups, that address similar issues in different ways. Second, the lack of oversight has caused these diverse schemes to evolve through decentralized interactions including competition and collaboration. The result is "networked governance" in two senses: many individual schemes are based on voluntary, reciprocal interactions among multiple participants, and the entire Triangle system reflects nuanced network relationships among schemes.[21] For these reasons, we rely on a broad understanding of distributive bargaining across the regulatory space of the Triangle to explain the emergence and structure of RSS.

RSS and State Regulation

We define the Triangle in terms of States, Firms, and NGOs because the interaction of these actor groups is the most striking and innovative feature of transnational RSS. Traditionally, as noted above, the state (acting singly or collectively) has been regarded as the appropriate institution to address the adverse consequences of production, with mandatory regulation as its characteristic instrument. In that view there is little need for a Governance Triangle. Yet serious structural issues constrain state regulation, providing the conditions for the emergence of RSS schemes.

Domestically, as discussed further below, advanced states may have impressive regulatory powers, but states as a group vary greatly in their will and capacity to regulate. Some governments are captured or corrupt. Governments in developing countries—where the negative externalities of transnational production largely fall—often view regulation as a

[20] Mattli and Woods, "In Whose Benefit? Explaining Regulatory Change in Global Politics," this volume.

[21] Compare the definition of "networks" in Kahler and Lake, "Economic Integration and Global Governance," this volume. However, institutions on the Triangle are controlled by non-state actors to a much greater extent than the examples of networking (e.g., the Basel Committee on Banking Supervision) discussed by Kahler and Lake.

trade-off against economic growth, and lack the information, resources, and technical competence to manage complex regulation.[22]

Globalization exacerbates these problems. Raymond Vernon's "Sovereignty at Bay"[23] encapsulated concerns over the ability of states to regulate MNEs, and similar concerns led to the adoption of instruments like the OECD Guidelines.[24] Over time, global supply chains have transformed production relationships in some sectors into transnational webs of contractors. In low-capital industries such as apparel, the ease with which firms can relocate production across states provides them significant leverage over regulators.[25] The existence of a regulatory "race to the bottom" is controversial, but these changes in global production have made it difficult for state regulation to rise to the top.[26]

Even developed states find regulation of global business practices challenging. Regulation is inherently a lower priority to the extent the adverse effects of production are felt abroad, making it more difficult to further the "public interest" in a proceduralist sense: workers in China or Indonesia do not vote in U.S. or European elections. Regulators have less adequate information on foreign business operations. Even limited efforts to regulate foreign operations are resented as disguised protectionism or the imposition of inappropriate standards. And the extent of na-

[22] Therefore, it is often difficult to distinguish between the "inability" of less developed states to regulate and their "unwillingness" to do so. See David Vogel, "The Private Regulation of Global Corporate Conduct," this volume.

[23] Raymond Vernon, *Sovereignty at Bay: The Multinational Spread of US Enterprises* (New York: Basic Books, 1971).

[24] The initial 1976 Guidelines applied only to a limited range of MNE activities in OECD states. They have been progressively expanded to other activities (e.g., environment and corruption), and in 2000 to supply chains in OECD and non-OECD countries.

[25] Leverage sometimes exists in capital-intensive industries as well. Theodore H. Moran, *Multinational Corporations and the Politics of Dependence: Copper in Chile* (Princeton, NJ: Princeton University Press, 1974), posits an "obsolescing bargain" whereby the balance of power shifts from a firm to a host country once the firm makes a large fixed investment. However, Eckhard Janeba, "Tax Competition When Governments Lack Commitment: Excess Capacity as a Countervailing Threat," *American Economic Review* 90 (2000), 1508–1519, shows that the ability to shift production across states preserves leverage for the firm.

[26] See Daniel Drezner, "Bottom Feeders" *Foreign Policy* 121 (November/December 2000), 64–70. One reason for the controversy is misleading terminology. As in the Cold War "arms race," which in its mature years became less a race to acquire arms than an inability to reduce existing arsenals, the "race to the bottom" need not mean a competitive decrease in standards; it can encompass pressures that prevent states from raising standards. In interviews for a related research project, numerous individuals involved in RSS described the adverse impact that actual or threatened relocations of production, especially to China, have on efforts to strengthen standards, notably in the area of worker rights. For further discussion, see Abbott and Snidal, "International 'Standards' and International Governance," 352–353.

tional legal authority is unclear, as the many battles over "extraterritorial" regulation attest.

Treaties and IGOs better match the scope of transnational production. They offer the potential to apply consistent standards across jurisdictions and to help overcome firms' threats of exit. IGOs can also build state capacity. Yet effective international regulation has proven elusive. Interstate negotiations are costly and contentious given widely divergent preferences and beliefs, especially between North and South. IGOs such as the ILO have created many international standards, yet ratification often fails to keep pace.[27] Traditional legal instruments depend on state implementation and enforcement.[28] IGOs lack the capacity to oversee implementation by firms, and states refuse to grant them the authority or resources to do so.

Actor Groups and the Governance Triangle

The symmetry of the Triangle—with the three main actor groups at the vertices—should not be taken to suggest that these three groups are equal. They are often highly unequal in their interests, power, and capacities; the Triangle merely depicts them as potential participants in RSS. Moreover, the location of schemes on the Triangle itself reflects the asymmetric participation and bargaining power of different actor groups.

Actors within each group also vary widely. For example, developed states generally have greater regulatory capacity than developing states; firms producing branded products are more vulnerable to NGO and public pressure than those producing intermediate goods; and labor unions have different motivations than human rights advocates. Each group also encompasses individual and collective actors: states and IGOs, firms and industry associations, NGOs and advocacy coalitions. We use the three groups to highlight broad similarities within each actor type, while discussing variations within them as needed.

As these diverse actors engage with one another in the regulatory space represented by the Triangle, we assume that each pursues its own interests and values. Simplifying greatly, we sketch here the characteristic preferences of the three actor groups.

Firms are by law and culture focused on profits. While a common view is that they prefer no regulation, firms in fact depend on some regulations—including standards and property rights—as the very basis of their

---

[27] The ILO's campaign for ratification of eight fundamental conventions responds to this problem.

[28] Instruments like the OECD Guidelines that address firms directly are intended to overcome this problem, albeit as soft law.

operations. Moreover, specific firms often benefit from regulations that promote their economic interests, for example, by creating monopoly power or otherwise limiting competition. Thus firms care more about the specific content than the mere fact of regulation. When advocates seek regulations that will conflict with profits—as in many contemporary calls for environmental, human rights, and social regulation—firms typically resist. In these circumstances, their favored fallback option is self-regulation. This allows firms to adopt more business-friendly rules and procedures, fine-tune rules to their individual situations, minimize compliance costs, and avoid potentially damaging intrusions by outsiders. In addition, more socially responsible firms may seek mandatory regulation to level the playing field vis-à-vis less socially responsible competitors.[29]

Firms are not immune to social values. In addition to their possible substantive commitments, firms, executives, and employees care about their reputations. Some firms strive to make CSR a competitive asset and a benefit for their employees. Conversely, no executive or employee wishes to be the target of an activist campaign depicting them as violating an important social norm. Such considerations can generate shared interests with activists, even if these are driven primarily by threats such as shaming. Yet here, too, firms prefer to pursue social goals in minimally intrusive ways, ideally through self-regulation.

Above all, firms' attitudes are shaped by their competitive environment. All firms must be wary of arrangements that increase costs, but this is especially true in competitive sectors involving standardized products where profit margins are thin; firms that control powerful brands or technologies and operate in differentiated markets have greater leeway. And all firms will be more open to RSS when competitors also participate. Key firms and industry associations can exercise leadership in developing sector-wide norms that promote social goals and preserve the industry's reputation without undermining any individual firm.

NGOs are even more diverse. This category includes advocacy groups, labor unions, consumer groups, socially responsible investors, social movements, and other noncommercial groups. Many are what we have called "value actors,"[30] motivated by principled beliefs rather than any direct stake in an issue. For example, WRC participants believe that

---

[29] Mattli and Woods, "In Whose Benefit? Explaining Regulatory Change in Global Politics," this volume. More cynically, firms that are not particularly socially responsible may support such regulation if it will advantage them by imposing greater costs on competitors.

[30] See Kenneth W. Abbott and Duncan Snidal, "Values and Interests: International Legalization in the Fight Against Corruption," *Journal of Legal Studies* 31, no. 1 (part 2) (2002), S141–178. We use the term "preference" broadly to cover any basis for action, including interests and principles.

failing to pay foreign workers a "living wage" is wrong, even though they are not themselves low-wage workers. Such norm entrepreneurs help mobilize regulatory action to assist often powerless beneficiaries. Value actors approach issues differently than interest actors. Driven by principle, value actors are less willing to make trade-offs and compromises that come naturally to interest actors. This can create conflict, for example, between value-driven NGOs and firms that are socially responsible but also care about profits; firms may view pure value NGOs as unsuitable collaborators.

NGOs do not necessarily represent the public interest or common interests. They may instead represent their own "private" values. This is evident in the fact that different NGOs pursue at least partially contradictory goals, such as economic development versus environmental protection. Even where NGOs share common goals, they represent only a segment of society's interests. Moreover, NGO efforts to represent the interests of others (e.g., northern NGO efforts to represent southern workers) raise issues of paternalism and accountability. NGOs also have organizational goals such as membership and fund-raising that may come into tension with their missions; like all organizations, they can develop "pathologies."[31] Finally, NGOs must compete with one another, not only over goals and strategies, but also for members, donors, and adherents to their standards.

Some actors in the NGO category have direct, material interests in the issues they address: unions, in particular, seek regulation to improve members' wages and working conditions. Such interest-based NGOs may use social commitments to disguise their material stakes. Often NGO motivations are mixed: for example, U.S. labor unions that protest the use of child labor in Central America may be motivated by altruistic considerations, but their emphasis on this issue may also derive from the implicit import protection such protests provide their members.

States are often viewed as arenas in which the interests and values of private actors play out—ideally to determine the public interest—rather than as actors with their own interests or values.[32] At the international level, however, states are better regarded as actors with preferences of their own. State attitudes toward regulation in areas like labor rights are determined not only by their situations (e.g., level of development) and domestic constituencies, but also by other international concerns, such as trade and strategic interests. Even where states share a common concern, economic and other forms of competition may impede cooperation.

---

[31] Michael N. Barnett and Martha Finnemore, *Rules for the World: International Organizations in Global Politics* (Ithaca, NY: Cornell University Press, 2004).

[32] Politicians, of course, face electoral and other incentives.

IGOs are important vehicles through which states manage competition and advance common interests.[33] Like NGOs, IGOs often internalize their missions within their organizational cultures and operate as value actors. But IGOs too must ensure their organizational survival, and may be forced to compromise their values. In particular, IGOs may be unwilling to take strong stands against their members, even if doing so is part of their fundamental raison d'être. IGOs can also develop organizational pathologies that divert them from their missions.

THE REGULATORY PROCESS AND INSTITUTIONAL COMPETENCIES

In this section we intensify the puzzles posed in the previous section—why are there so many RSS schemes, why have they emerged at different times, and why are they so widely and unevenly dispersed around the Triangle?—by asking which types of schemes can plausibly act as effective transnational regulators. Even without further analysis, one might reasonably speculate that the multiplicity and dispersion of schemes seen in figure 2.1 would produce inefficient gaps and overlaps in the regulatory coverage of issues, industries, and regions. One might also expect, as already suggested, that schemes controlled by particular actor groups would adopt structures of participation and deliberative procedures that further their narrow interests and values, rendering them deficient from a common interest perspective. Finally, the success of schemes depends on the informational, normative, and material resources they command. Here we identify criteria—based on inputs to the regulatory process—by which we can assess potential effectiveness.

In examining a highly political activity like regulation, effectiveness must be conceptualized broadly. Concrete means-ends effectiveness is crucial, although even that is complex: effectiveness may turn not only on material factors (e.g., resources), but also on subjective factors that influence legitimacy and public appeal. Effective regulatory institutions must also balance the interests of stakeholders and instantiate prevailing norms. Finally, to advance the public interest, institutions must adopt structures and procedures that are open, transparent, and fair.

It is difficult to assess effectiveness in any of these senses by measuring real-world impact: too many variables influence the outputs and effects of regulation, and the counterfactuals are too complex. We therefore ask instead what attributes, capacities, and skills—what inputs or "competencies"—an institution needs to operate successfully throughout the regula-

---

[33] Kenneth W. Abbott and Duncan Snidal, "Why States Act through Formal International Organizations," *Journal of Conflict Resolution* 42, no. 1 (1998), 3–32.

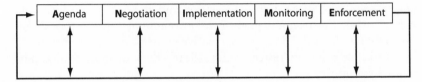

Figure 2.3. Stages of the regulatory process

tory process. By identifying competencies that are *necessary* to effectiveness, we can conclude that schemes lacking one or more of those competencies are likely to be ineffective. However, the competencies we identify are not *sufficient*: a scheme that possesses all of them might still be paralyzed by infighting, adopt an ineffective monitoring system or otherwise fail.

The Regulatory Process

As noted above, the regulatory process comprises five main stages: placing an issue on the regulatory agenda (Agenda-setting); negotiating, drafting, and promulgating regulatory standards (Negotiation); implementing standards within the operations of firms or other targets of regulation (Implementation); monitoring compliance (Monitoring); and promoting compliance and responding to noncompliance (Enforcement). Figure 2.3 presents these stages (A N I M E) graphically.[34]

To be sure, the five stages are neither as distinct nor as neatly ordered as figure 2.3 suggests: for example, some activities support multiple stages, and each stage is typically carried out with an eye to previous and subsequent steps. For analytical purposes, however, figure 2.3 captures essential features of the regulatory process. Certain actors focus on particular stages: some NGOs, for example, specialize in highlighting issues (A) or observing and critiquing firm behavior (M E) without promulgating any standard of their own. RSS institutions also emphasize particular stages: for example, many firms adopt company codes (N) without any follow-up procedures. Truly effective schemes, however, must address all five stages.

While terms such as Monitoring and Enforcement evoke the "logic of consequences," the ANIME process can also accommodate the "logic of appropriateness." In schemes built on consequences, for example, Monitoring might be designed to detect cheating and Enforcement to impose material costs. In schemes built on appropriateness, in contrast, Monitoring might aim to communicate the commitment and concern of managers

---

[34] Figure 2.3 also includes feedback loops, common in successful schemes. For a fuller discussion, see Abbott and Snidal, *The International Standards Process*.

and stakeholders, promoting socialization and an appropriate corporate culture, while Enforcement might invoke community approval or disapproval, enmeshing the firm in a normative conversation with customers, investors, and other interested groups. Clearly the two approaches can be mutually reinforcing.

Competencies

We begin with the specific competencies that are essential at each stage of the regulator process. From this analysis, we extract four general competencies.

Agenda-setting requires an ability to capture public attention, frame issues in politically powerful ways, gather and disseminate information, and formulate appropriate ways to proceed. Effective advocates must possess information and expertise about the normative issue being highlighted (normative expertise), the business context in which the issue arises (business expertise), and the political context in which a response must be negotiated (political expertise). Agenda-setters must also have legitimacy; this will stem from perceptions of normative commitment, expertise, and independence from the targets of regulation. Finally, some practical capabilities and resources are essential to support sustained public communication.

At the *Negotiation* stage, several types of expertise are essential. These include (a) normative expertise, to ensure that a standard furthers underlying norms, resonates with the prevailing fabric of norms, and appeals to relevant audiences, including consumers, the public, and employees who must internalize the standard and socialize their colleagues; (b) business expertise, to ensure that the standard will mesh with business practices and be cost-effective; (c) auditing expertise, to ensure that the standard can be effectively monitored; and (d) political expertise, to negotiate effectively. Participation of a range of stakeholders, directly or through representatives accountable to them,[35] and procedures that grant those stakeholders effective voice enhance the legitimacy of negotiations and any resulting standard: if business dominates, the standard may lack credibility; if issue advocates dominate, the standard may be too aggressive to attract adherents. Participation, accountability, and voice are likewise essential to public interest regulation. More concretely, some actors or institutions must have the resources and skill to initiate and manage negotiations.

[35] Ruth W. Grant and Robert O. Keohane, "Accountability and Abuses of Power in World Politics," *American Political Science Review* 99, no. 1 (2005), 29–43.

Implementation of RSS standards takes place within firms and along supply chains. To be effective, a standard must be incorporated into the policies, operations, contracts, technologies, and processes of target firms, including procedures for assessing employees and suppliers to ensure they take the standard seriously. This requires not only business expertise and managerial capacity, but also access to the inner workings of firms and legal and managerial authority.

Two forms of *Monitoring* figure in RSS. Managers conduct *internal* monitoring of employees and contractors as an adjunct to implementation: internal monitoring conveys management's commitment to a standard, helps managers determine if implementation procedures are effective, and lays the basis for penalties and rewards. Effectiveness and credibility may be enhanced if internal monitors possess normative and auditing expertise, appropriate incentives, and some degree of independence from general management.

Entities outside the firm conduct *external* monitoring as a basis for enforcement. A wide range of actors monitors RSS standards: NGOs, IGOs, commercial inspection firms, and auditing firms, among others. To be effective, monitors must have the capacity to gather and assess relevant information and the resources to act in diverse locations. They also need auditing, business, and normative expertise; training and accreditation procedures can help confirm or develop these skills. In addition, monitors must be credible to relevant audiences: the principal issue here is independence from the target firm. From the firm's perspective, a related issue is neutrality: firms are unlikely to grant access to organizations seen as unduly biased against business.

Enforcement typically refers to the application of rewards and penalties, although many schemes use "managerial" techniques such as remediation to respond to noncompliance. When sanctions are imposed, they may be material, normative, or both. Internally, for example, firms sanction employees through compensation (material) and promote a corporate culture that stigmatizes inappropriate behavior (normative).

Externally, since RSS schemes lack coercive power, they must rely on private actors for enforcement. Materially, various actors may condition important decisions on a firm's compliance with a standard: consumers and downstream firms may do so with purchasing decisions, potential workers with employment decisions, and socially responsible investors with financial decisions. Normatively, consumers, employees, and members of the public may view compliance as a central element in the reputation of a firm and its executives. Yet because these groups are diffuse, they must be "activated" to perform as sanctioners. Advocates must raise the salience of the issue, publicize noncompliance, suggest an appropriate response, and motivate individuals to action, much as in Agenda-setting.

To accomplish these tasks, schemes must be normatively committed, expert, and independent; representing a range of stakeholders rather than one narrow interest also strengthens a scheme.

From this analysis we extract four competencies essential to effective RSS:[36]

1. *independence*—especially important when the agenda is set and standards are invoked (A M E)
2. *representativeness*[37]—especially important to the promulgation and enforcement of standards (A N E)
3. *expertise* (of the several kinds mentioned above)—important at every stage of the regulatory process (A N I M E)
4. *operational capacity*—the practical abilities, resources, and authority to perform necessary tasks—especially important in the application of standards (I M E) but relevant in other stages (A N)

Competencies and Actor Groups

Each actor group possesses a constellation of competencies. Collective actors often possess competencies somewhat different from those of their members (e.g., industry associations may be relatively independent of particular firms). We discuss here the main actor competencies across the stages of the regulatory process, as summarized in table 2.2.

1. *In the domestic context*, developed states frequently possess all four competencies. They have strong operational capacity, including substantial resources, legal authority, and strong legislative and administrative procedures (A, N), inspection systems (M), and enforcement processes (E). But even strong states lack the authority and expertise to implement standards within firms (I); they must act indirectly, requiring management to implement. Advanced states also possess moderate to strong technical and normative expertise (but limited business expertise), particularly within specialized agencies, and have elaborate procedures for collecting and creating information and assembling the views of interest and advocacy groups. Many developing countries, however, have severe capability gaps in all these areas.

States also differ in their independence from firms. Capture and corruption are pervasive, but political, administrative, and judicial processes can be structured to promote independence and pursuit of the public interest. Democratic states represent a broad range of interests and values

[36] For a similar effort to connect the "regulatory capacities" of different actors to "regulatory functions," see Julia Black, "Enrolling Actors in Regulatory Processes: Examples from UK Financial Services Regulation," *Public Law* (2003), 63–91.

[37] Representativeness is a complex concept which we do not unpack here, except to note that it usually assumes that actors are in some way accountable to those they represent.

and are generally accountable, adding to their legitimacy as regulators and to the likelihood that they will act in the common interest, although again this varies widely.

In the transnational context, however, states have far less operational capacity (including authority for rule-making, monitoring, and enforcement), information (on foreign business operations and their effects), and expertise. From a transnational perspective, their independence is compromised to the extent that they act on behalf of particular domestic interests (e.g., exporters), while their representativeness is weak insofar as they pursue primarily national interests.

IGOs are more broadly representative in the transnational sense and more independent from particularistic interests. They often possess specialized expertise, both technical and normative. Although collective-action problems and divergent preferences impede interstate cooperation, some IGOs have fairly effective norm-generating machinery (N), including the ability to convene high-profile conferences (A). However, states grant IGOs only limited authority and resources for monitoring and enforcement (M E). Their implementation capacity (I) is even more limited than that of states, as they are more remote from firms. IGOs are at best indirectly representative (as the "democratic deficit" debate suggests), although they may be less subject than states to capture by private actors. Their independence and representativeness are diminished when powerful states exert disproportionate influence.

2. *Firms* (and industry associations) have strong operational capacity, including ample resources (at least in the case of large, profitable firms), internal authority and access, and managerial systems. These capacities are especially significant for implementation (I); indeed, only firms possess the competencies to manage this stage directly. Firms also possess unparalleled expertise on business, especially their own operations, which is valuable for the design of standards (N) and for implementation (I) and monitoring (M).

However, firms lack independence by definition, a weakness especially significant for monitoring (M). Most firms are relatively weak on normative expertise and commitment, although some have accumulated both through CSR activities. Firms are not generally representative beyond their economic stakeholders. Because of these deficiencies, firms are unlikely to produce regulatory standards and programs that serve common interests, and may lack legitimacy and credibility in the eyes of the public—and certainly those of activists—even when they are sincere about self-regulation.

3. *NGOs* have competencies of varying importance at the agenda-setting (A), negotiation (N), monitoring (M), and enforcement (E) stages, including the ability to raise the salience of issues, standards, and violations and to generate public responses. Many NGOs specialize in gather-

ing and disseminating credible information. Their independence often makes them the only actor able to gather accurate testimony from workers and others affected by firms' practices. Many NGOs have strong normative expertise and a level of normative commitment that enhance their legitimacy.

Yet NGOs' very commitment to principle may undercut their perceived independence. Firms view many NGOs not as independent or neutral, but as hostile. That perception has inhibited many firms from accepting NGOs as monitors and from adhering to NGO standards and even participating in some multi-stakeholder schemes. NGOs' perceived independence and normative commitment are further undercut if they are seen to be overly influenced by organizational goals. Finally, although NGOs often claim to speak for their members, disadvantaged groups, or particular values as such, their representativeness and accountability vary widely.

Table 2.2 summarizes actor competencies through the stages of the regulatory process. To illustrate, consider the negotiation stage (N). Here, States possess key operational capacities: domestically, to promulgate legislative and administrative rules; transnationally, to convene and organize negotiations. Firms have a crucial competency, business information, and expertise, including on the feasibility and cost-effectiveness of proposed standards. NGOs and often states have normative expertise. Finally, while NGOs and firms represent constituencies (narrow in the case of firms), only states and some multi-stakeholder schemes can be broadly representative and accountable. The "independence" box in the Negotiation column is blank to indicate that this competency is less important at that stage.

Table 2.3 summarizes the overall importance of the three actor groups in each regulatory stage, as derived from table 2.2. For example, in the Negotiation column of table 2.3, States are ranked High because of their operational capacity and representative character; Firms and NGOs are ranked Medium because of their distinctive expertise and operational capacities. In the Enforcement column, States are ranked High because of their authority to impose penalties for rule violations; NGOs are ranked Medium because of their ability to mobilize market and reputational sanctions; and Firms are ranked Low because of their lack of independence.

As tables 2.2 and 2.3 make clear, in transnational settings no actor group, even the advanced democratic state, possesses all the competencies needed for effective regulation. To be sure, if regulation required action only at one or two stages, a single actor group might have the necessary competencies: for example, States could effectively promulgate standards (N) and Firms could effectively implement them (I). But regulation requires action across all stages, and no actor group—and hence no single-actor scheme—possesses the full range of required competencies.

TABLE 2.2
Actor Competencies in Stages of Transnational RSS Schemes

	Agenda-Setting	Negotiation	Implementation	Monitoring	Enforcement
Expertise	States NGOs	Business: Firms Normative: States, NGOs	Firms	Firms NGOs (States)	States NGOs
Operational Capacity	States NGOs (Firms)	All	Firms	Firms NGOs (States)	States (NGOs)
Independence	States (NGOs)	—	—	NGOs States	States (NGOs)
Representativeness	States (NGOs)	States	—	—	States

(Parentheses) indicate a secondary capacity.

TABLE 2.3
Relative Importance of Actors at Different Stages of Transnational RSS Schemes

	Agenda-Setting	Negotiation	Implementation	Monitoring	Enforcement
Firms	*Low*	Medium	**High**	Low-Med	*Low*
NGOs	Medium	Medium	*Low*	Medium	Low-Med
States	**High**	**High**	*Low*	Low-Med	**High**

Actors and schemes may be able to acquire additional competencies; in particular, one can often acquire expertise by hiring expert employees or consultants. Yet neither Firms nor NGOs can acquire all essential competencies: Firms cannot acquire true independence (although they can improve the perception and fact of independence by, e.g., creating separate monitoring departments), and NGOs cannot acquire the authority to directly implement standards.

We conclude, therefore, that single-actor schemes, whose competencies are primarily derived from their sponsors, are implausible as transnational regulators. In Zone 1, it is the failures of traditional state and IGO regulation that have opened space for private and public-private RSS. Zone 1 does include a number of innovative soft law RSS initiatives, but these face serious problems of implementation. In Zone 2, self-regulation by firms and associations may make a significant contribution over time, especially through the logic of appropriateness. By itself, however, self-regulation is insufficient: firms lack the independence and representativeness to gain legitimacy and act in the public interest, and competitive incentives undermine meaningful self-regulation. In Zone 3, NGO schemes shape the discourse of CSR and the practices of some firms, but they too are insufficient: they depend on firm adherence and implementation, and typically lack resources. Collaborative schemes are more plausible regulators, as they can assemble needed competencies from their diverse participants, and are by their nature more open and representative.

Yet Zones 1 and 2 are far more densely populated than any of the collaborative zones. This intensifies the puzzles posed above: why do we see so many RSS schemes that are suboptimal in terms of regulatory effectiveness and the common interest? And under what circumstances can more propitious collaborative schemes emerge? We approach these questions by considering the bargaining processes through which schemes are created and shaped.

The Regulatory Standards Bargaining Game

The Bargaining Game

The Governance Triangle, representing the transnational regulatory space, is the site of a complex bargaining game among the three actor groups, with each seeking to control regulatory governance and hence the substance and form of regulatory outcomes.[38] This bargaining game largely determines which RSS schemes are created and what form they take.

---

[38] The regulatory space has multiple dimensions, such as the strictness and form of standards, but we analyze the competition in terms of actors.

Importantly, much bargaining on the Triangle is *implicit*, with actors pursuing unilateral strategies (with an eye to the actions of others) designed to produce regulatory outcomes that satisfy their preferences. For example, actors bargain implicitly by advocating particular forms of regulation (including the absence of regulation), seeking to minimize pressures for regulation, and—most important for present purposes—creating single-actor RSS schemes like those in Zones 2 and 3. In addition, schemes themselves are actors that bargain implicitly as they compete to control the regulatory space.

Actors also bargain *explicitly* over the creation of collaborative schemes, like those in Zones 6 and 7. Actors have incentives to collaborate when they share common interests with regard to regulation. However, actors from different groups are likely to differ sharply over the structure and governance of schemes and the scope and content of their standards and procedures. Moreover, collaboration entails risks: firms may increase their vulnerability to NGO pressures, while NGOs may be perceived as selling out. As a result, bargaining will be highly contentious and may well fail—or not be attempted at all. Explicit bargaining also occurs within ongoing collaborative schemes, as participating actors seek to influence or even capture them. Finally, single- and multi-actor schemes bargain explicitly among themselves over interscheme collaboration.

Bargaining is costly, so collaboration is not an efficient process even when it succeeds. This is especially true of bargaining among actors that are inherently suspicious of one another, as are many firms, NGOs, and state agencies. Bargaining among actors from the same category, for example, as part of an effort to develop a common front, may also be contentious and difficult. NGOs, for example, vary widely in their "radicalness"; they must bargain and compromise to create coalition schemes for greater influence, but may well be unable to agree. Similarly, firms facing different costs from social responsibility or differing vulnerabilities to external pressure must bargain and compromise to create industry schemes that have the potential for greater credibility, but the distributive implications of such negotiations may be hard to bridge.[39]

---

[39] Typically, larger firms—which have greater resources than smaller firms and are more visible to the public and more vulnerable to NGO pressure—support industry schemes such as SFI and Responsible Care. In both of those cases, the industry association made participation mandatory for members. While large firms must bargain with smaller ones over the design of such schemes, they often have the power to force their adoption. See Aseem Prakash and Matthew Potoski, *The Voluntary Environmentalists: Green Clubs, ISO 14001, and Voluntary Environmental Regulations* (Cambridge: Cambridge University Press 2006), 52; and Erika N. Sasser, Aseem Prakash, Benjamin Cashore, and Graeme Auld, "Direct Targeting as an NGO Political Strategy: Examining Private Authority Regimes in the Forestry Sector," *Business and Politics* 8, no. 3 (2006), 9–10.

The AIP (Zone 7) illustrates the difficulty of both inter- and intragroup bargaining. The AIP was a state-initiated effort to create a grand coalition of apparel industry stakeholders, from manufacturers and retailers to labor unions and human rights groups. Once bargaining turned from principles to implementation, however, there proved to be limited bargaining space between industry and NGO participants; the envisioned coalition had to be scaled back. Bargaining also collapsed within each group: while some moderate firms and NGOs combined to create the FLA, more radical NGOs split off to create the WRC and more conservative firms left to form WRAP.

Competencies and Bargaining Power

The competencies of actors determine what they can bring or deny to any potential RSS scheme; competencies therefore constitute power resources important in bargaining. Situational factors also advantage or disadvantage actors, while states (even if not bargaining directly) can strengthen or weaken the positions of other actors. In conjunction with diverse actor preferences and transactions costs, this combination of power and circumstance determines the outcomes of the bargaining game.

As noted earlier, actors and schemes sometimes acquire additional competencies to strengthen their operations and bargaining positions. An NGO might add auditing capacities that make it a more effective monitor and strengthen its claim for a role in collaborative RSS schemes. A firm might enhance its independence by hiring NGO veterans to staff its monitoring department, making its unilateral scheme somewhat more effective and strengthening its claim that this enhanced self-regulation is sufficient without state or other intervention. In addition, enhancing the competencies of parallel schemes may intensify competition among them in ways that reinforce, or perhaps undermine, the effectiveness of each.

As this discussion suggests, competencies give rise to two closely related forms of power that strongly influence bargaining outcomes. "Go-It-Alone-Power" (GIAP) refers to the unilateral ability of an actor to establish a scheme (or to take no action at all) that meets some or all of that actor's objectives, even if the scheme is not fully effective and does not further the public interest.[40] An NGO, for example, might draw on its

---

[40] Gruber's use of the term "GIAP" differs from ours by assuming that an actor with GIAP can force others into a new "cooperative" scheme that serves its interests, whereas we allow for other actors to remain outside such a scheme and even to establish competing schemes. Gruber's formulation is appropriate when there are strong incentives for all actors to join a single arrangement, but does not apply where multiple schemes can co-exist. See Lloyd Gruber, *Ruling the World: Power Politics and the Rise of Supranational Institutions* (Princeton, NJ: Princeton University Press, 2000).

normative expertise and independence to adopt a standard that shapes the dialogue on a regulatory problem, even if it does not directly change company practices. Similarly, a firm might draw on its business expertise and operational capacity to establish a self-regulatory code that excludes other voices and is only moderately effective, but heads off outside pressures. Each actor posses some competencies (and may acquire others) and thus has some GIAP, as reflected in the profusion of single-actor schemes.

"Inclusion Power" refers to an actor's importance to a collaborative scheme based on the competencies it could contribute. Inclusion power requires that those competencies be essential, and that other actors cannot readily acquire them. Thus, NGOs may find it necessary to include firms in schemes that involve workplace implementation because of their expertise and operational capacity; firms may find it necessary to involve independent NGOs as monitors if their schemes are to be seen as legitimate in the absence of state participation. As the latter example suggests, when multiple actor groups can provide a needed competency—for example, either states or NGOs may be able to supply independence—their individual inclusion power is diminished. The flip side of inclusion power is "veto power": actors with essential competencies can block creation of a scheme, or render it ineffective, by refusing to participate.

In summary, GIAP creates an "outside option" for independent action, whereas inclusion power creates an "inside option" for participation in a collaborative scheme. These two forms of power correspond closely to our discussion of unilateral versus collaborative strategies below.[41]

Situational factors also affect actors' bargaining power. The most important is the nature of a firm's products and market: firms that sell branded consumer products, for example, are therefore especially vulnerable to NGO pressure. A related consideration is visibility: certain products (e.g., Nike shoes), standards (e.g., child labor), and violations (the Bhopal disaster) are highly visible and salient to consumers and the public, and thus stimulate greater demand for regulation. Consumers in particular markets (e.g., Europe versus Japan; developed versus less developing countries) may be more concerned with particular issues or have higher expectations for business conduct. Finally, the number of actors on each side affects bargaining power; for example, firms with many strong competitors may be unable to adopt higher standards without impairing their competitiveness.

---

[41] Alternatively, by analogy to cooperative game theory, GIAP can be seen as reflecting the value an actor creates by acting alone, whereas inclusion power reflects the value it adds when it joins a coalition with other actors. In principle, such considerations can be aggregated into overall "power indices" (such as the Shapley-Shubik or Banzhaff indices), but those have significant limitations. We rely on the simpler notions here.

Implicit Bargaining and GIAP

Zones 1–3 on the Governance Triangle contain RSS schemes formed by actors from a single group, individually and collectively. These zones, especially Zones 1 (including domestic legislation) and 2 (firm codes), are densely populated. All schemes in these vertex zones are premised on GIAP; inclusion power is of secondary importance.[42]

STATES: LIMITED DIRECT ACTION

Zone 1 contains state-based regulatory and RSS schemes. Some schemes in this zone aspire to the traditional model of the regulatory state with substantial GIAP to impose regulatory solutions on other societal actors. Zone 1 is particularly dense with domestic laws, represented by IECA++. These core state measures vary substantially in effectiveness. Labor, environmental, and human rights laws are largely effective within developed states, although even the most sophisticated regulatory system is subject to gaps, failures, and capture. But even domestic regulation is relatively ineffective within many developing countries, and regulation in all states is significantly weakened when it addresses transnational problems. The globalization of production and issues of extraterritorial jurisdiction limit the state's concern and effective reach. Even within developed countries, then, mandatory regulation is increasingly being supplemented by private and public-private RSS regimes.

Other Zone 1 schemes have been adopted by IGOs, including the OECD, WHO (BM), and IFC.[43] The IFC, alone among these institutions, has the financial leverage to enforce its standards in its own operations; the others lack the necessary competencies. This is due partly to state reluctance to delegate supranational authority and partly to differences in preferences and capacities across states.[44] Indeed, the ineffectiveness of direct state regulation, both individual and collective, is a fundamental reason for the proliferation of Triangle schemes.[45] Thus we focus especially on schemes led by NGOs and firms (Zones 2, 3, and 6).

---

[42] Inclusion power may be relevant, however. For example, group schemes may find it necessary to include the most powerful states, largest firms, or most widely known NGOs, who will influence the scheme in their preferred direction.

[43] The ILO Declaration in Zone 7 and UN Global Compact in Zone 4 are both driven by states and IGOs, and so might also be included in this group.

[44] The EU illustrates the possibility of supranational regulation, as does the OECD among developed states on a few economic issues. Drezner argues that powerful states can impose their regulatory preferences abroad, but they seem unwilling or unable to do so in the cases we examine here. See Drezner, *All Politics Is Global: Explaining International Regulatory Regimes*. We argue below that states need not become directly involved to play an important role in shaping international regulation.

[45] We argue that entrepreneurs have created many private and public-private Triangle schemes because they do not regard any of the forms of state action identified by Kahler and Lake (this volume)—regulation by individual states, supranational regulation by IGOs,

Still, even when the state does not engage in effective *direct* regulation, it can play substantial *indirect* roles that shape bargaining among other actors. To take one example, by promulgating international standards (e.g., ILO conventions), states and IGOs shape the expectations and normative understandings that guide other actors engaged in RSS. They create levers by which NGOs hold firms accountable and focal points that simplify bargaining over the content of standards and reduce its cost.[46] We discuss indirect state roles at greater length later in the chapter.

FIRMS: UNILATERAL BARGAINING ADVANTAGES

Zone 2 is densely populated with codes and schemes adopted by individual firms and industry associations. All are self-regulatory, although they vary widely in content and form, and collective schemes may reflect somewhat greater independence and representativeness.

Firms have inherent advantages in the bargaining game. First, in the areas considered here, they typically prefer minimal regulation, which is often the default position. Thus, smaller and less visible firms and industries can often ignore regulatory issues in the hope that advocates for higher standards will overlook them or focus on larger, more vulnerable targets. The weak or nonexistent CSR codes of these firms and sectors constitute gaps in regulatory coverage within Zone 2.

Second, while large firms are more visible, they have a "first mover" *preemption* advantage. Firms are already directly involved in the production processes at issue; in addition, they can promulgate and (uniquely) implement standards through their internal management systems and other forms of operational capacity. This GIAP allows firms to blunt political pressures and preempt alternative forms of regulation by adopting standards that are minimally sufficient.[47] Many firm and industry codes of the 1980s–90s appear to be products of this strategy. Preemption may disarm NGOs and public advocates by undermining their case for exter-

---

hierarchical regulation by dominant states, or regulation by networks of national agencies—as providing or likely to provide satisfactory regulation.

[46] This is not to say that state-created international standards are uncontroversial. More radical NGOs push for even stricter standards (e.g., requiring payment of a "living wage"), while firms argue that international standards are already overly restrictive. However, it is striking that even schemes that set out to innovate in RSS increasingly accept international standards as their benchmark. As a result, many international norms that were originally intended to apply only to states now provide standards for firms.

[47] The sovereign debt restructuring issues discussed by Helleiner, unlike the issues of business conduct discussed here, turn on the actions of two parties: sovereign debtors and private creditors. In that context, Helleiner suggests that creditor associations and certain developing-country governments jointly adopted a voluntary code of conduct in large part to preempt a more formal and less business-friendly debt restructuring mechanism. Eric Helleiner, "Filling a Hole in Global Financial Governance? The Politics of Regulating Sovereign Debt Restructuring," this volume.

nal regulation, split moderate NGOs from more radical ones, and divert NGO attention to firms that have not adopted any standards—although there exists the countervailing possibility that preemptive action will raise a firm's or industry's prominence as a target for activists.[48]

Third, the same competencies give firms a "second mover" preemption advantage. In a variety of sectors, once an NGO-based or collaborative scheme has been created and begins to press firms to sign on, the relevant industry association creates a competing, business-friendly scheme. Examples include SFI and PEFC, forest industry schemes created in response to the FSC, and WRAP, an apparel industry labor rights scheme created in response to the FLA.[49] These alternative schemes allow firms to argue that they are actively implementing higher standards without acceding to more stringent and intrusive NGO schemes. Collective action through industry associations strengthens firms' external bargaining positions and protects the industry's collective reputation.[50]

When they act preemptively, firms or associations may adopt the trappings of effective self-regulation—including codes, responsible officers, outside auditors, and logos—without seriously implementing it. An early example was Nike's 1997 engagement of Andrew Young's Goodworks International to evaluate its Asian suppliers' production sites against its labor standards. Critics charged that Young was taken on a "carefully guided tour," spent too little time to do a serious evaluation, focused on the wrong issues, and even relied on translators provided by Nike.[51] Firms may also adopt standards that are easy to meet and avoid others that would be costly to satisfy. In the extreme case, they may adopt sham schemes intended mainly to mislead.

The inherent opacity of self-regulation (partially justified by a legitimate concern to protect production secrets) makes it hard for third parties to distinguish sincere schemes from preemptive moves and shams. This equally poses a dilemma for sincere firms that wish to self-regulate for reasons of efficiency and privacy or to avoid the perceived risks of dealing with NGOs. A few firms (including Body Shop and Levi Strauss) have

[48] David P. Baron and Daniel Diermeier, "Strategic Activism and Nonmarket Strategy," *Stanford GSB Research Paper* no. 1909 (2005).

[49] Benjamin Cashore, Graeme Auld, and Deanna Newsom, *Governing through Markets: Forest Certification and the Emergence of Non-State Authority* (New Haven, CT: Yale University Press 2004); Errol Meidinger, "Beyond Westphalia: Competitive Legalization in Emerging Transnational Regulatory Systems," in Christian Brütsch and Dirk Lehmkuhl, eds., *Law and Legalization in Transnational Relations* (London and New York: Routledge, 2007).

[50] Prakash and Potoski, *The Voluntary Environmentalists*, 52–56.

[51] Dana Canedy, "Nike Appoints Andrew Young to Review Its Labor Practices," *New York Times,* March 25, 1997; Bob Herbert, "Mr. Young Gets It Wrong," *New York Times,* June 27, 1997.

nevertheless pioneered fairly aggressive self-regulatory strategies, promoting them as a centerpiece of their corporate strategy. BP exemplifies a mixed case: it has attempted to redefine and rebrand itself around CSR ("beyond petroleum") and has implemented meaningful self-regulation, yet has been responsible for significant environmental harms.[52] When a self-regulating firm is found to have violated its own standards—as The Gap recently has been with respect to child labor in India—the issue will quickly become politicized, and it will be hard for consumers to evaluate the firm's performance.

NGOS: LIMITED GIAP

Zone 3 contains a modest number of NGO-based schemes. NGOs have limited GIAP, based on their normative expertise and independence. This allows them to promulgate standards such as the CERES and Sullivan principles and the WRC model code. NGO standards can raise awareness of issues, create expectations for firm behavior, and shape the regulatory dialogue and broader public discourse. More concretely, a significant number of firms have signed on to these and other NGO codes. Many NGOs have the operational capacity to administer product certification systems, monitor firm behavior against their own codes and other standards, and pressure firms to adhere and comply through tactics ranging from newspaper ads to sit-ins, blockades, and consumer boycotts. NGO GIAP is enhanced to the extent that such actions also advance organizational needs, such as fund-raising, publicity, and membership.

Ultimately, however, NGO GIAP is modest. Without cooperation from firms or support from states, NGOs often lack the resources to identify violations and the legitimacy to mobilize counteraction. Moreover, their occasional power to punish can be counterproductive: NGOs' use of GIAP, especially through adversarial campaigns, threatens firms, makes them wary of adhering to NGO codes, and stimulates the formation of weaker industry schemes.[53] Ultimately, NGOs can only achieve their goals by inducing firms to implement higher standards.

IMPLICIT BARGAINING AMONG SCHEMES

Unilateral action based on GIAP leads to a multiplicity of largely parallel RSS schemes.[54] Some multiplicity occurs within vertex Zones 1–3 on the Triangle, as many firms and industry associations adopt self-regula-

---

[52] The BP case also illustrates that, especially when dealing with large corporations, a firm can contain both "good" and "bad" actors, so that even "good" firms will violate standards on occasion— making it doubly hard for outsiders to evaluate firm schemes.

[53] Sasser, Prakash, Cashore, and Auld, "Direct Targeting as an NGO Political Strategy."

[54] Kenneth W. Abbott and Duncan Snidal, "Nesting, Overlap and Parallelism: Governance Schemes for International Production Standards." Memo presented at Workshop on Nested and Overlapping Institutions, Princeton University, February 2006.

tory codes, and NGOs establish schemes to regulate different problems. Schemes in different Zones also operate in parallel: for example, an apparel firm like Gap might be affected by nearly a dozen of the schemes in figure 2.1, in several Zones.[55]

Implicit bargaining takes the form of competition among parallel schemes to control the regulatory space. In some cases, competition exerts pressure toward higher standards. Sincere firms compete for recognition (and sometimes for consumer loyalty) by adopting self-regulatory schemes more stringent than the industry, as by authorizing external monitoring or expanding reporting; this puts pressure on laggard firms. Industry schemes such as SFI, PEFC, WRAP, and ICMM—which may have been created with the aim of preemption but must compete with NGO and multi-stakeholder schemes for legitimacy and public support—have over time strengthened their substantive standards, procedures (e.g., adding optional external auditing and reporting under GRI standards), and governance (e.g., adding stakeholder advisory or supervisory boards).[56] Changes such as these make even single-actor schemes more likely to reflect common interests. Thus, schemes like FSC and WRC can have important indirect effects through their influence on competing schemes as well as direct effects on participating firms.[57] Competition has even produced modest convergence across Zones, ameliorating the problem of multiple standards. Areas of convergence (all supportive of common interest regulation) include stakeholder input into standard-setting (N), external auditing and accreditation procedures (M), and reporting (I/E).

To strengthen their positions for implicit bargaining, schemes have adapted models of organization and operation that have proven successful in certain sectors or for certain problems for use in new areas. While emulation is not always successful, it can increase the effectiveness, legitimacy, and competitive strength of the new schemes. A notable example is fair trade certification and labeling, which began in 1988 when a Dutch NGO created the "Max Havelaar" label for certified fair trade coffee. This approach has now been adopted by at least twenty-one national

---

[55] In addition to having its own Code of Business Conduct and working for uniform industry codes (Zone 2), Gap Inc. is a member of UNGC (Zone 4), has worked with the ILO's Better Factories Cambodia project which monitors Gap suppliers (Zone 7), and has partnered with SAI (Zone 6) on several projects. For a self-reporting of its involvement in these and many other schemes, see "Gap Inc., 2005–2006 Social Responsibility Report" (August 16, 2007). Gap is also subject to the OECD Guidelines and ILO Declaration, as well as multiple national laws, and could potentially participate in additional schemes.

[56] Meidinger, "Beyond Westphalia," 8; Sasser, Prakash, Cashore, and Auld, "Direct Targeting as an NGO Political Strategy," 10–11.

[57] Cashore, Auld, and Newsom, *Governing through Markets*, 219.

schemes (all members of FLO) and applied to numerous products.[58] The FSC "stewardship council" model similarly has been adapted for marine (MSC) and farm products (Food Alliance Stewardship Council), and proposed for tourism. Many states have adopted national eco-labels (ECO) and environmental management systems (EMAS); the latter has also influenced the work of the ISO.

In other cases, however, competition exerts pressure toward lower standards. Because NGO schemes have an operational impact only if firms voluntarily adhere,[59] they face an incentive to compete by subtly weakening their standards or procedures. For example, even as competition has forced forest industry schemes to become stronger, it has led FSC to soften some standards to take account of business concerns.[60] In still other cases, the impact of competition is mixed: for example, NGO campaigns put pressure on firms to adopt higher standards, but also create incentives for firms to take preemptive action by creating alternative business-friendly schemes.

Unsurprisingly, implicit bargaining through unilateral action leads to a proliferation of highly diverse RSS schemes across the regulatory space, as depicted in figure 2.2. This can have positive consequences. Perhaps most significantly, certain types of schemes, such as those created by independent NGOs and highly representative collaborative groups, are resistant to capture by the targets of regulation. Moreover, whereas an industry operating in a traditional state regulatory context might gain complete control over regulation by capturing a single agency, in the decentralized world of RSS an industry is unlikely to succeed in capturing the several relevant RSS schemes—and new ones might arise if they did. Multiple schemes of different types also allow for normative and institutional learning and innovative forms of collaboration. In sectors where RSS is mature, competition has led to an overall strengthening of regulation, modest convergence, and the emergence of an interdependent network of schemes.[61]

At the same time, the rapid emergence of many diverse RSS schemes may produce more noise than clarity in the development of regulatory norms and confuse consumers and other audiences. In forestry alone there

---

[58] Margaret Levi and April Linton, "Fair Trade: A Cup at a Time?" *Politics & Society* 31 (2003), 415–416.

[59] We distinguish firm adherence to NGO standards from schemes that are firm-NGO collaborations.

[60] Cashore, Auld, and Newsom, *Governing through Markets*, 8.

[61] Meidinger, "Beyond Westphalia." This suggests both an extension of Kahler and Lake's analysis of networked governance to the broader set of private and public networks that link Triangle institutions, and a more positive view of these networks as less susceptible to capture.

are now over thirty non-state schemes, in tourism, over one hundred.[62] This multiplicity may be advantageous to firms that prefer weak regulation, allowing them to preempt stronger action by allying with less stringent schemes. It also causes ongoing conflict, as NGOs criticize and impose costs on firms that accept only weaker standards.

Collaborative Schemes

EXPLICIT BARGAINING TO CREATE MULTI-ACTOR SCHEMES

The inadequacy of unilateral action and the costs of implicit bargaining create possibilities for actors to improve their outcomes through collaboration in multi-actor schemes.[63] For example, a firm that prefers self-regulation and an NGO that favors higher standards may find it preferable to work together on a joint standard that will be more effectively implemented than an NGO scheme and more legitimate than a pure self-regulatory code. More generally, actors sharing such common interests may combine their competencies to create more effective, legitimate, and representative RSS institutions. As figures 2.1 and 2.2a–c demonstrate, a significant number of collaborative schemes in Zones 4, 6, and 7 have been created, especially since 1995.

Yet bargaining among actors with disparate goals and capacities will be costly and contentious, will sometimes fail, and may not even be attempted.[64] The problem is exacerbated by mistrust. From the NGO perspective, firms are targets precisely because they engage in normatively inappropriate practices for profit. Some firms may sincerely want to improve their social and environmental performance, but others have only paid lip service or even disguised their behavior through RSS schemes. From the firm perspective, NGOs do not understand the needs of business in competitive markets and have unrealistic conceptions of what standards and procedures are compatible with production. Many NGOs use confrontational tactics at least in part for organizational reasons; firms are wary that collaboration with such groups will render them more vulnerable.

[62] On forestry see Sasser, Prakash, Cashore, and Auld, "Direct Targeting as an NGO Political Strategy," 7; on tourism, see Cashore, Auld, and Newsom, *Governing through Markets*, 26.

[63] Actors of one type may also engage in explicit bargaining to create a collective (IGO, industry association, or NGO alliance) scheme.

[64] Subgroups of actors may find common ground with the other camp, however, so that bargaining will not be contentious for them. For example, makers of specialty coffee have endorsed fair trade certification as an additional way to distinguish their products (Levi and Linton, "Fair Trade," 409), and organic farmers form the base of IFOAM.

The bargaining power of actors in these situations depends on a number of factors. Each actor will insist that any collaborative scheme be at least as attractive as what it could achieve unilaterally using its GIAP. Each actor also has some inclusion power insofar as its competencies are necessary elements in the hoped-for scheme. These two sources of power are often closely related. When company products are branded or otherwise visible to consumers, for example, NGOs have significant GIAP, even as their independence, representativeness, and capacities for monitoring and enforcement make their inclusion more important.

Bargaining power also depends on situational factors, such as the numbers of actors on each side of an issue. As with implicit bargaining among schemes, firms facing multiple NGOs may be able to forge alliances with the most business-friendly groups; for example, when SFI created a more representative stakeholder board, it drew the board's NGO members from relatively conservative conservation groups. This prospect may heighten competition among NGOs to attract firm partners—although NGO cooperation may attenuate this effect. On the other hand, more "radical" NGOs excluded from collaborative schemes may target scheme participants with special vigor, undoing some of the benefit for firms: NGOs active in FSC still criticize SFI as a "historic greenwashing effort to blur the public's trust."[65] Scandals that focus public attention also increase the bargaining power of NGOs and states vis-à-vis firms.

Where bargaining power is relatively equal, we would expect to see collaborative schemes that balance NGO goals of higher and more effective standards with firm goals of avoiding adverse publicity and NGO campaigns. This will apply especially where NGOs have significant leverage, as with consumer branded sectors, prominent firms, and industries facing scandal. An important variant occurs where firms see opportunities to build market niches based on socially responsible behavior and so are eager to collaborate with NGOs that can legitimate their efforts.

In many situations, however, there will be no bargaining room between firms and NGOs; either or both will prefer unilateral action over collaboration. In particular, firms not subject to strong consumer scrutiny will prefer self-regulation or inaction, knowing that NGOs lack countervailing power and that consumers and the public find it difficult to distinguish strong from weak schemes. Because firms have the strongest unilateral position in the absence of state regulation, the most likely outcome in many areas—reflected in Zones 2 and 3 on the Triangle—will be modest firm self-regulation combined with noisy but often ineffective NGO critics and schemes.

[65] Sasser, Prakash, Cashore, and Auld, "Direct Targeting as an NGO Political Strategy," 3–4, 10.

COLLABORATION AMONG SCHEMES

RSS schemes bargain among themselves for a variety of purposes. Schemes that share similar goals can collaborate on standards and procedures while continuing to operate independently. Such cooperation provides mutual support and learning, facilitates harmonization to reduce the burden and confusion of multiple schemes, enhances the voice of the organizations in international forums, and helps establish shared practices as international standards, undercutting the legitimacy of less stringent schemes.

An important example is the ISEAL Alliance, whose members include FSC, MSC, SAI, FLO, IFOAM and other standard-setting and conformity assessment schemes. To enable these high-standards institutions to distinguish themselves from weaker schemes, ISEAL has promulgated a Code of Good Practice for Setting Social and Environmental Standards, with which all member organizations comply; members also commit to comply with ISO standards on accreditation of certifiers. ISEAL provides peer and technical support to members and new applicants, conducts research, and advocates for state and market recognition of high-standards schemes.

Even deeper collaboration occurs when like-minded schemes form umbrella organizations. These typically adopt common standards and procedures through bargaining among member groups; they often enhance members' legitimacy and impact by establishing a common label or mark that can gain wide recognition. For example, IFOAM is a loose umbrella for over 750 diverse organizations concerned with organic food; it accredits member schemes based on common substantive standards. FLO unites twenty national fair trade certification/labeling schemes and three producer networks. Both license a common mark to their members. PEFC is an umbrella for national industry-based forestry schemes; it "recognizes" schemes that meet its standards, including SFI in the United States. FSC also certifies national initiatives.

Finally, schemes sometimes collaborate across zones to gain complementary competencies, much as actors do. The UN Global Compact has urged firms that accept its principles to report on compliance using GRI standards, rather than attempting to promulgate its own. ICMM and TOI, both dominated by business, have committed to GRI reporting to enhance their legitimacy; in response, GRI has developed specific supplemental standards for the relevant sectors.

Yet interscheme collaboration often fails. This may be simply because otherwise like-minded schemes have slightly different areas of focus: for example, schemes supporting fair trade, shade-grown and organic coffee have much in common, but find it difficult to agree on common standards.[66] More often it is because of ideological differences. For example, in 2002 the FSC, SFI, PEFC, and other forestry schemes initiated the Forests Dialogue out of concern that mutual criticism would undercut public support for all of them. The Dialogue identified several areas of beneficial cooperation, but in the end was unable to bridge the gaps among NGO- and firm-dominated schemes. Again, the result is a multiplicity of parallel, competing schemes.

THE BACKGROUND ROLES OF THE STATE

So far our analysis has been equivocal as to the prospects for public interest regulation of transnational business. On one hand, the state's domestic regulatory capacity does not extend readily into the transnational realm, and states have been unwilling to grant IGOs sufficient authority to manage the problem. The GIAP of firms and NGOs and the bargaining advantages of firms have led to the proliferation of single-actor RSS schemes that are implausible regulators. Numerous parallel schemes may create confusion, and competition among them sometimes leads to a weakening of standards. On the other hand, a multiplicity of schemes can lead to learning and limit the possibility of complete capture. Competition among schemes can lead to higher standards, and schemes increasingly cooperate to reinforce and complement one another. Common interests in regulation, NGO bargaining leverage, and inclusion power have also produced promising collaborative schemes with a broad range of competencies. Still, successful RSS schemes typically depend either on the voluntary adherence of firms committed to CSR or on special circumstances that afford NGOs the leverage to push firms in a socially responsible direction. At present, neither of these forces is sufficiently prevalent to provide a sound basis for "common interest" regulation.

A more optimistic picture emerges when we take into account the entrepreneurial roles states and IGOs can play in enhancing the competencies and bargaining power of other actors and modifying the situational factors relevant to bargaining. The importance of such background roles is familiar from domestic settings, as where the potential for state regulation creates incentives for professional associations to police their members (although perhaps to a lesser extent than if the state regulated directly). The impact of background activities can also be considerable in transnational settings, increasing the feasibility of particular RSS schemes as well as putting pressure on actors, especially firms, to take social responsibility

---

[66] Levi and Linton, "Fair Trade," 425–426.

and the public interest seriously. We discuss here the impacts the state can have at each stage of the ANIME regulatory process.[67]

Agenda-Setting. The state can play an important catalytic role by placing regulatory issues on the political agenda and by convening, promoting, and supporting non-state RSS schemes as legitimate participants in their resolution. State support can be political and moral, as was the Clinton administration's role in convening the AIP. Because of growing civil society participation, IGOs too can play a major convening role. For example, by bringing together some 35,000 state delegates, 10,000 environmentalists, and 9,000 journalists, the 1992 Rio Conference heightened awareness of global environmental issues and increased pressure on firms to organize in response. The origin of the World Business Council for Sustainable Development can be traced directly to Rio. The 2002 Johannesburg Summit played a similar role in catalyzing public-private partnerships for sustainable development.

State support can also be material, as was the Dutch government's contribution of facilities and financial support for GRI. The tax-deductibility of contributions to NGOs in the United States is tantamount to government support of their activities, although that support is so indirect it gives the state little influence over NGO activities. Broader state action can affect the context of bargaining and the strength of particular actors. For example, a state guarantee of freedom of association for workers, and the right of domestic and international NGOs to operate, each provide an important underpinning for the competencies and bargaining power of those groups.

Negotiation. NGO- and firm-based schemes frequently draft their own standards, but they still typically root them in state-generated norms, such as those found in UN or ILO conventions. Indeed, even though private schemes often try to innovate in terms of standards, they increasingly return to international norms as the appropriate benchmarks. An example is the business group of Amnesty International, which promulgated its own human rights guidelines for firms, but then abandoned them to base their advocacy efforts instead on the UN Draft Norms on the Responsibilities of Transnational Corporations.

Reliance on state-generated norms is driven partly by the efficiency advantages of having a single standard, so that firms face fewer inconsistent and possibly conflicting demands. But public norms are more than convenient focal points. They are also highly legitimate because—except for

---

[67] In addition, as Vogel points out, developing countries can strengthen regulation both by operating directly as regulators and by strengthening civil society within their country so that private entrepreneurs can promote RSS schemes. David Vogel, "The Private Regulation of Global Corporate Conduct," this volume.

instances of regulatory capture—they have been developed through participatory processes by actors that (at least to some extent) represent a broad range of interests and values. By contrast, standards generated by firms are seen as biased toward their economic interests. And while NGOs may be other-regarding, they are not always representative, and their values may be disputed within civil society and between North and South.[68] The use of public norms ameliorates these problems.

The availability of legitimate public standards shifts the balance of power in implicit and explicit bargaining between firms and NGOs. When states agree on new standards—as in the recent wave of instruments addressing corruption and the successive revisions of the OECD Guidelines—they signal non-state actors that expectations for business conduct have changed. Firms find it harder to resist such standards or to substitute their own; NGOs can strengthen their position by framing their activities in those terms.

States and IGOs can also support non-state standards more directly. For example, the legitimacy and influence of GRI were strengthened symbolically by the organization's 2002 inauguration at the United Nations. GRI standards also receive political support from the participation of UNEP and their endorsement by the UNGC as the preferred framework for participants' communications on progress.

Implementation. The state's role in implementation is fairly limited, in the background as well as in the foreground. However, an important exception is government procurement. In some sectors, public institutions are large enough purchasers that their requirements for suppliers can set a trend for an entire industry. If a state agency or IGO requires suppliers to adopt a particular RSS standard—or requires satisfaction of a general standard that can most effectively be demonstrated through adherence to an RSS scheme—it will lead some firms to act accordingly to gain access to this market. The Procurement Division of the UN, for example, "strongly encourages" all vendors to actively participate in the Global Compact.[69]

In addition, some states and IGOs provide technical assistance that facilitates implementation. The ILO's Better Factories Cambodia Program (operated in conjunction with the Cambodian government and Garment Manufacturers' Association) organizes training programs designed to im-

---

[68] International (rather than national) standards have a similar legitimacy advantage in being developed through transnationally representative processes and thus presumably less shaped by narrow national interests. By contrast, ICANN Internet standards, developed by an agency that is nominally independent of but close to the U.S. government, are often perceived as biased by other states and their citizens.

[69] UN Procurement Division, "The Global Compact," http://www.un.org/Depts/ptd/global.htm.

prove both working conditions and productivity. Although the ILO has limited resources for such efforts and the Program is relatively small, it nevertheless exemplifies the possibility that states and IGOs can facilitate implementation by firms when capacity (not willingness) is the issue.

Monitoring. Most states have substantial monitoring capacity, but monitoring is expensive; its cost limits the ability of states to monitor even domestic regulations thoroughly. Even when the state itself cannot directly monitor business, however, it can create an environment that enables and increases the effectiveness of monitoring by others. Most important here are requirements for transparency and disclosure, including the requirement of some states that major corporations publish social responsibility reports. Examples include the 2005 United Kingdom Operating and Financial Review Regulations (S.I. 2005/1011), which require reporting on the community and environmental impact of corporate operations, and the 2002 French New Economics Regulations (Article 116), which require triple bottom line reporting. Such mandates increase the effectiveness of monitoring by NGOs and socially responsible investors, and shift the balance of power between actors by legitimating the underlying standards.

Enforcement. In principle, the threat of mandatory regulation and coercive sanctions—where credible—can induce firms to observe self-regulatory standards and enhance the enforcement leverage of weaker parties. In practice, however, the state's enforcement capacity is limited and is mainly exercised indirectly. Such pressure may be insufficient to produce strong action by individual firms because of the competitive pressures and collective-action problems they face. However, industry groups such as the International Council of Chemical Associations (sponsor of Responsible Care) may adopt and enforce sectoral standards (e.g., by expelling noncomplying members) to forestall state action. Again, because firm-based standards are often suspect, industry groups have an incentive either to incorporate public standards or to collaborate with NGOs.

NGOs sometimes utilize the enforcement power of the state in ways states did not intend. For example, firms that misrepresent their compliance with standards may in some jurisdictions be sued for false advertising, as Nike has been in California. Existing law may also provide other hooks for enforcement by non-state actors. The effectiveness of these tactics will often depend on the state's acquiescence, but this opens the possibility for states to actively create or support legal doctrines and procedures to strengthen NGO bargaining power. The U.S. Alien Torts Claims Act is a current example: an ongoing series of decisions and considerable debate is determining whether U.S. courts will become involved in rectifying private foreign wrongs. So far, however, doctrines like these remain weak factors in the enforcement of transnational standards.

Finally, although direct state involvement in enforcing transnational production standards has been limited, this remains a possibility. For example, although the WTO has rejected appeals to adopt enforceable labor and environmental standards, some preferential trade agreements (PTAs) have ventured in that direction. The labor and environment side agreements to NAFTA open novel enforcement strategies for private actors; participants could decide to tighten these agreements further because of true concern for regulatory standards and/or (as proposed in the 2008 U.S. presidential nomination campaign) for domestic political purposes.[70] A recent U.S. agreement between the Bush administration and congressional Democrats provided for stronger labor and environmental protections in new PTAs.[71] PTAs are also increasingly being used to induce developing countries to respect human rights.[72] Even where such leverage is not applied directly, its mere possibility may strengthen the observance of global standards.

Conclusion

The discussion of the background roles of the state brings us back to the issue with which we began: Who should regulate transnational production? Empirically, the Governance Triangle demonstrates clearly that when it comes to regulating the externalities of transnational production, the state is far from the only game in town, and may no longer be the most important game in town. Most Triangle institutions, except for those in Zone 1 and the upper regions of Zones 4, 5, and 7, were created without significant state mandate or involvement. And most were created precisely because their founders were frustrated with the state as regulator: not only by the failure of states and IGOs to address perceived problems, but by the structural weaknesses that seemed to prevent them from doing so. We still lack a clear picture of how effective Triangle schemes will be—if nothing else, many lack resources and must limit their efforts to narrow sectors, such as university apparel or luxury consumer goods—and how

[70] Vogel provides other examples of trade policy being used to punish unacceptable labor, environmental and human rights practices, but sees the WTO as more of an impediment than a help in this area. David Vogel "The Private Regulation of Global Corporate Conduct," this volume.

[71] John D. McKinnon and Greg Hitt, "Critics Target Trade Deal for Not Going Far Enough," *Wall Street Journal,* May 12, 2007.

[72] Emilie M. Hafner-Burton, "Trading Human Rights: How Preferential Trade Agreements Influence Government Repression," *International Organization* 59 (Summer 2005), 593–629.

well they will advance the public interest, but a significant number have assembled the necessary competencies.

Yet the state is not becoming obsolete as a regulator, either domestically or internationally. Instead, in both settings its role is evolving, from the centralized mandatory regulator of tradition (and to some extent of myth) to a more subtle role as catalyst, coordinator, and supporter of diverse regulatory activities. The state retains unique competencies, especially at the agenda-setting, negotiation, and enforcement stages. These competencies remain central even where non-state institutions are prominent, for example, through the widespread reliance on state-generated standards. The competencies of the state also operate in the background, often invisibly: many firm and industry codes have been adopted, in whole or in part, to preempt mandatory regulation, litigation, or some other action that depends on state authority. Somewhat more visibly, states and IGOs provide many forms of support to Triangle schemes, from monetary contributions to in-kind support to preferential status that gives access to information and political influence.

Thus, the glass of transnational state regulation is both half-full and half-empty. The extent of traditional state regulatory control over transnational production is dramatically less than over domestic production. But while the traditional statist model transfers poorly to the transnational level, the state can use its competencies both directly and indirectly to shape the regulatory space and influence the bargaining power of non-state actors and institutions. Thus, if states decide there is a need for greater regulation or regulation that better serves the public interest, they can use their competencies in many ways to support the RSS schemes depicted on the Governance Triangle, even if direct regulation is infeasible.

Filling a Hole in Global Financial Governance?
The Politics of Regulating Sovereign Debt
Restructuring

Eric Helleiner

MOST COUNTRIES with market-based economies have developed formal regulatory mechanisms, in the form of bankruptcy laws, to facilitate the orderly restructuring of unsustainable debts owed to private creditors within their territories. It is widely recognized that these mechanisms serve important public good functions at the national level. By imposing a standstill on payments, they can prevent creditors from engaging in a destructive "rush to the exit" when debtors are suffering financial difficulties. Equally important, they outline clear procedures for fostering the speedy and orderly restructuring of debts when necessary that can benefit debtors and creditors alike.

Why, then, has there been no formal counterpart mechanism at the global level to help restructure sovereign debts owed to private foreign creditors? The question was raised prominently in November 2001 by the IMF's deputy managing director, Anne Krueger, who described this situation as a "gaping hole" in the governance of international finance.[1] Her speech garnered enormous attention and helped generate an intense debate over the question of how best to facilitate a more orderly restruc-

Some portions of this chapter have been previously published in my article, "The Mystery of the Missing Sovereign Debt Restructuring Mechanism," *Contributions to Political Economy* 27, no. 1 (2008) (Oxford University Press).

I am grateful for research help to Asim Ali, Geoff Cameron, Masaya Llavaneras-Blanco, Troy Lundblad, Bessma Momani, Ian Muller, and Antulio Rosales. For their helpful comments, I thank two anonymous reviewers, and also Amar Bhattacharya, Tom Biersteker, Ariel Buria, Tom Callaghy, Randy Germain, Dierdre Kamlani, Bessma Momani, Layna Mosely, Tony Porter, Matthew Tubin, the participants in the Global Economic Governance seminar at the University of Oxford, and the contributors to this book, particularly Walter Mattli and Ngaire Woods. I also thank the Social Sciences and Humanities Research Council of Canada for assisting this research.

[1] Anne Krueger, *International Financial Architecture for 2002: A New Approach to Sovereign Debt Restructuring*, address given at the National Economists' Club Annual Members' Dinner, American Enterprise Institute, Washington, DC, November 26, 2001. Available at http://www.imf.org/external/np/speeches/2001/112601.htm.

turing of unsustainable sovereign debts. To date, this debate has generated two international regulatory initiatives. In a very short time, almost all new international bond issues have come to include a new set of standard legal clauses—"collective-action clauses" (CACs)—designed to facilitate a more orderly restructuring of unsustainable sovereign bond debt owed to foreign private creditors. At the same time, a new international code of conduct to govern sovereign bond restructuring episodes has been endorsed by the leading representatives of the international private financial community and public authorities in both "emerging market" and "creditor" countries.[2]

These initiatives represent a more limited international response than many, including Krueger herself, had hoped for. But they are still significant in having brought the restructuring of sovereign debts owed to private foreign creditors under new forms of regulation. Scholars of international political economy have not yet devoted much attention to these developments. This is unfortunate not just because of their potential practical significance whenever the next sovereign debt crises break out. These developments also have broader significance for scholarly debates about the politics of global economic regulation. How was it possible to foster such a rapid convergence of legal provisions in this sphere of the world economy? Why have leading actors been willing to cooperate in the development of an international code of conduct? And more generally, what does this episode teach us about the politics of global regulatory change?

This chapter addresses these questions, drawing on the analytical framework developed by Mattli and Woods for this volume.[3] The first section of the chapter explores the politics of international agenda-setting vis-à-vis this issue. It highlights how the creation of a formal international debt restructuring mechanism historically lacked a political champion because private creditors usually succeeded in serving their interests without such a mechanism, while sovereign debtors (especially wealthier ones) worried that their advocacy of the cause might undermine their creditworthiness. In this context, it took a third party—governments in creditor countries—finally to place the issue squarely on the international political agenda in the current age. Creditor governments were provoked by a set of international financial crises from the mid-1990s onward which demonstrated very publicly the negative externalities of the use of large-scale international bailout lending to resolve sovereign debt crises. While bail-

---

[2] I use the phrase "creditor countries" in this chapter to refer to home countries of private creditors involved in international lending to emerging market countries (rather than net external asset position of these countries).

[3] Walter Mattli and Ngaire Woods, "In Whose Benefit? Explaining Regulatory Change in Global Politics," this volume.

outs served private creditors' interests, they imposed considerable costs on others, including taxpayers in creditor countries, and seemed to do little to discourage further crises. As support for this model eroded in creditor countries, some key "public-sector entrepreneurs"—including Krueger—found an opportunity to promote international initiatives for regulating sovereign debt restructuring in ways that might better serve the global public interest.

The second section of the chapter examines the complicated and often conflictual politics associated with the negotiation and implementation of some of these initiatives from 2001 onward. Krueger's ambitious proposal to create a sovereign debt restructuring mechanism (SDRM) was opposed strongly and successfully not just by groups who had been wary of such schemes in the past—private creditors and wealthier sovereign debtors—but also by key U.S. officials who favored instead, largely on normative grounds, the introduction of CACs. These same three groups, led by some key entrepreneurs in each camp, quickly emerged as a "pro-change coalition" backing the CAC initiative. A narrower alliance of debtors and private creditors also took the lead in negotiating the international code of conduct. In a strategic sense, each of these groups hoped these initiatives might help defeat the SDRM proposal. Key debtors and private creditors also each saw these initiatives as potentially helpful in shifting the distributional impact of debt restructuring in their favor, particularly after the Argentine financial crisis of 2001 demonstrated the consequences of the lack of international regulation in a post-bailout context.

The chapter concludes with a brief discussion of the wider theoretical relevance of the episode. The analysis presented highlights the usefulness of various aspects of Mattli and Woods' framework for analyzing international regulatory change: the distinction between different stages of rule-making, the significance of "demonstration effects," the role of public and private "entrepreneurs" and pro-change coalitions, as well as the importance of demand- and supply-side determinants of negotiation and implementation outcomes. The episode also demonstrates the limitations of both functionalist and realist accounts of global regulation. The CACs and the international code of conduct emerged from a much more disorganized, conflictual, and intensively political process than traditional functionalist explanations predict. Actors were also motivated by various normative, distributional, and strategic concerns that went well beyond the objective of serving the global public good. The outcome also reflected not just the preferences of dominant states, as realists would anticipate, but those of key sovereign debtors and private international creditors as well. Indeed, many of the most important developments in this episode involved the strategic interaction between and within the latter two groups.

THE POLITICS OF INTERNATIONAL AGENDA-SETTING

Sovereign debt crises have been a recurring feature of the global economy for several centuries. It is not surprising, then, that economists as far back as Adam Smith have identified the case for endorsing sovereign bankruptcy or other formal restructuring mechanisms at the international level.[4] One function of a formal international debt restructuring mechanism would be to restrain the behavior of creditors during the lead-up to a debt crisis. When a sovereign debtor is facing financial difficulties, it is in the collective interest of private creditors to back a regime that would prevent each of them from "rushing to the exit" in the form of capital flight since the latter will only exacerbate the debtor's difficulties and thus undermine the value of creditors' assets. An international mechanism that restricts this kind of "asset grab," by such means as a standstill on payments, could keep the debtor solvent by giving it time to reorganize its affairs, arrange new borrowing, or negotiate a debt restructuring with creditors collectively. Without this, individual private creditors are faced with a classic collective-action problem: they each have an individual incentive to be the first to exit even though their collective behavior undermines the debtor's position and thus the value of creditors' assets as a whole.

An international debt restructuring mechanism could also help solve collective-action problems that arise among creditors *after* a crisis has broken out. When a sovereign debtor cannot repay its debts in full, creditors share a collective interest in agreeing to reschedule debts or extend new credits in order to strengthen the ability of the debtor to repay its debts. But individual creditors may be tempted to take advantage of such a situation by not participating in these activities, and demanding full repayment after these initiatives have borne fruit. In the immediate aftermath of a crisis, individuals may also "rush to the courthouse" in order to be the first to demand full repayment via litigation. A formal international debt restructuring mechanism could constrain these kinds of freeriding behavior in a number of ways: by forcing holdout creditors to accept the terms of debt restructuring, by imposing "stays" on litigation during the restructuring negotiations, and/or by outlining provisions for the extension of new credits during restructuring exercises.

These measures could benefit not just private creditors but also sovereign debtors. The latter could, of course, *unilaterally* prevent "rushes to

---

[4] See, for example, Kenneth Rogoff and Jeromin Zettelmeyer, "Bankruptcy Procedures for Sovereigns: A History of Ideas, 1976–2001," *IMF Staff Papers* 49, no. 3 (2002), 470–507.

the exit" by introducing exchange controls. Similarly, debtors can attempt to set the terms of debt restructuring through *unilateral* debt write-downs. But debtors undertaking these actions on their own face the threat of creditor retaliation and litigation, as well as damage to their reputation as a borrower. An international mechanism that legitimizes and supports these actions will minimize these risks.

Who Will Champion the Cause?

Given these potential benefits for creditors, debtors, and the global public interest, why was an international debt restructuring mechanism not created in the past? Past initiatives to fill this hole in international financial governance have failed to find a political champion who is able to mobilize a wide coalition of support at the international level. Private creditors have seen little gain from such initiatives because they have often succeeded in overcoming collective-action problems associated with debt restructuring on their own. In the pre–World War II era, bondholders from many countries negotiated with debtors through representative bodies that aggregated and protected their collective interests during debt restructuring episodes.[5] Private creditors were also sometimes successful in minimizing debt rescheduling altogether by mobilizing the power of their home state to coerce debtors into repaying their loans at times of crisis.

When the threat of sovereign defaults to private international investors arose again in the 1970s, the lead private creditors–now Northern banks– once again developed mechanisms for coordinating private creditor interests during sovereign debt restructuring episodes. Created in 1975, their creditor-controlled Bank Advisory Committees—soon nicknamed the "London Club"—quickly came to dominate the handling of sovereign debt crises on terms that were favorable to the banks' interests. With the outbreak of the international debt crisis in the early 1980s, these committees then took a center stage role in coordinating the interests of private creditors and preventing sovereign defaults.[6] They were aided in this task by Northern governments and the IMF, which not only helped to coordinate private creditor interests but also took a lead role in extending public funds to bail out bankrupt debtor governments. This broad "creditor cartel" succeeded in pushing the primary adjustment burden to the crisis on to the debtor countries as well as taxpayers in creditor countries.

[5] Paulo Mauro and Yishay Yafeh, *The Corporation of Foreign Bondholders*, IMF Working Paper no. 03/107 (Washington, DC: International Monetary Fund, 2003).

[6] Charles Lipson, "Bankers' Dilemmas: Private Cooperation in Rescheduling Sovereign Debts," *World Politics* 38, no. 1 (1995), 200–225.

Using the terminology of Mattli and Woods, private creditors have thus historically succeeded in "capturing" the international regulatory agenda in this area through their organization and power as well as through their political influence within their home states. Given this privileged position, they have seen little reason to change the status quo by proposing new formal international mechanisms to govern sovereign debt restructuring. Indeed, they have usually been wary that such proposals might provide sovereign debtors with more voice and influence over debt restructuring negotiations than the ad hoc creditor-controlled mechanisms they had developed. This latter attitude was apparent when they strongly and successfully opposed a 1979–80 proposal from the G-77—an organization representing developing-country governments—to create a new, independent "international debt commission" that could facilitate the restructuring of sovereign debts owed to both private and official creditors. The proposal was designed to replace the creditor-controlled informal London Club (as well as the Paris Club that handled official debts) with a more formal institutionalized mechanism that was friendlier to the interests of debtor countries, particularly their "development" goals.[7]

It is not just the asymmetries of power between private creditors and debtors that have allowed the former to capture the international regulatory agenda in episodes such as this. Divisions among debtor governments have also undermined efforts to promote international reform. These divisions were apparent in 1979–80 when a number of the wealthier developing countries expressed concerns that the proposed international debt commission might discourage future capital flows to the developing world. By October 1980, disagreements among the G-77 had even led the group to withdraw its support for the proposal.[8]

A similar division emerged vis-à-vis a previous proposal for an international debt restructuring regime in the 1930s. In the wake of the Latin American defaults of the early 1930s, the Mexican government proposed at a 1933 Pan American conference "the possibility of establishing public international organizations to take care of debt negotiations and agreements." Like the G-77's initiative, this proposal was explicitly designed to undermine the power of creditor committees by transferring debt restructuring negotiations to an international organization in which

---

[7] Susanne Soederberg, "The Transnational Debt Architecture and Emerging Markets: The Politics of Paradoxes and Punishment," *Third World Quarterly* 26, no. 6 (2005), 927–949; Lex Rieffel, *Restructuring Sovereign Debt* (Washington, DC: Brookings, 2003), chaps. 5–6.

[8] Rieffel, *Restructuring*, 146; Rogoff and Zettelmeyer, "Bankruptcy Procedures"; Kathryn Lavelle, "Governing Sovereign Debt: Formal and Informal Alliances in Emerging Market Financial Politics." Paper presented to the annual meeting of the Canadian Association for the Study of International Development, June 2–4, 2005, London, Ontario, Canada.

sovereign debtors and creditor *governments* were represented. As the Mexican foreign minister put it, the goal was "to exclude thereby the intervention of Bankers' Committees."[9] But once again, a number of Latin American governments refused to back the Mexican proposal for fear that it would undermine their countries' creditworthiness in the eyes of foreign investors.[10]

These episodes highlight an important collective-action problem that has prevented debtor country governments from pushing proposals for a formal international debt restructuring mechanism more strongly at the international level. Although the creation of such a mechanism promised benefits to all debtors, any individual debtor government that indicated support for its construction faced large potential costs. Their support could be interpreted by private creditors as signaling willingness to default and thus damage the debtor's financial reputation in ways that increased borrowing costs or made it more difficult to raise funds abroad. Although they might gain from the creation of such a mechanism, individual debtors thus faced strong incentives to pretend to be disinterested in, or to oppose, the initiative.

On the International Political Agenda in 1995–1996

If private creditors and sovereign debtors have been historically reluctant to champion the cause of a formal international debt restructuring mechanism, how did the issue get placed on the international political agenda in the current period? It took a change in the attitude of a third party—creditor country governments—in the wake of the Mexican financial crisis of 1994. The Mexican crisis was handled in the same manner that others had been over the previous decade; that is, a default was prevented through the extension of an IMF-led international rescue package. But the massive scale of the international rescue provoked a substantial political backlash within creditor countries' policymaking circles.

It was not just the close to $50 billion size of the lending package that acted as a direct "demonstration effect" of the costs of handling sovereign debt crises in this way. The Mexican crisis was also the first to highlight very publicly how international lending to developing countries had shifted in the early 1990s largely to bond finance. When Latin American

[9] Both quotes in this paragraph are from José Manuel Puig, "VII Conference International Americana, Delegacíon de México" [no date], 2, U.S. National Archives, Record Group 43, International Conference Records, U.S. Delegation to the Seventh International Conference of American States, General Records, 1933–34, Reports of Delegates, Comm. On Initiatives, 2–4, Box No. 5, File: 4th Committee Economic and Financial, no. 1.

[10] Eric Helleiner, "The Mystery of the Missing Sovereign Debt Restructuring Mechanism," *Contributions to Political Economy* 27, no. 1 (2008).

governments threatened to default on loans to the largest northern banks in the early 1980s, there was a clear risk of a meltdown in the Northern financial system. But there was much less of this risk if the Mexican government defaulted to thousands of individual Northern holders of Mexican bonds. Bailouts now appeared simply to reward investors for their poor investment choices at the taxpayers' expense. The handling of the Mexican crisis thus symbolized to its critics how international financial policymaking had been increasingly captured by the interests of private creditors.

The critics of the Mexican bailout included many top-ranking European financial officials, particularly those from Germany and Britain.[11] But the issue became particularly politicized within the United States, which had shouldered the largest portion of the rescue package. Congressional Republicans, in particular, voiced strong concerns about the cost to U.S. taxpayers, and the Clinton administration was forced to retract its initial request to Congress for loan guarantees and to raise the required funds instead from its Exchange Stabilization Fund.[12] The U.S. support helped Mexico avoid default, but the political viability of future bailouts had been called into serious question.

In this context, governments in creditor countries began to consider ways to encourage private investors to assume more of the costs associated with sovereign debt crises. Because bondholders were more numerous and decentralized than banks, financial regulators in creditor countries recognized that it would not be easy to twist the arms of these private creditors in informal ways to support bailouts and other initiatives designed to resolve sovereign debt crises. It would be necessary instead to consider more formal mechanisms to prompt the private sector to assume more of the burden of adjustment in sovereign debt restructuring episodes.

Two alternative mechanisms were immediately considered. At their June 1995 Halifax summit, G-7 governments briefly discussed a proposal by the prominent economist Jeffrey Sachs to transform the IMF from a lender-of-last-resort into an international bankruptcy court. In this role, the Fund would be able to sanction payments standstills and then, if necessary, encourage a restructuring of debts. In the same month, the IMF Executive Board discussed a document prepared by the IMF legal

[11] Paul Blustein, *The Chastening* (New York: Public Affairs, 2001), 172–174.

[12] Robert Rubin and Jacob Weisberg, *In an Uncertain World* (New York: Random House, 2003); Barry Eichengreen and Brad Delong, "Between Meltdown and Moral Hazard: Clinton Administration International Monetary and Financial Policy," in Jeffrey Frankel and Peter Orszag, eds., *American Economic Policy in the 1990s* (Cambridge, MA: MIT Press, 2002).

department that outlined an IMF-led international bankruptcy mechanism which would have enabled debtors to initiate a payments standstill and stay of litigation until an "international debt adjustment facility" (operating as an independent affiliate of the IMF) backed a restructuring plan that had been approved by the debtor and a qualified majority of creditors.[13]

These proposals for an international bankruptcy mechanism initially went nowhere. They encountered a mixed reaction from the IMF Board and were rejected by a subsequent G-10 report in 1996 that had been commissioned by the G-7 summit.[14] In addition to opposition from many European officials, the Clinton administration was also wary of these proposals. As one observer later put it, U.S. officials regarded "the bankruptcy court as a political non-starter, [and] preferred to focus on the only crisis-management tool it had—in other words, bailouts. In the Clinton view, a fruitless debate on bankruptcy would only have underlined the lack of official confidence in the bailout option."[15] The proposals also generated little enthusiasm from private financial interests since they could interfere with the free cross-border flow of capital and force writedowns of private loans, whereas bailouts had the effect of socializing investor risks.

Although the proposal for an international bankruptcy mechanism failed to gain official support, a second mechanism for fostering debt restructuring did gain a little more traction. The G-10 "Rey Report" of 1996 backed the idea of encouraging international bond issues to be rewritten to include "collective-action clauses" (CACs). These clauses, which had been common in the London bond market since the late nineteenth century, would encourage more orderly restructuring of debts after a default by allowing for such things as: debtor-initiated restructuring and payments suspensions, the collective representation of creditors in a crisis, qualified majority voting by bondholders to alter terms and conditions of bond contracts, and restrictions on the ability of individual creditors to sue debtors or demand full repayment. As their name suggested, these clauses were explicitly designed to solve collective-action problems on the creditor side, and they were seen as a more politically feasible tool to encourage bondholders to be "bailed-in" to future financial crises. The

[13] Rogoff and Zettelmeyer, "Bankruptcy Procedures." For the document, see Legal Department, "Note on an International Debt Adjustment Facility for Sovereign Debtors," May 25, 1995, IMF Archives, Washington DC.

[14] For the IMF Board discussion, see "Minutes of the Executive Board Seminar 95/2, June 23, 1995," IMF Archives, Washington DC. The Group of 10 involves financial policymakers from eleven countries: Belgium, Canada, France, Germany, Italy, Japan, Netherlands, Sweden, Switzerland, the United Kingdom, and the United States.

[15] "A Question from Argentina," *Washington Post*, December 11, 2001.

idea of pushing for a universalization of CACs beyond London is usually attributed to Barry Eichengreen and Richard Portes, who had written a background study on this issue for the G-10 report.[16]

Political support among creditor country governments for CACs was, however, still very tepid. The Rey Report suggested that the incorporation of these CACs into bond contracts should be a market-led process rather than being forced on private actors. This recommendation was destined to be ignored because, beyond the London market, both investors and sovereign debtors had shown little interest in CACs. Debtor governments worried that their borrowing costs would rise if they suddenly incorporated CACs into bonds issued in New York and other non-London markets. This fear was only compounded by the fact that international investors had made clear their lack of enthusiasm for the Rey Report's recommendations, particularly its advocacy that standstills be endorsed in exceptional circumstances within CACs. From the investor standpoint, such a provision would give undue power to debtors by forcing creditors to the bargaining table.[17]

Renewed Interest in the Wake of Two Further Crises

While the Mexican crisis had placed international debt restructuring mechanisms back on the international political agenda, it took two further international financial crises to raise the political profile of the issue to a higher level. The first was the 1997–98 crisis which struck the East Asian region and beyond. Once again, very large international bailouts were offered to various countries to stem the crisis, and they provoked further opposition within many European countries and especially the United States. This opposition was particularly apparent during the 1998 debate within U.S. Congress concerning an IMF quota increase, a debate in which congressional Republicans almost succeeded in blocking approval because of dissatisfaction with the IMF's crisis lending.

Some of the discontent with the United States reflected the same distributional concerns about preventing taxpayers from bearing the costs of private lending mistakes. Concerns were also expressed about the costs borne by the debtor countries that were undergoing IMF-supervised adjustment programs as a condition of the loans they received. But opposi-

---

[16] See, for example, Rogoff and Zettelmayer, "Bankruptcy Procedures," 488. For the study, see Barry Eichengreen and Richard Portes, *Crisis? What Crisis? Orderly Workouts for Sovereign Debtors* (London: Centre for Economic Policy Research, 1995).

[17] Reiffel, "Restructuring," 224; Anna Gelpern and G. Mitu Gulati, "Public Symbol in Private Contract: A Case Study," *Washington University Law Review* 84 (2006), 1627–1715.

tion to bailouts, particularly among U.S. Republicans, increasingly also reflected the concern among free-market advocates that international bailouts were distorting proper market signals at the global level. By encouraging investors to see lending to developing countries as risk-free, bailouts were said to generate reckless lending and thus the negative externality of increased global financial instability. This "moral hazard" problem, it was argued, could only be addressed by scaling back—or even ending altogether—international bailouts in ways that both changed market expectations and forced investors to accept sovereign defaults and debt restructuring at the outset of debt crises.[18]

In the face of this criticism, the IMF began to push more actively for "bail-ins" of private investors during the 1998 South Korean financial crisis and then during several subsequent crises in Ecuador, Pakistan, and Ukraine in the 1999–2000 period. The election of George W. Bush as U.S. president then gave a large boost to those calling for greater private-sector involvement in the resolution of sovereign debt crises. Key officials in the new Bush administration embraced the "moral hazard" critique of IMF bailouts, including the new Treasury Secretary Paul O'Neill and his undersecretary for international affairs, John Taylor.[19] Many also had concerns about the distributional consequences of bailouts. O'Neill, a successful industrialist, was particularly critical that international investors gained from bailouts at taxpayers' expense. As he put it: "As we in the finance ministries of the world talk glibly about billions of dollars of support for policies gone wrong, we need to remember that the money we are entrusted with came from plumbers and carpenters who sent 25 percent of their $50,000 annual income to us for wise use." He was especially opposed to the manner in which "the IMF rides in on its horse and throws money at everybody, and the private-sector people get to take their money out."[20]

Upon assuming power, Bush administration officials quickly stated that they would not bail investors out of future sovereign debt crises.[21] In late 2001, they carried through on this commitment in the context of Argenti-

---

[18] For these debates, see, for example, Blustein, *The Chastening*.

[19] Ron Suskind, *The Price of Loyalty: George W. Bush, the White House, and the Education of Paul O'Neill* (New York: Simon & Schuster, 2004), 173, 175, 243–244; John Taylor, *Global Financial Warriors* (New York: Norton, 2007), 104.

[20] Quoted in Paul Blustein, *And the Money Kept Rolling In (and Out)* (New York: Public Affairs, 2005), 117–118.

[21] U.S. House of Representatives, *The State of the International Financial System and IMF Reform*, Hearing before the Committee on Financial Services, U.S. House of Representatives, 107th Congress, 1st session, May 22, 2001 (Washington, DC: U.S. Government Printing Office, 2001), 8, 13–16; Michael Sesit, "Who'll Blink First: Bush Administration or Bold Debtholders?" *Wall Street Journal*, February 16, 2001.

na's dramatic financial crisis.[22] After supporting an IMF loan to Argentina in August 2001, U.S. officials pulled away from supporting further IMF assistance to the country when its government did not meet IMF targets. When the Argentine government then defaulted on its loans—marking the largest sovereign default in world history—the United States did not push the IMF to intervene, and they defended this approach on moral hazard grounds.[23] U.S. officials also did little to protect the interests of private creditors during the latter's subsequent negotiations with the Argentine government which culminated in most investors accepting very large write-downs on the value of their bonds in 2005.[24]

As part of their new policy, some top Bush officials also began to look again at the proposals for an international debt restructuring mechanism. Faced with the impending Argentine crisis, in September 2001 O'Neill suggested to senior IMF management—and then to Congress—that attention should be given to the idea of an international bankruptcy law for sovereign debtors. As he told the Senate Banking Committee, "We need an agreement on an international bankruptcy law, so that we can work with governments that, in effect, need to go through a Chapter 11 reorganization instead of socializing the cost of bad decisions."[25]

The IMF's deputy managing director, Anne Krueger, then formally proposed a "sovereign debt restructuring mechanism" (SDRM) in November 2001.[26] Appointed to her position only a few months earlier with the strong support of the Bush administration, Krueger was a free market–oriented U.S. Republican who was less supportive of IMF bailouts than her predecessor, Stanley Fischer.[27] Unlike IMF staff in 1995, who had never made their proposal for an SDRM public, Krueger chose a very public and high-profile speech to outline this idea and her backing for it. Although she acknowledged that her proposal would not be available in time for Argentina's crisis, the speech attracted enormous attention and is rightly credited with placing the construction of an international mechanism for debt restructuring prominently on the international political agenda.

[22] They had passed up an earlier opportunity in Turkey, which experienced a financial crisis in early 2001 and had received a large IMF loan.

[23] See, for example, U.S. Senate, *Argentina's Economic Crisis*. Hearing Before the Subcommittee on International Trade and Finance of the Committee on Banking, Housing and Urban Affairs, U.S. Senate, 107th Congress, 2nd session. February 28, 2002 (Washington, DC: Government Printing Office, 2002), 33.

[24] Taylor, *Global Financial Warriors*, 93.

[25] Quoted in Sean Hagan, "Designing a Legal Framework to Restructure Sovereign Debt," *Georgetown Journal of International Law* 36, no. 2 (2005), 28. See also Blustein, *And the Money*, 176–178.

[26] Krueger, *International Financial Architecture*.

[27] "Kohler's New Crew," *The Economist*, June 16, 2001.

Under Krueger's initial proposal, a sovereign debtor that was facing the prospect of defaulting could request that the IMF endorse a standstill on payments. In return, the debtor would be required to introduce sound economic policies and negotiate debt restructuring in good faith with its creditors. These commitments would be monitored by the IMF, which might also provide further financial backing to the debtor. While private creditors and the debtor government would negotiate a restructuring of the debts, these negotiations might "occasionally" require more formal adjudication via an agency, whose members were selected by the IMF, but which was independent of the Fund.[28] During the negotiations, a stay on litigation would exist and any debt settlement that was agreeable to a supermajority of private creditors would be binding on all creditors.

As her subsequent high-profile advocacy of these ideas highlighted, Krueger was clearly a strong believer in the case for the SDRM. It could, she argued, help minimize bailouts of private creditors and address the moral hazard problem, and it would provide benefits to both debtors and investors. As an institution, the IMF also had important bureaucratic reasons to support this idea. Since the early 1980s, one of its central functions had been to manage sovereign debt crises. The SDRM would maintain this role in the post-bailout era.

A number of Northern governments initially supported the SDRM idea, including Britain and Canada, whose own central banks advanced a similar, though less ambitious, idea a few months earlier.[29] Within the U.S. government, however, O'Neill's deputy, John Taylor, did not share O'Neill's enthusiasm. To be sure, he had come into office with the strong belief that debt restructuring needed to be made more orderly in the post-bailout age. But he questioned whether the specific SDRM plan was the most appropriate approach. In February 2002, he publicly contrasted Krueger's "statutory" approach to his preferred "contractual" approach of encouraging CACs in all international bond contracts.[30] He also emphasized that he was ready to promote the use of CACs much more actively than governments had done in the wake of the 1996 Rey Report. Influential Republicans in Congress, such as the chair of the Joint Economic Committee, Jim Saxton, echoed Taylor's views. Because Congressional approval would likely be necessary to implement the SDRM (since it

---

[28] Quote from Krueger, *International Financial Architecture*, 7.

[29] Andy Haldane and Mark Kruger, *The Resolution of International Financial Crises*, Bank of Canada Working Paper 2001-20 (Ottawa: Bank of Canada, 2001). For other European support, see Lavelle, "Governing Sovereign Debt"; Gelpern and Gulati, "Public Symbol."

[30] U.S. Joint Economic Committee, *Reform of the IMF and World Bank*, Hearing Before the Joint Economic Committee, Congress of the United States, 107th Congress, 2nd session, February 14, 2002. (Washington, DC: U.S. Government Printing Office, 2002), 6.

would require changes to the IMF's Articles of Agreement), their stance was politically significant.

By early 2002, then, the two proposals first put forward in 1995–96 had been placed on the international political agenda in a more serious manner. As in the earlier period, international financial crises had raised the profile of the issue of the regulation of sovereign debt crises. Like the 1994 Mexican crisis, the 1997–98 financial crisis had provided a very visible demonstration of what critics argued were the negative externalities—to taxpayers in creditor countries, to debtor countries, and to global financial stability more generally—of the existing approach to handling debt crises. The Argentine crisis then provided the catalyst for thinking about how to implement a new approach (even if it could not in fact be implemented fully in that specific crisis). In this context, three key "public entrepreneurs" rose to the challenge—Anne Krueger, Paul O'Neill, and John Taylor—and their ideas built on the earlier mid-1990s work of IMF and G-10 officials as well as that of academics such as Sachs, Eichengreen, and Portes.

THE POLITICS OF NEGOTIATION AND IMPLEMENTATION

Although there was now serious interest in the reform of the regulation of sovereign bond restructuring, the path forward remained unclear. Which of the two proposals first put forth in 1995–96 would be implemented? Let us begin by examining the fate of the SDRM proposal.

The Fate of the SDRM: 2001–2003

Many aspects of the politics surrounding this proposal were in fact quite reminiscent of past initiatives to construct a formal international debt restructuring mechanism. To begin with, representatives of private creditors quickly emerged as very strong critics of Krueger's ideas. One line of criticism was that the SDRM could override contract provisions and restrict creditors' freedom by imposing standstills and/or restrictions on the freedom to litigate.[31] A second critique was that the SDRM would bolster sovereign debtors' bargaining position during restructuring negotiations. From the perspective of some creditors, even the very idea of an official endorsement of sovereign default through the creation of a

---

[31] See, for example, Lavelle, "Governing Sovereign Debt"; Gelpern and Gulati, "Public Symbol"; Josef Ackermann, "Time to Strengthen Emerging Markets Finance," *Financial Times*, February 17, 2004.

formal mechanism would tilt the balance too far in favor of debtors. Many creditors also argued that the IMF would not always be a neutral party because of its own exposure to sovereign debtors. The IMF's accommodating behavior toward Argentina—one of the IMF's largest debtors at the time—during the 2002–05 debt restructuring negotiations only reinforced this critique.[32]

Krueger's proposal was also controversial among developing-country governments. Although many African countries supported it, wealthier debtors such as Brazil and Mexico feared the SDRM would reduce capital inflows and increase the cost of borrowing from abroad.[33] As the Mexican deputy finance minister Agustin Carstens noted in early 2003, "The issue is that as this mechanism is perceived as increasing the probability of default, that will increase the pricing of debt."[34] Even if they saw its merits, many debtor governments were wary of supporting the SDRM proposal because investors might interpret this support as a willingness to default. These concerns only grew when private investors began to highlight their opposition to the SDRM.[35]

Alongside this familiar private creditor and debtor opposition, Krueger's ideas also encountered opposition within the U.S. official circles. Although U.S. policymakers were being lobbied by the private creditor community, it is important to recognize that the wariness of figures such as Taylor had important ideational roots. Taylor had long been a critic of the IMF; indeed, he had even called for the institution's abolition at the height of the East Asian crisis. To him, the SDRM proposal was an overly bureaucratic solution that would give the IMF too much power (and which also had little chance of being approved by Congress).[36] He preferred the more decentralized, market-oriented solution offered by the CACs.

[32] See, for example, Michele Wucker, "Searching for Argentina's Silver Lining," *World Policy Journal* 19, no. 4 (2002), 55; Martin Wolf, "If the Debt Is Unpaid," *Financial Times*, March 8, 2004.

[33] Ariel Buria, "The IMF at Sixty: An Unfulfilled Potential?" in Ariel Buira, ed., *The IMF and World Bank at Sixty* (London: Anthem, 2005), 20; Nouriel Roubini and Brad Setser, *Bailouts or Bail-ins?* (Washington, DC: Institute for International Economics, 2004), 196. In the 1995 discussion at the IMF Executive Board, the Executive Director from Colombia, Alberto Calderón, had expressed similar concerns, although the Executive Directors from Venezuela (Luis Berrizbeitía) and Peru (Carlos Saito) had been more sympathetic to the idea of an international debt adjustment mechanism. See "Minutes of the Executive Board Seminar 95/2, June 23, 1995," 34–35, 43–45, 52, IMF Archives, Washington, DC.

[34] "IMF Sovereign Bankruptcy Plan Needs More Work, Conference Told," *International Business and Finance Daily*, January 27, 2003.

[35] Lavelle, "Governing Sovereign Debt"; Gelpern and Gulati, "Public Symbol."

[36] Taylor, *Global Financial Warriors*, chap. 4.

Influential Republicans in Congress such as Saxton shared these views. Saxton had been an opponent of the IMF quota increase in 1998 and a strong supporter of the recommendations of the 2000 report of the Congressionally appointed Meltzer Commission, which had called for a dramatic scaling back of the IMF's activities, including bailout lending. He worried that Krueger's proposal "would have the effect of compensating the IMF for the reduction in its influence arising from a more restricted policy towards international bailouts." He saw the promotion of CACs as a better and more market-oriented approach than the SDRM, which was destined to result in "a greatly expanded role for the IMF."[37]

A different kind of normative opposition emerged from many not-for-profit, non-governmental organizations (NGOs) involved in the debate. In one respect, prominent NGOs such as the Jubilee movement were encouraged to see the IMF taking an interest in the idea of an international bankruptcy court. Many of their members had been promoting this idea for years without having any concrete impact on international public policy debates. Suddenly, their cause was front and center, and they found themselves invited to participate in many IMF and intergovernmental forums debating the issue. But they were critical of many of the details of Krueger's proposal, such as the prominent role assigned to the IMF and the fact that it did not include Paris Club debt. They also criticized that fact that Krueger had failed to address what they considered to be the illegitimacy of much developing-country debt and that her proposal did not guarantee citizen input and the protection of basic government services during debt restructuring negotiations.[38]

What was the impact of these various critiques of the SDRM proposal? They did not initially derail it. In April 2002, the G-7 and the IMF's International Monetary and Financial Committee permitted IMF staff to continue to develop the idea. The September 2002 IMF/World Bank annual meetings even instructed the IMF to prepare a concrete draft by April 2003. But Krueger and other IMF staff were also very aware of the opposition, and they modified the SDRM throughout 2002 and early 2003 to address criticisms. The changes proved insufficient to garner the support of the financial community or developing countries such as Mexico and Brazil. Most important, U.S. policy shifted away from supporting the IMF's plans with the resignation of Paul O'Neill in December 2002 and the swearing in of John Snow as U.S. Treasury Secretary by early February

[37] Jim Saxton, "IMF Sovereign Bankruptcy Supervision Is Unnecessary: New Analysis Rejects More IMF Mission Creep." Press Release, April 19, 2002 (Washington, DC: Chairman Jim Saxton, Joint Economic Committee, Congress of the U.S., 2002).

[38] See especially Ann Pettifor, *Chapter 9/11* (London: Jubilee/New Economics Foundation, 2002).

2003. Unlike O'Neill, Snow was much more sympathetic to Taylor's views than Krueger's on this issue.[39] In April 2003, the International Monetary and Financial Committee of the IMF finally declared that there was no longer enough support for the proposal.

The Spread of CACs as an International Standard

The shelving of Krueger's proposal did not, however, put an end to the international efforts to bring greater regulatory order to sovereign bond restructuring. Indeed, it was at this very time that momentum finally began to build in favor of the international promotion of collective-action clauses. The initiative was remarkably successful. At the end of 2002, only 30 percent of sovereign bonds issued by emerging markets had CACs, and most had been issued in London. By 2004, close to 90 percent of new international bond issues had CACs, and the figure had approached close to 100 percent by the first half of 2005.[40]

Supporters of the SDRM were keen to highlight the limitations of CACs. While the former would have covered all international bond issues, CACs only applied to the new bonds being issued with these provisions. The SDRM also enabled the terms of a country's debt restructuring to be extended across all categories of bonds, whereas most CACs do not include provisions for this kind of aggregation. In addition, CACs do not usually endorse standstill provisions (although Taylor suggested in April 2002 that perhaps they should,[41] as had the Rey Report). And finally, CACs leave many of the key decisions concerning debt restructuring in the hands of the private creditors, rather than allocating them to an independent arbiter or sharing power more equally with sovereign debtors in a formal institutional setting.

Despite these limitations, the sudden emergence of CACs as a standard provision in international bond issues was a striking development. What explains it? The phenomenon was *not* a product of a formal international agreement or treaty. It was initiated by the unilateral decision of the Mexican government in February 2003 to issue a bond in New York with CACs. Before this announcement, most developing-country governments

[39] Taylor, *Global Financial Warriors*, 128; Gelpern and Gulati, "Public Symbol."

[40] International Monetary Fund, *IMF Survey Supplement* (Washington, DC: International Monetary Fund, 2003), 12; International Monetary Fund, "Progress Report to the International Monetary and Financial Committee on Crisis Resolution," September 28, 2004 (Washington, DC: International Monetary Fund, 2004); International Monetary Fund, "Progress Report to the International Monetary and Financial Committee on Crisis Resolution," September 21, 2005 (Washington, DC: International Monetary Fund, 2005).

[41] John Taylor, "Sovereign Debt Restructuring: A U.S. Perspective, April 2, 2002" (Washington, DC: U.S. Treasury, 2002). Found at www.ustreas.gov/press/releases/po2056.htm.

had been nervous that such a move would discourage investors and raise the cost of borrowing.[42] But their attitude changed dramatically after the Mexican issue because the latter was oversubscribed and the CACs did not affect the price of the bonds. When a similar issue by Brazil in April had the same successful results, many other countries quickly followed the lead of these two countries. And in all these subsequent issues, there was no evidence that CACs affected the price of the bonds or levels of subscription.[43]

In this way, the Mexican government assumed a leadership role in overcoming the kind of collective-action problem that had plagued debtor coordination in the past. By taking the initiative and highlighting the absence of reputational costs associated with CACs, the Mexican government acted as a "public entrepreneur" promoting this new regulatory initiative. What led it to take to this "courageous step" as Taylor later called it?[44] As late as September 2002, the Mexican finance minister had declared definitively that Mexico had no intention of including CACs in its bond issues. What changed the government's mind?

The U.S. Treasury—and particularly Taylor—was certainly pressuring strongly. As we have seen, Taylor had serious misgivings about the SDRM proposal and saw CACs as the better way to usher in a more orderly sovereign debt restructuring process. To encourage developing countries to begin to issue CAC bonds, the U.S. government could have used a legal route of requiring all bonds issued in New York to include these provisions. Because the New York market was the largest for developing-country sovereign bonds, that move would have set the standard for international markets as a whole. But Taylor chose instead a more indirect route of actively lobbying developing-country borrowers and investors.[45]

---

[42] See, for example, Nicolás Eyzaguirre, *Statement by the Honourable Nicolás Eyzaguirre, Minister of Finance of Chile Speaking on Behalf of the Southern Cone Countries* (Washington, DC: IMF, International Monetary and Financial Committee, 2002). These worries might seem odd given that investors had not been scared off by the CACs already in use in London markets, but governments worried that a CAC issue in New York markets, where they had not been common, might be perceived as showing a willingness to default.

[43] Effie Psalida and Yan Liu, "IMF Promotes Wider Use of Collective Action Clauses," *IMF Survey*, June 2, 2003, 166–168.

[44] Taylor quote from John Taylor, "The IMF's Virtuous Lona Cycle," *Wall Street Journal*, April 19, 2006. Despite the perception at the time, the Mexican government was not in fact the first developing-country government to issue bonds with CACs in New York. There had been a few previous cases between 1997 and 2001 that involved smaller sovereign borrowers: Bulgaria, Egypt, Kazakhstan, Lebanon, and Qatar. But Gelpern and Gulati ("Public Symbol") highlight that the clauses had not been noticed by most market participants. (See also Psalida and Liu, "IMF Promotes.")

[45] Taylor, *Global Financial Warriors*, chap. 4. See also Gelpern and Gulati, "Public Symbol."

For the former, he encouraged the IMF to begin to promote the issue of CACs in annual country and multilateral surveillance efforts, a suggestion it followed from July 2002 onward.[46] Taylor also engaged in some intense direct lobbying of developing-country governments. As he later noted, "We, the Bush administration, promoted the collective-action clauses very actively, a very time-consuming process, and we had a lot of help from many people . . . we kept on getting on the phone, kept calling ministers, kept calling our colleagues, and then thanks to our good friends from Mexico, they issued in New York, and it was a great success."[47]

The Mexican central bank president Guillermo Ortiz said later that the initiative was undertaken not just because of U.S. pressure but also to derail the SDRM: "We were worried because it [the SDRM] would increase our financing costs. The truth is we did it because it was a way to get rid of the SDRM."[48] The timing of the Mexican move was very significant in this respect; it was announced shortly before the April 2003 meeting of the IMFC that was to decide the fate of the SDRM. If the bond issue was successful, it would take some of the wind out of the sails of the SDRM proposal by highlighting the viability of the CAC alternative. Not coincidently, the other leading Latin American critic of the SDRM proposal, Brazil, was the first to follow the Mexican lead.

The Mexican government also came to the conclusion that the risks of the issuing international bonds with CACs were overstated. Particularly important was the fact that representatives of private creditor interests had suddenly emerged as champions of CACs. Although many private investors had been wary of proposals to expand the use of CACs in the wake of the Rey Report, there were important signs of a change in attitude after Taylor made clear his support for the initiative in February 2002. A widely noticed and early sign came when Charles Dallara of the Institute of International Finance (IIF) backed the initiative in April 2002.[49] The Washington-based IIF had been established in 1983 to coordinate creditor interests at the height of the international debt crisis of the early 1980s, and it had quickly emerged as one of the key groups representing private international financial interests with a membership of over three hundred international banks. By late January 2003, a set of model CACs was endorsed publicly by a coalition of the IIF and the six other (mostly U.S.-

[46] Psalida and Liu, "IMF Promotes," 166–67.

[47] Quote from American Enterprise Institute, *Argentina: Economic Challenges in the Wake of Default. March 31* (Washington, DC: American Enterprise Institute, 2004), 4. Found at: www.aei.org/include/event_print.asp?eventID=767.

[48] Quoted in Lavelle, "Governing Sovereign Debt," 27. Taylor (*Global Financial Warriors*, 127) also notes that Mexican officials requested that the United States publicly oppose the SDRM if Mexico agreed to go ahead with the CAC issue.

[49] Taylor, *Global Financial Warriors*, chap. 4.

based) leading industry associations representing the private international investor community involved in the market for emerging market sovereign debt.[50] While Mexico's leadership helped to overcome collective-action problems on the debtor side, the new stance of these groups performed the same function for the creditors. It signaled that the key players in the private creditor community were willing to embrace an international initiative designed to bring greater order to sovereign debt restructuring, even if that initiative imposed some new legal constraints on the behavior of individual investors.

What explained this change of perspective among private investors? Financial officials in creditor countries were certainly pressing investors to accept the new provisions. In addition to Taylor's strong encouragement, the G-7 finance ministers and central bank governors had embraced CACs as part of their April 2002 "Action Plan" on crisis prevention and resolution.[51] Both the United Kingdom and Canada had even included CACs within their foreign jurisdiction bonds in 2000 in an effort to boost the acceptance of these provisions. All EU finance ministers undertook a commitment to do the same in September 2002.

But private creditor groups also had some self-interested reasons to throw their weight behind CACs. To begin with, like Mexico, they began to see this support as a way to stop the more ambitious SDRM proposal. As Blustein puts it, "Only when the more radical SDRM reared its head did private financiers come around to backing CACs as the lesser evil."[52] Many analysts in fact noted that the United States and G-7 seemed to be deliberately keeping the SDRM proposal on the table until early 2003 as a way of prompting private financial interests to accept CACs. When private financial interests finally endorsed CACs, these interests were particularly keen to highlight that these clauses could address many of the problems that the IMF claimed the SDRM was needed to solve.[53]

Also important was the fact that the costs of not having a more orderly process of sovereign bond restructuring had become more apparent. Some high-profile lawsuits had highlighted the damaging role that minority creditors could play. The best known involved the "vulture fund" Elliot Associates, which had purchased discounted Peruvian bonds and then successfully sued the Peruvian government for full repayment (and capi-

---

[50] See www.emta.org/ndevelop/Final_merged.pdf.

[51] Gelpern and Gulati, "Public Symbol."

[52] Blustein, *And the Money*, 230. For further evidence, see Gelpern and Gulati, "Public Symbol."

[53] See, for example, Robert Gray, "Collective Action Clauses: The Way Forward." Unpublished paper, February 2004. Gray was from the International Primary Market Association.

talized interest). The case had finally been settled only after the Peruvian government agreed to pay $58 million to the firm in 2000.[54]

The outcome of the Argentine crisis was even more significant in highlighting the costs to private creditor interests of the status quo. The crisis had made clear that the IMF and G-7 were now quite prepared to allow very large-scale sovereign defaults and to provide only minimal support to bondholders in the subsequent debt restructuring negotiations. It also demonstrated how a sovereign debtor could exploit the disorganization among thousands of bondholders spread across many countries, each with distinct circumstances and interests. In this episode, investors scrambled to create various committees to represent their interests, but divisions among them prevented the creation of a fully unified front. In this context, creditors were forced to acknowledge their limited bargaining power and the potential benefits of efforts to make sovereign debt rescheduling more orderly through CACs.[55]

Using Mattli and Woods' terminology, leading financial industry associations thus began to act as "private entrepreneurs" promoting the CAC initiative primarily because they were "corporations at risk."[56] The risks they faced stemmed partly from their own governments, who had withdrawn official support to private creditors during sovereign debt crises and now even threatened to create the SDRM, which the private creditors opposed. Also important was the changing nature of the international lending market; that is, the move from centralized bank lending to more decentralized bond finance. The risks facing investors should not be overstated. It would be going much too far to say that the economic viability of private creditor groups *depended* on the emergence of the CACs. But their new willingness to support the CACs certainly reflected their changed circumstances.

---

[54] Helen Thompson and David Runciman, "Sovereign Debt and Private Creditors," *New Political Economy* 11, no. 4 (2006), 541–555. These kinds of lawsuits had been much less common when international lending had been bank-dominated because banks had ongoing relationships with developing-country governments and because syndicated bank loans included "sharing clauses" which promised that any proceeds from legal challenges would have to be shared with other banks; see Barry Herman, "Mechanisms for Dialogue and Debt-Crisis Workout that Can Strengthen Sovereign Lending to Developing Countries," in Ariel Buira, ed., *Challenges to the World Bank and IMF* (London: Anthem, 2003).

[55] See, for example, Andrew Cooper and Bessma Momani, "Negotiating Out of Argentina's Financial Crisis," *New Political Economy* 10, no. 3 (2005), 305–320. Gelpern and Gulati ("Public Symbol") cite evidence that the first-model CAC to be proposed by a private-sector association (the Emerging Markets Creditors Association) in May 2002 reflected frustration with the Argentine situation.

[56] Mattli and Woods, "In Whose Benefit? Explaining Regulatory Change in Global Politics," this volume.

With this new private-sector support, the risk to the Mexican government and that of other developing countries of including CACs in their bond issues diminished considerably. Investors would no longer interpret this move as a provocative signal that the issuing government was contemplating a future default. It would now be seen as supporting an emerging norm that was being promoted by the international private financial community itself—a norm that was designed at least in part to forestall the more ambitious SDRM proposal.

The fact that the international private financial community was suddenly promoting this initiative provided one final and more strategic reason for Mexico to launch its issue in early 2003. If CACs were indeed about to emerge as an international market norm, Mexico and other developing-country governments had an important stake in the debate about their specific content. CACs could clearly benefit debtors by legitimizing debt restructuring and making it more orderly, but there was a risk that the clauses might be written in such a way that they bolstered the bargaining power of the creditors too much. If, for example, the threshold for majority amendments was set at too high a level, debtors would find themselves forced to make too many concessions to potential holdouts in the investment community in order to secure a deal.

Already, in the fall of 2002, a G-10 working group, chaired by Taylor's deputy Randy Quarles, had influenced the terms of this debate by publishing model CACs that could be used in the market. That initiative had been followed by the private-sector coalition's proposal of model clauses in late January 2003. The Mexican government saw its bond issue as a way to ensure that the debate remained friendly to debtor interests. Specifically, they were able to set the threshold for majority amendment clauses at 75 percent of bondholders (which was consistent with British convention) instead of the higher figure of 85–90 percent that the industry associations (although not the G-10) had been pressing for.[57] Their objective was successful; this threshold became the standard for most subsequent CACs.[58]

Summing up, what explains the sudden embrace of CACs since 2003? In a process and institutional sense, it was certainly not a typical story involving international negotiations among government policymakers. Formal intergovernmental negotiations had centered instead on the SDRM proposal, and they had failed in the face of opposition from

---

[57] Dierdre Kamlani, *Systemic Change, Structural Power and Sovereign Bankruptcy Regimes (1982–2005)*, M.Sc. (Politics of the World Economy), London School of Economics, 2005. Gelpern and Gulati ("Public Symbol") also note the concern that a higher threshold might have been perceived by the markets as a sign of Mexican weakness.

[58] Brazil used 85 percent in its April 2003 issue, but shifted later to 75 percent.

groups that had often opposed initiatives of this kind in the past—private creditors and wealthier sovereign debtors—as well as from the U.S. government. Instead, the rapid spread of CAC bonds resulted from the combination of the unilateral decisions of debtor governments to issue them and the embrace of these bonds by private creditor interests.

The new enthusiasm for CACs among these two groups of actors partly reflected the encouragement by public entrepreneurs in the U.S. government, most notably John Taylor. This encouragement was itself a product of distributional (encouraging private-sector involvement), normative (moral hazard/neoliberal), and strategic (undercutting the SDRM) motivations. But the embrace of CACs also emerged from the leadership of the Mexican government and the leading industry associations that helped to overcome collective-action problems on both the debtor and private creditor sides. These public and private entrepreneurs were thrust into the role of agents of change partly by the threat of the SDRM, a threat they hoped could be undermined by the strategic tool of the CACs. The views of private financial actors were also influenced by the growing recognition, particularly after the Argentine default, of the costs that disorganized bondholders could face when confronting sovereign bond default. Mexican officials also saw their CAC issue in distributional terms, as a way of influencing the terms of the debate in the debtors' favor.

Developing an International Code of Conduct

The growing use of CACs was not the only important international development in this period. In late 2002, the IIF began to promote the development of a voluntary code of conduct for debt restructuring that could be endorsed by both investors and developing-country governments. The IIF hoped the code could outline principles to encourage: (1) information sharing and transparency, (2) close debtor-creditor dialogue and cooperation, (3) good faith actions in debt restructurings, and (4) equal treatment of all investors in case of defaults. The code would be designed to complement the CAC initiative. Indeed, when the IIF and the six other financial industry associations released their model CACs in late January 2003, they accompanied it with a draft of a "Code of Conduct for Emerging Markets" which they suggested could be monitored by representatives of sovereign debtors, investors, creditor countries, the IMF, and the BIS.[59]

The idea for such a code is often attributed to Jean-Claude Trichet of the Bank of France, who had mentioned it in a fall 2002 speech.[60] But the

[59] See www.emta.org/ndevelop/Final_merged.pdf.

[60] See, for example, Alonso Garcia Tames, "New Hopes for Debt Crisis Avoidance," *The Banker*, February 1, 2005. Trichet later highlighted that he drew inspiration from the nonbinding agreements struck within the Paris Club; Paris Club Secretariat, *Fifty Years of Orderly Sovereign Debt Restructuring. Proceedings of the International Policy Forum,*

initiative also clearly built on efforts the IIF had undertaken since 1999 to promote better relations between investors and sovereign debtors. These efforts took on a greater urgency for the IIF and other investor groups in the context of both the SDRM debate and the Argentine government's aggressive bargaining stance vis-à-vis the restructuring of its debts after 2001. Regarding the former, the development of the code provided an additional way to preempt the SDRM and shift the terms of the international debate regarding bond restructuring mechanisms to terms that were more friendly toward private creditor interests.[61] Regarding the latter, the proposed code was designed to discourage other debtor governments from following Argentina's lead. As an IIF official put it, the development of the code "is especially important against the backdrop of Argentina, which has called into question basic concepts of international finance, such as fair play and the rule of law, as well as the role of the IMF."[62]

As with the issuing of CACs, it was the Mexican and Brazilian governments that proved most interested in the IIF's initiative.[63] The development of the code offered them a way not just to stop the SDRM proposal but also to distinguish, in the eyes of investors, their approach to debt issues from that of Argentina. This motivation was interesting given how debtors had often worried in the past that their support for the creation of more formal debt restructuring mechanisms would hurt their international financial reputation. In this instance, the dynamic was quite different since the proposal was coming from the private creditor interests themselves and it was explicitly designed to encourage more creditor-friendly behavior on the part of debtor governments. Not surprisingly, Argentina refused to back the initiative, seeing it as a criticism of their behavior.[64]

During the initial discussions of the Code, IMF and World Bank officials were involved. But the discussion was soon restricted to a narrower dialogue between a small group of private financial interests—primarily the IIF and International Primary Market Association (which represented debt underwriters)—and emerging market governments, particularly

June 14, 2006 (Paris: Paris Club Secretariat, 2006), 75. His speech was followed up by a Bank of France proposal for a "Code of Good Conduct" in January 2003: Bank of France, *Towards a Code of Good Conduct on Sovereign Debt Re-Negotiation* (Paris: Bank of France, 2003).

[61] Andrew Balls, "IIF Seeks Extra Support for Fair Debt Restructuring Principles," *Financial Times*, January 18, 2005.

[62] Josef Ackermann, "Time to Strengthen Emerging Markets Finance," *Financial Times*, February 17, 2004.

[63] "G20 Voluntary Code of Conduct on Debt Restructuring Leaves Argentina Isolated," *Financial Times*, November 22, 2004.

[64] Ibid.; Andrew Balls, "IIF Seeks Extra Support."

Mexico and Brazil but also Turkey and Korea. Discussion among these parties lasted for more than two years before an agreement was finally reached in November 2004. In a public statement at the time, the voluntary code—covering the four areas that the IIF had initially proposed—was released and formally endorsed by Mexico, Brazil, Turkey, Korea, the IIF, and the International Primary Market Association.[65]

To secure the debtor governments' agreement, the IIF had had to water down a number of clauses, particularly regarding provisions to bring debtor governments to the negotiating table after a default. Some fund managers and groups representing investors were initially skeptical of the code, arguing that the language of the code had been diluted too far to get developing-country governments' agreement. But it was also clear that some of the debtors were still wary of the constraints that the code might impose on their freedom of action. After the November 2004 announcement, Mexican government officials went out of their way to highlight the voluntary nature of the code and argued that it was too early to implement the recommendations.[66]

While the code had been developed through direct negotiations between debtor governments and representatives of private creditor interests, the initiative also quickly earned some important official backing. U.S. Treasury Secretary John Snow welcomed the initiative, as did French, British, and German officials.[67] So too did the G-20—an organization comprising financial officials from both rich countries and the leading "emerging market" countries—which noted in November 2004 that "such principles, which we generally support, provide a good basis for strengthening crisis prevention and enhancing predictability of crisis management now, and as they further develop in future."[68] By fall 2006, over thirty countries had backed the code. They were also supported by the Paris Club creditors.[69]

Most of the provisions in the code—formally titled "Principles for Stable Capital Flows and Fair Debt Restructuring in Emerging Markets"—concern the behavior of debtors and private creditors. But the Principles also prescribe a role for the IMF in resolving crisis, although it is hardly the central one that Krueger had proposed. In addition to noting that the

---

[65] The Principles can be found at www.iif.com/data/public/principles_1104.pdf. See also Josef Ackermann, "Precautionary Principles," *Wall Street Journal*, April 14, 2005, A18.

[66] Andrew Balls, "IIF Seeks Extra Support."

[67] Alonso Garcia Tames, "New Hopes for Debt Crisis Avoidance," *The Banker*, February 1, 2005.

[68] Group of 20, "Communique: Meeting of Finance Ministers and Central Bank Governors," Berlin, November 20–21, 2004, p. 2.

[69] Principles Consultative Group, *Report on Implementation* (Washington, DC: Institute of International Finance, 2006), 2.

IMF should not give "any appearance of encouraging a debtor to default," the document also encourages the IMF to "lend in arrears"; that is, to provide financial support (backed by an IMF economic program) to a government that has defaulted but which is undertaking good faith negotiations with private creditors.[70] Interestingly, IIF officials have also been keen to highlight that the Principles allow for the use of standstills, if endorsed by private creditors, as a means of supporting "a borrowing country's efforts to avoid a broad debt restructuring."[71]

To what extent have the Principles been implemented so far? The IIF has tried to boost their profile since the 2004 agreement. In December 2005, they began publicly evaluating the extent to which emerging market governments were complying with the Principles in areas such as investor relations and information sharing.[72] In March 2006, the IIF also established a "Group of Trustees" to review the implementation and possible further development of the Principles. The Group, which met in September 2006 for the first time, included senior representatives of the private international financial sector as well as prominent officials (including Trichet) and ex-officials from industrialized and emerging market countries.[73]

The Group also provides guidance to a "Principles Consultative Group" (PCG), a seventeen-member body made up only of senior private financial sector executives and emerging market government officials (with the former in the majority).[74] It was established a few months earlier to evaluate individual country situations and provide advice to private creditors and governments about compliance with the Principles and any possible amendments of them.[75] The PCG's work is supported technically by the IIF secretariat, which also presents the PCG's country assessments and recommendations privately to the country authorities. One represen-

[70] The IMF had been allowed to "lend into arrears" vis-à-vis bank debt since 1989 and bond debt since 1998.

[71] Diana Gregg, "IIF 'Principles' for Emerging Markets Aim to Ease Crises, Improve Debt Process," *International Business and Finance Daily*, November 23, 2004.

[72] IIF press release, "Emerging market sovereign bond issuers strengthen investor relations and release more key data, but numerous countries still fall short of market needs," December 8, 2005.

[73] Its co-chairs were Trichet, Toyoo Gyohten (former Vice-Minister of Finance in Japan), and Henrique de Campos Meirelles (Governor of the Central Bank of Brazil). Its members include ex-officials from Chile, Brazil, Indonesia, Mexico, Morocco, Poland, Nigeria, China, Peru, India, South Africa, the United States, Saudi Arabia, and Turkey.

[74] Of the seventeen members, only seven are public officials, and they are from the following countries: Brazil, Korea, Mexico, Turkey, China, Russia, and South Africa.

[75] IIF Press Release, "Trichet, Meirelles and Gyohten to lead new group of trustees for emerging markets finance initiative," March 30, 2006.

tative of the Federal Reserve Bank of New York and staff from the IMF's policy and capital markets departments are also invited as observers to the PCG discussions. With respect to the latter, the PCG noted in September 2006 that it is considering whether "synergies could develop between the PCG's discussions and the Fund's own policy advice," including in areas such as the implementation of the IMF's data standards. It is also discussing whether to encourage bond raters to examine compliance with the Principles when evaluating countries' creditworthiness.[76]

It is not the objective of this chapter to evaluate the effectiveness of the Principles to date, but a few words on this question may be appropriate. Some analysts are skeptical of their significance because of the Principles' voluntary nature and because their content is ambiguous in places. These are of course the very features that have helped the Principles gain such wide acceptance by minimizing the kinds of collective-action problems and distributional disputes that have plagued past initiatives to build an international debt restructuring mechanism. Despite these weaknesses, the IIF suggests that the Principles have already had some impact in changing investor and debtor behavior, and have even been applied in recent debt rescheduling cases involving the Dominican Republic and Grenada.[77] At the very least, the initiative is significant in the long history of efforts to regulate sovereign debt restructuring because it represents an effort by leading sovereign debtors, private financial actors, and creditor governments to agree to an international set of principles of engagement in this area. In a more specific sense, the negotiation, implementation, and monitoring of the Principles has already been creating a set of social networks that bring representatives of debtor governments, private financial interests, and creditor country governments into closer contact with each other. These networks were built first in the context of a relatively small "club," but they are now extending to include a much wider set of actors in all three groups.

It is in this latter respect that the Principles may have their most important lasting impact. Instead of constructing a new international institution, this initiative is cultivating a more informal, networked form of governance. As Kahler and Lake's chapter highlights, networks have often played an important role in financial governance, but the focus is usually on networks of central banks or official financial regulators.[78] In this case,

[76] Principles Consultative Group, *Report*, 7, 13.

[77] Principles Consultative Group, *Report*.

[78] See also Anne Marie Slaughter, *A New World Order* (Princeton, NJ: Princeton University Press, 2005). For a broader discussion of emerging hybrid networks and regulatory arrangements in global finance, see Layna Mosely, "Privatizing Global Governance? Dilemmas in International Financial Regulation." Paper presented at De Nederlandsche Bank,

the networks that are being cultivated extend wider to include various private-sector representatives as well as ex-officials (thereby complicating the private-public distinction). Particular emphasis is being placed on the development of networks between representatives of investors and sovereign debtors which could play a role in cultivating trust and shared understandings in advance of the outbreak of the next sovereign debt crisis. Given the leadership role of the IIF, some might be tempted to describe the Principles as an example of a "private regime."[79] But this would be misleading not just because debtor governments are key partners, but also because northern public authorities have played, and continue to play, an important role in supporting the development of, and implementation and monitoring of, the Principles. Rather than acting as regulators, however, these officials are serving more as coordinators in the building of this odd voluntarist public-private hybrid networked form of governance.

Like the spread of CACs, the creation of the Principles did not emerge from a conventional story of intergovernmental negotiations. They were a product of an unusual set of discussions involving a few self-selected debtor governments and private-sector lobby groups. The IIF was the key "entrepreneur" in launching these discussions, and it was motivated by similar goals as those that encouraged it to back CACs. The development of the Principles provided a further strategic tool with which to undermine the SDRM and it could help protect private creditors from future debtors that might choose to emulate the Argentine government's approach to debt negotiations. In a supportive role were the same key sovereign debtors, Mexico and Brazil (along with Turkey and Korea), who had backed CACs, and who found in this initiative a way of differentiating themselves from Argentina's behavior.

Other actors got involved only after these negotiations took place, and they did so only by endorsing the outcome the smaller group had already reached. These actors have included not just other debtor governments and private creditor interests driven by similar motivations. Government officials in creditor countries have also supported the outcome, and have even agreed to assume formal positions in bodies mandated with the implementation of the Principles. From their standpoint, the Principles serve to provide at least some of the functions that they were unable to gain through formal interstate negotiation.

Amsterdam, September 27, 2006; Tony Porter, *Globalization and Finance* (Cambridge: Polity, 2005).

[79] For important discussions of the growing significance of "private regimes," see Claire Cutler, Virginia Haufler, and Tony Porter, eds., *Private Authority and International Affairs* (Buffalo: State University of New York Press, 1999).

CONCLUSION

Taken together, the near universal adoption of CACs and the development and wide embrace of the Principles are a sign that a new pattern of regulation of sovereign debt restructuring is taking shape. What does this episode teach us about the politics of global financial regulation? To begin with, it highlights the usefulness of the framework for analyzing international regulatory change outlined by Mattli and Woods. As their framework predicts, the process of regulatory change was initiated by a set of crises—the international financial crises of 1994 and 1997–98—which demonstrated very publicly the costs associated with the old bailout model of handling sovereign debt crises. The latter was suddenly seen by critics as serving the narrow interests of private creditors at the expense of taxpayers in creditor states, debtors, and global financial stability more generally. This "demonstration effect" of the costs of regulatory "capture" opened a political window for various private and public "entrepreneurs" to press the case for the new regulatory initiatives, particularly after the 2001 Argentine crisis demonstrated the costs of the absence of regulation in the post-bailout world.

In the case of the CACs, the lead entrepreneur initially was the U.S. Treasury's John Taylor. But he was soon joined by officials in key sovereign debtors (especially Mexico) and private-sector industry groups (especially the IIF) who also took the lead in developing the Principles. While Taylor was inspired in large part by the idea that the reforms he was promoting were global public welfare-enhancing, the other entrepreneurs were thrust into role of agents of change by motivations that were more strategic (defeating the SDRM) and distributional (boosting the respective interests of debtors or private creditors). Regardless of their different motivations, these entrepreneurs succeeded in mobilizing a considerable pro-change coalition behind both the CACs and the Principles that included a wide collection of private creditor interests, sovereign debtors, and financial officials in creditor states.

The significance of the new pattern of global regulation ushered in by this pro-change coalition should not be overstated. As Mattli and Woods' framework suggests, the limitations of the CACs and the Principles are a product of both demand- and supply-side features of these regulatory initiatives. On the demand side, the range of groups interested in regulatory change after 2001 was much wider than the pro-change coalition that eventually backed the CACs and Principles. Many backed the more ambitious SDRM proposal, but found that they were unable to overcome the powerful opposition of the private creditor community, wealthier sovereign debtors, and especially the United States after early

2003. The more limited regulatory outcome reflected not just the power asymmetry between the advocates of the two different proposed courses of action, but also the fact that many backers of the successful initiative to promote CACs and the Principles were inspired to promote change in part for the simple defensive reason of forestalling the more ambitious SDRM proposal.

On the institutional supply side, the initial SDRM debate had taken place in quite an inclusive context involving "access points" not just for various government actors within official international meetings but also for the private sector and not-for-profit nongovernmental groups in various international forums involving IMF and government officials. But when consensus could not be reached on that proposal, the negotiation and implementation of the CACs and Principles took place in a very different institutional context. In the case of the issuing of CACs, the key processes involved informal lobbying of market "insiders" and unilateral actions (in the case of Mexico's issue). In the case of the Principles, the process was dominated by private negotiations between a small, self-selected informal "club" of sovereign debtors and representatives of the private creditor interests. These contexts left each process closed to the wide range of actors who had contributed to the SDRM debate and more vulnerable to capture by the very groups—wealthier sovereign debtors and private creditors—who historically had been most wary of the construction of international rules in this area.

If this episode highlights how Mattli and Woods' model helps us to understand the nature of regulatory change, it also reveals the limitations of some other models. Studies of the regulation of international finance sometimes assume a rather functionalist quality. As financial markets have globalized, it is suggested that financial policymakers have increasingly identified the public good functions to be served by coordinating regulation at the international level. With this recognition, these officials have then efficiently negotiated and implemented international regulatory coordination to serve the global public good. It may be tempting to see these most recent international regulatory initiatives in the financial sector in a similar manner, since they emerged in the wake of a set of debt crises that highlighted the costs of the absence of clear rules for facilitating international debt restructuring.

But a functionalist perspective overlooks the intensely political nature of international rule-making in this episode. To be sure, some key policymakers saw these initiatives as serving global public good functions. But the process that generated the CACs and Principles was a much more disorganized, conflictual, and intensively political one, and the key actors were driven by various normative, distributional, and strategic concerns that went well beyond the objective of serving the global public good.

The new regulatory frameworks also did not emerge from the kinds of formal intergovernmental negotiations that functionalists predict. The negotiations of that kind which did take place—concerning the SDRM proposal—failed, and the successful regulatory initiatives emerged instead from a more disorganized process involving unilateral government decisions and informal negotiations between various private financial actors and governments. Finally, at the level of outcomes, the CACs and the Principles represent styles of global economic regulation that are a far cry from the kinds of interstate agreements, formal international regimes, and international organizations that traditionally have been the focus of functionalist analyses.

What about more realist explanations of global economic regulation? From this tradition, Daniel Drezner has suggested that global regulatory change usually follows the preferences of dominant powers.[80] As we have seen, the United States and other dominant northern powers did play a key role in setting the agenda in this episode. Indeed, although private-sector actors and debtor governments played important roles in establishing the new patterns of global regulation, their initiatives emerged very much within the "shadow" of dominant states, especially the United States. At the same time, there are some aspects of the story that fit less well with Drezner's predictions. He notes that a dominant state will usually promote regulatory coordination that is centered on its domestic standards in order to minimize adjustment costs for its domestic actors. In the case of the CACs, however, the United States promoted British standards rather than its own; indeed, a number of observers have noted that Krueger's SDRM proposal came much closer to embracing the U.S. tradition of addressing bond defaults with bankruptcy laws. As we have seen, the eventual rejection of Krueger's ideas by U.S. officials suggests that normative sentiments—the preference for a more market-based mechanism, in this case—can trump the fear of domestic adjustment costs. To be sure, this outcome was certainly facilitated by the fact that the domestic actors who needed to "adjust" to the new rules—the U.S. private financial community—were very strong supporters of its creation. But more generally, it is worth noting that the distributional issue that drove U.S. officials—and those of other northern powers—to put this issue on the international political agenda was not that of minimizing adjustment costs for domestic private actors. It was, in fact, the opposite. These officials sought from the mid-1990s onward to force private investors to assume a *greater* share of the adjustment costs associated with sovereign debt restructuring in order to minimize the burden on the taxpayer.

---

[80] Daniel Drezner, *All Politics Is Global* (Princeton, NJ: Princeton University Press, 2007).

The significance of U.S. power also should not be overstated. One of the most important roles of the United States in this episode was an indirect role—or "background" role, to use Abbott and Snidal's wording—of signaling that the era of guaranteed large-scale bailouts was coming to an end, a move that transformed the context of the debate for debtor governments and private creditor interests. A second background role was that of providing enough support for Krueger's SDRM between 2001 and 2003 to frighten debtors and investors into backing the CACs and Principles as a less-bad alternative. U.S. officials had more direct influence through their active promotion of CACs, but they did so through informal persuasion rather than via the kinds of coercive means, such as denial of access to U.S. markets, that Drezner highlights. This informal mechanism of influence was effective largely because sovereign debtors and private creditors found their own reasons to support CACs. These last two groups have also played a much more significant role than the United States in developing the Principles. The roles of these actors highlight that the study of international economic rule-making should not be too narrowly focused on the role of dominant states. Many of the most important developments in the agenda-setting, negotiation, and implementation stages of this episode involved the strategic interaction *between* sovereign debtors and the private international financial community and *within* each of these respective groups. The further implementation and monitoring of the new rules will also be heavily dependent on the activities of these groups.

From State Responsibility to Individual Criminal Accountability: A New Regulatory Model for Core Human Rights Violations

Kathryn Sikkink

ALTHOUGH THE TERM "regulation" is rarely used in the literature on human rights, the core issues in the human rights area involve "making, implementing, monitoring, and enforcing of rules" to organize and control activities, which is the definition of regulation used in this volume. The concept is thus a useful and not unfamiliar way to think about standard-setting and rule enforcement in the human rights realm.

The area of human rights has experienced a dramatic increase in international regulation in the post–World War II period. In 1945, this area was virtually unregulated; by 2000, states had ratified many treaties involving diverse human rights, and those treaties had entered into effect. The human rights issue, however, is characterized by relatively weak enforcement mechanisms. Where accountability existed, it focused mainly on reputational accountability via moral stigmatization of state violators.[1] In the few cases where stronger enforcement mechanisms existed, especially the regional human rights courts in Europe and the Americas, the model of regulation was one that focused on state legal accountability for human rights abuses. That is, for example, when the European Court of Human Rights finds violations of human rights, it says that a *state* is in violation of its obligations under the Convention, and the state is asked to provide some kind of remedy, usually in the way of changed policy.

This regulatory model of state accountability with weak enforcement continues to be the main model for international human rights violations. But for a small set of core human rights and war crimes, states are

---

[1] I use Grant and Keohane's definition of accountability that implies that "some actors have the right to hold other actors to a set of standards, to judge whether they have fulfilled their responsibilities . . . and to impose sanctions if they determine that these responsibilities have not been met." Legal and reputational accountability are two of the seven forms of accountability they discuss. Ruth Grant and Robert O. Keohane, "Accountability and Abuses of Power in World Politics," *American Political Science Review* 99, no. 1 (February 2005), 29–43.

increasingly using a new regulatory model of individual legal criminal accountability for human rights violations.[2] In this model, for example, when the Ad Hoc Tribunal for the Former Yugoslavia (ICTY) finds violations of human rights, it convicts a particular *individual* of these violations, and sentences that individual to time in prison. This change in regulatory model has emerged gradually over the last twenty years in domestic, foreign, and international judicial processes.[3] I will argue that these regulatory changes, from no regulation to a weak regime without enforcement, and the gradual increase in enforcement via individual criminal accountability represent a movement toward more effective public interest regulation.

The bulk of enforcement is occurring in domestic courts applying a combination of domestic criminal law, international human rights law, and international humanitarian law. Because of this combination of forms of law, we could think of this as an example of "legal integration" of the type discussed by Burley and Mattli, in reference to the penetration of EC law into the domestic law of member states.[4] In the human rights case, however, the individual criminal accountability model is the dominant model in domestic legal systems, and it has penetrated the international legal arena, rather than the other way around. Norms scholars have long recognized that powerful domestic norms may have a prominence that makes them likely candidates for international norms.[5] In this chapter, I provide a description and initial explanation of this new regulatory development in the area of core political rights.

[2] See Steven Ratner and Jason Abrams, *Accountability for Human Rights Atrocities in International Law: Beyond the Nuremberg Legacy*, 2nd ed. (Oxford: Oxford University Press, 2001).

[3] Jenny Martinez argues that nineteenth-century antislavery courts were the first international human rights courts. These courts indeed applied individual accountability for a human rights violation, in that slave ships were confiscated from owners and sold, but they did not apply individual criminal accountability, since neither crews nor owners were held criminally accountable in these international tribunals. We might call this a form of individual civil accountability, in which slave traders were forced to pay damages, not to their victims, the people they enslaved, but to the governments that established the tribunals and were intercepting slave ships. Jenny S. Martinez, "Antislavery Courts and the Dawn of International Human Rights Law," *Yale Law Journal* 117, no. 4 (January 2008), 550–641.

[4] Anne-Marie Burley and Walter Mattli, "Europe Before the Court: A Political Theory of Legal Integration," *International Organization* 47, no. 1 (Winter 1993), 41–76.

[5] Ann Florini, "The Evolution of International Norms," *International Studies Quarterly* 40, no. 3 (1996), 363–389; David H. Lumsdaine, *Moral Vision in International Politics: The Foreign Aid Regime, 1949–1989* (Princeton, NJ: Princeton University Press, 1993); and Martha Finnemore and Kathryn Sikkink, "International Norm Dynamics and Political Change," *International Organization* 52, no. 4 (Autumn 1998), 906.

THE PROCESS OF REGULATION OF HUMAN RIGHTS

The history of the evolution of the human rights regime has been told at length elsewhere, so I will provide only the briefest sketch to situate the current shift in earlier regulatory stages. Using the regulation stages put forward by the editors of this volume, the first stage of the process of regulating human rights began shortly after World War II. The Holocaust was the shock or demonstration effect that led states and non-state actors to identify the problem as a complete lack of international standards and accountability for massive human rights violations, and initiate action through the newly formed United Nations. The drafting and passage of the Universal Declaration of Human Rights in 1948 can be seen as setting the agenda for human rights regulation. In the second phase, the regulatory solution that states and non-state actors initially negotiated was a state accountability model that relied on standard-setting through international human rights treaties with weak enforcement. States negotiated and produced dozens of human rights treaties in the second half of the twentieth century. As late as 1975, however, effective international regulation of human rights was quite thin; only two human rights treaties had entered into effect—the Genocide Convention and the Convention on the Elimination of All Forms of Racial Discrimination. Relatively ineffectual international institutions, like the United Nations Human Rights Commission and the various committees established by most treaties, were assigned the task of overseeing the implementation of the new norms. There were few human rights NGOs, no government agencies devoted to human rights, and virtually no countries with bilateral human rights foreign policies.[6] Only in Europe could we say that international regulation existed through the European Commission of Human Rights and the European Court of Human Rights.

During the 1970s and 1980s, the third and fourth phases of regulation came into effect. States implemented the rule-based solutions of a state accountability model, and states, international organizations, and increasing numbers of NGOs began to monitor compliance. The Covenant on Civil and Political Rights entered into force in 1976, which in turn created the UN Human Rights Committee to oversee the implementation of the Covenant. Over the next thirty years, the number of human rights

[6] For documentation of these claims, see Kathryn Sikkink, "The Idea of Internationally Recognized Human Rights" and "Introduction to the Effectiveness of Human Rights Policies," in *Mixed Signals: U.S. Human Rights Policy and Latin America* (Ithaca, NY: Cornell University Press, 2004), 23–47, 79–105.

treaties increased dramatically, as did the number of international and regional institutions to oversee compliance with those treaties, the number of international and domestic human rights NGOs, and the number of domestic institutions devoted to regulating civil and political rights. Most of these human rights treaties reflect a state accountability regulatory model. It continues to be the model used by virtually the entire human rights apparatus in the United Nations, including almost all of the treaty bodies. It is also the model employed by the regional human rights courts: the European Court of Human Rights, the Inter-American Court of Human Rights, and the African Court of Human Rights. Likewise, even some of the new developments in the area of human rights, such as an increase in government reparations to past victims of human rights abuses, also reflect a state accountability model, with the reparations serving as a form of state remedy for past abuse.[7]

By the early 1990s, the human rights field had passed through the four first stages of the regulatory process, but there was still a great weakness in the area of enforcement. The human rights regime had been launched with high expectations in 1948, but a half century later, human rights violations had not subsided, and if anything, the perception was the human rights violations were on the increase. This was especially heightened by the demonstration effect of the conflict in the Balkans, since the discovery of concentration camps and perhaps genocide in the heart of Europe fifty years after World War II suggested that the regulatory model had failed. The ineffectiveness of the international response to the genocide in Rwanda in 1994 proved yet another demonstration effect of the failure of regulation to prevent major human rights violations. The new model of individual criminal accountability thus may have emerged as a way to provide additional enforcement mechanisms for the human rights regime in the wake of the perception that the current enforcement mechanisms were inadequate and new tools were needed.

The main changes in regulation involve *who* is being held accountable and *how* these actors are held accountable.[8] Both models may involve legal accountability, but the old model involves *state civil* legal accountability, while the new regulatory model involves *individual criminal* legal accountability.[9] Under a state civil accountability model, the state pro-

---

[7] See, for example, Maria José Guembe, "Economic Reparations for Grave Human Rights Violations: The Argentinean Experience," in *The Handbook of Reparations*, Pablo de Greiff, ed. (Oxford: Oxford University Press, 2006), 21–54.

[8] Ratner and Abrams, *Accountability for Human Rights*, 15.

[9] Legal accountability is the requirement that "agents abide by formal rules and be prepared to justify their action in those terms in courts or quasi-judicial arenas." Grant and Keohane, "Accountability and Abuses," 36.

vides remedies and pays damages, while under a criminal model, the convicted go to prison.[10] The new regulatory model has emerged over the last twenty years, alongside of the state accountability model, and recently it has grown more dramatically than the state accountability model. States are beginning to hold individuals, including heads of state, accountable for past human rights violations. This trend has been described by Lutz and Sikkink as "the justice cascade."[11]

This new regulatory model is not for the whole range of civil and political rights, but rather for a small subset of political rights sometimes referred to as the "rights of the person," especially the prohibitions on torture, summary execution, and genocide, as well as for war crimes and crimes against humanity.[12] Prior to the 1970s, it appears to be a classic case of regulatory capture, where state officials protected themselves from any individual legal accountability either during the repressive regime or after transition to another, more democratic regime. In principle, the citizens of any country could have held their past leaders legally accountable for human rights violations, but the continuing power of these leaders, and the fear of coups and instability, almost always prevented such accountability.

I argue that this process of regulation reflects a movement on the regulatory continuum discussed in the framework chapter of this volume toward a more public interest form of regulation. Individual criminal accountability is not necessarily more in the public interest than the state accountability model. But the addition of individual criminal accountability alongside of the existing state accountability model means that there is now significantly more enforcement of human rights norms than existed previously. Both the compliance literature in international relations and the deterrence literature in sociology suggest that an increase in the probability of enforcement is likely to reduce human rights violations.[13] The

[10] Although I focus on individual *criminal* legal accountability, there is also an increase in individual *civil* legal accountability, especially in U.S. courts, where individuals found guilty of human rights violations are required to pay damages to their victims. These are cases brought mainly under the Alien Claims Tort Act, which permits tort claims for violations of international customary law.

[11] Ellen Lutz and Kathryn Sikkink, "The Justice Cascade: The Evolution and Impact of Foreign Human Rights Trials in Latin America," *Chicago Journal of International Law* 2, no. 1 (Spring 2001), 1–33.

[12] These include rights from only two or three of the twenty-seven substantive articles of the International Covenant on Civil and Political Rights, those protecting the right to life and prohibiting torture. The new model also provides enforcement of the Genocide Convention, the Convention against Torture, and those parts of the Geneva Conventions prohibiting war crimes.

[13] See, for example, George W. Downs, David M. Rocke, and Peter N. Barsoom, "Is the Good News about Compliance Good News about Cooperation?" *International Organization* 50, no. 3 (1996), 379–406; and Daniel S. Nagin, "Criminal Deterrence Research at the

movement toward more enforcement thus should lead to greater compliance with human rights norms and deterrence of future human rights violations, although this is beyond the scope of this chapter.[14]

To determine the actual dimensions of the global justice cascade, Carrie Booth Walling and I have created a new data set of domestic, foreign, and international judicial proceedings for individual criminal responsibility for past human rights violations.[15] We define *domestic trials* as those conducted in a single country for human rights abuses committed in *that* country. *Foreign trials* are those conducted in a single country for human rights abuses committed in *another* country—the most famous of which are Spain's trials for human rights violations that have occurred in Argentina and Chile. *International trials* also involve trials for individual criminal responsibility for human rights violations in a particular country or conflict and result from the cooperation of multiple states, typically acting on behalf of the United Nations. Examples include the International Criminal Tribunal for the former Yugoslavia (ICTY) and the International Criminal Tribunal for Rwanda (ICTR). The international trials category also includes hybrid criminal bodies defined by their mixed character of containing a combination of international and national features, such as those in Cambodia, Sierra Leone, and Timor-Leste (formerly East Timor).

Our data reveal an unprecedented spike in state and international efforts to address past human rights abuses by focusing on individual criminal responsibility since the mid-1980s (see figure 4.1).[16]

Most previous discussions of these issues have only looked at parts of this trend, examining just international trials, or specific international tribunals, or just foreign trials, or domestic trials in certain countries.[17] I believe that these different tribunals and doctrines are all part of a related global phenomenon that I refer to here as a new model of global regulation of core political rights.

Outset of the Twenty-First Century," in M. Tomry, ed., *Crime and Justice: A Review of Research* (Chicago: University of Chicago Press, 1998), 1–42.

[14] See Hunjoon Kim and Kathryn Sikkink, "Do Human Rights Trials Make a Difference?" Paper presented at the American Political Science Association Annual Meetings, Chicago, Illinois, September 2007.

[15] I am indebted to Carrie Booth Walling for her permission to use material from our joint data set, and for preparing the three figures based on that data for this chapter.

[16] We have created two data sets on human rights trials, one for all human rights trials and one for human right trials in transitional countries. The data reported here are from the data set for all human rights trials. For a full discussion of the data set for transitional countries only, see Kathryn Sikkink and Carrie Booth Walling, "The Impact of Human Rights Trials in Latin America," *Journal of Peace Research* 44, no. 4 (July 2007), 427–445.

[17] Stephen Macedo, ed., *Universal Jurisdiction: National Courts and the Prosecution of Serious Crimes under International Law* (Philadelphia: University of Pennsylvania Press, 2004); and Naomi Roht-Arriaza, *The Pinochet Effect* (Philadelphia: University of Pennsylvania Press, 2005).

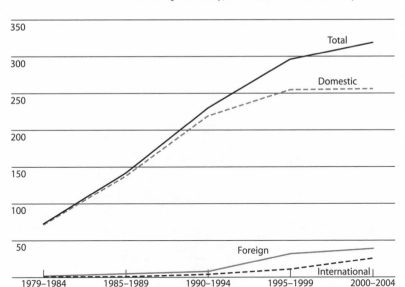

Figure 4.1. Human rights trials, 1979–2004

In figure 4.2, we divide all the trial years in the data set and find that 88 percent occur in the country where the crime was committed, and fully 96 percent of the trial activity takes place either in domestic or foreign courts, that is, in domestic judicial systems, either in the country where the crime occurred or in another country.

The doctrine of universal jurisdiction and the creation of the ICC are an important part of this new model of regulation, but it is much more than that. Given how new and embattled that ICC has been, it would be unpersuasive if the new model rested primarily on its shoulders. But because of the importance of domestic courts, the ICC is *not* the main institution through which regulation of the new model is enforced. The doctrine of complementarity in the ICC can be seen as a broader expression of the new model of enforcement. Contrary to the Ad-Hoc Tribunals, or to the European Court of Justice, which have primacy or supremacy over domestic courts, under the doctrine of complementarity the ICC can only exercise jurisdiction if domestic courts are "unwilling" or "unable" to prosecute.[18]

The primary institutions for enforcement of the new model thus are domestic criminal courts, and the ICC and foreign courts are the backup institutions or the last resort when the main model of domestic en-

[18] William A. Schabas, *An Introduction to the International Criminal Court* (Cambridge: Cambridge University Press, 2001), 13, 67.

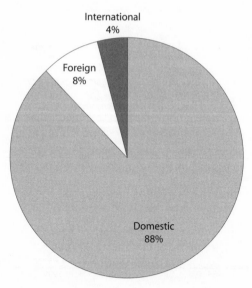

Figure 4.2. Percentage of total human rights trials

forcement fails.[19] Such backup institutions, however, are necessary to create a fully functioning international model. If the model depended only on domestic courts, perpetrators could always escape either by blackmail and veto in the domestic constituencies (for example, the rattling of the sabers and coup attempts that former military leaders in Argentina and Chile tried each time they faced the possibility of domestic prosecution), or by retirement abroad in a friendly third country. The backup provided by foreign and international trials makes such options less possible than before. In the language of this volume, while regulation was only domestic, it was more subject to capture by domestic repressors, whereas the move to create a more transnational system of regulation reduced the opportunity for capture by domestic repressive forces. Thus, it is not the case that foreign and international trials are more in the public interest than domestic trials. But the existence of international and foreign trials make the overall decentralized system more effective and less open to regulatory capture.

Many critics of the ICC or the specialized courts have not understood their role as the backup institutions in a global system of regulation. For

[19] Orentlicher calls this "domestic enforcement with an allowance for 'fallback' international jurisdiction," and Naomi Roht-Arriaza refers to foreign trials as a "back-stop" for domestic justice. Diane F. Orentlicher, "Settling Accounts: The Duty to Prosecute Human Rights Violations of a Prior Regime," *Yale Law Journal* 100 (1991), 2537–2618; Roht-Arriaza, *The Pinochet Effect*, 200.

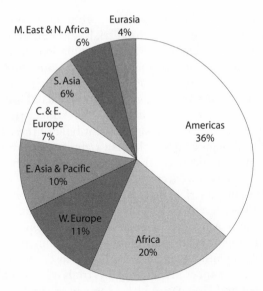

Figure 4.3. Regional distribution of human rights trials

example, Helena Cobban in *Foreign Policy* argues that international tribunals "have squandered billions of dollars" and that domestic solutions would be more cost-effective.[20] It would indeed be costly if international tribunals or the ICC were designed to provide a comprehensive system of individual criminal justice by themselves, but that is not how the model is currently working. The use of international tribunals or foreign courts as a backup is the exception, not the rule, in the new model of regulation. For the most part, the new model uses a decentralized system of enforcement that depends primarily on enforcement through domestic courts. In the Introduction to this volume, Mattli and Woods suggest that decentralized regulatory structures may be less open to capture, and this appears to true in the human rights case. Because the system is decentralized, however, the quality of the enforcement varies with the quality of criminal justice systems in different countries. At the international level, there are also concerns about the quality of regulation. Since the criminal justice model was transferred from domestic politics to international politics, it was sometimes not adapted to the different needs of international courts with international criminals.

There is significant variation in the frequency of human rights trials in different regions of the world. As figure 4.3 indicates, this trend toward

[20] Helena Cobban, "Think Again: International Courts," *Foreign Policy* (March/April 2006), 22.

domestic human rights trials has been most pronounced in Latin America, which accounts for 36 percent of total trials, although it only accounts for approximately 8 percent of the world's population. Not only do Latin American countries account for the plurality of domestic human rights trials, but they are also the subject of the largest number of foreign human rights trials. Most of the 101 foreign trials in our database were held in the domestic courts of European countries for human rights violations committed largely in the Americas. The great bulk of these foreign trials were brought to foreign courts by human rights organizations acting on behalf of human rights victims or their relatives from the country in which the human rights violations occurred.

But, even in Latin America, there is significant variation among different countries in the degree to which they have adopted the new regulatory model. Some Latin American countries such as Argentina and Bolivia were among the very first to start making use of human rights trials in the mid-1980s. Argentina was both the leader in the region and also a global leader in the number of human rights trials it has held. Argentina's neighbors, Brazil and Uruguay, which experienced similar authoritarian regimes and transitions to democracy at roughly the same time as Argentina, made different choices about trials. Brazil has held no human rights trials for violations during the authoritarian government, and Uruguay held no trials for the first fifteen years after the transition, only to begin a handful of prosecutions in the early 2000s.

In the final section of this chapter, I will explore explanations for the emergence of the new regulatory model and for the particular institutional forms and regional patterns that we see in the database. In particular, explanations need to address the prominence of human rights trials in some regions, like Latin America or Africa, and their relative rarity in some other regions of the world.

Key Actors in Human Rights Regulation and Change over Time

The cast of key actors in the human rights realm has long included states, international organizations, and NGOs. In this issue area, the private sector has played a less important role and NGOs have played a more important role than in many other international issue areas. The shift in regulatory model has led to the involvement of new kinds of actors, in particular the addition of international and domestic criminal courts and individual litigants to the cast of actors. Human rights NGOs, some governments, and parts of international organizations, form the "pro-change alliance," in favor of greater regulation of human rights, and in particular, of more enforcement. The inclusion of litigants and domestic courts in the pro-change alliance multiplies by hundreds the number of potential actors who could intervene in core human rights issues. The inclusion of this vast new array of potential actors thus increases the volatility and unpredictability of the issue area. Individual judges, such as Judge Garzon in Spain, suddenly are potentially actors on the international human rights stage. As the Spanish government found out, much to its dismay, foreign policy is no longer completely under the control of the foreign ministry.

Human rights NGOs are also active in the new regulatory framework, working domestically, and linked together in transnational networks. These human rights NGOs and networks have been the most important source of timely information in the process of human rights regulation. Even when international organizations and domestic and international courts became more deeply involved in the process of human rights regulation, NGOs often provided the original sources of information about human rights violations. To the degree that effective oversight requires costly information, these nonprofit NGOs have often taken on the burden and the cost of providing this information. The quality of this information may vary greatly; some NGOs produce very high-quality information, while others do not.

The NGO networks in turn are often closely linked to the transgovernmental networks, especially of the so-called like-minded states that have supported human rights regulation.[21] In this sense, the pro-change alliance behind the regulatory shift discussed here is a hybrid creature—including elements of transgovernmental networks, advocacy networks, and epistemic communities of legal experts. So, for example, the drafting of the ICC was the product of a transgovernmental network of foreign ministry lawyers from a core group of like-minded countries, including Canada, Argentina, Sweden, Norway, and the Netherlands. This transgovernmental network worked in close collaboration with an NGO network, supporting and often participating informally in the drafting process of the ICC Statute.[22]

---

[21] See Ann-Marie Slaughter, *A New World Order* (Princeton, NJ: Princeton University Press, 2004); Eric Voeten, "The Politics of International Judicial Appointments: Evidence from the European Court of Human Rights," *International Organization* 61, no. 4 (October 2007), 669–701.

[22] William R. Pace and Mark Thieroff, "Participation of Non-Governmental Organizations," in Roy S. Lee, ed., *The International Criminal Court: The Making of the Rome Statute: Issues, Negotiations, Results* (The Hague: Kluwer Law International), 391; and interview with Silvia Fernandez, Argentine foreign ministry official and key participant in all phases of the ICC negotiations, December 11, 2002, Buenos Aires.

Contrary to what Realist theory would predict, international human rights regulation was not the result of regulatory innovation in a dominant state. The United States, though it supported the ICTY and the ICTR as well as some domestic human rights trials, has been the major opponent of the ICC, the main embodiment of the new regulatory model. Rather, the hybrid network, with the crucial support of like-minded states, often worked without U.S. support, and sometimes in direct opposition to the United States, to develop the new model.

THE TURN TO THE NEW MODEL OF REGULATION: CHANGING NORMS AND LAWS

The gap between the domestic and international realms, what Ian Clark calls "the great divide" that saw domestic society as "rule-bound" and the international system as anarchy, once made domestic criminal law and international human rights law two completely separate realms. When these separate realms began to converge, it was difficult for some to see the convergence because of the continuing grip that the great divide has on our imagination.[23] I argue that this divide has made it difficult for scholars to recognize and understand the initial emergence of a unified system of international regulation of core political rights with often decentralized and fragmented enforcement primarily in domestic courts.

For many years, there was a huge disjuncture between the treatment of crime in the domestic and the international realms. Domestically, there was a clear hegemony of the individual criminal justice model, while this model was absent internationally. If an individual killed one person, there was an expectation and an apparatus to permit that he would stand trial for murder, and possibly be convicted and imprisoned. But if that individual was a head of state, and gave orders for thousands of individuals to be killed, the expectation was that nothing would happen. When their regimes were replaced by another, former dictators like Idi Amin, Jean Claude (Baby Doc) Duvalier, or Alfredo Stroessner traditionally lived a comfortable exile without any expectation of facing criminal trials for human rights violations committed during their regimes.

Thus, the oldest model of human rights regulation is a "no-accountability" model, or what we could call an impunity model. The Nuremberg and Tokyo trials, and the domestic and foreign World War II successor trials, were the important exceptions to this rule, but they were also exceptions that proved the rule. If the leaders ordered such crimes and then

---

[23] Ian Clark, *Globalization and International Relations Theory* (Oxford: Oxford University Press, 1999), 16.

utterly lost a war, they could indeed be held individually criminally responsible for their crimes by the victors of the war or by domestic or foreign courts. Since these were exceptional circumstances, they did not break the hegemony of the impunity model.[24]

After World War II, we began to see the emergence of the state accountability model where the state was occasionally held responsible for human rights violations carried out by its officials. Why did states initially adopt a state accountability model for human rights violations? This state accountability model is simply the application of standard international law principles to the realm of human rights. When a state breaches any international obligation under international law, it incurs responsibility and must provide some remedy to the injured party, be it a state or an individual. Thus, when states began regulating human rights as part of international law, they simply applied to the area of human rights the state accountability model that was used in the rest of international law. But human rights issues were quite different from most other international law issues. Most international law regulated interactions among states. Human rights law regulated interactions mainly between a state and it own citizens. This disjuncture between most international law and human rights law created some tensions in the state accountability model for human rights.

Nevertheless, these differences were initially ignored, and a state accountability model was adopted for international human rights law. In this model, determining state responsibility has always involved *attributing* conduct to the "act of the State," as opposed to individuals or groups.[25] For many years, the state accountability model accepted that one could attribute to the state significant violations of core human rights carried out by individuals and groups associated with the state. The advocates of the new model argued that a gross violation of human rights could not be a legitimate "act of state" and thus it must be a criminal act carried out by individuals (even heads of state like Pinochet or Milosevic) acting in their individual capacity and thus criminally liable. This argument was made in the Nuremberg Judgment, which argued that "the principle of international law, which under certain circumstances protects the representative of a State, cannot be applied to acts which are condemned

---

[24] Jon Elster, who writes about historical cases of transitional justice, says that there are no important episodes of transitional justice between classical Athens and the post–World War II trials, and then again no human rights trials until the Greek trials in the mid-1970s. *Closing the Books: Transitional Justice in Historical Perspective* (Cambridge: Cambridge University Press, 2004), 47–48, 61.

[25] Louis Henkin et al., *International Law: Cases and Materials*, 2nd ed. (St. Paul, MN: West Publishing, 1986), 522.

as criminal by international law."[26] Despite Nuremberg, international and domestic law and practice continued to protect state officials from prosecution for human rights violations.

Two key legal developments permitted the move from the state accountability model to the individual criminal accountability model. First was the simple argument that the fact that an individual has been a head of state or a state official shall not exempt him from criminal responsibility for gross violations of human rights. The second and related legal development was the idea that victims of human rights violations have a right to judicial remedies. The International Covenant on Civil and Political Rights and the American Convention on Human Rights both specify that states shall ensure that people have a right to an effective remedy for a human rights violation, even if such a violation has been committed by a state official. The right to a remedy does not necessarily imply a duty to punish, but it provides a basis for human rights trials. Finally, the Torture Convention and the Inter-American Convention to Prevent and Punish Torture, both of which entered into effect in 1987, specify that states have a duty to punish. Indeed, the notion of punishment is so important that it is part of the title of the Inter-American Convention. Human rights organizations, especially Amnesty International and Human Rights Watch; legal scholars and jurists, such as Professor M. Cherif Bassiouni; regional organizations, such as the Inter-American Court of Human Rights; and the governments of like-minded states, especially Canada, Norway, the Netherlands, and Argentina, proposed the treaty language and helped develop the jurisprudence that put the new model into place.

The drafters of various treaties, especially the Genocide Convention of 1948 and the Convention against Torture (CAT) negotiated in the late 1970s and early 1980s, managed to insert clear references to individual criminal accountability.[27] These treaties did not create a new legal framework all at once, but rather contributed gradually and in an understated way to the development of the new norms. The CAT refers to various state obligations, but the actual offender in most of the treaty is "a person"—specifically a public official who either inflicts torture directly or instigates, consents, or acquiesces to it. The Convention requires states to ensure that acts of torture are offenses under domestic criminal law, and to investigate alleged cases of torture and either to extradite or prosecute the accused and grant universal jurisdiction in the case of torture. The lan-

---

[26] *Trial of the Major War Criminals, before the International Military Tribunal* 1 (Nuremberg 1947), 223.

[27] United Nations Convention of the Prevention and Punishment of the Crime of Genocide, 78 U.N.T.S. 277 (1948).

guage granting universal jurisdiction is unobtrusive, simply saying that a State Party shall take measures to establish its jurisdiction over torture if the alleged offender is present in its territory. Universal jurisdiction provides for a system of decentralized enforcement in any national judicial system against individuals who commit or instigate torture. Legal experts from Amnesty International were very involved in proposing language about individual criminal accountability and universal jurisdiction to the states drafting the Torture Convention. Many states, including the United States, supported the inclusion of universal jurisdiction in the treaty.[28] But, at the time of drafting and ratification, it is not clear that all State Parties understood the ramifications of this provision buried in section 2 of article 5. For example, when Pinochet himself approved the Chilean ratification of the treaty in 1989, he could not have understood that it could lead to his arrest in the future.

Meanwhile, at the same time as the CAT was being drafted and ratified, and well before the Ad-Hoc Tribunals, the Pinochet case, or the ICC, legal developments were occurring in domestic polities around the world that began to reinforce the idea of individual criminal accountability for state officials for human rights violations. Thirty-three countries initiated domestic human rights trials before the ICTY began working in 1993. We don't know the exact legal reasoning courts used in each of these countries to justify the trials, but they were beginning to implement an individual criminal accountability model for human rights violations.

These domestic developments are all the more surprising because both scholars of transitions to democracy and many policymakers generally concluded that domestic trials for past human rights violations were politically untenable and likely to undermine new democracies. These scholars, such as Huntington, and O'Donnell and Schmitter, referred in particular to the cases of transition in Latin America.[29] But over time, as it became clear that trials in Latin America neither blocked transitions to democracy nor led to coups, the initial hesitance to adopt trials may have moderated. Since 1978, when the first trials were initiated in the region, there have been only three examples of coups in Latin America, and none was provoked by human rights trials. The remaining fourteen countries that used trials have not had a successful coup attempt since the use of

---

[28] Herman Burgers and Hans Danelius, *The United Nations Convention Against Torture: A Handbook on the Convention Against Torture and Other Cruel, Inhuman or Degrading Treatment or Punishment* (Dordrecht, Netherlands: Martinus Nijhoff Publishers, 1988), 78–79, also see 58, 62–63.

[29] Samuel P. Huntington, *The Third Wave: Democratization in the Late Twentieth Century* (Norman: University of Oklahoma Press, 1991); Guillermo O'Donnell and Phillipe C. Schmitter, *Transitions from Authoritarian Rule: Tentative Conclusions about Uncertain Democracies* (Baltimore: Johns Hopkins University Press, 1986).

trials, and in many cases, are increasingly considered consolidated democratic regimes. The argument that trials undermine democracy came largely from observations of a single case: the early coup *attempts* in Argentina against the Alfonsin government after it carried out far-reaching trials of the three juntas for past human rights violations. But twenty years after those failed coup attempts, Argentina has had more transitional human rights trials than any other country in the world and has enjoyed the longest uninterrupted period of democratic rule in its history.[30]

Although the CAT granted universal jurisdiction in the case of torture, this power wasn't exercised until the Pinochet case in 1998–99. The Law Lords determined that a head of state of Chile was not immune from extradition to Spain for torture committed while he was head of state, since both countries had ratified the Torture Convention recognizing international jurisdiction for the crime of torture. The Law Lords limited their decision only to the Torture Convention because the letter of treaty law ratified by all parties clearly stated that universal jurisdiction existed for torture.

Finally, the ICC Statute must be seen as the clearest statement of the new doctrine of individual criminal accountability. The statute is explicit in that it deals with individual criminal responsibility and individual punishment, and that the fact that an individual has been a head of state, or a member of government "shall in no case exempt a person from criminal responsibility" nor lead to a reduction of sentence.[31] The ICC, as the clearest distillation of new rules, came relatively late in the regulatory process and benefited from and drew upon the experience of other efforts at individual criminal accountability, especially the ad-hoc tribunals, but also individual country experiences. A pro-change alliance of like-minded states and human rights NGOs promoted the ICC and eventually persuaded a large number of states to sign and ratify the Statute, despite strong U.S. opposition to the final draft. The NGOs organized The Coalition for the International Criminal Court, a global network of over 2,000 NGOs advocating for the ICC and ratification of the Rome Statute. The like-minded states, initially a small group of states chaired by Canada, eventually expanded to include more than sixty states by the time the Rome Conference began. The like-minded were motivated by human rights ideals, and by their opposition to a court controlled by permanent members of the Security Council.[32] Lloyd Axworthy, Ministry of Foreign Affairs of Canada at the time the ICC was established, explained that

---

[30] For more support of this argument, see Sikkink and Walling, "The Impact of Human Rights Trials in Latin America."

[31] Rome Statute of the International Criminal Court, U.N. Doc. 2187 U.N.T.S. 90 (2002).

[32] Schabas, *An Introduction*, 15.

Canadian support for the ICC reflected its broader human security agenda. Central to that agenda was not only protecting individuals from risk, but also holding accountable those responsible for human rights violations.[33] The Statute of the International Criminal Court opened for signature in 1998, and by early 2008, 106 states had ratified it.

This new regulatory model involves an important convergence of international law (human rights, humanitarian, and international criminal law) and domestic criminal law.[34] This blurring of the distinction between international law and domestic law is not unique to this issue area, but characterizes many areas of global regulatory governance or global administrative law, as it is also termed.[35] In some cases, international human rights law might be absent from the reasoning of the judges. Domestic criminal law prohibiting murder may be perfectly adequate to prosecute individual government officials accused of carrying out summary executions in their official capacity. But the idea that heads of state were immune from individual criminal prosecution kept the model from being applied to state officials either in domestic courts or international courts. What created the political conditions and legal conditions to hold former government officials accountable for crimes?

EXPLANATIONS FOR THE EMERGENCE OF THE NEW REGULATORY MODEL

How do we account for this striking agenda change from a state accountability model to a criminal justice model of human rights regulation?

Two different kinds of explanations are required. We need to explain the general phenomenon of the dramatic rise of individual criminal accountability in the world, and account for the significant variation in the use of such forms of accountability, both across regions and among countries in a single region. The factors that can explain the general increase in human rights trials in the world are not necessarily the same factors

[33] Lloyd Axworthy, "Afterword: The Politics of Advancing International Criminal Justice," in Stephen Macedo, ed., *Universal Jurisdiction: National Courts and the Prosecution of Serious Crimes Under International Law* (Philadelphia: University of Pennsylvania Press, 2004), 261.

[34] Rattner and Abrams, *Accountability for Human Rights*, 9–14, refer to four interrelated bodies of law that underpin the move toward individual accountability for human rights violations: international human rights law, international humanitarian law, international criminal law, and domestic law.

[35] See Nico Krisch and Benedict Kingsbury, "Introduction: Global Governance and Global Administrative Law in the International Legal Order," *European Journal of International Law* 17, no. 1 (February 2006), 11.

that explain variation among regions and countries. Nevertheless, in both cases, demonstration effects and negative externalities form part of the explanation. The fact that the ICTY and the ICTR were responses to the crises in the Balkans and genocide in Rwanda, and the ICC Statute was drafted also in the wake of these events, points to the importance of the demonstration effects and the negative externalities of inadequate regulation as the final impetus for the new regulatory model at the global level. In the Latin American regional context, demonstration effects were also important. The human rights violations of the 1970s and 1980s in many countries in Latin America were the highest recorded levels in the twentieth century, and in many cases, we would have to go back to the colonial period to find equally high levels of repression. The fact that violations occurred in countries like Chile and Uruguay that had experienced decades of democracy and rule of law was particularly troubling and called into question the existing regulatory model.

The factors that may help explain the increase of human rights trials in Latin America, for example, include the demonstration effects of the severity of human rights violations, as well as institutional features such as the nature of the transition to democracy, the strength of domestic human rights organizations, and types of legal systems in many countries in the region.

But these factors can't necessarily explain the general increase in the number of trials in the world, or the variation between regions. So, for example, although there are more trials in Latin America than elsewhere in the world, it is *not* because Latin America has experienced more severe forms of human rights violations than other developing regions in the world. Nor can we explain the general increase in trials in the world as a result of the increase in global human rights violations. To the degree that we have a measure of human rights violations in the world, there is a general agreement that such violations have stayed at a relatively constant high level during the entire period under study. And yet, despite the relatively stable level of human rights violations, there has been a very dramatic change in how states respond to them. So, the changes are due not to the increase in human rights violations, but to increased information about such violations, made available through human rights NGOs and the media, and to changing ideas about the legitimacy of governments that engaged in or tolerated such human rights violations.

In this initial discussion of the phenomena, I will focus on the factors that can explain the adoption and the initial growth of the new model of regulation rather than those that explain the variation among countries and among regions. Why would actors choose to initiate and increasingly regulate and enforce standards in this area of human rights, and why did they choose this particular model of regulation?

Who are the relevant groups in the process of regulation of core human rights issues, and how do they understand their interests in this process? The core set of actors I will consider include different states, different agencies within states, including the judiciaries and the military and police perpetrators of human rights violations, and victims of human rights violations and their NGO/transnational network allies. These actors often have strong preferences about the primary question of whether or not there should be some form of accountability for human rights violations. In addition, they may also have preferences about the particular form of accountability, that is, state versus individual. We can assume for purposes of simplicity that victims of human rights violations prefer some kind of retributive justice, while state perpetrators of such violations (usually the military and police) will always work to block accountability.

Victims are important because they are often the litigants who bring human rights cases to the courts. As Mattli and Slaughter argue in the case of Europe, "Without individual litigants, there would be no cases presented to national courts and thus no basis for legal integration."[36] Victims and their families want accountability, but it is not obvious why human rights victims and their families should prefer a criminal accountability model instead of a state accountability model. From the point of view of material benefits, a state (civil) accountability model would be more likely to provide financial compensation to a victim than an individual criminal model. Nevertheless, in the countries where I have conducted field research—Argentina, Uruguay, Chile, and Guatemala—victims and their families have been at the forefront of demanding individual criminal accountability, while some have rejected financial compensation, or accepted it with hesitance and guilt. I argue that victims prefer individual criminal accountability (retributive justice) and that these are "ideational" preferences rather than "material" ones.[37]

Victims, in turn, had NGO allies that also had strong preferences for accountability. In most countries of the world, victims become litigants when they receive assistance from lawyers associated with human rights NGOs. Eventually, in addition, a transnational network of small groups of activist lawyers began to emerge working in favor of accountability for human rights violations. These lawyers helped pioneer the strategies, develop the legal arguments, often recruit the plaintiffs and/or witnesses, marshal the evidence, and persevered through years of legal challenges.

[36] Walter Mattli and Anne-Marie Slaughter, "Revisiting the European Court of Justice," *International Organization* 52, no. 1 (Winter 1998), 186.

[37] Mattli and Slaughter, "Revisiting," use the term "ideological preferences," but I prefer the term ideational, to signal that these preferences have to do with strongly held beliefs, which may or may not be connected to particular political ideologies.

These groups of lawyers resemble an *advocacy network*, in that they are interconnected groups of individuals bound together by shared values and discourse who engage in dense exchanges of information and services.[38] The transnational justice network tended to be confined to lawyers with appreciable technical expertise in international and domestic law who systematically pursued the tactic of human rights trials. This network had strong ideational preferences for accountability but not necessarily for individual criminal accountability. Network members were equally at home working on cases in the European Court of Human Rights or the Inter-American Court of Human Rights (state accountability) and for human rights trials in domestic or foreign courts. But since the network has strong preferences for more accountability, the addition of individual criminal accountability to existing state accountability models allowed them to expand dramatically the reach of accountability. To the extent that the continued existence of these groups depended on the continuation of human rights trials, we could say that these groups of lawyers had both material and ideational interests in trials.

The institutional features of the countries also affect the ability of victims and their NGO allies to successfully pursue lawsuits. First, democratic countries with rule of law systems that are at least minimally fair, transparent, and open are more likely to hold human rights trials. Although the data set surveyed above includes some human rights trials in nondemocratic countries, the great bulk of human rights trials occurred in democratic countries or countries in transition to democracy. In this sense, the "Third Wave" of democratic transitions is part of the explanation for regional patterns of the new system of global regulation. Since Latin America has experienced the most significant wave of transitions to democracy in the last decades, it is not surprising that it is also the region with the most trials.[39]

But just attributing the level of trials to the number of transitions would be misleading. Latin America experienced a similar wave of transitions to democracy between 1945 and 1975, but that wave of transitions was not accompanied by a new system of regulation of human rights violations.[40] Prior to the mid-1980s, the expectation after transition to democ-

[38] Margaret Keck and Kathryn Sikkink, *Activists beyond Borders: Advocacy Networks in International Politics* (Ithaca, NY: Cornell University Press, 1998), 2.

[39] Ninety-one percent of the countries of Latin America and the Caribbean are now democratic. See table 5, "Democracy and Freedom by Region, 2002," in Larry Diamond, "Can the Whole World Become Democratic? Democracy, Development, and International Policies" (Irvine: Center for the Study of Democracy, University of California, Irvine, 2003), Paper 03'05.

[40] For an overview of waves of transition in Latin America, see Frances Hagopian and Scott Mainwaring, eds., *The Third Wave of Democratization in Latin America: Advances and Setbacks* (Cambridge: Cambridge University Press, 2005).

racy was that the new governments would pass an amnesty law, and there would be impunity for past human rights violations.[41] Other institutional and ideational factors were also necessary to lead to the changing model of regulation.

Another institutional feature of the legal system also appears to be important. Civil law systems with provisions for private prosecution in criminal cases give victims and their allies more access to domestic courts than common law systems or civil law systems without provisions for private prosecutors. Judicial institutions where the government controls access to criminal prosecutions will be more open to capture than judicial institutions where private citizens have some ability to initiate criminal trials. This may help explain why more human rights trials occurred in Latin America than in other regions, because there were many countries in transitional democracy with relatively open civil law systems that included some provisions for private prosecution.

Finally, regional institutional features also play a role. Latin America has a more propitious legal context for human rights activism than Asia or the Middle East, for example, because of the existence and density of the Inter-American human rights norms and institutions, while Asia and the Middle East have no such regional human rights regime.[42] And while not generally considered a highly judicialized region, Africa has the third most significant regional human rights regime in the world after that of Europe and Latin America. So the regional propensity to hold human rights trials may be related to levels of regional judicialization or legalization, especially as regards human rights law. These regional institutions give victims and their allies an opportunity to bring forward human rights cases against their governments. In Latin America, the decision of the Inter-American Court that amnesty laws were contrary to the American Convention on Human Rights has had an important impact on opening more space for domestic human rights trials.

For government officials or members of the security forces that have already carried out human rights abuses, the strategic landscape is initially straightforward: it is in their interests to prevent prosecution for past human rights violations. These are the so-called spoilers, who are often

[41] This pattern has been documented very carefully in Chile, for example, but similar patterns exist throughout the region. See Brian Loveman and Elizabeth Lira, *Las suaves cenizas del olvido: Vía Chilena de Reconciliación Política 1814–1932* (Santiago: LOM Ediciones, 1999); *Las ardientes cenizas del olvido: Vía Chilena de Reconciliación Política 1932–1994* (Santiago: LOM Ediciones, 2000); and *El Espejismo de la Reconciliación: Chile 1990–2002* (Santiago, Chile: LOM Ediciones, 2002).

[42] On the low level of legalization in Asia, see Miles Kahler, "Legalization as Strategy: The Asia-Pacific Case," in Judith L. Goldstein and others, eds., *Legalization and World Politics* (Cambridge, MA: MIT Press, 2001), 165–187.

willing to go to great lengths to capture the regulatory process and prevent prosecution. Given a choice, they will always prefer no transitional justice at all, preferably guaranteed by an amnesty. They very often succeed in blocking domestic trials, through threats, coup attempts, or stalemated peace processes.[43] These former repressors have resisted all forms of accountability, but they have been much more forceful in rejecting individual criminal accountability than state accountability. While their motives include a mixture of ideological and material concerns, it is not difficult to understand why these officials would prefer to avoid trials and individual punishment.

But the motivations of other actors are more complex. Newly democratic governments are often portrayed as primarily interested in stability, continuity, and political survival. If they believe that human rights trials will undermine stability by provoking military coups, for example, they will oppose them. But, if they believe that trials will limit the power of veto players and thus promote stability, democratic governments may promote them.

The roles of lawyers, judges, and courts are even more complex. As parties interested in the growth of rule of law, we might expect such actors to support legal accountability over other forms of accountability. Resolving accountability issues in courts could contribute to the growth, power, and influence of the judicial sector and increase its autonomy vis-à-vis the executive. But it is less clear why judges would support individual criminal accountability over state accountability. In some cases, judges are part of transgovernmental networks that embrace new forms of judicial activism. In other countries, however, taking up a human rights case or trial could be dangerous and could undermine one's career. For example, during and after the dictatorship in Chile, involvement in such trials had a negative effect on judicial careers, and thus judicial actors tended to shun trials.[44] Elsewhere, as Judge Baltazar Garzon discovered, despite the animosity his arrest warrants provoked with the conservative Spanish government, he became an international celebrity as a result of his stand on human rights. Judges in Argentina under suspicion of corruption charges have also found that human rights trials have a way of burnishing their corroded images.

---

[43] Jack Snyder and Leslie Vinjamuri, "Trials and Errors: Principle and Pragmatism in Strategies of International Justice," *International Security* 28, no. 3 (Winter 2003/04), 5–44; and Leslie Vinjamuri and Jack Snyder, "Advocacy and Scholarship in the Study of International War Crimes Tribunals and Transitional Justice," *Annual Review of Political Science* 7 (May 2004), 345–362.

[44] See, for example, Elisabeth Hilbink, *Judges beyond Politics in Democracy and Dictatorship: Lessons from Chile* (New York: Cambridge University Press, 2007).

Although state officials accused of perpetrating human rights violations oppose trials, states more generally have not opposed the move to create law and ratify treaties that underpin individual criminal accountability models. If we look at the state ratification of the treaties that include some provisions for individual criminal accountability, we see many states ratify these treaties, but somewhat fewer states ratify human rights treaties calling for individual criminal accountability than treaties without these provisions. Of the three treaties that form the backbone of individual criminal accountability, 146 countries have ratified the Torture Convention, 136 countries have ratified the Genocide Convention, and 105 countries have ratified that Statute of the ICC, which was only opened for ratification in 1998. This compares to the most highly ratified of the core human rights treaties, the Convention on the Rights of the Child, with 192 ratifications. Only nineteen countries have not ratified at least one of the three treaties that underpin the move toward individual criminal accountability, and the list reads more like an inventory of small island countries with scarce state capacity than a coherent movement against the practice of individual criminal accountability. The relatively high number of ratifications of the ICC in a short time is especially significant, since the U.S. government has initiated a campaign against the ICC, and uses political and economic sanctions against countries that ratify and refuse to sign bilateral agreements promising not to turn U.S. personnel over to the ICC. We could argue that it is in the interests of states not to ratify the ICC Statute and thus avoid possible sanctions.[45] Yet, it appears that the great majority of states supported the development of general legal underpinnings of the individual criminal accountability model. Why would states do this? It seems possible that most states believed that individual criminal accountability would be reserved for individuals in other states, not their own (this, for example, was the position of the United States in the drafting of the Torture Convention). Second, since the ICC can only examine violations that occur after a country has ratified the statute, current state officials know that they are safe from prosecution for any past crimes. So, for example, the Argentine armed forces supported the move toward the ICC because it allowed them to support the cause of human rights without any fear that it would lead to their prosecution for past human rights violations.[46]

Even so, it is difficult to find a strong interest-based motivation for why states would have supported the move toward individual criminal

[45] On this issue, see Judith Kelley, "Why Do States Keep International Commitments? The International Criminal Court and Non-surrender Agreements," *American Political Science Review* 101, no. 3 (August 2007), 573–589.

[46] Interview with Silvia Fernandez, Buenos Aires.

accountability for human rights violations. Rather, we need to suggest that states too may be motivated by ideational or reputational concerns, and they may believe (except in the case of the ICC) that there are relatively low costs to treaty ratification.

We could make a rational argument that states would want to pass accountability from the state to individuals previously associated with the state. This permits the state itself to avoid accountability, perhaps avoid payment of remedies, and allows the state to scapegoat certain individuals. It may lower reputation costs of human rights violations if, for example, the crimes of Serbia are associated with Milosevic instead of Serbia.

But such an intuitively simple rationalist solution is not persuasive. If it were so rational, why did it take governments so long to make the move to individual criminal responsibility, and why have some governments, the Bush administration in particular, resisted the move so strenuously? Why would the socialist government of Chile fight so hard against Augusto Pinochet's detention in the United Kingdom and seek his return to Chile?

Targeted states did, however, resist specific international, foreign, or domestic trials for individual criminal accountability. In virtually all cases of foreign trials, the governments of the countries where the human rights violations have occurred have argued, often vehemently, that foreign trials for individual criminal accountability for human rights violations are either illegitimate or unnecessary or both. Their arguments varied, but generally, the arguments were *not* against the *concept* of individual criminal accountability per se, but against individual criminal accountability in foreign courts. This often led these governments to advocate individual criminal accountability in domestic courts, even if they had not initially taken this position. The Chilean government, for example, after Pinochet was detained in London argued forcefully that Pinochet could and should be tried at home, even though such trials were initially blocked by domestic amnesty legislation.

The interests of state actors often changed when individual criminal accountability moved from being a one-level game to a two-level game. When Pinochet thought that he was just in a domestic game, it was clear that his interest (and those of his military colleagues) was to block domestic trials at all costs, and he was able to do so with threats of coups and shows of military strength. When he was arrested in London, on the basis of an arrest warrant from Spain, it became clear that he was operating in a more complicated two-level game. The Chilean foreign ministry was unable to use the standard tools of diplomacy to get him released. It was at this point that the interests of some of those who opposed trials in Chile began to change. It was no longer the question of trials or no trials (in Chile), but now a question of trials in Spain, trials in the United Kingdom, or (perhaps) a trial in Chile. Under these circumstances, the option of a trial in Chile started looking better than before. This is why the possibility of international and foreign trials is a necessary backup system in the regulatory model. It is this possibility that converts the one-level game into a more complicated two-level game and changes the interests of the players in question.

In these circumstances, foreign and international trials may also have the strategic impact of changing calculations of past and current members of the security forces to make them more favorable to domestic trials than they would have been otherwise. Once perpetrators believe that they cannot prevent trials completely, the accused may decide that they prefer domestic courts to foreign or international courts. Along these lines, domestic trials opened up not only in Chile with the arrest of Pinochet in London, but the threat of extradition to Spain also led to new trials in Argentina, and more recently, the threat of extradition of Uruguayans to Argentina to stand trials has given impetus to the first human rights trials in Uruguay.

The discussion of interests, however, misses what is most interesting about this issue, and those are the very beliefs about what people think is possible. In the human rights area, for years, people didn't advocate individual criminal responsibility for human rights violations because they didn't think it was possible or realistic. Even months before Pinochet was arrested in London, most experts in this area didn't think it was politically possible to arrest him, even though it was legally possible in principle. This issue area illustrates that before we can think of the obvious or natural interests of actors, we have to understand the conditions of what they thought was possible. First it had to become possible to imagine that powerful leaders could face consequences for their human rights violations. Only then could actors begin to consider what kind of model of regulation should be adopted.

Most victims of human rights violations historically did not imagine that it was possible to turn their deeply felt need for justice into any practical form. Even when groups spoke out for justice, it wasn't always clear what that meant. So, for example, when human rights organizations in Argentina began to call for "trials and punishment for all those guilty of human rights violations" ("Jucio y Castigo a Todos los Cupables"), it wasn't clear exactly what justice and punishment meant or what they should mean.[47] It wasn't clear because in 1983, there was no history in Latin America, and little experience in the entire world, with how domestic courts might hold former government officials responsible for human

---

[47] Elizabeth Jelin, "La política de la memoria: el movimiento de derechos humanos en la Argentina," in *Jucio, Castigo, y Memoria* (Buenos Aires: Nueva Vision, 1995), 119–120.

rights violations. The "transitional justice mechanisms" that eventually emerged during the Alfonsín government were the result of interactions of the human rights movement, the government, and the political opposition, each engaged in forms of improvisation in this uncharted realm. The treatment of human rights violations in Argentina during this period "was a process with a life of its own, the course and results of which escaped the calculations and desires of each of the actors directly involved."[48]

When we try to understand why governments chose to use the criminal accountability model, there is a striking fact that comes to our attention. Once it became possible to imagine accountability for individual leaders, the model of regulation chosen (individual criminal accountability) was an extension of the criminal model already used for domestic crimes. It is possible that a logic of appropriateness was at work here rather than a logic of consequences.[49] For hundreds of years, most societies have regulated crimes like murder or kidnapping with domestic trials for individual criminal accountability. Many people never questioned what form accountability for past human rights violations should take, but took for granted that the criminal accountability model would be used.

The first trials for individual criminal accountability (after the World War II trials) took place in the domestic judicial systems of individual countries (Greece, Argentina, and Bolivia). While leaders in those countries could have chosen other models of accountability than individual legal criminal accountability (and they sometimes did choose other models), they increasingly focused on criminal trials. For example, Carlos Nino, the brilliant legal theorist who was President Alfonsin's adviser on the trials in Argentina, considered many factors (such as how many members of the military should be tried), but did not seriously consider an option other than individual criminal accountability.[50] Because the enforcement was happening through domestic criminal courts, these same courts just took a process they know well—individual criminal accountability—and used it on a new set of perpetrators: past government officials. They did not do this without substantial legal and political difficulties, but over time, domestic courts established that it was possible to hold government officials criminally accountable for human rights violations.

These domestic trials began to create a certain precedent, and the weight of example. When international actors searched for a solution to

[48] Oscar Landi and Inés González Bombal, "Los derechos en la cultura política," in *Jucio, Castigo, y Memoria*, 163 (translation mine).

[49] James G. March and Johan P. Olsen, "The Institutional Dynamics of International Political Orders," *International Organization* 52, no. 4 (Autumn 1998), 943–969.

[50] Carlos Santiago Nino, *Radical Evil on Trial* (New Haven, CT: Yale University Press, 1996).

the problem in the Balkans in the early 1990s, the possibility of a court using individual criminal accountability for past human rights violations was on the agenda, having been put there by high-profile domestic examples. The ethnic cleansing in the Balkans, followed shortly after by the genocide in Rwanda, created the kind of international demonstration effect that pointed to the weaknesses of the human rights regime. While trials weren't the only possible solution (indeed, military intervention was another response to massive human rights violations that was increasingly proposed), the move to criminal accountability represented one effort by the international community to find more effective models of enforcement of human rights norms. The justice cascade in domestic politics contributed to increasing the salience of the individual criminal accountability as an option for the international community.

We therefore cannot explain changing trends in regulation of human rights without reference to changing ideas about justice and the embodiment of those ideas in international law and institutions. As Mattli and Woods point out, ideas are a key explanatory variable for changes in regulation. These include both ideas about what is desirable and about what is possible. Gary Bass attributes international war crimes tribunals primarily to the legalism of wealthy liberal states, as well as to their unwillingness to sacrifice their own soldiers and citizens in actually intervening to stop war crimes from happening. But the fact that domestic human rights trials first began as domestic trials in countries of the periphery, such as Greece, Argentina, and Bolivia, suggests that these liberal ideas about trials and human rights did not necessarily derive from the wealthy northern countries. Nevertheless, I agree with Bass that one can not understand the emergence of the model of individual criminal accountability "without reference to ideas drawn from domestic politics."[51] Bass also argues that domestic trials are the most sincere indication of the strength of ideas and norms, since it is more difficult to put one's own leaders and soldiers on trial than those of another country, especially one vanquished in war.[52]

The ideas that underpin both international and domestic trials are mainly liberal ideas about human rights, due process, and in particular, individual responsibility for human rights violations. Latin America is a particularly interesting region in this regard because it has a long tradition of liberal thought that coexisted with increasingly authoritarian regimes. In Latin America there was a tradition of support for human rights and international law.

[51] Gary J. Bass, *Stay the Hand of Justice: The Politics of War Crimes Tribunals* (Princeton, NJ: Princeton University Press, 2000), 12.
[52] Ibid., 14.

There were various counter-ideas to individual criminal jurisdiction. The first was to propose a continuation of the impunity model. This idea was increasingly discredited. Essentially changing ideas about the desirability and possibility of some form of accountability for human rights violations had become sufficiently entrenched that they have made it more difficult to advocate a return to a pure impunity model. The most powerful counter-idea to the individual criminal accountability, however, was the idea that countries should focus only on "restorative justice" via truth commissions and reparations, but should eschew "retributive justice" through human rights trials. The proponents of this idea claimed that restorative justice could promote reconciliation and satisfy victims with truth and reparations without causing divisions and rancor through retributive trials. The South African case, with its Truth and Reconciliation Commission, is held up as the paradigmatic example of how restorative justice should function. Because the impunity model has been discredited, many prior advocates of impunity have now embraced restorative justice. Because restorative justice ideas have a much more positive connotation than impunity, opponents of trials find it more legitimate to oppose them by proposing reconciliation. The restorative justice model also finds strong support from activists and legal scholars who have long criticized harsh retributive punishment in their domestic legal systems as counterproductive. The restorative justice idea thus also has a strong alliance behind it. Once again, debates about domestic legal systems are transposed to the international arena.

Finally, can the factors discussed in the framework chapter help explain the degree or speed of the adoption of individual criminal accountability in different Latin American countries? First, transition to democracy is the most important predictor of the use of human rights trials in the region. All of the countries that held human rights trials were democracies or were in the process of a transition to democracy. This is consistent with the point made by Mattli and Wood in the framework chapter that an institutional context offering participatory mechanisms is a necessary condition for public interest regulation. Second, the level of severity of human rights violations also affected the decision to use trials, so that countries with more severe violations, like Argentina and Guatemala, were more likely to use trials than countries with less severe violations, such as Brazil. This fits with the argument of Mattli and Woods that the scale and scope of the negative externalities of existing regulatory models may influence the demand for a change in regulation. Third, the nature of the transition has effects on the use and timing of trials, because some transitions gave more power to perpetrators of human rights violations. The transitions literature called our attention to the differences between the so-called negotiated or "pacted" transitions, where the military negotiate the transition, and ensure significant protections and guarantees for themselves from prosecution for human rights violations, and the "society-led" transitions, where the military are forced to exit from power without negotiating specific protections.[53] Countries that had negotiated or pacted transitions to democracy are less likely to use trials than those that have had society-led transitions forcing authoritarian regimes out of power.[54] Again, this is consistent with the Mattli and Woods argument that the relative power of the pro-change alliance vis-à-vis the agents of capture helps determine regulatory outcomes. Basically, in pacted transition, the military used their power to ensure their continued capture of regulation. In Latin America, Argentina, Bolivia, Peru, and Panama are all examples of ruptured transitions, and all are examples of countries where trials occurred more promptly after transition. Chile, Uruguay, El Salvador, Guatemala, and Brazil are examples of pacted transitions. Pacted transitions can lead to no trials (in the case of Brazil, for example), fewer trials than we might expect given the level of prior human rights violations (as is the case of El Salvador), or delayed trials (as in the case of Chile, Uruguay, and Guatemala). Nevertheless, what is most striking is that even in most pacted transitions, over time, the military have not been able to completely block human rights trials. Changing ideas and norms about appropriate transitional justice made the impunity model increasingly untenable, and with the passage of time, human rights trials became increasingly common throughout the hemisphere. These ideas did not just emerge from dominant countries but from a diverse pro-change alliance of like-minded governments, including many newly democratic Latin American governments, human rights NGOs, and judges and lawyers in many parts of the world.

Conclusions

The demonstration effect of the Holocaust first led to the emergence of a human rights regime focused on state accountability with weak enforcement mechanisms. States negotiated a series of increasingly precise human

---

[53] Alfred C. Stepan, "Paths Towards Redemocratization: Theoretical and Comparative Considerations," in Guillermo O'Donnell, Philippe C. Schmitter, and Laurence Whitehead, eds., *Transitions from Authoritarian Rule* (Baltimore: Johns Hopkins University Press, 1986).

[54] Rene Antonio Mayorga has argued that only with ruptured transitions "has it historically been possible to open space necessary to bring military dictators to justice." "Democracy Dignified and an End to Impunity: Bolivia's Military Dictatorship on Trial," in A. James McAdams, ed., *Transitional Justice and the Rule of Law in New Democracies* (Notre Dame: University of Notre Dame Press, 1997), 67.

rights treaties that began to enter into effect in the 1970s, 1980s, and 1990s. At the same time, networks of human rights NGOs multiplied, and they found allies among the governments of like-minded states and increasing numbers of lawyers and legal experts to form a powerful pro-change alliance in favor of more enforcement of existing human rights norms. This created the ideational, legal, and political conditions in some transitional countries to first experiment with human rights trials, starting with Greece in 1974–75, but picking up steam and legitimacy in particular after the Argentine trials of the juntas in 1985. While these trials had mixed results, the accumulation of trials in over thirty transitional countries eventually created an ideational and political context where trials were seen as a salient and workable solution to the failure of the existing regulation model in the Balkans and Rwanda. Human rights NGOs lobbied for more accountability, including individual criminal accountability, and diffused the ideas and practices being used by state actors in domestic trials.

In the end, these processes led to an important but still incomplete change in ideas and practices at both the domestic and international levels. Before the 1970s, state officials and publics alike took the impunity model for granted, and did not imagine it was possible to hold state officials accountable for human rights violations. Now in many parts of the world, repressors are no longer certain they can block domestic or international trials. This change is too recent to say with any certainty whether government and security forces around the world are actually persuaded by the new ideas or simply constrained by them. But the dramatic increase in human rights trials in the world and their geographical spread suggest that the individual criminal accountability model will not be easily reversed and will continue to grow together with state accountability to provide greater enforcement for human rights law.

The Private Regulation of Global Corporate Conduct

David Vogel

THIS CHAPTER explores the dynamics of regulatory change associated with new forms of transnational non-state governance designed to make global firms more responsible and accountable.[1] It begins by defining "civil regulation," describing its growth and placing its development, structure, and purposes in a broader historical and institutional context. It then explains the development of civil regulation as a response to the shortcomings of the global and national governance of global firms and markets. The "demonstration effects" associated with these perceived policy failures have in turn created a demand for the development of new regulatory vehicles to control the social conduct of international firms. The third section describes how various policy entrepreneurs, led by non-governmental organizations (NGOs) and often supported by some national governments and international organizations, have, through a complex process of conflict and cooperation, persuaded large numbers of global firms to accept non-state regulatory standards.

The uneven impact of civil regulation, and the factors that underlie it, are then explored in case studies of relatively effective, moderately effec-

---

[1] The term civil regulation comes from Simon Zadek, *The Civil Corporation* (London; Earthscan, 2001). It is also used by Dale Murphy and Jem Bendell, *Partners in Time?* (Geneva: United Nations Research Institute for Social Development, 1999). The scholarly literature on non-state regulation is beginning to increase. There are now five books on this subject by political scientists, four published since 2004: Benjamin Cashore, Geame Auld, and Deanna Newsom, *Governing through Markets: Forest Certification and the Emergence of Non-State Authority* (New Haven, CT: Yale University Press, 2004); Virginia Haufler, *The Public Role for the Private Sector: Industry Self-Regulation in a Global Economy* (Washington, DC: Carnegie Endowment for International Peace, 2001); Ronnie Lipschutz with James Rowe, *Globalization, Governmentality and Global Politics; Regulation for the Rest of Us?* (London and New York: Routledge, 2005); Aseem Prakash and Matthew Potoski, *The Voluntary Environmentalists: Green Clubs, ISO 14004, and Voluntary Environmental Regulation* (Cambridge: Cambridge University Press, 2006); and David Vogel, *The Market for Virtue: The Potential and Limits of Corporate Social Responsibility* (Washington, DC: Brookings Institution Press, 2005). For a review of the literature on civil regulation by political scientists and other scholars, see David Vogel, "Private Global Business Regulation," *Annual Review of Political Science* (2008), 261–282.

tive, and relatively ineffective private global regulations. These studies demonstrate that it has proven far easier to develop new regulatory instruments than to either persuade significant numbers of firms to adhere to them or to develop effective monitoring and enforcement mechanisms to assure compliance with them. This chapter concludes by specifying the changes in both corporate practices and public policies that would be necessary to strengthen the effectiveness of civil regulation and measurably contribute to ameliorating the current shortcomings of the governance of global firms and markets.

This chapter argues that the growth in the supply of civil regulation both reflects and has contributed to new expectations, values, and ideas regarding both the shortcomings of existing regulatory mechanisms as well as the need for new strategies for ameliorating them. In this sense, activists have effectively challenged the legitimacy of existing regulatory arrangements. Public pressures on firms as well as demonstrations of the business benefits of more responsible corporate behavior have, to some extent, in the words of this project's framework study, "changed the mind-set of [at least] some former agents of capture, reshaping their understanding of what regulatory arrangements are best for them [and potentially] bolstering a more public-interest basis for regulation."[2]

But to what extent and under what circumstances has the demand for new approaches to global business regulation been accompanied by the development of new governance or institutional mechanisms capable of giving the "public interest" a more effective voice in global regulation? In other words, what has been the effectiveness of the monitoring and enforcement mechanisms of civil regulations in addressing the shortcomings of global business regulation—which include both industry capture of existing regulatory institutions as well as business opposition to their expansion and effective enforcement—that prompted the political demand for their emergence in the first place? As Mattli and Woods note in the framework chapter of this volume, supply does not create its own demand: the ability of regulations to achieve their public interest objectives also requires adequate mechanisms of enforcement and accountability.

Because such mechanisms are lacking for many civil regulations, their success in challenging the regulatory status quo has been both limited and uneven. The problem they face is primarily due to the lack of sufficient economic and political "demand" for more responsible global corporate conduct on the part of both firms and governments. This limitation has constrained the ability of pro-regulation activists to develop effective vehicles for changing how global firms are governed.

---

[2] Walter Mattli and Ngaire Woods, "In Whose Benefit? Explaining Regulatory Changes in Global Governance," this volume.

To explicitly draw on the framework of the introductory chapter, NGOs and their supporters have been relatively successful in demonstrating the shortcomings of the regulatory status quo, in mobilizing sufficient political support to create new regulatory mechanisms, and in changing both business and public expectations about how corporations should respond to many of the political and market failures associated with economic globalization. In doing so, they have added an important new nonstate dimension to global governance: they have created a new political setting in which corporate policies can be scrutinized and corporate priorities can be challenged. But these new private regulatory instruments typically lack the capacity to bring about sufficient changes in corporate behavior to compensate for the shortcomings of state-based regulations.

Global civil regulation—and the principles and practices of global corporate social responsibility (CSR) to which it is often linked—has become a highly visible and increasingly legitimate dimension of global economic governance. Making many global corporate practices much more transparent has increased public pressures on firms to behave more "responsibly." It has also provided important new vehicles for nonbusiness constituencies, primarily in western countries, to participate in the regulation of global firms and markets, and forced some global firms to internalize some of their negative social and environmental externalities.

But while civil regulations can compensate for some of the shortcomings of national and international governance, they are not a substitute for the more effective exercise of state authority at both the national and international levels. The long-term impact of private global business regulation depends on the extent to which its standards for business conduct and its mechanisms for holding firms accountable are integrated with and reinforced by state-based regulatory policies at both the national and international levels.[3]

Defining Civil Regulation

Civil regulations employ private, non-state, or market-based regulatory frameworks to govern multinational firms and global supply networks. A defining feature of civil regulation is that its legitimacy, governance,

---

[3] See, for example, Halina Ward, *Public Sector Roles in Strengthening Corporate Social Responsibility: Taking Stock* (Washington, DC: World Bank, International Finance Corporation, 2004); *Partnering to Strengthen Public Governance: The Leadership Challenge for CEOs and Boards* (Geneva: World Economic Forum, 1998); and Jane Nelson, "Leadership, Accountability and Partnership: Critical Trends and Issues in Corporate Social Responsibility," Report of the CSR Initiative Launch Event, Corporate Social Responsibility Initiative, Report No. 1. Cambridge, MA: John F. Kennedy School of Government, Harvard University.

and implementation are not rooted in public authority. Typically operating beside or around the state rather than through it, civil regulations are based on "soft law" or private law rather than legally enforceable standards: violators typically face social or market penalties rather than legal sanctions.[4] Civil regulation extends regulatory authority "sideways" beyond the state to global non-state actors.[5] Its recent growth reflects an expanded "public role for the private sector," as well as the growing importance of "private authority in global governance."[6] Global corporate codes constitute part of an "emerging global public domain." Civil regulation does "not replace states, but . . . (rather) embed(s) systems of governance in broader global frameworks of social capacity and agency that did not previously exist."[7] Its growth reflects, as Abbott and Snidal's chapter in this volume suggests, the emergence of a more complex global "governance triangle," in which states are no longer the exclusive source of global regulatory authority.[8]

At the same time, there are important linkages between civil and state regulations. For example, civil regulations typically include commitments by their corporate signatories to obey host country laws, and many private regulatory standards are based on those of intergovernmental organizations such as the Organization for Economic Cooperation and Development (OECD), the International Finance Corporation (IFC) of the World Bank, and the International Labor Organization (ILO). A number of developed-country governments, including the United States (U.S), the European Union (EU), Great Britain, Belgium, France, Austria, and Germany, have promoted the development of global industry codes of conduct, as has the United Nations.

---

[4] For excellent analysis of the role and importance of "soft law" in global governance, see John Kirton and Michael Trebilock, "Introduction: Hard Choices and Soft Law in Sustainable Global Commerce," in John Kirton and Michael Trebilock, eds., *Hard Choices, Soft Law: Voluntary Standards in Global Trade, Environment and Social Governance* (Aldershot: Ashgate, 2004); and the essays in Ulrika Moth, ed., *Soft Law in Governance and Regulation* (Cheltenham: Edward Elger, 2004). Both edited volumes contain essays on both private and public soft law. See also Kenneth Abbott and Duncan Snidal, "Hard and Soft Law in International Governance," *International Organization* 54, no. 3 (Summer 2000), 421–456.

[5] Virginia Haufler, "Globalization and Industry Self-Regulation," in Miles Kahler and David Lake, eds., *Governance in A Global Economy: Political Authority in Transition* (Princeton, NJ: Princeton University Press, 2003), 226.

[6] See Virginia Haufler, *The Public Role for the Private Sector*; and Rodney Hall and Thomas Biersteker, eds., *The Emergence of Private Authority in Global Governance* (Cambridge: Cambridge University Press, 2002).

[7] John Ruggie, "Reconstituting the Global Public Domain—Issues, Actors and Practices," *European Journal of International Relations* 19, no. 4 (2004), 519.

[8] Kenneth Abbott and Duncan Snidal, "The Governance Triangle: Regulatory Standards Institutions and the Shadow of the State," this volume.

There are also important structural similarities between civil regulations and a subset of government regulations. Many governments employ voluntary agreements or market-based mechanisms as vehicles of business regulation. The market-based regulatory mechanisms typically employed by civil regulations, namely, producer certification, product labeling, third-party auditing, and information disclosure, are also used by governments, especially in the area of environmental policy.[9]

However, the labeling, disclosure, auditing, and certification components of civil regulations are not subject to state scrutiny. Moreover, many "voluntary" agreements between firms and governments are voluntary in name only, as the state retains final legal authority.[10] This is not the case for civil regulations for which there is typically no state "backup." Rather, civil regulations rely primarily, if not exclusively, on voluntary compliance. As Grant and Keohane observe, "When standards are not legalized, we would expect accountability to operate chiefly through reputation and peer pressure, rather than in more formal ways."[11] Finally, while regulatory alternatives to command and control typically govern only domestic producers, many civil regulations address the international dimensions of business conduct, for which there are fewer effective state or interstate regulations.

Still, the boundaries between "voluntary" and mandatory regulations, state and non-state regulations, private and public law, and hard and soft law cannot always be sharply drawn.[12] It is also a fluid one: soft laws can become "harder," and norms can become more law-like, as has occurred with respect to human rights.[13] The Uruguay Round agreement

[9] See, for example, Neil Gunningham and Peter Grabosky, *Smart Regulation: Designing Environmental Policy* (Oxford: Clarendeon Press, 1978) and *Voluntary Approaches for Environmental Policy* (Paris: OECD, 2003).

[10] Patrick ten Brink, ed., *Voluntary Environmental Agreements: Process, Practice and Future Use* (Sheffield, UK: Greenleaf Publishing, 2001).

[11] Ruth Grant and Robert Keohane, "Accountability and Abuses of Power in World Politics," *American Political Science Review* 99, no. 1 (February 2005), 35.

[12] For a detailed analysis of both private and public voluntary codes and the relationships between them, see Kernaghan Webb, ed., *Voluntary Codes: Private Governance, the Public Interest and Innovation* (Carleton, Canada: Carleton Research Unit for Innovation, Science and Environment, 2004). See also Jon Birger Skjaerseth, Olav Schram Stokke, and Jorgen Wessestaad, "Soft Law, Hard Law, and Effective Implementation of International Environmental Norms," *Global Environmental Politics* 6, no. 3 (2006), 104–120.

[13] See, for example, Thomas Risse, Stephen Ropp, and Kathryn Sikkink, *The Power of Human Rights: International Norms and Domestic Change* (Cambridge: Cambridge University Press, 1999); Thomas Risse, "International Norms and Domestic Change: Arguing and Communicative Behavior in the Human Rights Area," *Politics and Society* 27, no. 4 (December 1999), 529–550; and Ethan Naderman, "Global Prohibition Regimes: The Evolution of Norms in International Society," *International Organization* 44, no. 3 (Autumn 1990), 429–526.

that established the World Trade Organization (WTO) granted international legal recognition to the food safety standards of the Codex Commission, a private industry body, while the standards of both the Forest Stewardship Council (FSC) as well as ISO 14001 have been accorded legal recognition by some national and local governments. In several countries, formerly voluntary corporate social reporting has become mandatory. In a few exceptional cases noted below, civil regulations have been enforced by trade policies.

The Political Dynamics of Civil Regulation

Throughout the history of capitalism, business self-regulation has existed in parallel with government regulation; indeed, historically the former often preceded the latter. The medieval guilds exercised a wide variety of regulatory functions, including price, market entry, and quality controls. In contemporary economies, private regulations govern a wide variety of business activities, most notably in the areas of electronic commerce, maritime transportation, bond ratings, and financial services. Numerous technical standards have been developed by private organizations, and these play an important role in the global economy.[14]

Civil regulations are distinctive from traditional forms of industry self-regulation in three important respects. First, in contrast to many technical standards whose primary purpose is to lower the transactions costs of market transactions, civil regulations require firms to make expenditures that they would not otherwise make. They typically seek to protect interests not directly involved in the market chain by ameliorating some of the negative externalities of market transactions. Second, compared to traditional forms of business self-regulation, civil regulations are more likely to be politicized: they have typically emerged in response to political and social pressures on business, often spearheaded by national and transnational activists who have embarrassed global firms by publicizing the shortcomings of their social and environmental practices. Third, the governance of civil regulations is more likely to be transparent, contested, and to either formally or informally involve nonbusiness constituencies—

---

[14] For the importance of technical international standards, see Walter Mattli, "Public and Private Governance in Setting International Standards," in Miles Kahler and David A. Lake, eds., *Governance in a Global Economy* (Princeton, NJ: Princeton University Press, 2003), 199–225; and a Special Issue of *The Journal of European Public Policy* 8, no. 3 (2001) on "Governance and International Standards Setting," Walter Mattli, guest editor. See also the case studies in A. Claire Cutler, Virginia Haufler, and Tony Porter, eds., *Private Authority and International Affairs* (Albany: State University of New York, 1999).

in contrast to traditional business self-regulation, which is typically exclusively governed and controlled by firms.

Civil regulation does not privatize business regulation in the sense of removing it from public scrutiny. Rather, it is associated with the development of new non-state, political mechanisms for governing global firms and markets. "Private governance helps empower global civil society by providing activist groups with political levers that exist outside state systems."[15] The expansion of global civil regulation is closely linked to the emergence of a global "civil society," an increasingly sophisticated and extensive international network of NGOs based primarily in North America and Europe that monitor and seek to influence a wide range of global business practices.[16]

"NGOs' role and influence have exploded in the last-half decade."[17] NGOs have also become more global in scope: more than a thousand draw their membership from three or more countries. Many such organizations have become influential and legitimate global political actors. While much of their political activity has focused on public policies and institutions, over the last decade they have increasingly sought to directly influence the practices of many firms, markets, and industries. The participants in the movement for global corporate accountability are wide-ranging: they include unions, environmental organizations, human rights and labor activists, religious and consumer groups, student organizations, consumer groups, as well as social or ethical mutual funds and socially oriented institutional investors.

Western activists primarily seek to improve business practices in developing countries by placing public pressures on global firms that have a highly visible presence in the United States and Europe—in effect bypassing both their own governments and those of developing countries. Civil regulation thus turns globalization on its head, making the global scope of business activity into a source of political vulnerability for global firms. A key objective of the movement for CSR is to politicize consumer and financial markets in developed countries in order to socialize market practices in developing ones.

[15] Robert Falkner, "Private Environmental Governance and International Relations: Exploring the Links," *Global Environmental Politics* 3, no. 2 (May 2003), 79.

[16] For the emergence and impact of global civil society and global citizen activism, including its efforts to address corporate conduct, see Robin Cohen and Shirin Rai, eds., *Global Social Movements* (London: Continuum, 2000); Michael Edwards and John Gaventa, eds., *Global Citizen Action* (Boulder, CO: Lynne Rienner, 2001); Margaret Keck and Kathryn Sikkink, *Activists Beyond Borders* (Ithaca, NY: Cornell University Press, 1998); Marjorie Mayo, *Global Citizens* (Toronto: Canadian Scholars Press, 2005); and Sidney Tarrow, *The New Transnational Activism* (Cambridge: Cambridge University Press, 2005).

[17] Jessica Mathews, "Power Shift," *Foreign Affairs* (January/February 1997), 53.

Global civil regulations are thus engaged in a non-state, market-based, variant of "trading up." By attempting to transmit more stringent regulatory standards from developed countries to firms, industries, and markets in developing ones, they are seeking to privatize the "California effect," a term coined to describe the dynamics of the transmission of more stringent standards among states via international trade.[18] Their emergence and impact has been facilitated both by the growth of global brands—which make firms more vulnerable to threats to their reputations in important consumer markets—and the expansion of international communications—which enables activists to more easily acquire information about global business practices, and then to rapidly disseminate it.

The number and scope of global civil regulations began to expand significantly during the 1990s. Private regulations that define standards for "responsible" business practices now exist for virtually every global industry and internationally traded commodity, including forestry, fisheries, chemicals, computers and electronic equipment, apparel, rugs, coffee, cocoa, palm oil, diamonds, gold, toys, minerals and mining, energy, tourism, financial services, and athletic equipment—though most formally govern only a portion of these global products or sectors.[19]

There are now more than 300 industry or product codes, nearly all of which address labor or environmental practices; many sectors and products are governed by multiple codes. More than 3,000 global firms now regularly issue reports on the social and environmental practices, and many of these firms have developed their own codes and/or subscribe to one or more industry or cross-industry codes. The largest private business code, the UN Global Compact, has more than 3,500 corporate signatories. More than 2,300 global firms have endorsed the Business Charter for Sustainable Development developed by the International Chamber of Commerce, while over 46,000 firms have been certified as ISO 14001 compliant. More than seventy major global financial institutions from sixteen countries, representing assets of $4.5 trillion, have signed the United Nations Principles for Responsible Investment.

[18] David Vogel, *Trading Up: Consumer and Environmental Regulation in Global Economy* (Cambridge, MA: Harvard University Press, 1995).

[19] For the growth of civil regulation, see Gary Gereffi, Ronie Garcia-Johnson, and Erike Sasser, "The NGO-Industrial Complex," *Foreign Policy* (July–August 2001), 56–65; Mathias Koenig-Archibugi, "Transnational Corporations and Public Accountability," *Government and Opposition* 39, no. 2–3 (2004): 234–259; Ans Kolk and Rob van Tulder, "Setting New Global Rules? TNCs and Codes of Conduct," *Transnational Corporations* 14, no. 3 (December 2005), 1–27; and Rhys Jenkins, "Corporate Codes of Conduct: Self-Regulation in a Global Economy" (Geneva: UN Research Institute for Social Development, 2001).

During the 1960s and 1970s, interest in the global dimensions of CSR was primarily an American phenomenon.[20] However, over the last decade civil regulation has become more internationally based. In fact, in a number of respects, global CSR is now more important in Europe than in the United States.[21] Ethical brands or certifications for coffee, rugs, flowers, and wood products have larger market shares in many European countries than in the United States. London has replaced New York as the global center of CSR conferences, activism, research, reporting, and monitoring. Europe is also home to more global NGOs than is the United States. The "Europeanization" of CSR is an important development as it has significantly expanded the international scope of civil regulations and number of global firms that have agreed to accept them.[22]

GOVERNANCE FAILURES AND THE GROWTH OF CIVIL REGULATION

Why has civil regulation grown? The growth of global civil regulation in part represents a political response to the recent expansion of economic globalization and the firms and industries that have fostered and benefited from it.[23] During the last two decades, the dynamics of economic globalization have significantly transformed the international economic landscape in two respects. First, they have shifted the locus of manufacturing from developed to developing countries. Second, the production and supply networks of global firms increasingly transcend national boundaries: most international trade is now among firms or interfirm networks, with the higher value-added components of the value chain primarily located in developed countries and the lower value-added portions in developing ones.

[20] David Vogel, *Lobbying the Corporation: Citizen Challenges to Business Authority* (New York: Basic Books, 1978).

[21] For a comparative overview of government efforts to promote CSR, see Susan Ariel Aaronson and James Reeves, *Corporate Responsibility in the Global Village: The Role of Public Policy* (Washington, DC: National Policy Association, 2002). For the role of European governments in promoting CSR, and the importance of CSR in Europe, see Francesco Perrini, Stafano Pogutz, and Antonio Tencati, eds., *Developing Corporate Social Responsibility: A European Perspective* (Cheltenham, UK: Edward Elgar, 2006). The role of governments in partnering with firms to support private business regulation is explored in more detail in Abbott and Snidal, "The Governance Triangle: Regulatory Standards Institutions and the Shadow of the State," this volume.

[22] For the growth and impact of CSR in Europe, see Andre Habisch, Jan Jonker, Martina Wegner, and Rene Schmidpeter, eds., *Corporate Responsibility Across Europe* (Berlin: Springer, 2005).

[23] See Gary Gereffi and Frederick Mayer, "Globalization and the Demand for Governance." Unpublished paper, June 2006.

The emergence of global civil regulation has been motivated by a widely held perception that economic globalization has created a structural imbalance between the size and power of global firms and markets, and the capacity and/or willingness of governments to adequately regulate them. According to this argument, economic globalization and the increased legitimacy and influence of neoliberal values and policies, has undermined both the willingness and capacity of governments to make global firms politically accountable. Accordingly, transnational corporations are said to "wield power without responsibility. They are often as powerful as states and yet less accountable."[24] Another critic observes: "Corporations have never been more powerful, yet less regulated."[25] Civil regulation proposes to fill the regulatory gap between global markets and global firms on the one hand, and government regulation of multinational firms on the other. It is intended to "compensate for the decreasing capacities of national governments for providing public goods [as] . . . internationalization yields an increasing gap between territorially bound regulatory competencies at the national level and emerging problems of international scope."[26]

The claim that the state is "in retreat" is contestable, as the scope and extent of business regulation continues to expand in many countries, as well as at the international level. But arguably the global economy is characterized by systemic regulatory failures or a structural "governance deficit."[27] As Abbott and Snidal argue in their contribution to this volume, the structure and scale of global production *has* challenged the existing capacities of governments to regulate the growing share of business activities that take place beyond their borders.[28] There are four important ways in which additional or more effective government controls over global firms and markets could address many, if not all, the criticisms of economic globalization. *It is the inability or unwillingness of states to adopt or enforce them that has contributed to the development and growth of non-state-based governance institutions.*

The first potentially important public policy mechanism is trade policy. Developed countries with relatively stringent and extensive domestic

---

[24] Peter Newell, "Environmental NGOs and Globalization," in Cohen and Rai, *Global Social Movements*, 121.

[25] J. Vidal, quoted in ibid.

[26] Christoph Knill and Dirk Lehmkuhl, "Private Actors and the State: Internationalization and Changing Patterns of Governance," *Governance* 15, no. 1 (January 2002), 42, 44.

[27] The phrase is from Peter Newell, "Managing Multinationals: The Governance of Investment for the Environment," *Journal of International Development* 13, no. 7 (2002), 908.

[28] Abbott and Snidal, "The Governance Triangle: Regulatory Institutions and the Shadow of the State," this volume.

product and production standards could, in principle, restrict imports of products produced by "irresponsible" labor or environmental practices, or from countries with poor records on human rights, while rewarding countries with better practices with preferential market access. Some governments have in fact done so. For example, the United States has restricted imports of both tuna and shrimp harvested in ways that violated American animal protection standards. Both the United States and the European Union have imposed restrictions on trade with Burma because of its human rights policies, while the United States has restricted American investments in the Sudan. Both the European Union and the United States have extended preferential trade privileges to countries with stronger domestic labor and environmental standards and human rights practices.[29] However, the cumulative impact of trade policy as either a carrot or a stick to strengthen the regulations of developing countries remains limited, in part because few western governments have been willing to effectively link trade liberalization to improvements in the regulatory practices of their trading partners. Although several recent bilateral trade agreements entered into by the United States do incorporate linkages to labor and environmental standards, their provisions have been poorly enforced.

Moreover, the rules and rulings of the WTO constrain the ability of governments to link trade liberalization to domestic social and environmental practices—even if more were willing to do so.[30] As many critics of the WTO have noted, there is a clear imbalance between the scope of the WTO's jurisdiction over domestic policies that protect producers and those that regulate them. WTO rules and rulings require signatory countries to adequately protect intellectual property rights, to not discriminate against "like products," to avoid technical barriers to trade, and in some cases to demonstrate scientific justification for nontariff barriers to trade. But WTO rules do not permit a nation to restrict imports if its trading partners do not protect domestic working conditions, human rights, or the quality of its domestic environment.

WTO rules could certainly be changed to more closely link global trade liberalization to domestic environmental, labor, or human rights

---

[29] See Emilie M. Hafner-Burton, "Trading Human Rights: How Preferential Trade Agreements Influence Government Repression," *International Organization* 59, no. 3 (Summer 2005), 593–629; Der-Chin Jorng, "The Human Rights Clause in the European Union's External Trade and Development Agreements," *European Law Journal* 9, no. 3 (December 2003), 677–701; and Susan Aaronson and Jame Zimmerman, *Trade Imbalance: The Struggle to Weight Human Rights Concerns in Trade Policymaking* (Cambridge: Cambridge University Press, 2008).

[30] See Ken Conca, "The WTO and the Undermining of Global Environmental Governance," *Review of International Political Economy* 7, no. 3 (Autumn 2000), 484–494.

practices.[31] Many western activists have strongly supported such a change in WTO rules, and, in the case of labor standards, so have many western labor unions. Domestic firms facing competition from less expensive imports from developing countries have also supported extending the legal basis for trade restrictions. But global firms have strongly opposed such linkages on the grounds that it would raise their costs and disrupt their supply chains. Equally important, many developing countries regard efforts to link their access to western markets to their domestic environmental, human rights, or labor practices as a disguised form of protectionism. To date, the preferences and influence of MNCs and developing-country governments have prevented a change in WTO rules that would link trade liberalization with the improvement of national environmental, labor, and human rights practices.

A second way in which governments could more effectively control the conduct of global firms and ameliorate the negative social impacts of global markets is by expanding the scope and improving the effectiveness of international regulations. While scores of environmental treaties exist, they still cover a relatively small portion of global trade and production. Most include few enforcement provisions and many of those that do are poorly enforced. Moreover, the adoption of additional international environmental agreements has often proven difficult. For example, the International Tropical Timber Organization has refused NGO requests to adopt a forest certification and labeling system, largely due to opposition from developing countries.[32] When former U.S. Secretary of Labor Robert Reich proposed that the ILO develop a system for labeling garments based on the labor conditions under which they were produced, his initiative was strongly criticized by representatives from developing countries, and it was not adopted. Compliance with the ILO's labor standards is entirely voluntary, and this international treaty contains no enforcement mechanisms. To date, the scope of international human rights treaties does not extend to international firms.[33]

A legally enforceable international code of conduct for global firms has been under discussion in various international forums.[34] During the

[31] For some specific suggestions as to what these changes would look like, see Michael Trebilock, "Trade Policy and Labour Standards: Objectives, Instruments, and Institutions," in Kirston and Trebilock, eds., *Hard Choices, Soft Law*, 170–188.

[32] Ronnie Lipschutz, "Why Is There No International Forestry Law?" *UCLA Journal of Environmental Law and Policy* 19 (2000/2001), 155–192.

[33] For an analysis of how global firms might be made legally accountable for human rights, see Steven Ratner, "Corporations and Human Rights: A Theory of Legal Responsibility," *Yale Law Journal* (December 2001), 443–545; and David Kinley and Junko Tadaki, "From Talk to Walk: The Emergence of Human Rights Responsibilities for Corporations at International Law," *Virginia Journal of International Law* 44, no. 4 (2004), 1005–1015.

[34] See Kolk and van Tulder, "Setting New Global Rules? TNCs and Codes of Conduct."

1970s, the ILO, the UN Commission on Transnational Corporations, and the OECD all attempted to adopt legally binding codes of global corporate conduct; none of these efforts were successful. The OECD did adopt comprehensive guidelines for multinational corporations, but they are nonbinding. In 1992, the issue of transnational corporation (TNC) regulation was dropped from the agenda of the United Nations Conference on Environment and Development (UNCED), largely due to the strong opposition of global firms. For its part, the EU briefly considered adopting a legally binding "Code of Conduct for European MNCS Operating Abroad," but because of strong business opposition, it decided to make it voluntary. The dearth of legally binding standards for multinational firms also reflects a lack of international consensus about the content of such codes as well as how sanctions against noncompliant companies would be enforced.

A third way governments could better govern global business activity is to regulate more of the international behavior of global firms headquartered in their countries. The U.S. government has done so in one important policy area: the Foreign Corrupt Practices Act restricts the bribery of foreign government officials by American firms. Thanks to American pressures, in 1999 the OECD required all its members to impose similar restrictions. But two-thirds of the countries that signed this anti-bribery convention "have achieved little or no enforcement."[35] American law also restricts investments in some countries on either national security or human rights grounds. However, international law generally restricts the ability of home country governments to establish rules governing the conduct of the subsidiaries of global firms when they operate outside their borders.[36]

The fourth and most important way in which the negative impacts of economic globalization could be ameliorated is for developing countries themselves to enact and enforce laws to better protect the welfare of their citizens and their domestic environment. This certainly has been the historical pattern in developed countries, whose controls over business labor

[35] Hugh Williamson and Michael Peel, "Nations 'Shamed' over Bribery," *Financial Times*, June 27, 2006, 4. For an update, see Jose Angel Gurria, "Rich Must Set the Example in Bribery," *Financial Times*, September 3, 2006, 5.

[36] See Jennifer Zerk, *Multinationals and Corporate Social Responsibility: Limitations and Opportunities in International Law* (Cambridge: Cambridge University Press, 2006). There have been several attempts to use the American judicial system to hold global firms legally accountable for human rights abuses under the provisions of the 1789 Alien Torts Claims Act, but they have largely been unsuccessful. See, for example, Kerrie Taylor, "Thicker Than Blood: Holding Exxon Mobil Liable for Human Rights Violations Committed Abroad," *Syracuse Journal of International Law and Commerce* 31, no. 2 (2004), 273–297.

and environmental practices became progressively stronger as they industrialized and extended the franchise. Presumably, many developing countries will eventually adopt similar regulations for both foreign and domestic firms that sell or produce within their borders as these countries become more affluent and their governments more democratic and accountable. Some are already doing so, but many are not. In most cases, the problem is not so much the lack of regulations, but the inability or unwillingness of governments to adequately enforce them.

Moreover, these governments often face trade-offs. For example, many fear that tighter or better enforced domestic labor or environmental standards would restrict foreign investment or outsourcing by geographically mobile MNCs, thus reducing much needed capital inflows and domestic employment. Equally important, some developing-country governments restrict or discourage civic organizations, such as independent trade unions, that could play an important role in making both foreign and domestic firms more politically accountable. In the case of "failed states," public authority itself is problematic: many governments, including those in countries with substantial natural resources, lack the capacity and in many cases, any interest, in protecting the welfare of their citizens.

In sum, regulatory failures at the global and national levels are pervasive, in large measure because both global firms and national governments have been either unable or unwilling to develop adequate mechanisms to effectively govern the social and environmental dimensions of global commerce. The growth of civil regulation reflects an effort to *extend* regulation to a wide range of global business practices for which the scope or effectiveness of national and international government authority currently is weak, limited, or nonexistent due to the political influence of global firms in developed countries and the preferences of developing-country governments and/or their domestic producers.[37]

THE POLITICAL DEMAND FOR CIVIL REGULATION

The fact that there are numerous regulatory failures with respect to many important global business activities does not necessarily mean that new mechanisms will emerge to address it. As the introductory chapter to this volume argues, the development of new global regulatory arrangements also requires "public entrepreneurs" who are capable of defining and asserting the interests of previously underrepresented political constituen-

[37] For a comprehensive analysis of the growth of civil regulation in the context of a global governance deficit, see Mathias Koenig-Archibugi, "Transnational Corporations and Public Accountability," *Government and Opposition* no. 2–3 (2004), 234–259.

cies and persuading firms, governments, and international organizations to support new regulatory arrangements. In short, the demands for civil regulations must be accompanied by the willingness of organizations and institutions to supply them.

Where have civil regulations come from? Who has initiated them? The organizational or institutional sources of civil regulations vary widely.[38] They include NGOs such as the World Wildlife Fund, Greenpeace, the Clean Clothes Campaign, Amnesty International, the Council on Economic Priorities, and Oxfam; trade associations for coffee, chemicals, mining, apparel, electronics, toys, and cocoa; trade unions such as the International Textile Workers Association; and international standards bodies such the International Standards Organization. Some civil regulations have been established with the support of governments or interstate organizations. For example, the United Nations Environmental Program helped establish the Electronics Industry Code of Conduct, the British and American governments worked with firms in extractive industries to develop Voluntary Principles on Security and Human Rights, the Fair Labor Association emerged from an initiative of the American government, and the Austrian government supported the development of the Forest Stewardship Council. However, states have not participated in the enforcement of these regulations, which remain voluntary. Rather, they have primarily served as facilitators, bringing firms and, in some cases, labor unions and NGOs together, helping them agree on common standards and, in some cases, providing civil regulatory organizations with initial funding.

This in turn poses two additional questions: what has motivated NGOs, governments, and international organizations to promote civil regulations, and why have many firms agreed to adopt or accept them? The motivation for western NGOs is straightforward: they regard civil regulations as an important source of leverage over global business activity. The international impact, and thus the potential leverage, of many large western firms are substantial. Changing the procurement policies and practices of firms such as Wal-Mart, Starbucks, and Home Depot would have major global social and environmental impacts—comparable

---

[38] For detailed case studies of the political and institutional development of codes in the apparel and timber sectors, see Tim Bartley, "Institutional Emergence in an Era of Globalizations: The Rise of Transnational Private Regulation of Labor and Environmental Conditions," *American Journal of Sociology* 113, no. 2 (2007), 297–351; and Tim Bartley, "Certifying Forests and Factories: States, Social Movements, and the Rise of Private Regulation in the Apparel and Forest Products Fields," *Politics and Society* 3, no. 3 (September 2003), 433–464. For forestry, see Lors Gulbrandsen, "Overlapping Public and Private Governance: Can Forest Certification Fill Gaps in the Global Forest Regime?" *Global Environmental Politics* 4, no. 3 (May 2004), 75–99.

to if not greater than that of many national regulations. At the same time, many NGOs have been repeatedly frustrated by their inability to strengthen international treaties. Thus, for global activists, lobbying corporations has come to represent a viable, though clearly second-best, alternative to pressuring for changes in public policies.[39] While some NGOs continue to emphasize the "naming and shaming" of global firms, others have chosen to cooperate with firms and industry associations to develop voluntary standards and participate in their enforcement. Their willingness to enter into alliances with global firms has been critical to the emergence, legitimacy, and relative effectiveness of many civil regulations.[40]

As noted above, some western governments, especially in Europe, have played an important role in promoting civil regulations. Several European governments have indirectly promoted CSR by requiring companies that trade on their stock exchanges to issue annual reports on their social and environmental practices and encouraging, or in some cases, requiring, public pension funds to consider corporate social and environmental practices in making investment decisions. The procurement policies of some governments give preference to privately certified products. For its part, the EU has been a strong supporter of global CSR.[41] Many aspects of civil regulation are consistent with the European approach to business regulation: the EU and many European governments make extensive use of voluntary agreements and soft regulation and frequently rely on private organizations to develop regulatory standards.[42] For many European governments, promoting global civil regulations represents a way of responding to pressures from domestic activists and trade unions, many of which are hostile to economic globalization, in a world whose dominant neoliberal institutions and doctrines, as well as the pressure of

[39] For examples of an earlier version of this strategy among American NGOs, see David Vogel, *Lobbying the Corporation*; and *Citizen Challenges to Business Authority*.

[40] See Philipp Pattberg, "The Institutionalization of Private Governance: How Business and Nonprofit Organizations Agree on Transnational Rules," *Governance* no. 4 (October 2005), 589–610; Gereffi, Garcia-Johnson, and Sasser, "The NGO-Industrial Complex," 589–610; and Dennis Rondinelli and Ted London, "How Corporations and Environmental Groups Cooperate: Assessing Cross-sector Alliances and Collaborations," *Academy of Management Executive* 17, no. 1 (2003), 61–76.

[41] On the EU's role, see, for example, Kristina Herrmann, "Corporate Social Responsibility and Sustainable Development: The European Union Initiative as a Case Study," *Indiana Journal of Global Legal Studies* 11, no. 2 (2004), 205–232.

[42] See, for example, Michelle Egan, *Constructing a European Market* (Oxford: Oxford University Press, 2001); Christian Joerges and Ellen Vos, eds., *EU Committees: Social Regulation, Law and Politics* (UK: Hart Publishing 1999); Jonathan Golub, ed., *New Instruments for Environmental Policy in the EU* (London: Routledge, 1998); and Christopher Ansell and David Vogel, eds., *What's the Beef? The Contested Governance of European Food Safety* (Cambridge, MA: MIT Press, 2006).

global competition, constrain their ability to expand legal controls over global firms.

In this context, an important advantage of civil regulations as a global regulatory vehicle is that their provisions are not currently governed by the WTO, whose rules only apply to regulations formally adopted by governments.[43] For example, while state eco-labels are regarded by the WTO as (potential) technical barriers to trade, private product labels and certifications are not.[44] Likewise, firms can demand adherence to labor and environmental standards by their global suppliers as a condition for doing business with them; governments generally cannot make such requirements a condition for market access. This means that foreign producers who have been disadvantaged by private regulations or standards have no legal remedy: they must comply with them or risk losing export markets. The reliance of civil regulations on private, market-based standards and enforcement thus represents a major "loophole" in international trade law—one that civil regulation has exploited.

For the UN, the Global Compact provides it with a vehicle to address some of the criticisms of the social impact of economic globalization voiced by many activists and some developing countries—without engaging in the more controversial challenge of enacting legally binding business regulations. The voluntary CSR standards adopted by the OECD and promoted by the World Bank follow a similar logic. These organizations primarily affect governmental policies through soft law; civil regulations essentially extend this same regulatory approach to corporations. The same dynamic holds for the ISO, whose development of ISO 14001, an environmental process standard, flowed from the recent focus of this international standards body on process standards.

What about corporations? In some cases, industries have adopted or accepted private global regulations to avoid additional government regulation. For example, Responsible Care was adopted by several national chemical industry associations in part to forestall national laws establishing more stringent plant safety standards following the chemical plant explosion at Bhopal, India in 1984. An international "Code of Pharmaceutical Marketing Practices" was developed by global drug firms as a response to the imminent threat of public regulation at the international level, including by the World Health Organization.[45] The International

---

[43] For an extensive discussion of this issue, see Steven Bernstein and Erin Hannah, "Non-State Global Standard Setting and the WTO: Legitimacy and the Need for Regulatory Space." Unpublished paper, March 2006.

[44] For an extensive discussion of both private and public social and environmental labels and their role in the global economy, see *Informing Consumers of CSR in International Trade* (Paris: OECD, 2006).

[45] Karsten Ronit and Volker Schneider, "Global Governance through Private Organizations," *Governance* 12, no. 3 (July 1999), 252.

Chamber of Commerce's Business Charter for Sustainable Development was initiated by global firms who feared that the 1992 Rio "Earth Summit" would lead to an expansion of global environmental regulations. The global confectionary industry adopted a code of conduct governing forced child labor in part as a response to the threat of American trade sanctions on imports of cocoa from West Africa. During the 1990s, many highly visible apparel producers and retailers endorsed voluntary international labor standards in order to secure congressional support for the renewal of China's most favored nation status as a trading partner.

As noted above, business opposition has played a critical role in preventing western governments and international agreements from more effectively regulating global firms. But typically, firms have not agreed to accept civil regulations to avoid additional government regulation as there has been little prospect of additional regulations being enacted, let alone enforced, especially at the global level or by developing countries. Nike, for example, did not agree to improve health and safety conditions in its factories in Vietnam because it wanted to prevent the government of Vietnam from strengthening its own occupational and safety standards. The more than 3,500 firms who have signed onto the UN Global Compact did not do so in order to prevent the UN from adopting legally binding regulations for global corporations since there was no likelihood that it would do so.

Why, then, have an increasing number of global firms and industries accepted the legitimacy of voluntary regulations? Most civil regulations have their origin in citizen campaigns directed against particular companies, industries, and business practices.[46] Such campaigns have proliferated over the last decade, focusing on such issues as working conditions and wages, child labor, the income of agricultural workers, unsustainable forestry practices, business investments that support corrupt governments, and natural resource developments that adversely affect human rights and environmental quality. These public campaigns of "naming and shaming" have been directed at highly visible European and American-based firms such as Nike, Home Depot, Shell, Ikea, C & A, Gap Inc., Tiffany & Co., Nestlé, Starbucks, Hennes & Mauritz, Rio Tinto, Freeport Mining, and Citibank, which then became public symbols of "corporate irresponsibility." Such widely publicized demonstrations of corporate ir-

---

[46] For an analysis of activist targets and strategies, see Tim Bartley and Curtis Child, "Shaming the Corporation: Reputation, Globalization, and the Dynamics of Anti-Corporate Movements," Working paper, Department of Sociology, Indiana University, 2007; and Dara O'Rourke, "Market Movements: Nongovernmental Organization Strategies to Influence Global Production and Consumption," *Journal of Industrial Ecology* 9, no. 1–2 (2005), 115–129. See also Naomi Klein, *No Logo* (London: Flamingo, 2001).

responsibility have played a critical role in placing political pressures on global firms to act more "responsibly." Indeed, for many global firms CSR stands for "Crisis Scandal Response."

Few of these public campaigns, even when accompanied by product boycotts, adverse media coverage, and pressures from socially concerned investors, have adversely affected either the sales or share prices of targeted firms.[47] Nevertheless, many firms have chosen to respond to them by either adopting industry self-regulations or participating in multistakeholder codes involving NGOs. Their motives are complex. Firms that market to consumers are particularly risk adverse as they are especially vulnerable to public criticisms that might adversely affect the value of their brands. "NGOs have become highly sophisticated in using market-campaigning techniques to gain leverage over recalcitrant firms" that sell directly to consumers.[48] For targeted firms, investing some resources to comply with civil regulations makes obvious business sense, while for firms that have not yet been targeted, accepting voluntary standards regulations reduces the likelihood that they will also be targeted.

But even some global firms that do not market to consumers are concerned about their reputations: they value public approval and dislike negative media attention. For many global firms, CSR has become a component of their risk management policies and their marketing, public, employee, and investor relations. In some cases, the values and concerns of critics of economic globalization are personally shared by some executives, particularly those who manage corporations whose traditions and cultures have historically emphasized a strong commitment to corporate responsibility. Some firms have also developed or agreed to accept civil regulations in response to pressures from employees or prospective employees.[49]

This in turns raises a more interesting question. Why don't firms simply adopt their own codes of conduct? Why do they frequently encourage the formation of, or endorse, civil regulations that also govern their competitors? The two are not incompatible; many large global firms have also adopted their own regulations, and in some cases, these go beyond industry standards. But for "targeted" firms, industry-wide regulations make business sense. Adopting higher social or environmental standards can raise a firm's costs, while persuading their competitors to adopt similar standards creates a more level playing field. Moreover, the public often does not distinguish among the social or environmental practices of firms

---

[47] See Vogel, *The Market for Virtue*, chapter 3: "What Is the Demand for Virtue?"

[48] Gereffi, Garcia-Johnson, and Sasser, "The NGO-Industrial Complex," 64.

[49] C. B. Battacharya, Sankar Sen, and Daniel Korschun, "Using Corporate Social Responsibility to Win the War for Talent," *MIT Sloan Management Review* (Winter 2008), 37–44.

in the same industry. For example, in the fine jewelry industry, when some diamond retailers were accused of selling "blood diamonds" sold by warlords in conflict zones, the reputation of the entire industry was damaged.

In addition, "herd effects" play an important role in disseminating many management practices.[50] Accordingly, when an industry leader agrees to a voluntary code, other firms in its sector often decide that they should do so as well. This dynamic also operates across industries. The greater the number of global industries that agree to develop or accept voluntary codes, the more likely it is that other industries will follow their example. The growth of civil regulations among global firms and industries has thus created its own momentum: few global firms or industries headquartered in the United States or Europe want to be regarded as less "responsible" or "enlightened" than their peers. As the *Financial Times* observed in describing the growth of industry-wide social standards, "Industries seek safety in numbers."[51]

Finally, changes in norms can affect policy preferences. What begins as a primarily defensive response or largely rhetorical commitment can, over time, become viewed as legitimate. "Corporate preferences are driven in part about norms about the appropriate approaches to [managing] a business."[52] For many highly visible global firms, engaging in various forms of global CSR, including having a CSR office, issuing a CSR report, cooperating with NGOs, and agreeing to one or more voluntary industry codes, has become an accepted part of managing a global firm in a more politicized and transparent global economy.[53] As non-state governance systems become more institutionalized, corporate motivations to participate in them have shifted from a "logic of consequences" to a "logic of appropriateness."[54] The growth of civil regulation has not reduced the importance firms place on profit-maximization; rather, many global firms have now concluded that it is now in their interest to profess their commitment to "good global corporate citizenship" by subscribing to a private regulatory code.

[50] Marvin Lieberman and Sgigeru Asaba, "Why Do Firms Imitate Each Other?" *Academy of Management Review* 31, no. 2 (2006), 366–385.

[51] Alison Maitland, "Industries Seek Safety in Numbers," *FT Responsible Business, Special Report,* November 18, 2005, 1.

[52] Haufler, "Self-Regulation and Business Norms: Political Risk, Political Activism," 201.

[53] For a discussion of the importance of changes in business norms, see Kelly Kollman, "The Regulatory Power of Business Norms: A Call for a New Research Agenda." Unpublished paper, (2006); Claire Moore Dickerson, "How Do Norms and Empathy Affect Corporation Law and Corporate Behavior? Human Rights: The Emerging Norm of Corporate Social Responsibility," *Tulane Law Review* (June 2002), 26–40; and ibid.

[54] Steven Bernstein and Benjamin Cashore, "Can Non-state Global Governance Be Legitimate: An Analytical Framework," *Regulation & Governance* 1, no. 4 (2007), 349.

In sum, the growth of civil regulation has stemmed from a multiplicity of factors, each of which has contributed to expanding existing regulatory arrangements governing global firms and markets. Demonstration effects have been critical: the last fifteen years have witnessed a steady stream of widely publicized allegations that have effectively dramatized numerous negative externalities associated with the failures of governments at both the national and international levels to adequately protect the global environment, the welfare of workers, and human rights. But while public outrage may be a necessary condition for creating regulatory change, it is not a sufficient one. Accordingly, a critical role has been played by NGOs whose anti-corporate campaigns have creatively taken advantage of the vulnerability of global firms to threats to their public reputation and the value of their brands. Playing a role similar to that of public interest groups and Green political parties at the national level, these organizations have effectively mobilized the diffuse interests of those adversely affected by the shortcomings of existing regulatory mechanisms. Their efforts to create new forms of business regulation have been often supported by foundations, trade unions, social movements, and in some cases, governments.[55]

To protect their reputations and enhance the credibility of their public commitment to CSR, many industries have either adopted their own standards or entered into alliances or partnerships with NGOs to establish new regulatory standards. What was originally largely a defensive response to public criticism has in many cases been transformed into a change in norms as civil regulation has become recognized as increasingly legitimate. Finally, in some cases, voluntary regulations have been supported by national governments and international organizations, who regard them as a politically acceptable strategy for ameliorating some of the negative social and environmental impacts of economic globalization and to enable its benefits to be distributed more fairly—without enacting legally binding regulations.

THE EFFECTIVENESS OF CIVIL REGULATIONS

Under what conditions have civil regulations been effective in addressing the regulatory and market failure they were established to address? A useful way of beginning to answer this critical question is to examine a few important case studies of civil regulations. This section looks at three categories of civil regulations—those that have been relatively effective,

[55] Bartley, "Institutional Emergence in an Era of Globalization."

those whose impact has been mixed, and those that have been relatively ineffective in achieving their professed goals—and then seeks to explain these variations.

Relatively Effective Civil Regulations: "Conflict Diamonds" and Labor Practices in Cambodia

Two of the most important accomplishments of civil regulation have been to significantly reduce international trade in "conflict or blood diamonds" and to strengthen labor standards in the textile export sector in Cambodia. The issue of "conflict diamonds" first emerged during the late 1990s in connection with the civil war in Angola.[56] In 1998, at the request of the UN, Portugal, Russia, and the United States, the UN Security Council voted to prohibit the purchase of rough diamonds from UNITA, a rebel group, as their proceeds were being used to finance its civil war against the government of Angola. Similar trade restrictions were subsequently extended to diamonds from another conflict zone, Sierra Leone. In 2000, the U.S. Congress passed the Clean Diamond Trade Act, which prohibited the import of "blood diamonds" from conflict zones. While both De Beers, which dominates the global diamond market (and which withdrew from Angola under pressure in 1999) , and Tiffany & Co., a major diamond retailer, indicated their full support for these measures and declared that they did not deal in conflict diamonds, several NGOs expressed concern that their systems for monitoring the sources of diamond purchases was flawed.

Both De Beers and diamond retailers had an important reputational stake in assuring the public that they were not selling irresponsibly produced diamonds. In the case of De Beers, there was an additional motivation: their business strategy rests on controlling the supply of diamonds, which meant that the marketing of "conflict diamonds" threatened both their reputation *and* their quasi-monopolistic control of the global diamond market. In 2000, a joint resolution by an association of international diamond retailers declared a zero tolerance policy for trading in conflict diamonds and announced that any firm found to be doing so would be expelled from the World Diamond Council.

That same year, the Republic of South Africa launched the Kimberley Process (KP), named after the mining town at the heart of diamond production in the nineteenth century. KP brings together the world's major diamond producers and retailers, as well as diamond exporting and importing countries, seventy of whom have signed this agreement. KP has

---

[56] Carole Kantz, "The Power of Socialization: Engaging the Diamond Industry in the Kimberly Process," *Business and Politics* 9, no. 3 (2007), Article 2: 1–20.

established a certification system which requires that all countries that trade or produce diamonds must issue certificates of origin that guarantee that the diamonds do not come from a conflict zone. While compliance by diamond exporting countries is not mandatory, each country that has endorsed the KP has agreed to on-site monitoring. The KP has expelled some countries for noncompliance, which effectively bans their diamond exports from states that have endorsed the KP—a trade restriction for which the WTO has granted a waiver.

Most diamonds are not individually certified; rather, bags of them are certified by and in the countries in which they are produced. The process is far from perfect, since some noncertified diamonds are smuggled into KP member countries, mixed with legitimate stones, and then re-exported. The existence of gaps in the enforcement of the KP means that illicit rough diamonds still find their way into global markets. Nonetheless, according to the KP, its members account for 99.8 percent of all diamond production, though other estimates place the percentage of certified diamonds somewhat lower.[57] But on balance, the KP has made substantial progress in addressing a major deficit in global economic governance. Equally important, its effectiveness appears to be steadily increasing as monitoring and enforcement are improving and the level of civil conflict in African diamond-producing countries has declined. Accordingly, "KP stands as a positive example of active cooperation between governments, non-governmental organizations and the private sector."[58]

Labor relations in Cambodia provide a second example of a relatively effective civil regulation. Improving working conditions in factories supplying products for western retailers and manufactures has emerged as a major focus of civil regulation. Over the last decade, scores of private codes governing labor standards have been developed by global firms. Such codes primarily work through business-to-business markets: groups of western firms establish standards for policies such as child labor, overtime, gender discrimination, wages, and freedom of association and then monitor the adherence of their suppliers through periodic inspections.

While several of these codes appear to have made progress in reducing some abuses, most notably unsafe working conditions and the employment of child labor, effective and credible enforcement remains a serious problem, especially with respect to wages and forced overtime.[59] This is

[57] Nicol Degli Innocenti, "Time to Review the Monitoring System," *Financial Times*, July 17, 2006, 2.

[58] Nicol Degli Innocenti, "A Positive Example of Co-operations on Conflict Stones," *Financial Times*, June 28, 2005, 4. For more on the problems of conflict diamonds from the Ivory Coast, see Nicol Degli Innocenti, "Accord on Conflict Diamond Smuggling," *Financial Times*, November 16, 2005, 11.

[59] For a summary of the literature on the impact and enforcement of labor codes, see Vogel, *The Market for Virtue*, chapter 4: "Working Conditions in Developing Countries."

due to both the large number of suppliers and subcontractors in major sectors and the fact that western firms have conflicting incentives. They want to protect their reputations, but at the same time face competitive pressures to keep their costs as low as possible and to assure a rapid and continual flow of goods from their suppliers to retail outlets. While some firms have ended their contracts with suppliers who have violated their labor codes, their unwillingness to pay more for products produced by code-compliant contractors also constrains the ability of the latter to improve their labor standards.

Between 1994 and 1998, apparel exports from Cambodia grew from virtually zero to more than half a billion dollars. The success of this industry attracted the attention of American textile unions for two related reasons: the unions were concerned about reports of abusive working conditions, and they wanted to bring these exports under the American textile quota system in order to protect domestic employment. While the United States had previously entered into a number of trade agreements that provided for penalties unless appropriate labor standards were enforced, it had never established positive incentives for countries that did so. It now decided to employ an economic carrot: the United States agreed to increase Cambodia's annual textile quota, provided that the Cambodian government was able to ensure substantial compliance with national labor laws and internationally agreed labor rights by *all* its apparel factories.[60]

As the Cambodian government lacked any enforcement capacity, monitoring compliance presented a formidable problem. While several private organizations were already monitoring the labor practices of suppliers to western firms, their inspections lacked sufficient credibility to satisfy the American government. Accordingly, both the United States and Cambodia turned to the ILO, which for the first time agreed to establish a system for monitoring workplaces. (Previously, this intergovernmental organization had only reviewed the conduct of governments.) Financial support for the ILO was in turn provided by the American and Cambodian governments and western apparel firms. For its part, the ILO agreed to make the results of all its inspections public.

At the outset, supplier participation in the ILO inspection program was voluntary. This presented a serious free-rider problem, since nonparticipating firms faced lower costs, but enjoyed equal market access, as the American quota was awarded to the country as a whole. Subsequently, the Cambodian government agreed to limit exports to the United States

---

[60] Sandra Polaski, "Protecting Labor Rights through Trade Agreements: An Analytical Guide," *UC David Journal of Law & Policy* 10, no. 13 (2003), 13–25.

to those firms that agreed to participate in the monitoring program. Because all producers involved in the inspection program stood to suffer if any major violations were reported, all now had a common stake in adhering to the labor provisions of the trade agreement. The agreement essentially aligned the influence of the American government with the interests of the Cambodian government, local producers, and western retailers and manufacturers. The result was a measurable and cost-effective improvement in labor conditions in one of the world's poorest countries.

The U.S.-Cambodia Textile Agreement formally expired with the end of the multi-fiber agreement. Yet the regulatory systems it established remain in place. Significantly, many western firms, most notably Gap Inc., the largest purchaser of garments from factories in Cambodia, as well as Nike, continue to outsource from Cambodia, even though such products no longer receive preferential trade treatment. The fact that textile production in Cambodia has continued to increase demonstrates the importance of civil pressures for corporate accountability: those firms that continue to outsource from Cambodia presumably have a stake in maintaining responsible labor standards and a credible, transparent system for monitoring the compliance of their suppliers. The latter is particularly critical.

> If there is one aspect of the Cambodia monitoring program that can be singled out as indispensable to its success, it is the higher level of transparency that the ILO provided through its reports. . . . [The reports served a multiplicity of purposes in the hands of different actors and reinforced the common interests they shared.][61]

While some private labor regulations have become more transparent, few provide the detailed plant-by-plant disclosures of specific labor practices and conditions that characterize the work of the ILO in Cambodia. However, The Cambodian regulatory arrangement has yet to be effectively replicated in any other country, in part because no other country has been able to establish a credible system for monitoring supplier compliance. There have been negotiations among representatives of different labor codes to harmonize their standards in particular countries in order to improve the efficiency of monitoring and enforcement, but to date no such agreements have been reached.[62]

---

[61] Sandra Polaski, "Combining Global and Local Forces: The Case of Labor Rights in Cambodia," Global Economic Governance Programme Working Paper, 2005/13, (2005), 16.

[62] However, a pilot program has been developed in Turkey. "Gap Inc's Crusade Against Sweatshops," ICFAI case, Reference no. 707-048-1 (2006), 10.

Moderately Effective Civil Regulations: Fair Trade
and Forest Certification

In two other important cases of civil regulation, namely Fair Trade International (FTI) and the Forest Stewardship Council (FSC), the effectiveness of private global governance has been mixed. Both have attracted a significant number of business participants and have effective private compliance mechanisms. But when measured against the scope of global business activity in their respective sectors, their impact has been constrained by the limited number of producers who participate in them. Both FTI and FSC are market-based: they employ private labeling and certification to align the interests of western consumers with socially responsible global producers or exporters. Each represents a private response to a serious global governance deficit: the former seeks to ameliorate the impoverishment of farmers due to low global commodity prices, while the latter attempts to fill the regulatory gap created by the absence of an effective international forestry treaty.

In 1997, seventeen national Fair Trade certification programs in Europe, North America, and Japan established an international consortium, Fairtrade Labeling International. This organization certifies products produced in developing countries and then markets them to consumers in developed countries using the "Fair Trade" (FT) label. While this social label has been used to market several agricultural products, including bananas, cocoa, tea, flowers, oranges, nuts, sugar, chocolate, and most recently cotton, the most important ethical label is for coffee, an $80 billion industry and the world's second most widely traded commodity. The primary purpose of FT coffee is to increase the prices paid to farmers for this commodity, many of whose expenses barely cover the costs of production. FTI guarantees these farmers above world market prices for their products—a commitment that is financed by selling FT-labeled products at a premium price.

FTI exhibits both the strengths and weaknesses of consumer-based global governance. On one hand, there is a market for virtue: a growing number of consumers in the United States and Europe purchase FT coffee, often due to a sense of social commitment, and several coffee firms, such as Proctor & Gamble as well as coffee retailers such as Starbucks, offer FT coffee, among other kinds, to their customers. Cafedirect, which only sells FT coffee, is the sixth largest British coffee brand, and nearly one-fifth of the British ground and roast coffee market is FT.[63] Thirty-five thou-

---

[63] Margaret Levi and April Linton, "'Fair Trade' a Cup at a Time?" *Politics and Society* 31, no. 3 (2003), 419; Alan Beattie, "Follow the Thread," *Financial Times*, July 22/23, 2006, W1.

sand firms sell FT coffee in the United States and sales have tripled since 1999, making it the fastest-growing segment of the specialty or premium coffee business.[64] In 2005, 60 million pounds of FT coffee were imported by the United States.

On the other hand, the economic impact of FT is limited by consumer demand for its products. Consumers typically purchase products on the basis of price, convenience, and quality, not on whether they were produced "responsibly"; most consumers are happy to benefit from the lower costs of production in developing countries. While FT coffee has an important advantage compared to other ethically labeled products, namely, that it is not more expensive than other premium coffees, though it is more expensive than commodity coffee, it still occupies a niche market. FT certified coffee represents 2 percent of American coffee sales, and 3.5 percent in some European countries. Accordingly, while ethical labels have benefited some producers in developed countries, their overall redistributive impact remains limited.

Forestry regulation provides a second example of the strengths and shortcomings of market-based civil regulations. Frustrated by the failure of the 1992 Rio Summit to develop an effective international agreement governing forestry practices, a group of NGOs attempted to develop a private global forestry "treaty." Their efforts were supported by a number of foundations as well as the government of Austria, whose effort to develop a labeling standard for tropical forestry products was withdrawn following complaints from developing countries to the WTO. After several years of negotiations among foresters, scientists, and firms, the Forest Stewardship Council (FSC) was established in 1993, and began operations three years later. Arguably the most ambitious example of the "privatization of environmental governance," the FSC is an international private standard-setting body.[65] Its goal is to create a global market for wood harvested in a socially and environmentally sound manner. The FSC has developed standards for forestry management and accredits and monitors organizations that in turn carry out assessments of wood production practices. It then issues certificates that guarantee a chain of custody for wood products from certified forests to their end users.

---

[64] Jennifer Alserver, "Fair Prices for Farmers: Simple Idea, Complex Reality," *New York Times*, March 16, 2006, Business Section, 5. For a comprehensive analysis of the growth of ethical product certification including Fair Trade, see Michael Conroy, *Branded! How the "Certification" Revolution Is Transforming Global Corporations* (British Columbia: New Society Publishers, 2007).

[65] Benjamin Cashore, "Legitimacy and the Privatization of Environmental Governance: How Non-State Market-Driven (NSMD) Governance Systems Gain Rule-Making Authority," *Governance* 15, no. 1 (2002), 514. See also Cashore et al., *Governance through Markets*. More scholarly articles have been written on the FSC than on any other civil regulation.

While originally conceived as a product labeling scheme, relatively few wood products sold to consumers are actually labeled, largely because relatively few consumers value certification. Nor, in contrast to FT products, are consumers willing to pay a market premium for certified wood. Rather, as in the case of labor codes that certify producers in developing countries, FSC operates primarily in the business-to-business market. It relies on sales of certified wood products to retailers and builders, rather than to individual consumers, few of whom have ever heard of FSC. For firms such as Home Depot, the world's largest retailer of wood products, their willingness give preference to FSC certified products often represents a key component of their public commitment to CSR; many agreed to do so only after extensive grassroots pressures from activists, often accompanied by actual or threatened boycotts.

But many forestry firms regard FSC certification as too expensive and burdensome, especially given that certified products do not command a price premium from either retailers or builders. In large measure as a response to FSC, more than forty industry-dominated alternative certification schemes have been developed, and their requirements are generally less stringent than those of FSC, though many have gradually been strengthened.[66] In 2006, FSC's global market share of certified wood stood at 30 percent, while that of the two major industry-based and governed certification schemes totaled 57 percent.[67] Worldwide, 4 percent of all managed forests are FSC certified, accounting for 7 percent of the global forest-product market. This is an important accomplishment—the number of hectares of FSC certified wood grew from 500,000 in 1994 to more than 70 million in 2006, while between 1998 and 2006, the number of chain of custody certifications increased from 268 to 4,500.[68] However, virtually all FSC certified forests are located in temperate zones, and 84 percent of them are located in Europe and North America, where forestry practices were already extensively regulated by governments.

FSC may well have improved the social and environmental management of temperate forests, especially in Europe and North America. But the most egregious forestry management practices are taking place in tropical forests, only 2.4 percent of which are certified by the FSC or any other private certification scheme. The limited geographic scope of private forestry certification has seriously limited its ability to adequately address what is arguably the most critical forestry governance failure, namely,

[66] Errol Meidinger, "The Administrative Law of Global Private-Public Regulation: The Case of Forestry," *European Journal of International Law* 17, no. 1 (2006), 47–97.

[67] Philipp Pattberg, "The Influence of Global Business Regulation: Beyond Good Corporate Conduct," *Business and Society Review* 111, no. 3 (Fall 2006), 247.

[68] Ibid., 248.

the accelerating rate of tropical deforestation.[69] In fact, only 6–8 percent of global timber production is traded and most of this trade occurs between environmentally sensitive developed countries, rather than from developing countries to developed ones, thus weakening the international leverage of western firms and activists.[70]

Relatively Ineffective Civil Regulations: Curbing Corruption

One of the most critical governance deficits in the global economy involves the misuse by developing countries of the royalty payments received from extractive industries. These payments are often squandered by corrupt government officials and, as a result, many of the people living in countries with the most abundant deposits of oil, natural gas, and minerals are among the world's most impoverished.[71] In 2002, a global coalition of 200 NGOs launched a "Publish What You Pay" (PWYP) campaign to pressure global firms in extractive industries to reveal their royalty payments to host country governments.[72]

The results of this voluntary initiative have been disappointing.[73] Only seven global oil companies—all based in Europe or the United States—have agreed to disclose their payments, and not all have actually done so, largely due to the opposition of host country governments. For example, when British Petroleum (BP) announced that it would disclose its royalty payments to the government of Angola, that government threatened to terminate BP's exploration rights and it took two years of negotiations before a compromise was reached. An equally striking limitation of PWYP is the failure of any state-based global energy firm to endorse it, even though such firms, as well quasi-private energy firms based in the former Soviet Union and Asia, account for a growing share of foreign investments in this sector, especially in Africa.[74] As a result, governments that benefit from the misuse of royalty payments from natural resources

[69] See Peter Dauvergne, *Shadows in the Forest: Japan and the Politics of Timber in Southeast Asia* (Cambridge, MA: MIT Press, 1997); and *Loggers and Degradation in the Asia-Pacific* (Cambridge: Cambridge University Press, 2001).

[70] Philipp Patttberg, "The Forest Stewardship Council; Risk and Potential of Private Forest Governance," *Journal of Environment and Development* 14, no. 3 (September 2005), 366–367.

[71] See Erika Weinthal and Pauline Jones Luong, "Combating the Resource Curse: An Alternative Solution to Managing Mineral Wealth," *Perspectives on Politics* 4, no. 1 (March 2006), 35–43.

[72] "The Paradox of Plenty," *Economist*, December 24, 2005, 46–47.

[73] Peter Davis, "Extracting Transparency Promises," *Ethical Corporation* (May 2005), 35–36.

[74] See, for example, Andrew Yeh, "China Ventures on Rocky Roads to Trade with Africa," *Financial Times*, June 20, 2006, 2.

can continue to offer exploration or production concessions to global firms that have less demanding ethical standards.

The challenge faced by energy companies attempting to behave more responsibly in failed or highly corrupt states is illustrated by the experience of ExxonMobil in Chad. In 1998, an unprecedented agreement was reached among the government of Chad, one of the world's poorest countries, the World Bank, which helped finance ExxonMobil's $4.2 billion energy investment project, and several NGOs. Its terms provided that all royalty payments would be monitored: 10 percent would be held in trust, 80 percent earmarked for education, health, and rural development, 5 percent distributed to the oil-producing regions, and 5 percent to the central government.[75] The agreement was hailed as groundbreaking and a model for responsible energy development.

But in December 2005, the government of Chad decided to take advantage of increased oil prices by breaking its terms.[76] It took a portion of the funds held in trust for development and allocated them to military spending, and also demanded increased royalty payments. The terms of the agreement were subsequently renegotiated, providing the government of Chad with more control over oil revenues and in 2008, Chad severed its ties with the World Bank. Significantly, there has been no effort to establish similar programs in other countries, and for its part, ExxonMobil does not view the effort as a success. There is also no evidence that the agreement has improved the welfare of the citizens of Chad, which remains among the world's most corrupt countries and recently has faced increasing civil unrest. The Chad case illustrates an important limitation of global civil regulation, namely, the difficulty of promoting more responsible corporate practices when the objectives of civil regulations are opposed by host country governments.

There have also been other voluntary corporate initiatives to reduce corrupt payments. For example, concerned about numerous corruption allegations, forty-seven major global firms, representing $300 billion in global revenues, have signed a "zero-tolerance" pact against paying bribes.[77] But these firms represent only a small portion of MNCs, and their compliance with this pact is not independently monitored. For its part, the UN Global Compact has made eliminating corruption one of its ten key previsions, and along with the World Economic Forum, the

[75] Jerry Useem, "Exxon's African Adventure," *Fortune*, April 15, 2002, 102–114.

[76] Lydia Polgreen, "Chad Backs Out of Pledge to Use Oil Wealth to Reduce Poverty, *New York Times*, December 3, 2005, A15; and Chip Cummins, "Exxon Oil-Fund Model Unravels in Chad, *Wall Street Journal*, February 28, 2006, A4.

[77] Glenn Simpson, "Multinational Firms Unite to Fight Bribery," *Wall Street Journal*, January 27, 2005, A4, A8.

International Chamber of Commerce, and an NGO, Transparency International, it has established a private regulatory standard: Business Principles for Countering Bribery.[78] But it also lacks any enforcement mechanisms or provisions for independent auditing.

Notwithstanding the endorsement of the Global Compact by more than 3,500 firms and the nearly fifty global firms who have signed a "zero-tolerance" pledge, cases of corrupt payments by American and European firms continue to surface, though such payments are now more likely to be made public.[79] There is no evidence that the extent of such payments has declined.[80] The misuse of royalty payments by corrupt governments remains pervasive, as does the civil unrest such corruption often fosters. In short, the impact of these civil regulations on both business conduct and the citizens in developing countries whose welfare they were intended to enhance has been extremely modest, and, as a result, virtually all the regulatory and governance failures they were intended to ameliorate persist.

Explaining Relative Effectiveness

The growth of many civil regulations initially follows a roughly similar trajectory. First, a governance deficit is identified and second, one or more NGOs, firms, and/or governments then proposes a voluntary code to ameliorate it. These demonstration effects include abusive labor practices, the funding of civil conflict by international trade, economic hardships for coffee and other developing-country agricultural producers, irresponsible forestry practices, widespread corruption, and the misuse of royalty payments by developing-country governments.

Some global firms then initially agree to help establish or endorse a civil regulation that is designed to address this perceived governance deficit. These private-sector "CSR entrepreneurs" are often firms whose current policies or policy goals are already similar to those of the proposed code or who have been targeted by NGOs and thus support such regulations in order to make their CSR commitments more credible. It is at this point that the effectiveness of civil regulations begins to diverge. The first critical divergence emerges at the negotiation stage and is associated with the number of firms or producers that agree to be bound by a particular code.

---

[78] Jem Bendell and Jonathan Cohen, "Not Banking on Corruption," *The Journal of Corporate Citizenship* (May–June 2006).

[79] See, for example, Raymond Bonner and Jane Perlez, "Controller Charges Mining Company with Filing False Statements," *New York Times*, January 26, 2006, A6.

[80] Hugh Williamson, "West Failing to Curb Bribery Overseas," *Financial Times*, September 26, 2006, 5.

In the two most successful cases, all the relevant producers had a collective interest in supporting the terms of the proposed civil regulation, though it is important to note that Cambodia accounts for only a small share of global textile production. In the case of the KP, no other civil regulation has been endorsed by such a large share of global producers—a factor to which the economic concentration of the diamond export industry clearly contributed. FSC and FTI did attract a sufficient number of firms to have a discernible impact, but these still constitute a relatively small portion of relevant global producers. While the most stringent anti-corruption code, PWYP, has attracted very few corporate adherents, other weaker anti-corruption codes have been endorsed by relatively large numbers of global firms, though these still constitute only a relatively small proportion of global producers.

The benefits of the Cambodia labor agreement to both developing-country producers and western firms were relatively clear: they provided market access to the former and reputation benefits to the latter. Likewise, diamond exporters wanted continued global market access while diamond processors and retailers were anxious to protect the reputation and image of their luxury product. The business benefits of FSC were more mixed: it provided privileged market access for some forestry firms, but for most producers these benefits were not sufficient to encourage them to bear the additional costs of securing FSC certification, especially when they had less burdensome private regulatory alternatives. FLI did provide economic benefits to developing-country producers, but the lack of adequate consumer demand for certified products has limited the number of producers who have benefited from FLI certification.

The relatively large number of firms that have endorsed the various anti-corruption codes suggests that such codes did provide important benefits to many firms as well as offer a potential solution to the collective-action problem: many global firms based in countries with anti-corruption statutes and which face intense media scrutiny would clearly prefer not to pay bribes if they could be assured that their competitors would behave similarly. But this is not the case, especially as a growing number of multinational firms are based in countries where there is little domestic pressure to reduce corrupt payments.

However, the most important differences among codes emerge at the implementation, monitoring, and enforcement stages. What distinguishes the KP from many other global producer codes and the Cambodia agreement from other labor codes was the willingness of other actors, including national governments and international organizations, to actively participate in their implementation, monitoring, and enforcement. It is impossible to overstate the significance of this development. By making monitoring and enforcement credible and more effective, both the benefits of participation and the costs of noncompliance were enhanced. *The relative effectiveness of these civil regulations is in large measure due to the fact that they were embedded in agreements between or among governments.* Thus, private and public enforcement mechanisms complemented one another. In the case of the KP, countries can be expelled for contravention, making the KP highly distinctive and substantially contributing to its relative effectiveness. Similarly, the United States could deny market access if the ILO's labor standards were violated in Cambodia, as Cambodia was not then a WTO member. These state-backed enforcement mechanisms make these codes very atypical.

By contrast, no developed-country government has denied market access to products from countries that misuse their royalty payments, and their enforcement of their own anti-corruption statutes has been uneven. For their part, relatively few developing-country governments have been willing or able to either enforce anti-corruption policies or commit to using their royalty payments responsibly, notwithstanding the efforts of the Extractive Industry Transparency Initiative, an initiative launched by the British government in 2003 to promote the monitoring and responsible use of revenues from energy and mineral firms by host country governments. Elites in many countries, particularly those with substantial natural resources, continue to benefit from misusing their royalty payments, and paying bribes remains critical to doing business in many countries. This has significantly weakened the business benefits of compliance with anti-corruption and royalty disclosure agreements and explains why the civil regulation whose compliance can be independently monitored, namely PWYP, has attracted the least business support.

In the case of FTI and FSC, their standards appear to be relatively effectively monitored and enforced. In essence, both operate as nonprofit firms. They have developed a brand or certification standard that is both visible and valued, and which links a complex network of suppliers and retailers. As a result, numerous firms have a stake in effective monitoring and enforcement, and both organizations have developed sufficient resources and expertise to effectively regulate producers and distributors. Yet precisely because they rely exclusively on market incentives, a relatively small portion of global producers participate in them.

In sum, in all three categories of cases, both the business case for compliance and the establishment of effective monitoring and enforcement mechanism parallel one another, and together explain much of the divergence in their effectiveness. Both were strongest in the case of the KP and the Cambodia agreement and weakest in the case of the various anti-corruption civil codes, with FTI and FSC falling in between. On balance, civil regulations have been most successful at influencing agenda-setting; they have placed a wide array of global regulatory failures on the agenda of the international community. Many also have been relatively effective at the negotiation stage, persuading relatively large numbers of firms to subscribe to them. But for many civil regulations, implementation, and effective monitoring and enforcement represent a serious structural weakness.

CONCLUSION

The growth of global civil regulation and CSR has been both hailed as a highly promising solution to the shortcomings of state regulation and sharply criticized on the grounds that voluntary business regulations are inherently incapable of addressing market and regulatory failures—especially when these failures were created by global firms in the first place.[81] However, any realistic assessment of civil regulation should compare it not to an ideal world of effective global economic governance, but to actual policy alternatives. When compared to most government regulations in developed countries, civil regulation is clearly less effective. In fact, civil regulations exhibit many of the well-documented shortcomings of industry self-regulation at the national level, with whom they share many important characteristics.[82] Both remain weaker than well-enforced command and control regulations in changing corporate behavior.

But the effectiveness of civil regulations *is* roughly comparable to that of many intergovernmental treaties and agreements, many of which are also based on soft law and the "naming and shaming" of noncompliant countries; their effectiveness in improving environmental protection, labor practices, and human rights is also mixed and uneven.[83] In a number of cases, most notably with regard to labor standards and forestry, civil regulations, for all their shortcomings, have been considerably *more* effective than intergovernmental treaties. At the same time, their scope is much more limited as they primarily affect the way some products exported to highly visible western firms are produced.

---

[81] For the former, see, for example, Andrew Savitz, *The Triple Bottom Line: How Today's Best-Run Companies Are Achieving Economic, Social and Environmental Success—and How You Can Too* (San Francisco: Jossey-Bass, 2006). For the latter, see Lipschutz and Rowe, *Globalization, Governmentality and Global Politics.*

[82] See, for example, Michael Lenox and Jennifer Nash, "Industry Self-Regulation and Adverse Selection: A Comparison Across Four Trade Association Programs," *Business Strategy and the Environment* 12, no. 3 (2003), 343–356; *Voluntary Approaches for Environmental Policy: An Assessment* (Paris: OECD, 1999); and Richard Morgenstern and William Pizer, eds., *Reality Check: The Nature and Performance of Voluntary Environmental Programs in the US, Europe, and Japan* (Washington, DC: Resources for the Future, 2007).

[83] See, for example, David Victor, Kal Raustiala, and Eugene Skolnikoff, eds., *The Implementation and Effectiveness of International Environmental Commitments: Theory and Practice* (Cambridge, MA: MIT Press, 1998).

For all their shortcomings, civil regulations are undoubtedly *more* effective than the labor, human rights, and environmental regulations of many developing countries. For some developing countries, they constitute the *only* effective form of business regulation. The environmental, social, and human rights practices of firms in developing countries that either produce for global supply chains or are directly owned by western MNCs are frequently better than those of domestic producers, and this is largely due to the impact of global civil regulations. By providing a political vehicle for the export of more effective regulatory practices from developed to developing countries, civil regulation has played a role, albeit a limited one, in socializing economic globalization.

Civil regulations have challenged the capture of existing regulatory institutions described in the introductory chapter in this volume in three important ways. First, by creating private international standards for many processes and products, they have helped compensate for the failure of states to enact and/or enforce international treaties governing these products and processes. Second, through the expansion of soft law international standards governing MNCs, western governments have taken more responsibility for the conduct of their global firms outside their borders, thus challenging the dominance of multinational firms over their foreign economic policies. Third, private global labor, environmental and human rights standards have enabled western activists to bypass the governments of developing countries, many of whom have been unable or unwilling to regulate the conduct of global firms and their supply networks within their borders.

These three challenges to industry capture of existing regulatory institutions are not a panacea, but neither are they an unimportant component of global governance. By creating new expectations of global corporate conduct and by establishing new regulatory institutions to address them, civil regulations have *partially reduced* the governance deficits and regulatory failures that characterize many global firms and markets. If "accountability . . . implies that some actors have the right to hold other actors to a set of standards, to judge whether they have fulfilled their responsibilities in light of these standards, and to impose sanctions if they determine that these responsibilities have not been met," then civil regulations have made some global firms *more* accountable.[84]

What would it take to make civil regulation a more effective form of global economic governance? Two factors are critical in strengthening demand. First, the business case for compliance with civil regulations would need to become stronger.[85] For all the widespread and widely be-

---

[84] Grant and Keohane, "Accountability and Abuses of Power in World Politics," 29.

[85] For a critical assessment of the business case for CSR, see Vogel, *The Market for Virtue*, chapter 2: "Is There a Business Case for Virtue?"

lieved rhetoric about the "win-win" case for CSR, many developing-country producers regard the civil regulations imposed by western firms as a burden: meeting the requirements of western codes raises their costs, but does not increase the prices they receive. (FT branded products are a notable though clearly limited exception.) This means that such firms have every incentive to do as little as possible to accommodate the demands of their western contractors. Many have developed an adversarial relationship with private inspectors, and often seek to deceive them.[86]

A similar logic holds for western firms. They have accepted civil regulations for a variety of reasons, including public and peer pressures, changes in business norms, and in some cases a more sophisticated understanding of the basis for profitable business activities. But because the financial benefits of CSR remain for the most part either modest or elusive, few firms have integrated the standards of civil regulation into their core business practices. Many global CSR commitments and policies remain akin to corporate philanthropy or community or public relations, remaining on the periphery of their business strategies.[87] They typically represent more a form of insurance against public opprobrium than a source of competitive advantage. As long as more "responsible" global firms do not enjoy consistently stronger financial performance than their less responsible competitors, and to date they do not, the incentives of firms to invest substantial resources into complying with civil regulations will remain limited, and the incentive of some firms to free ride on industry codes will remain a serious problem.

In many global industries, a handful of highly visible firms based in North America and Western Europe have emerged as CSR leaders, making good faith efforts to comply with relatively high standards for respect of labor, environmental protection, and human rights, and often seeking to persuade other firms in their industries to behave more responsibly. But to the extent that many of their competitors are either less able or unwilling to effectively comply with the civil regulations to which they have nominally agreed, these firms' own efforts to behave more responsibly are constrained. Peer and public pressures have promoted business adoption of many civil regulations, but in most cases such pressures have not been an effective tool for promoting compliance with them. The growing economic prominence of MNCs based in non-western countries, who face fewer domestic pressures from NGOs and who have been less willing

---

[86] See, for example, Dexter Roberts and Pete Engardio, "Secrets, Lies and Sweatshops," *Business Week*, November 27, 2006, 50–58.

[87] See, for example, Michael Porter and Mark Kramer, "Strategy and Society: The Link between Competitive Advantage and Corporate Social Responsibility," *Harvard Business Review* (December 2006), 78–92.

to accept civil regulations, has also exacerbated the competitive challenges faced by more responsible western firms.

The second critical determinant of the future impact of civil regulation has to do with their relationship to governments. Some developing-country governments, such as Cambodia, recognize the value of civil regulation; others, such as Chad, do not. Unfortunately, the latter is more typical than the former: most developing countries tend to be indifferent to voluntary labor standards, and many are not supportive of codes that seek to reduce corruption. The KP is a notable exception, but that is primarily because it can be enforced by trade sanctions. In the case of FSC, the pattern is more mixed: some developing-country governments closely cooperate with its rules, while others are indifferent to them.[88] The laws of some countries, such as China, do not permit local firms to comply with labor codes that guarantee the right of workers to choose their own representatives, while some Central and Latin American countries have been unwilling or unable to protect independent labor organizations. In the long run, civil regulations must be more closely integrated into the domestic regulatory policies and the competitive strategies of developing-country governments if they are to become more effective.[89] Equally importantly, developing-country governments need to promote or at least permit the strengthening of civil society so that their citizens are able to define and defend their own social, political, and environmental interests vis-à-vis business firms, without having to rely on western activists to do so in their name.

The future effectiveness of, or demand for, effective civil regulations also depends on the policies of developed-country governments. As noted above, some western governments have assisted the development of civil regulations.[90] But there is much more they could do to improve the behavior of global firms. For example, they could make greater efforts to promote compliance by developing-country governments with the wide array of international treaties governing labor conditions and human rights that already exist as well as support legally binding standards for the conduct

[88] For an analysis of the critical importance of the local political and economic environment in affecting the willingness of firms to comply with civil regulations, see Ralph Espach, "When Is Sustainable Forest Sustainable? The Forest Stewardship Council in Argentina and Brazil," *Global Environmental Politics* 6, no. 2 (May 2006), article 3.

[89] For a discussion and analysis of how some developing countries are seeking to integrate civil regulation into their competitiveness strategies, see Simon Zadek, Peter Raymond, and Christano Olivera, *Responsible Competitiveness: Reshaping Global Markets' Responsible Business Practices* (Accountability, December, 2005). See also Alex MacGillivray, Johan Sabapathy, and Simon Zadek, *Aligning Corporate Responsibility and the Competitiveness of Nations* (Accountability and The Copenhagen Centre, December 2003).

[90] See note 21 above.

of global firms—both of which would "harden" public and private international soft law.[91] They could also impose global corporate reporting requirements, develop procurement policies that give priority to more globally responsible firms, establish voluntary but legally enforceable labeling requirements and certification standards, and provide financial assistance to strengthen the regulatory capacity of developing-country governments—as some countries have done. They could also support changes in trade rules that would integrate voluntary CSR initiatives into the WTO.[92] Until the world's developed countries are willing to more closely integrate the norms of civil regulations into their domestic laws and international relations, the global regulatory failures private social regulation was intended to redress will persist.

Voluntary business regulation has emerged as a response to the failures or shortcomings of existing legal mechanisms of regulatory governance in the global economy. Civil regulation has played a critical role in highlighting the ineffectiveness of existing state regulations and in persuading many firms that they have a responsibility to help ameliorate them. But ironically, many of the shortcomings of global economic governance are themselves due to the political influence of the very same global firms who, while often agreeing to adopt voluntary standards, have typically opposed stronger international treaties, extra-territorial business regulations, and links between trade liberalization and labor, environmental, and human rights practices. Global business activity can only become more effectively governed if the inadequacies of both government regulation *and* civil regulation are recognized by both firms and governments. The effectiveness of global business regulation ultimately depends on the extent to which private and public authority, civil and government regulation, and soft and hard law, reinforce one another.

---

[91] See "Noreena Hertz, "Corporations on the Front Line," *Corporate Governance* 12, no. 2 (April 2004), 202–209; and John Ruggie, "Business and Human Rights: The Evolving International Agenda," A Working Paper of the Corporate Social Responsibility Initiative, Harvard University, June 2007. For an excellent analysis of the legal challenges and opportunities of holding global firms legally responsible for CSR standards, see Jennifer Zerk, *Multinationals and Corporate Social Responsibility*. See also the references in note 33.

[92] For a wide range of creative proposals to achieve this, see Susan Ariel Aaronson, "A Match Made in the Corporate and Public Interest: Marrying Voluntary CSR Initiatives and the WTO," *Journal of World* Trade 41, no. 3 (2007), 629–659.

CHAPTER SIX

Racing to the Top . . . at Last: The Regulation of Safety in Shipping

Samuel Barrows

THE REGULATION of safety in shipping has increased dramatically over the past forty years. Although the industry has always been hazardous, as late as the 1960s there was little effective regulation. Today, nearly fifty international conventions and agreements exist, widely enforced by numerous regulators.

For centuries every ship has been obliged to register with and fly the flag of a state, which has then been responsible for its regulation. Until recently such regulation was extremely limited; however, in the 1970s, a number of major conventions were negotiated. In the 1980s, European states started to enforce these conventions for the ships visiting their ports, and in the 1990s, an increasing number of states began to apply these conventions to the ships on their registries. In recent years these developments have attracted the attention of international relations scholars.

These scholars have drawn heavily on the literature on "races to the top" and "races to the bottom" in analyzing these developments. Murphy, for example, identifies a "race to the bottom" and seeks to determine the characteristics of the shipping industry that explain this regulatory outcome.[1] DeSombre, in contrast, identifies a "race to the middle" and examines the effectiveness of different strategies in driving up regulatory standards.[2] No one, however, has sought to explain the timing of regula-

I am grateful to Miles Kahler, Nik Winchester, Ngaire Woods, and especially Walter Mattli for their excellent comments. I benefited greatly from discussions with John Astbury of the U.K. Maritime and Coastguard Agency, Agustín Blanco-Bazán of the International Maritime Organization, Angelo Mouzouropoulos of the International Merchant Marine Registry of Belize, as well as Donald Chard, William Gallagher, Andrew Meiklejohn, Tracy Murrell, and John Ramage. I also thank Inderjit Arora, Scott Bergeron, Michael Davies, Gary Hockham, Timothy Keegan, Tor Møinichen, David Pascoe, Chris Sawyer, and Bertrand Smith for their detailed correspondence. I gratefully acknowledge the financial support provided by St. John's College, Oxford.

[1] Dale Murphy, *The Structure of Regulatory Competition: Corporations and Public Policies in a Global Economy* (Oxford: Oxford University Press, 2004).

[2] Elizabeth DeSombre, *Flagging Standards: Globalization and Environmental, Safety, and Labor Regulations at Sea* (Cambridge, MA: MIT Press, 2006).

tory change. In the literature on races to the top and bottom, the process of globalization triggers regulatory change.[3] However, the shipping industry has been globalized for centuries and has seen extensive regulatory change in the past forty years. What explains this development?

In this chapter, I address this question drawing on Mattli and Woods' analytical framework. I begin by outlining the movement toward "public interest" that has taken place in shipping and also describe its limitations. I argue that an increasingly extensive institutional context at the supranational level has helped to bring about this change but is not sufficient to explain it. Demand-side factors have also played a crucial role. Disasters have triggered regulatory initiatives, and the emergence of a pro-change coalition has sustained the process of change. I identify the developments that have brought about this coalition and the roles that different entrepreneurs of regulatory change have played. Finally, I explain why there have been limitations to regulatory change.

The Development of Safety Regulation in Shipping

During the past forty years, an effective global regime for regulating safety in the shipping industry has emerged for the first time. The industry had previously remained largely unregulated for millennia, despite posing large and obvious risks.

In 1914, the first International Convention for the Safety of Life at Sea (SOLAS) set the agenda for regulating safety in shipping. It did not, however, come into force until 1933, and an organization was not created to implement it until the establishment of the International Maritime Organization (IMO) in 1948.[4] During this time, Honduras and Panama set up the first "open registries" and began to attract large numbers of ships.[5] Open registries, in contrast to national registries, accept ships with no connection to the state in terms of crewing or ownership.[6] Since Honduras

---

[3] See, for example, David Vogel, *Trading Up: Consumer and Environmental Regulation in a Global Economy* (Cambridge, MA and London: Harvard University Press, 1997), 3; and Miles Kahler, "Modelling Races to the Bottom." Paper presented at American Political Science Association, Boston, September 3–6, 1998, 2–3.

[4] John Braithwaite and Peter Drahos, *Global Business Regulation* (Cambridge: Cambridge University Press, 2000), 420.

[5] Rodney Carlisle, *Sovereignty for Sale: The Origins and Evolution of the Panamanian and Liberian Flags of Convenience* (Annapolis, MD: Naval Institute Press, 1981), 1, 132.

[6] In this chapter I use the term "open registry" rather than "flag of convenience" because there is considerable debate surrounding the definition of the latter. For a discussion of definitional issues, see Angelo Bergantio and Patrick O'Sullivan, "Flagging Out and International Registries: Main Development and Policy Issues," *International Journal of Transport Economics* 16, no. 3 (October 1999), 449–452; and Kevin Cullinane and Mark Robert-

and Panama had no connection to the ships on their registries, they failed to enforce any safety standards.[7] Thus, by the end of the 1960s, there was still little regulation of the shipping industry.

Major regulatory change first took place in the 1970s, when states negotiated several conventions, most notably the 1974 SOLAS convention, the International Convention for the Prevention of Pollution from Ships (MARPOL) (1973), and the International Convention on Standards of Training, Certification and Watchkeeping for Seafarers (STCW) (1978). These conventions were widely ratified, both by states with open registries and by traditional maritime states (industrialized states with historic national registries).[8] By the end of the 1970s, therefore, a comprehensive and widely accepted regulatory regime existed on paper. In practice, however, effective regulation remained limited. While traditional maritime states did apply the conventions they had ratified to the ships on their registries, enforcement by open registries remained ineffective. The IMO lacked the power to compel states to properly enforce conventions or to do so itself.[9]

In the 1980s, the new regulatory regime became increasingly effective as numerous states with ports (port states) began to implement, monitor, and enforce conventions. Although a flag state (a state with a shipping registry) is responsible for regulating the ships on its registry, states retain the right to inspect the ships visiting their ports and to detain them if they are not in compliance with conventions.[10] In 1982, seeing little sign of flag states exercising their responsibilities, fourteen European states adopted the Paris Memorandum of Understanding on Port State Control, which aimed to create a harmonized system of port state control (PSC).[11]

---

shaw, "The Influence of Qualitative Factors in Isle of Man Ship Registration Decisions," *Maritime Policy and Management* 23, no. 4 (1996), 322–325.

[7] Carlisle, *Sovereignty for Sale*, 139–141.

[8] See *www.imo.org/includes/blastDataOnly.asp/data_id%3D14744/9193.pdf*, accessed October 24, 2006.

[9] Joseph Vorbach, "The Vital Role of Non-Flag State Actors in the Pursuit of Safer Shipping," *Ocean Development and International Law* 32, no. 1 (2001), 31; see also International Commission on Shipping, *Ships, Slaves and Competition* (2000) (*www.icons.org.au/images/ICONS-fullreport.pdf*, accessed October 26, 2006).

[10] Kenneth Abbott and Duncan Snidal, "The Governance Triangle: Regulatory Standards Institutions and the Shadow of the State" (this volume), point out that "issues of extraterritorial jurisdiction limit the state's concern and effective reach." Shipping is unusual for a globalized industry in that, because ships enter states' waters and ports, issues of extraterritorial jurisdiction can to a degree be circumvented.

[11] PSC provides a good example of different regulatory schemes collaborating. PSC primarily enforces existing IMO standards, and the IMO has taken steps to support PSC; Keith Hindell, "Strengthening the Ship Regulating Regime," *Maritime Policy and Management* 23, no. 4 (1996), 373; www.imo.org/Safety/mainframe.asp?topic_id=159, accessed October 26, 2006. Abbott and Snidal, "The Governance Triangle" (this volume), identify a number of examples of collaboration between other regulatory standard-setting schemes.

Monitoring was carried out by inspecting a proportion of the ships visiting ports in the PSC region, and enforcement through the detention of ships that did not meet the standards required by conventions. While the effects of PSC were initially limited to ships sailing to the participating European states, PSC regimes now cover all of the world's oceans.[12] However, in developing regions they are largely ineffective. Furthermore, the 1980s saw the establishment in many developing states of new open registries with lax safety standards.

Regulation became even more effective in the 1990s as previously lax open registries began to implement, monitor, and enforce the conventions to which they were signatories. This extended the reach of conventions to many of the ships that did not sail to regions covered by effective PSC. To monitor compliance, registries increased the frequency and effectiveness of inspections of their vessels. They enforced conventions by fining deficient ships and, if they consistently failed to improve, expelling them. Belize, for example, imposed fines of up to $50,000 and expelled 40 percent of the ships on its registry.[13] However, as some open registries improved new ones were established, again based in developing states, to fill the lax niche left vacant.

In the terminology of Mattli and Woods' framework, the regulatory change outlined above constitutes a movement toward "public interest."[14] Prior to this change, the shipping industry was a paradigm of regulatory capture. Open registries, at the behest of shipowners, made no attempt to regulate their fleets.[15] In some cases, such as St. Vincent and the Grenadines, states contracted the management of their registries to private companies owned by the very shipowners who registered with them.[16] The resulting lax standards imposed huge costs on seafarers, civilians using

[12] Tokyo Memorandum of Understanding (1993), United States Coast Guard PSC Regime (1994), The Acuerdo de Vina del Mar (1992), Caribbean Memorandum of Understanding (1996), Mediterranean Memorandum of Understanding (1997), Indian Ocean Memorandum of Understanding (1998), Abuja Memorandum of Understanding (1999), Black Sea Memorandum of Understanding (2000), Riyadh Memorandum of Understanding (2004).

[13] Angelo Mouzouropoulos, Director General and Senior Deputy Registrar, International Merchant Marine Registry of Belize, interviewed in Belize City, September 6, 2006; see also Lloyd's List, January 16, 2002, 3.

[14] It is only by adopting a procedural understanding of public interest that I can unambiguously make this claim. There is considerable debate about whether stricter regulation in shipping is in the public interest in an idealist sense; see, for example, Daniel Mitchell, "The Threat to Global Shipping from Unions and High-Tax Politicians: Restrictions on Open Registries Would Increase Consumer Prices and Boost Cost of Government," Prosperitas 4, no. 3 (August 2004), 1–26.

[15] A state's fleet is all of the vessels on its registry.

[16] Tony Alderton and Nik Winchester, Flag State Audit 2003 (Cardiff: Seafarers International Research Centre, 2003).

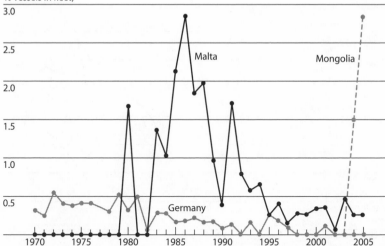

Figure 6.1. Overview of casualty rate trends, 1970–2005. Source: Casualty Return (1970–1995), World Casualty Statistics (1996–2005), Statistical Tables (1970–1992), World Fleet Statistics (1993–2005)

sea transport, and the populations of coastal states.[17] Yet these actors had little or no input into the regulatory process. During the past forty years, those affected by the negative externalities of the shipping industry have gained access to the regulatory process and have successfully demanded regulatory change.

Data provide clear evidence of the developments outlined above. Trends in the effectiveness of regulation can be observed in the casualty rates of three representative registries (see figure 6.1). A high casualty rate is indicative of lax safety regulation and a low casualty rate of effective regulation, though other factors can also affect a registry's casualty rate.[18] Germany, a traditional maritime state, has had a consistently low casualty

[17] For example, in 1967, the coastlines of southern England and Brittany were devastated when the *Torrey Canyon*, a Liberian flagged vessel, ran aground in the English Channel, spilling her entire cargo of 120,000 tons of crude oil. The cost of the cleanup alone has been estimated at £7.7 million, in 1967 prices, yet the British and French governments were only able to claim £3 million in compensation; Paul Burrows, Charles Rowley, and David Owen, "Torrey Canyon: A Case Study in Accidental Pollution," *Scottish Journal of Political Economy* 11, no. 3 (November 1974), 237–238, 242, 256.

[18] A registry's casualty rate, for a given year, is the total losses of vessels in its fleet as a percentage of its total fleet. Safety regulation is here defined as any piece of regulation that reduces the probability that a vessel in compliance with it will be recorded as a total loss in any given year.

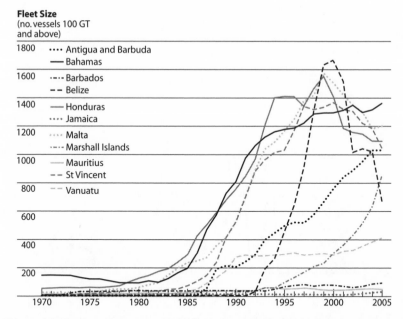

Fleet Size
(no. vessels 100 GT and above)

Figure 6.2. Improved open registry fleet sizes, 1970–2005. Source: Statistical Tables (1970–1992), World Casualty Statistics (1993–2005)

rate, which has declined further since the early 1980s.[19] Malta set up an open registry in the early 1980s. This registry initially had a high casualty rate, which subsequently declined. Mongolia recently established an open registry to fill the niche abandoned by states such as Malta. Its casualty rate is extremely high.

Data for fleet sizes show the growth of different types of registry. Figure 6.2 shows the growth of many open registries from the early 1980s onward, and a decline in their size from the late 1990s, as their standards improved. Figure 6.3 shows the second wave of open registries that have sprung up to fill the lax niche that the first group has abandoned.[20]

Data also show that the accounts of regulatory change put forward in the existing literature are incorrect. Murphy argues that "international

[19] Other traditional maritime states include France, the Netherlands, Norway, the United Kingdom, and the United States.

[20] In this chapter I take the International Transport Workers' Federation list of flags of convenience, as of August 2006, as the sample of open registries to be considered (www.itfglobal.org/flags-convenience/flags-convenien-183.cfm, accessed October 24, 2006). Whether a registry effectively enforces conventions is primarily assessed using casualty rate data. As this is unreliable for small fleets, I also used the *Shipping Industry Flag State Performance Table* (2003–2005) (www.marisec.org/flag-performance, accessed September 26, 2006); Alderton and Winchester, *Flag State Audit*; and detention statistics supplied by the European, Tokyo, and U.S. PSC regimes.

Fleet Size
(no. vessels 100 GT
and above)

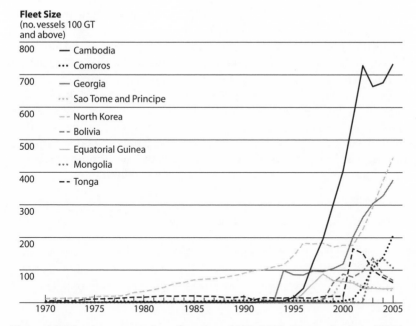

Figure 6.3. New lax open registry fleet sizes, 1970–2005. Source: Statistical Tables (1970–1992), World Casualty Statistics (1993–2005)

shipping offers an archetypal case of competition-in-laxity."[21] Yet the casualty rate of the world fleet fell by more than 75 percent from 1970 to 2005.[22] DeSombre argues that a "race to the middle" has taken place, with traditional maritime states establishing lax "second registries" and open registries being forced to adopt moderate standards.[23] The data, however, do not show that second registries have lower safety standards than national registries. Denmark's second registry, for example, had a lower casualty rate than its national registry in three of the five years from 2001 to 2005.[24] DeSombre is correct in saying that the open registries that have improved have achieved only moderate standards; however, she ignores the declining trend their casualty rates exhibit and the fact that they are "on a steep learning curve."[25]

---

[21] Murphy, *The Structure of Regulatory Competition*, 46.

[22] *Casualty Return* (London: Lloyd's Register of Shipping, 1970); *Statistical Tables* (London: Lloyd's Register of Shipping, 1970); *World Casualty Statistics* (London: Lloyd's Register—Fairplay, 2005); *World Fleet Statistics* (London: Lloyd's Register—Fairplay, 2005).

[23] DeSombre, *Flagging Standards*, 41–46.

[24] *World Casualty Statistics* (London: Lloyd's Register—Fairplay, 2001–2005); World Fleet Statistics *World Casualty Statistics* (London: Lloyd's Register—Fairplay, 2001–2005).

[25] Chris Sawyer, Principal Registrar, Barbados Maritime Ship Registry, London, correspondence received November 23, 2006.

In sum, over the past forty years an effective global regime for regulating safety in shipping has emerged for the first time. SOLAS (1914) set the agenda for regulatory change, but significant change did not take place until the negotiation of several conventions in the 1970s. Regulation became increasingly effective in the 1980s as port states started to enforce conventions. Many open registries followed them in the 1990s. At every stage, however, there have been limitations to regulatory change: open registries initially chose not to enforce conventions; PSC has been ineffective in developing regions; and several open registries still do not enforce conventions. In the rest of this chapter, I explain what caused regulatory change to take place, and why this change has had limitations.

Explaining Regulatory Change

The factors identified by Mattli and Woods have strong explanatory power with respect to the regulatory change outlined above. Both supply- and demand-side factors have played an important role in bringing about this change.

Institutional Supply

An increasingly extensive institutional context at the supranational level has been crucial in facilitating regulatory change. The development of more accessible participatory mechanisms at the supranational level, beginning in the 1960s, played a major role in bringing about broad-based negotiations leading to the adoption of key conventions. The IMO consists of an Assembly made up of all member states, an executive Council elected by the Assembly, and four main committees.[26] In 1961, the IMO adopted Rules Governing Relationship with Non-Governmental International Organizations. This allowed the IMO to grant "consultative status" to NGOs, which entitled them to speak and submit written statements on any item on the agenda of the Assembly or its subsidiary bodies; it also gave NGOs access to IMO documents.[27]

Since 1961, the IMO has granted consultative status to a number of environmental NGOs, trade union, insurance, and classification organ-

---

[26] See www.imo.org.

[27] See Rules 6 and 7, Rules Governing the Relationship with Non-Governmental International Organizations, in volume 1 of the "Basic Documents"; see Rémi Parmentier, "Review of the Rules and Practice for Civil Society Organisations (CSOs) Participation in Regional Seas Conventions and Action Plans." Paper presented at the United Nations Environment Programme 7th Global Meeting of the Regional Seas Conventions and Action Plans, Helsinki, October 18–20, 2005, 5.

izations.[28] Granting consultative status, as opposed to the observer status used by many other organizations, encourages a qualitative difference in the expectations of member states toward NGOs, and in the NGOs' own sense of responsibility.[29] In 2003, the success of public pressure in thwarting an attempt by several open registries to remove Greenpeace's consultative status demonstrated the strength of the position of organizations with this status.[30]

An increasingly extensive institutional context at the supranational level also helped to bring about the Paris MOU. In 1976, the International Labor Organization (ILO) passed the Merchant Shipping Convention, which sought to inspect vessels visiting the ports of member states to check the living and working conditions on board. In 1978, eight North Sea states signed the Hague Memorandum of Understanding, which primarily aimed to ensure that the Merchant Shipping Convention was enforced.[31] The Paris Memorandum of Understanding then expanded the content of the Hague Memorandum of Understanding and added six more signatories.[32]

Increasingly accessible participatory mechanisms at the ILO were a key factor behind the passing of the Merchant Shipping Convention. In 1948, the ILO introduced consultative status, which it granted to three international union organizations.[33] These organizations were particularly influential because the commission within the ILO with responsibility for maritime matters comprised employers' and employees' representatives only.[34] In 1956, the ILO also set up a Special List of Non-Governmental

---

[28] Friends of the Earth International (1973), International Union for the Conservation of Nature and Natural Resources (1981), Greenpeace International (1991), World Wide Fund for Nature (1993), International Confederation of Free Trade Unions (1961) (the International Transport Workers Federation is one of several Global Federation Unions allied with the International Confederation of Free Trade Unions), International Association of Classification Societies (1969), International Union of Marine Insurance (1961), International Association of Producers of Insurance and Reinsurance (1975).

[29] Parmentier, "Review of the Rules and Practice for CSOs," 6.

[30] See www.greenpeace.org.uk/toxics/victory-at-the-imo, accessed March 21, 2008.

[31] Meltem Güner-Özbek, "Paris Memorandum of Understanding—an Example of International Cooperation and Its Perspectives," in Peter Ehlers and Rainer Lagoni, eds., *International Maritime Organisations and their Contribution towards a Sustainable Marine Development* (Münster: Lit Verlag: 2006), 61.

[32] See www.parismou.org/ParisMOU/Organisation/About+Us/History/xp/menu.3950/default.aspx, accessed March 21, 2008.

[33] These organizations were the International Confederation of Free Trade Unions, the World Federation of Trade Unions, and the World Confederation of Labour; Victor-Yves Ghebali, *The International Labour Organisation: A Case Study on the Evolution of U.N. Specialised Agencies* (Dordrecht: Martinus Nijhoff Publishers, 1989), 31.

[34] Bruce Farthing and Mark Brownrigg, *Farthing on International Shipping* (London: LLP, 1997), 77.

International Organizations to "establish working relations with international NGOs other than employers' and workers' organizations." This list includes several international maritime NGOs.[35]

The implementation of the Paris Memorandum of Understanding gave NGOs and unions further access to the regulatory process. The executive body of the Paris Memorandum of Understanding is composed of representatives from the participating authorities and the European Commission, and representatives from the IMO and the ILO participate in meetings as observers.[36] NGOs, unions, and other actors thus have indirect access to the regulatory process within the Paris Memorandum of Understanding, via their access to these other supranational organizations.

In sum, the increasing accessibility of participatory mechanisms at the supranational level has been an important cause of regulatory change. Institutional change at the IMO and the ILO has given NGOs, unions, and other actors affected by the shipping industry greater influence over the regulatory process, which has led to regulatory change. This change has, in turn, helped to make the institutional context more extensive. However, an increasingly extensive institutional context alone is not sufficient to explain the huge regulatory change that has taken place. Demand-side factors have also played a crucial role.

Demand-Side Factors

THE ROLE OF DEMONSTRATION EFFECTS

Demonstration effects have helped to bring about regulatory change at every stage, by revealing the costs of inadequate regulation. The sinking of the *Titanic*, in 1912, exposed the risks posed by increasingly large steamships and triggered the setting of an agenda for regulatory change, in the form of SOLAS (1914).[37]

Fifty years later, further disasters induced the negotiation of several conventions, by calling attention to the growing danger that shipping posed. The running aground of the *Torrey Canyon*, in 1967, caused the biggest pollution incident ever recorded up to that time and highlighted the danger posed by increasingly large tankers.[38] This resulted in the

[35] For example, the International Christian Maritime Association, the International Federation of Shipmasters' Associations, and the United Seamen's Service (www.ilo.org/public/english/bureau/exrel/civil/ngo/index.htm, accessed March 21, 2008).

[36] See www.parismou.org/ParisMOU/Organisation/About+Us/Structure/xp/menu.3958/default.aspx, accessed March 21, 2008.

[37] Braithwaite and Drahos, *Global Business Regulation*, 430.

[38] See note 17.

negotiation of MARPOL.[39] Disasters have subsequently prompted the refinement of existing treaties, by bringing to light their limitations. The sinking of the *Herald of Free Enterprise*, in 1987, demonstrated that existing regulations did not effectively cover roll-on-roll-off ferries.[40] This made a "strong impression on public opinion" and led to a series of amendments to SOLAS (1974).[41]

A disaster also gave rise to PSC. The grounding of a Liberian flagged tanker, the *Amoco Cadiz*, in 1978, demonstrated the failure of open registries to enforce the newly negotiated conventions.[42] This generated a "strong political and public outcry" that helped bring about the adoption of the Paris Memorandum of Understanding.[43] Demonstration effects prompted many open registries to enforce conventions by making clear the costs of failing to do so. In 1999, an uproar over the deaths of four British seafarers on board a Belizean registered vessel and a U.S. Drug Enforcement Administration investigation into the registry convinced Belize to raise its standards.[44]

Disasters have triggered every stage of regulatory change; however, the initial public and political outcries that they have produced could not have sustained the process of change. To explain this change, it is necessary to consider how the diffusion of information from demonstration effects, and other developments, have brought about the formation of a pro-change coalition.

THE EMERGENCE OF A PRO-CHANGE COALITION

Since the 1970s, a number of actors have emerged as entrepreneurs of regulatory change. These entrepreneurs, though they have rarely cooperated directly, have effectively formed a pro-change coalition. Three common causes underlie the emergence of these entrepreneurs: the growing size of ships and consequent increased liability prior to and during the

[39] Ronald Mitchell, "Regime Design Matters: International Oil Pollution and Treaty Compliance," *International Organization* 48, no. 3 (Summer 1994), 431–432.

[40] *The Herald of Free Enterprise* was a roll-on-roll-off ferry that sank en route from Belgium to England, with the loss of 193 lives.

[41] IMO, "IMO and Ro-Ro Safety," *Focus on IMO* (January 1997) (www.imo.org/includes/blastDataOnly.asp/data_id%3D718/RORO.pdf, accessed June 22, 2007), 11; see also Michael Clarke, *Regulation: The Social Control of Business between Law and Politics* (London: MacMillan, 2000), 210–211.

[42] The *Amoco Cadiz* was an oil tanker that ran aground off the coast of Brittany, spilling 223,000 tons of crude oil.

[43] See www.parismou.org/ParisMOU/Organisation/About+Us/History/xp/menu.3950/default.aspx, accessed June 22, 2007.

[44] Andy McSmith, "Ashcroft Linked to Ship Enquiry," *The Observer*, August 15, 1999; Ewen MacAskill and Duncan Campbell, "Tories Admit to Damage of Ashcroft Belize Affair," *The Guardian*, July 19, 1999.

1970s; recession, surplus capacity, and an increase in competition in the 1970s and early 1980s; and the impact of PSC from the 1980s to the present day.

Environmental NGOs. These NGOs emerged as "non-governmental entrepreneurs of regulatory change" in the early 1970s. They helped to bring about the negotiation of conventions by lobbying governments and international bodies and by raising public awareness.[45] Many environmental NGOs had only recently been established.[46] They increased their political influence by setting up organizations to facilitate the coordination of their efforts.[47]

In the decades prior to the 1970s, ships had grown massively in size; for example, tanker sizes rose from 30,000 deadweight tons in the 1950s to over 500,000 deadweight tons in the 1970s.[48] This increased the potential magnitude of environmental disasters, as accidents such as the *Torrey Canyon* demonstrated. At the same time, the rising number of ships in the world fleet increased the probability of disasters.[49] These developments put safety in shipping high on the agenda of the newly formed environmental NGOs.

The increasing effectiveness of environmental NGOs as entrepreneurs of regulatory change helped to bring about the enforcement of conventions by open registries. By the 1990s, environmental NGOs were showing a growing activism in the South, where most open registries are based.[50] Environmental NGOs also took a leading role in using computer

[45] Jon Burchell and Simon Lightfoot, *The Greening of the European Union? Examining the EU's Environmental Credentials* (London: Sheffield Academic Press, 2001), 18–19.

[46] For example, the International Union for the Conservation of Nature and Natural Resources (1948), the World Wide Fund for Nature (1961), Greenpeace (1971).

[47] Friends of the Earth International was founded in 1971 by organizations from France, Sweden, England, and the United States as a federation of grassroots environmental groups; the Environment Liaison Centre was established in 1972 to monitor the activities of the United Nations Environment Programme and help NGOs work more effectively with this organization; and in 1974, the European Environmental Bureau was set up to monitor and respond to the European Union's emerging environmental policy; Sally Morphet, "NGOs and the Environment," in Peter Willetts, ed., *The Conscience of the World: The Influence of Nongovernmental Organisations at the United Nations* (Washington, DC: Brookings Institution Press, 1996), 128.

[48] Clarke, *The Social Control of Business*, 205.

[49] Between 1955 and 1975, the number of ships in the world fleet almost doubled, from 32,492 to 63,724; *Statistical Tables* (London: Lloyd's Register of Shipping, 1955, 1975).

[50] For example, the Southeast Asian Programme in Ocean Law, Policy and Management, formed in 1981, sought to facilitate the exchange of information and ideas related to current ocean law, policy, and management in the region; Lee Kimball, "The Role of NGOs in the Implementation of the 1982 LOS Convention," in Alfred Soons, ed., *Implementation of the LOS Convention through International Institutions. Proceedings of the 23rd Annual Conference of the Law of the Sea Institute* (Honolulu: University of Hawaii, Law of the Sea Institute, 1990), 149–150.

and telecommunications systems to collect and widely disseminate information.[51] They further strengthened their influence by forming networks and active coalitions with other types of organizations. In 1999, and again in 2002, Greenpeace cooperated with the International Transport Workers' Federation (ITF) and other trade union organizations to publish a joint report criticizing open registries.[52]

The International Transport Workers' Federation. In the 1970s, the ITF emerged as another powerful entrepreneur of regulatory change. It supported the negotiation of conventions through a political campaign that it had the advantage of fighting as a single body and with almost unlimited resources, in contrast to shipowners' organizations.[53] The ITF ostensibly is a nongovernmental entrepreneur: it is a federation of 621 trade unions and works "to improve the conditions for seafarers of all nationalities."[54] However, in the terms of Mattli and Woods' framework, the ITF is more akin to a "corporate leveller of the playing field." Its campaigns have sought to protect the jobs of seafarers from industrialized states by limiting the cost advantage of ships employing nationals from developing states.[55]

The strengthening of the ITF's desire to level the playing field explains why it emerged as an entrepreneur of regulatory change in the 1970s. When the ITF inaugurated its campaign against flags of convenience, in 1948, it initially had little impact. Unions from the capital-exporting United States and Nordic states supported the campaign, but unions from low-wage, labor-exporting European states opposed it. These European trade unions made up 56 percent of the ITF membership. By the 1970s, however, Europe had transformed from a labor-exporting to a capital-exporting region and was under pressure brought about by cheap

[51] Kimball 1990, "The Role of NGOs," 156–158.

[52] *Troubled Waters: Fishing, Pollution and FOCs: Major Group Submission for the 1999 CSD Thematic Review: Oceans and Seas* (London: International Transport Workers Federation, 1999). Likewise, in 2002, following the *Prestige* disaster, Greenpeace, the ITF, and the World Wide Fund for Nature wrote a joint appeal to the UN Secretary General urging him to take action to improve the effectiveness of regulation in shipping (www.greenpeace.org/international/news/leaked-oil-blackening-spain-s, accessed June 22, 2007).

[53] Herbert Northrup and Peter Scrase, "The International Transport Workers' Federation Flag of Convenience Shipping Campaign: 1983–1995," *Transportation Law Journal* 23 (1996), 421.

[54] See www.itfglobal.org/seafarers/index.cfm, accessed October 24, 2006.

[55] The ITF's General Secretary acknowledged, in a 1994 address, that their campaign "has been and still is led by the desire of . . . unions to defend and maintain their jobs"; David Cockroft, "The ITF and the Maritime Industry." Paper presented at the North American Maritime Ministry Conference, 1994. Similarly, Abbott and Snidal, "The Governance Triangle" (this volume) argue that protests by labor unions in developed countries against the use of child labor in Central America are, at least in part, motivated by the implicit import protection such protests may provide their members.

labor from Asia. This led European trade unions to support the campaign, while the Asian unions that now opposed it lacked political clout within the ITF.[56]

The ITF also played an important role in supporting the enforcement of conventions by open registries, through an industrial campaign that gave shipowners strong incentives to raise their standards. ITF inspectors boarded ships in port and organized boycotts of the handling of vessels whose owners refused to sign an agreement on wages and conditions dictated by the ITF.[57] The increasing effectiveness of the ITF campaign helps to explain the timing of enforcement by open registries, which were responding to pressure from shipowners. The number of ITF inspectors rose from 42 in 18 states in 1989, to 111 in 39 states in 1998.[58] The number of collective bargaining agreements rose from 1,565 in 1989, to 4,500 in 1998.[59]

Insurance Companies and Classification Societies. Insurance companies also began to push for regulatory change in the 1970s. They coordinated their efforts through the International Union of Marine Insurance.[60] The growing size of ships, as well as legal developments, turned insurers into "corporations at risk." Alongside the previously mentioned increase in the size of tankers, cargo ships went from about 10,000 deadweight tons to 200,000 deadweight tons in a two-decade period.[61] This greatly increased the potential costs of an accident, as disasters demonstrated.[62] Legal developments, notably the Convention on Limitation of Liability for Maritime Claims (1976), further increased shipowners', and thus their insurance companies', exposure to risk. The potential for higher payouts on a single accident raised the possibility of insurance companies facing

[56] Sigrid Koch-Baumgarten, "Trade Union Regime Formation Under the Conditions of Globalization in the Transport Sector: Attempts at Transnational Trade Union Regulation of Flag-of-Convenience Shipping," *International Review of Social History* 43 (1998), 381–382, 393–394.

[57] Northrup and Scrase, "Flag of Convenience Shipping Campaign," 376; see also *ITF Standard Collective Agreement* (January 2006) (www.itfglobal.org/files/seealsodocs/1467/ITF%20Standard%20CBA%202006.pdf, accessed October 24, 2006).

[58] Koch-Baumgarten, "Trade Union Regime Formation," 395.

[59] Northrup and Scrase, "Flag of Convenience Shipping Campaign," 377; Koch-Baumgarten, "Trade Union Regime Formation," 398.

[60] The International Union of Marine Insurance was formed in the nineteenth century, but was strengthened in 1946 when individual membership was replaced by membership of National Associations, making it possible for Lloyd's to join (www.iumi.com/index.cfm?id=7136, accessed March 17, 2008).

[61] Alistair Couper, *Voyages of Abuse: Seafarers, Human Rights, and International Shipping* (London: Pluto Press, 1999), 10.

[62] For example, the *Torrey Canyon* disaster cost insurance companies nearly £10 million, in 1967 prices; Burrows, Rowley, and Owen, "Torrey Canyon," 242, 256.

costs that they could not absorb. Insurance companies therefore sought conventions in order to minimize the risks they faced.

Classification societies, which assess the safety of a vessel's construction on behalf of insurance companies, joined the pro-change coalition in the 1990s. The main classification societies worked together through the International Association of Classification Societies, which they strengthened in 1992 by establishing a permanent secretariat in London.[63] The International Association of Classification Societies, for example, set up a scheme to help lax registries enforce conventions.[64]

In the 1990s, classification societies found, for the first time, that they too were corporations at risk. In many states the law was "edging more and more towards acknowledging that there may be nothing preventing a classification society from being held liable to third parties."[65] PSC gave classification societies a direct incentive to ensure that the ships they classed were registered with states that enforced conventions, by targeting classification societies whose vessels had poor detention statistics. The Paris Memorandum of Understanding also began to publish the detention statistics of classification societies.[66]

Shipowners. The growing size of ships, and consequent legal developments increasing shipowners' liability, meant that the owners of large ships also emerged as corporations at risk in the 1970s. These shipowners formed a particularly well-resourced segment of the industry and further strengthened their influence by establishing a number of industry organizations.[67]

The rising potential cost of accidents gave shipowners an incentive to raise standards. The owners of large ships came under additional pressure to reduce risk because, as the size of ships grew, they increasingly needed to secure finance from banks, or to list their companies on

[63] Farthing and Brownrigg, *Farthing on International Shipping*, 45.

[64] See *www.iacs.org.uk/press/2004/Press14Apr04.PDF*, accessed November 26, 2006.

[65] See, for example, *Otto Candies LLC v. Nippon Kaiji Kyokai Corporation* (September 17, 2003), United States Court of Appeals for the Fifth Circuit; Barbara Vaughan, "The Liability of Classification Societies" (University of Cape Town, 2006), 12, 6–7 (http://web .uct.ac.za/depts/shiplaw/assign2006/vaughan.pdf, accessed June 22, 2007).

[66] Paris Memorandum of Understanding Secretariat, *Paris Memorandum of Understanding on Port State Control: Annual Report* (1999), 2–3 (www.parismou.org/upload/anrep/ PMOU99AR.pdf, accessed June 22).

[67] The Oil Companies International Marine Forum was established in 1970, in response to the *Torrey Canyon* incident, to ensure that the views of the oil industry could be represented to governments and intergovernmental bodies. Other examples include the European Community Shipowner's Association (1965), the Federation of ASEAN Shipowners' Associations (1967), and the International Association of Independent Tanker Owners; Farthing and Brownrigg, *Farthing on International Shipping*, 49–55.

stock markets.[68] These shipowners also became corporate levelers of the playing field, giving them an even stronger incentive to support more stringent regulation. As corporations at risk, they had to ensure that their own vessels adopted high standards, but if they raised their standards unilaterally they would lose business to low-cost competitors with smaller vessels. They therefore sought regulation to force their competitors to improve as well.

In the early 1980s, the owners of smaller vessels registered with traditional maritime states also surfaced as corporate levelers of the playing field. These shipowners, along with others with high safety standards, had increased their influence since the mid-1970s by amalgamating existing shipowners' organizations and creating new organizations for groups not previously represented in this way.[69] As traditional maritime states forced the ships on their registries to raise their standards, the owners of these ships had the choice of reregistering their vessels with open registries, or complying with the conventions and being placed at a cost disadvantage. Though some chose to reregister, a large number stayed put. They did so because surplus capacity and increased competition, aggravated by a global recession in the shipping industry, put them under pressure to improve, and not just maintain, their competitive positions.[70]

Ships registered with traditional maritime states already had higher safety standards than ships on open registries, prior to the introduction

---

[68] William Gallagher, "Ship Mortgages as a Financing Vehicle: The Flag State's Role in Protecting the Security Interests of Lenders." Paper presented at the Marine Money China Ship Finance Forum, Shanghai, October 15, 2004; see also Angela Bergantio and Peter Marlow, "Factors Influencing the Choice of Flag: Empirical Evidence," *Maritime Policy and Management* 25, no. 2 (1998), 164; and Couper, *Voyages of Abuse*, 9–11.

[69] In 1975, owners concerned about the imbalance between supply and demand in the tanker sector established the International Maritime Industries Forum. The International Association of Dry Cargo Shipowners was formed in 1980. The merger of existing shipowners' organizations created the Council of European and Japanese Shipowners' Associations (1974) and the General Council of British Shipping (1975); Farthing and Brownrigg, *Farthing on International Shipping*, 33–34, 43–45.

[70] In the 1960s and 1970s, an abundance of cheap oil increased the demand for ocean transport. At the same time, increased financing of vessels enabled shipowners to purchase larger and greater numbers of ships, and competition in the shipbuilding industry led governments to subsidize shipbuilders. When demand fell sharply as a result of global recession, there was huge surplus capacity: by 1983, approximately 80 million gross register tonnage of shipping lay idle. The 1970s also saw the decline of shipping cartels, as containerization introduced competition among different modes of maritime transport and facilitated the growth of Asian shipping firms; Couper, *Voyages of Abuse*, 9–11; Alan Cafruny, "The Political Economy of International Shipping: Europe Versus America," *International Organization* 39, no. 1 (Winter 1985); Mark Zacher and Brent Sutton, "Governing Global Networks: International Regimes for Transportation and Communications" (Cambridge: Cambridge University Press, 1996), 68, 71–75.

of conventions. Their owners realized that if they could force shipowners with lax standards to incur costs in raising their standards, or if they were able to restrict the operations of those that did not, then they would gain a competitive advantage. PSC provided an ideal mechanism, forcing the owners of ships on open registries to raise their standards or be excluded from trading in the regions it covered. Indeed, at the time critics accused it of being a "nontariff barrier."[71] The addition of these shipowners to the pro-change coalition helps to explain both the timing of PSC and why it was traditional maritime states that originally implemented it.

Shipbuilders based in traditional maritime states joined the pro-change coalition as corporate levelers of the playing field for similar reasons. They also felt the squeeze of the global recession, with orders in 1980 at less than one-third of their level in 1975.[72] In 1976, Europe had threatened to put greater obstacles in the way of Japanese-built ships.[73] PSC served this purpose while avoiding overt protectionism. Though PSC targeted ships that did not meet certain standards, rather than ships made in a particular region, Japan was mass-producing "unsophisticated vessels as quickly and cheaply as possible."[74] Thus, Japanese-made ships were precisely the sorts of vessel likely to fall foul of PSC. PSC also served to prevent shipbuilding industries emerging in developing states that might have competed by producing ships to lower standards. Furthermore, by keeping out old substandard vessels, PSC created demand for new ships. The influence of shipbuilders helps to explain why PSC developed first in Europe, as protectionist measures already supported the United States' shipbuilding industry.[75]

PSC turned many of the owners of ships on open registries into corporate levelers of the playing field. It forced the owners of ships that sailed to the regions covered by effective PSC to raise their standards. When they then sailed to regions where PSC was nonexistent or ineffective they were at a commercial disadvantage compared to shipowners who had maintained lower standards. The owners of ships sailing to regions covered by effective PSC, therefore, pressured their registries to enforce conventions, in order to remove this disadvantage. They wielded great influence over their registries through the threat of exit. PSC also deliberately encouraged shipowners to pressure open registries to enforce conventions,

---

[71] Murphy, *The Structure of Regulatory Competition*, 64.

[72] Cafruny, "The Political Economy of International Shipping," 85.

[73] Susan Strange, "The Management of Surplus Capacity: or How Does Theory Stand up to Protectionism 1970s Style?" *International Organization* 33, no. 3 (Summer 1979), 325.

[74] David Osler, "A Saga of Single Hulls, Double Standards and Too Many Flags of Convenience," *The Independent*, November 20, 2002, 18.

[75] Strange, "The Management of Surplus Capacity," 327.

by targeting ships on substandard registries for inspection. For example, in 1999, the Paris Memorandum of Understanding introduced a "Black List" of flags whose ships were targeted for inspection, and a "White List" whose ships were inspected less than the ships on other flags.[76]

In sum, the emergence of a pro-change coalition has been crucial in bringing about regulatory change. Actors have joined this coalition as a result of three common causes, corresponding to the three stages of regulatory change in this period. The growing size of ships caused the emergence, in the 1970s, of environmental NGOs as nongovernmental entrepreneurs of regulatory change, and shipowners and insurance companies as corporations at risk. These actors then pushed for the negotiation of conventions. Recessions in shipping, in the mid-1970s and early 1980s, led shipowners and shipbuilders from traditional maritime states to join the pro-change coalition as corporate levelers of the playing field and press for PSC. In the 1990s, PSC meant that classification societies also became corporations at risk, and that many shipowners from open registries became corporate levelers of the playing field. They have pressured open registries to enforce conventions.

Explaining Limitations to Regulatory Change

Limitations to the impact of demonstration effects and to the effectiveness of the pro-change coalition help to explain why many port states and flag states in developing regions still fail to enforce conventions. The institutional context in some developing states has also limited regulatory change. Traditional maritime states could, nonetheless, have compelled developing states to enforce conventions, but norms of state sovereignty have constrained them.

In most developing states disasters have had little impact because the media have not broadly revealed them and the public has not been politically empowered, potential limitations that Mattli and Woods identify. All of the disasters and scandals that have triggered regulatory change have revealed the costs that lax regulation imposes on the populations of industrialized states. The *Titanic* was sailing from the United Kingdom to the United States, and both the *Torrey Canyon* and the *Amoco Cadiz* ran aground in the English Channel. In the same year as the *Herald of Free Enterprise* sank en route from Norway to Britain with the loss of 193 lives, the *Dona Paz* sank in the Philippines with 4,375 casualties, yet it was the *Herald* disaster that led to regulatory change.[77]

---

[76] Paris Memorandum of Understanding Secretariat, *Annual Report*, 9.
[77] See note 41.

Some developing countries, however, have found it in their self-interest to enforce international shipping regulation. Belize, for example, decided to enforce conventions because demonstration effects revealed the cost to the United Kingdom and the United States of its failure to do so, and it feared that the bad publicity "could have a destabilising effect on the Belize economy."[78]

The considerations that led many shipowners to join the pro-change coalition have not applied to all. There are still numerous owners of small vessels intent on avoiding liability who have captured the regulatory process in several developing states with open registries. The influence of these shipowners is evident in the smaller average size of vessels on open registries that do not enforce conventions, compared to those that do, and in the lower regard for the "Rule of Law" in states that do not enforce conventions.[79] Shipowners trying to avoid liability seek to register with states with poorly functioning legal systems since "if you want to sue the shipowner you have to do it in the courts of the flag state."[80]

Shipowners with lax standards have opposed PSC because it threatens the competitive advantage they gain from these standards. Such shipowners dominate in developing regions, where they have been able to capture the regulatory process. Shipowners with lax standards whose vessels do not sail to, or have been able to avoid, regions covered by effective PSC have continued to press their registries not to enforce conventions.

In developing states where there has been demand for regulation, a limited institutional context has frequently prevented this from bringing about the enforcement of conventions. Access to the regulatory process is inherently more limited in states with open registries than it is in states with national registries, because there is a greater distance between the regulator and those affected by accidents. Ships on open registries are less likely to sail to their own ports or to be crewed by their own nationals, and several states with open registries are landlocked.[81] The domestic political

---

[78] MacAskill and Campbell, "Tories Admit to Damage." Belize is no isolated case. Like many former British colonies, it retains close economic and other ties to the United Kingdom. Strikingly, nine of the eleven open registries that have begun to enforce conventions are Commonwealth members. In contrast, of the nine open registries that remain lax, only one is a Commonwealth member (see www.thecommonwealth.org/Internal/142227/members/, accessed October 26, 2006; the sample of states used here is the same as in figures 6.2 and 6.3).

[79] *World Fleet Statistics* (London: Lloyd's Register—Fairplay, 2005); World Bank, *Worldwide Governance Indicators* (2006) (http://siteresources.worldbank.org/INTWBIGOVAN TCOR/Resources/1740479-1150402582357/2661829-1158008871017/gov_matters_5_tables.pdf, accessed October 26, 2006).

[80] Agustín Blanco-Bazán, Senior Deputy Director Legal Affairs, IMO, interviewed in London, December 7, 2006.

[81] Anthony Lane, "Flags of Convenience: Is It Time to Redress the Balance?" *Maritime Review* (1999), 31–35.

context often compounds this inaccessibility of the regulatory process. Some authoritarian Asian states, for example, prohibit ITF membership and include no-strike clauses in contracts of employment.[82] The better performance on an index of "Voice and Accountability" by those open registries that enforce conventions shows the importance of an extensive institutional context for facilitating regulatory change.[83]

Shortcomings and limitations on both the demand and institutional supply sides could have been circumvented if traditional maritime states had pressured lax states to enforce conventions. Actors in the pro-change coalition have pushed for such pressure to be applied, and traditional maritime states would have benefited from such an improvement, as it would have reduced the cost advantage of registries competing with their own and reduced the chances of accidents affecting their coastlines or the ships on their fleets. Furthermore, there were obvious and feasible means by which pressure could have been applied to developing states. The IMO could have been given a mandate to monitor the enforcement of conventions by flag states, simply by including a relevant provision in conventions; port states could have denied access to all ships registered with open registries, rather than just detaining those found to be deficient; and the *Member State Audit Scheme* could have been made compulsory.[84]

Traditional maritime states, however, have been constrained by state sovereignty. The IMO has not been given the power to monitor how effectively states implement conventions because "the implementation of IMO treaties is a matter well within the sovereignty of state parties, and state parties in general have always been reluctant to accept interference from outside bodies to double check this compliance."[85] Port states did not prohibit all ships registered with open registries from entering their ports since this would, in effect, have meant that they no longer recognized the right of every state to regulate the vessels flying its flag. Similarly, states with open registries successfully persuaded traditional maritime states that making the *Member State Audit Scheme* compulsory would be too great an infringement upon state sovereignty.[86]

[82] Koch-Baumgarten, "Trade Union Regime Formation," 399.

[83] World Bank, *Worldwide Governance Indicators*; Similarly, Kathryn Sikkink, "From State Responsibility to Individual Criminal Accountability" (this volume) finds that "the great bulk of human rights trials occurred in democratic countries or countries in transition to democracy."

[84] Under the *Voluntary Member State Audit Scheme*, states agree to a comprehensive assessment by the IMO of how effectively they administer and implement IMO instruments; Hindell, "Strengthening the Ship Regulating Regime," 379–380.

[85] Blanco-Bazán interview.

[86] Mouzouropoulos interview; Lawrence Barchue, "Making a Case for the Voluntary IMO Member State Audit Scheme." Paper presented at the World Maritime University, October 17–19, 2005, 5–6.

CONCLUSION

Over the past forty years, shipping has gone from being largely unregulated to having an extensive framework of conventions, widely enforced by many states. The agenda for regulatory change was set in 1914, but major conventions were not negotiated until the 1970s. In the 1980s, port states began to enforce these conventions, and in the 1990s, numerous open registries joined them in this. However, many open registries and port states in developing regions still fail to enforce conventions.

The increasing supply of participatory mechanisms at the supranational level has been one cause of regulatory change. Demand-side factors have also been influential. Disasters have triggered every stage of regulatory change by revealing the growing costs of lax regulation. Regulatory change has then been sustained by the emergence of a pro-change coalition. Three common causes, corresponding to the different stages of regulatory change, have led to the emergence of this coalition.

In the 1970s, growth in the size of ships and an increase in shipowners' liability caused the owners of large ships and their insurance companies to emerge as corporations at risk and environmental NGOs to mobilize for regulatory change. Shipowners and shipbuilders from traditional maritime states joined the pro-change coalition as levelers of the playing field as a result of recessions in the 1970s and early 1980s. In the 1990s, when port states began to enforce the conventions in earnest, classification societies became corporations at risk and shipowners from open registries became corporate levelers of the playing field.

The enforcement of conventions has remained limited in many developing states. Disasters have had little impact and the developments that caused a pro-change coalition to emerge have not affected many of the ships that sail between or are registered with developing states. Where there has been demand for stricter regulation, the limited institutional context in many developing states has curbed its impact. Traditional maritime states could have compelled developing states to enforce conventions, but they have been constrained by norms of state sovereignty.

The explanation of regulatory change presented in this chapter differs strikingly from the existing literature in its implications for the future of shipping regulation. Unlike Murphy, this chapter does not suggest that the characteristics of the shipping industry make a competition in laxity inevitable.[87] Some further movement in the direction of public interest is likely to occur; for example, those open registries that have begun to enforce conventions are likely to become more effective at doing so. In con-

---

[87] See Murphy, *The Structure of Regulatory Competition*, 45–71.

trast to DeSombre, this chapter does not imply that the open registries that do not currently enforce conventions will alter their approach.[88] The open registries that do not enforce conventions have different characteristics than those that do: an ineffective legal system, a limited institutional context, and weak links to the United Kingdom and the United States. These traits will continue to insulate them from pressure to change.

[88] See DeSombre, *Flagging Standards*, 228.

CHAPTER SEVEN

Regulatory Shift: The Rise of Judicial Liberalization at the WTO

Judith L. Goldstein and Richard H. Steinberg

INTERNATIONAL TRADE TRANSACTIONS are among the most regulated activities in the world. Indeed, the history of international trade since the seventeenth century cannot be understood without accounting for the changing ways by which public authority has interacted with, and influenced, private transactions.[1] In the contemporary era, we have witnessed a significant change in the locus of that regulation, from country-specific policies to rule-setting on the global, multilateral level, primarily through the emergence and evolution of the General Agreement on Tariffs and Trade and the World Trade Organization.[2]

A specific change in global regulation has taken place in recent years. We argue below that the form of global rule-setting has shifted, even as it has remained within the GATT/WTO. In the early years of the institution, trade regulation occurred through a negotiated legislative process associated with trade rounds. Over the last fifteen years, however, the focus of GATT/WTO trade regulation has moved from trade rounds to a judicial process. This shift is attributable largely to the increasing participation of developing nations in WTO negotiations, which has not only deadlocked the legislative process that for half a century liberalized

We thank Karen Alter, Curtis Bradley, Mark Busch, Christina Davis, Joanne Gowa, Oona Hathaway, Larry Helfer, Miles Kahler, Judith Kelly, Robert Keohane, Giovanni Maggi, Walter Mattli, Andrew Moravcsik, Helen Milner, Kalypso Nicolaides, Douglas Rivers, Duncan Snidal, Ngaire Woods, and workshop participants at Duke, Oxford, and Princeton for useful comments on earlier drafts. Parts of this essay were previously published in Richard H. Steinberg, "Judicial Lawmaking at the WTO: Discursive, Constitutional, and Political Constraints," *American Journal of International Law* 98 (April 2004).

[1] Eli F. Heckscher, *The Continental System: An Economic Interpretation*, ed. Harald Westergaard (Gloucester, MA: Peter Smith, 1964); Robert Pahre, *Politics and Trade Cooperation in the Nineteenth Century: The "Agreeable Customs" of 1815–1913* (Cambridge: Cambridge University Press, 2008).

[2] John Barton et al., *The Evolution of the Trade Regime: Politics, Law and Economics of the GATT and WTO* (Princeton, NJ: Princeton University Press, 2006).

global trade, but has also dampened the legislative check on judicial law-making. It is a shift that is consequential and not likely to be reversed anytime soon.

The varying effect of regulation is a well-mined topic in both political science and law. Scholars have contrasted regulation by courts with regulation by administration or legislative bodies, evaluating their relative effects according to metrics like economic efficiency, optimal deterrence, capture by particularistic interests, and justice.[3] But as Mattli and Woods explain in the framework chapter of this volume, regulation has become increasingly global because "elements of the regulatory process have migrated to international or transnational actors."[4] This migration of the locus of regulatory activity is clearly evidenced in the WTO, where the line between domestic and international regulation has become increasingly blurred.

We ask below whether or not this change in regulatory structure has policy effects. We find that it does: the regulatory shift taking place at the WTO, from the legislative to the judicial, has given a new set of actors the authority and autonomy sufficient to set policy. The result has been that the organization has supported more trade liberalization than would have occurred otherwise.[5] We argue that the judiciary has been efficacious, not because of an increase in its authority alone but because judicial oversight has increased the freedom of action for member-state governments, previously captured by entrenched domestic interests at home.[6]

What explains this regulatory shift at the WTO? Although created with great hope and fanfare in 1995, the WTO has been unsuccessful at advancing a broad legislated trade deal among members. In the last decade, creating a consensus among WTO members has become increasingly difficult. Developing nations, often speaking as a bloc, have exacerbated disjuncture in U.S. and EC preferences on trade policy. The result

---

[3] David Vogel, *National Styles of Regulation: Environmental Policy in Great Britain and the United States* (Ithaca, NY: Cornell University Press, 1986); Robert A. Kagan, *Adversarial Legalism: The American Way of Law* (Cambridge, MA: Harvard University Press, 2003); Susan Rose-Ackerman, "Regulation and the Law of Torts," *American Economic Review* 81 (May 1991), 54–58.

[4] Walter Mattli and Ngaire Woods, "In Whose Benefit? Explaining Regulatory Change in the Global Economy and Polity," this volume.

[5] Judith L. Goldstein and Richard H. Steinberg, "Negotiate or Litigate? Effects of WTO Judicial Delegation on U.S. Trade Politics," *Law and Contemporary Problems* 71 (Winter 2008), 257–82.

[6] We do not argue that market opening will always move states away from capture. For example, in sectors characterized by high barriers to entry and declining marginal costs, market opening could favor cartelization.

has been an impasse at the negotiating table and little progress in the current Doha Round. These same divisions, however, help explain the increasingly active role being played by the Appellate Body. Legislative gridlock and judicial lawmaking may be related phenomena in a domestic or international context.[7]

The failure of multilateral negotiations has quietly ceded authority to an alternative institution for regulation. We argue that in the wake of failed trade negotiations, WTO lawmaking has moved out of the legislative venue of member-states and into the courtroom. Delegation to the judiciary, established with the creation of the WTO, has been unexpectedly accompanied by considerable agent slack.[8] The same divisions that have undermined trade talks have made it increasingly difficult for the membership to provide a check on judicial lawmaking. As the prospects for legislative lawmaking have declined, judicial lawmaking has become more common, especially through interpretation of unclear rules and the filling of gaps within WTO agreements. Judicial lawmaking has been particularly evident in cases challenging subsidies or countervailing measures, antidumping duties, and safeguards measures, with considerable effect on the steel and agriculture sectors.

Taken together, these developments suggest that we are entering a period of "judicial liberalization" at the WTO, led by the Appellate Body. As discussed in the conclusion, this development may have some parallels to the period of "negative harmonization" in the EC, led by the European Court of Justice (ECJ) from the mid-1960s through the mid-1980s, when the Luxembourg Compromise and more limited availability of qualified majority voting constrained harmonization through Council directives.

---

[7] George Tsebelis, *Veto Players: How Political Institutions Work* (Princeton, NJ: Princeton University Press, 2002); George Tsebelis and Geoffrey Garrett, "The Institutional Foundations of Intergovernmentalism and Supranationalism in the European Union," *International Organization* 55 (Spring 2001), 357–390; Anne-Marie Burley and Walter Mattli, "Europe Before the Court: A Political Theory of Legal Integration," *International Organization* 47 (Winter 1993), 41–76.

[8] Our basic delegation model is drawn from Moe, who argues that "the principal-agent model is an analytic expression of the agency relationship, in which one party, the principal, considers entering into a contractual relationship with another, the agent, in the expectation that the agent will subsequently choose actions that produce the outcomes desired by the principal." Terry M. Moe, "The New Economics of Organization," *American Journal of Political Science* 28 (November 1984), 739–777, 756. We assume that the relationship between the GATT/WTO and its principals, nations, or customs territories, always held some degree of a principal-agent relationship, although the membership exerted far more oversight over the agents (the secretariat or the dispute settlement panels) than is common with other international agencies.

To examine the relationship between judicial lawmaking, legislative paralysis, and the regulation of trade, we proceed in four steps. The first section of this chapter examines the collapse of the legislative process: the origins of and explanation for the contemporary legislative stalemate in the WTO. Our second section examines the dispute settlement system and argues that it has become an increasingly and unexpectedly important venue for lawmaking with a liberalizing bias. Next we argue that this lawmaking has operated to free WTO members from capture by entrenched domestic protectionist interests in a way that negotiated liberalization efforts may not be able to do. Fourth, we explain why WTO judicial liberalization persists, suggesting that it may be favored by developing countries that now join together to block WTO legislative proposals that would diminish the Appellate Body's agent slack. Hence, we suggest that the decline in consensus at the ministerial level and the rise of judicial lawmaking are related and have made trade policy less prone to capture by protectionist interests.

LIBERALIZATION THROUGH NEGOTIATION (1947–1995) AND THE EMERGENCE OF LEGISLATIVE DEADLOCK

The GATT/WTO created a rule-based system, which facilitated the worldwide lowering of trade barriers and the growth of world commerce.[9] The efficacy of the regime, however, rested on a consensus among its largest members. In its earliest years, the GATT/WTO reflected U.S. power; as U.S. market share receded, the organization continued to prosper because of a transatlantic bargain between Europe and the United States. However, after 1995, as the transatlantic powers began demanding reciprocity from the South and accelerated their conclusion of preferential trade agreements (PTAs), consensus-building became increasing difficult. As northern cohesion evaporated, the South took a more unified and intransient position on trade openness, making demands on the North to provide access in previously closed sectors of their economy as a quid pro quo for their cooperation. Shifting alliances, however, is not the only explanation for the stalemate in trade talks. The issues on the agenda after the Uruguay Round were now tied to domestic regulatory structures, making agreement far more difficult than in the past, when negotiators focused on external barriers to trade.

---

[9] Judith L. Goldstein, Douglas Rivers, and Michael Tomz, "Institutions in International Relations: Understanding the Effects of the GATT and the WTO on World Trade," *International Organization* 61 (Winter 2007), 37–68.

The Basic Design

The GATT/WTO was created to solve what Bagwell and Staiger identify as a terms-of-trade–driven Prisoners' Dilemma.[10] According to this logic, large nations have an interest in shifting the cost of their trade protection on to their trade partners, thereby depressing foreign export prices and improving their own terms of trade. The problem, however, is that when all nations pursue this strategy, it gives rise to great inefficiencies: too much trade protection is produced and too little market access is available for growth. The literature on regimes points to a variety of ways in which international cooperation can change this individual calculation of interest.[11] In the case of trade regimes, the problem was ameliorated through the adoption of two fundamental principles: most-favored-nation (MFN) and reciprocity. These principles, however, did not equally affect the behavior of all members. Only those nations with large markets participated in the reciprocal lowering of tariffs, initially through the mutual exchange of benefits between principal suppliers of goods. Through a process of horse-trading market access in one set of goods for another, the large nations ratcheted down their tariff levels. This focus on the large markets is consistent with the explanation for the origins of the regime given by Bagwell and Staiger, since the terms-of-trade dilemma exists for a country with a market that is large enough to set the world price in a product.

Of course, the regime was created to include both big and small nations. At its inception in 1947, half of the nations that would join GATT were developing and not developed countries. These nations also benefited from regime participation but via the MFN provision in the GATT/WTO. Even in the absence of a commitment by the developing world to increase access to their own market, the MFN provision assured them of new export markets. Some southern countries did liberalize their markets in the pre-WTO period, either in a Round or in the process of accession, but the majority of these GATT members eschewed liberalization at home and grew their foreign trade through MFN-garnered export access.

Reliance on a norm–reciprocity (at least among big countries), and a rule–MFN, to fuel trade liberalization had long-term implications. The reciprocity norm made bargaining power in the GATT/WTO a function of market size and a nation's willingness to use the threat of market clo-

[10] Kyle Bagwell and Robert W. Staiger, "An Economic Theory of GATT," *American Economic Review* 89, no. 1 (March 1999), 215–248; Bagwell and Staiger, *The Economics of the World Trading System* (Cambridge, MA: MIT Press, 2002).

[11] See, for example, Robert Keohane, "The Demand for International Regimes," *International Organization* 36 (Spring 1982), 325–355.

sure as a means to influence others. Figure 7.1 shows actual market size (measured in GDP) of the biggest GATT/WTO members from 1949 through 2004, and projected market size from 2005 through 2034, as a percentage of GATT/WTO market size.[12] In the GATT's early years, U.S. GDP accounted for about 65 percent of GATT GDP; the United Kingdom accounted for another 10 percent. Since then, the relative size of the U.S. market has consistently declined; beginning in 1957, that of the EC has grown. Foreshadowing current problems, both Stephen Krasner and Lloyd Gruber have argued that this unequal power relation in the GATT system was part of the reason for the regime's success.[13]

To predict future growth, we used the projections of the Goldman Sachs Global Economic group. The Goldman Sachs model predicts growth as a function of growth in employment, growth in the capital stock, and total factor productivity (TFP) growth. TFP is modeled as a process of catch-up on the developed economies. The Goldman Sachs model forecasts for GDP growth in the next ten years are similar to IMF estimates of potential growth in the economies evaluated here.[14] We adjusted the Goldman Sachs growth rate projections downward for China and Russia in order to be conservative and to countervail implicit assumptions in the model about stable domestic political institutions and sound macroeconomic policies in those countries.

Shifting market share parallels coalition behavior in the GATT. The early years, 1947 to 1973, were a time of almost complete economic dominance by the United States. While the EC's market share was growing, it only accounted for an average of 15 percent of GATT GDP during

[12] National GDP figures for 1949–2004 are from the World Bank; they were converted into U.S. dollars at the annual average prevailing exchange rate, using IMF data. World Bank, *World Development Indicators* (Washington, DC: World Bank, 2005). Projected figures for 2005–2035 assume rates of national GDP growth for the largest WTO members that are similar to those used by the Global Economics group at Goldman Sachs. Dominic Wilson and Roopa Purushothaman, *Dreaming With BRICs: The Path to 2050*, Goldman Sachs Global Economics Paper no. 99 (New York: Goldman Sachs, 2003). Its projections are also close to those using the Levine and Renelt econometric model that explains average 30-year GDP growth as a function of initial per capita income, investment rates, population growth, and secondary school enrollments. Ross Levine and David Renelt, "A Sensitivity Analysis of Cross-Country Growth Regressions," *American Economic Review* 82 (September 1992), 942–963. For China, we assumed two shocks, one in 2010 (that would reduce growth from around 8% to 0% for that year, 3% in 2011, and 7% in 2012) and a large political shock in 2015 (resulting in -5% growth that year, returning to projected levels by 2019). For Russia, we assumed only the former shock.

[13] Stephen D. Krasner, "State Power and the Structure of International Trade," *World Politics* 25 (April 1976), 317–347; Lloyd Gruber, *Ruling the World: Power Politics and the Rise of Supranational Institutions* (Princeton, NJ: Princeton University Press, 2000).

[14] International Monetary Fund, *International Financial Statistics Yearbook* (Washington, DC: IMF, 2005).

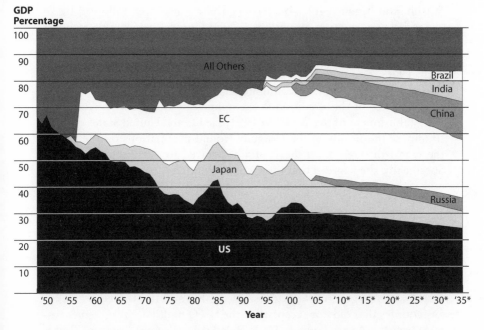

Figure 7.1. GDP of the largest WTO members as a percentage of GATT/WTO GDP, actual and projected, 1949–2034

the period. The establishment of the GATT itself best exemplifies U.S. dominance of the GATT negotiating process in these early years. The United States drafted the instrument that became the GATT 1947. It made accommodations to the United Kingdom, enabling the maintenance of colonial preferences, but the General Agreement was fundamentally U.S.-designed.[15]

By 1973, the U.S. share of GATT GDP had fallen below 40 percent and the EC share had grown to more than 20 percent. Other changes had occurred in the interim. Before 1973, EC institutions were insufficiently developed to enable Brussels to partner with Washington to govern the GATT system. By the mid-1970s, however, the role of the Commission in coordinating Europe's external commercial negotiations, and that of the 113 Committee in overseeing the Commission, were clearly established, enabling the EC to speak with a single voice.[16] As a result of both shifting market shares and better coordination among EC members, Brussels and

[15] Barton et al., *The Evolution of the Trade Regime.*
[16] Richard H. Steinberg, "The Transformation of European Trading States," in Jonah D. Levy, ed., *The State after Statism: New State Activities in the Age of Liberalization* (Cambridge, MA: Harvard University Press, 2006).

Washington began regular bilateral consultations, often followed by an expanded conversation among the "Quad Group," which also included Canada and Japan. Decisions of the "Quad Group" were then often presented as a fait accompli to the other GATT contracting parties. By the early 1970s, commentators had begun to suggest that U.S.-EC cooperation was necessary for successful negotiations at the GATT.[17]

The power of this coalition is exemplified by the events surrounding the establishment of the WTO. In 1991, the EC and United States decided to impose the results of the Uruguay Round negotiations on the rest of the world through what they initially referred to as "the power play." Specifically, they agreed that they would withdraw from the GATT 1947 and sign a substantively identical but legally distinct instrument, the GATT 1994. This would disengage Europe and the United States from their GATT 1947 MFN commitments to the rest of the world, and would replace them with new MFN commitments in the GATT 1994. The EC and U.S. negotiators agreed that these new commitments would be conditioned on third countries' acceptance of all the WTO multilateral agreements. The effect of this maneuver was to threaten closure of the world's two largest markets (those of the EC and the United States) to any country that did not accept *all* of the WTO multilateral agreements— including the Agreement on Trade-Related Intellectual Property Rights (TRIPs), the General Agreement on Trade in Services (GATS), the Understanding òn Balance-of-Payments Provisions of the GATT 1994, and other agreements, which most developing countries had previously refused to accept.[18] This transatlantic maneuver, which became known diplomatically as the "Single Undertaking" approach to closing the Uruguay Round, allowed the EC and United States to set the terms of the new organization. Now, all the regime's principles would be applicable to the developing world.

The Creation of Stalemate

For those favoring rapid and deeper liberalization, the WTO's biggest contemporary problem is an inability to gain consensus on a negotiated outcome. Stalemate in multilateral trade negotiations is the order of the day. Three developments explain the creation of stalemate.

[17] Gerard Curzon et al., "GATT: Trader's Club," in Robert W. Cox and Harold K. Jacobsen, eds., *The Anatomy of Influence: Decision-Making in International Organization* (New Haven, CT: Yale University Press, 1973).

[18] Richard H. Steinberg, "In the Shadow of Law or Power? Consensus-Based Bargaining and Outcomes in the GATT/WTO," *International Organization* 56 (Spring 2002), 339–374.

First, in recent years the norm of reciprocity has become generalized across all countries. Robert Hudec showed that throughout most of GATT history, North-South negotiations were characterized by non-reciprocity—an absence of expected reciprocity from poorer countries—a norm that he speculated might have started breaking down in the mid-1980s.[19] As of 1994, the norm of non-reciprocity became the exception, not the rule. Before then, the GATT made policy through an implicit bargain between the developed and the developing world. The northern countries opened up their markets but only in the range of products of their choosing; the South gained access to Northern markets without having to give reciprocal access. The cost of this deal was that the South could not choose what products gained access. In the 1970s, the GATT responded to the growing economic gap between the groups by expanding the number of preferences granted to developing nations, allowing access over and above that offered by MFN.

At the same time, starting in the 1970s, and increasingly by the mid-1980s, powerful constituencies in the North were demanding deeper liberalization that would discipline behind-the-border measures in such areas as technical barriers to trade, services regulations, and intellectual property protection. Moreover, as the U.S. trade balance deteriorated and the Asian Tigers emerged, various groups in the United States began demanding reciprocity from all countries. With this change in the focus of the trade regime and U.S. demands for a "level playing field," the North-South bargain became unstable. In return for agreement on a set of new rules, a developing world bloc began asking for changes in the negotiating agenda, especially for negotiations on a range of goods of their choosing. Unable or unwilling to offer much in return, negotiations have become attenuated and increasingly difficult.

Second, developing countries have adopted institutional strategies to sustain their coalitional behavior. Trade negotiations have always been difficult, and developing countries have in the past episodically joined together to influence negotiations. But the sustenance of contemporary developing-country coalitions is unprecedented. Developing countries are continuously acting in concert with each other, sustaining blocs that have successfully vetoed a range of various proposals favored by the EC and the United States.

The developing countries are not a unified bloc with identical interests, but they have figured out an institutional solution to remaining more unified and cohesive than ever before. Specifically, they are agreeing to bundle issues together, creating linkages across the interests of varying types of

---

[19] Robert E. Hudec, *Developing Countries in the GATT Legal System* (Aldershot, UK: Gower, 1987).

developing countries. In trade negotiations, efforts by countries to sustain a common and unified position on a single issue are unstable, susceptible to the "divide the dollar" problem. When a position is taken on a single issue by two or more countries, a third country may offer a coalition member a more attractive commercial concession to catalyze withdrawal from the common position. This was a common problem for the EC and United States in the early years of the Uruguay Round. For example, the EC and the United States had taken a common position in the TRIPs negotiations on the single issue of protecting pharmaceuticals in the regulatory pipeline; India was able to pry apart that coalition by offering the EC a politically valuable tariff concession in exchange for its shift of position on the pipeline issue. Europe and the United States solved the problem of being split asunder by agreeing to bundle issues, taking a common position on a host of issues of interest to each of them. In the Uruguay Round, the developing countries did not bundle and they were frequently frustrated in efforts to take a common position on individual issues.

In the Doha Round, the South seems to have learned this lesson. For example, the G-77 plus China took a common position opposing negotiation on issues such as competition policy, the environment, labor, and investment, and agreeing to support northern country industrial tariff and agricultural subsidy cuts, aid for trade, and access to medicines. The Africa Group meets annually to determine the set of issues that it will bundle together; Dr. Supachai has said that he is using his leadership of UNCTAD to help coordinate this bundling, with the knowledge that it is crucial for the cohesiveness of the Africa Group in the Doha Round. Similarly, the Newly Acceding Group of Countries in the G-20 has also done some bundling.

Since 1995, the developing world has been more successful than ever before at ending northern hegemony of the GATT/WTO system. Although not able to force the developed world into compliance to their wishes, they have become effective veto players, a role they have repeatedly played with success in the Doha Round. In other episodes of GATT/WTO history, developing countries have also displayed unity, particularly when they successfully blocked conclusion of the Tokyo Round negotiations unless they were given a free ride on the MTN agreements (which were concluded as codes and accorded MFN treatment). But until the Doha Round, the developing world never sustained cooperation in both the early and middle stages of a Round, when the agenda is typically set and the texts of the agreements themselves are being negotiated.

Third, beginning in the 1990s, the EC and then the United States began accelerating their conclusion of PTAs, which has had the apparently unintended and unanticipated consequence of diminishing their bargaining power at the WTO. Largely in pursuit of a strategy of "competitive liberalization," the conclusion of PTAs became a cornerstone of EC and U.S.

trade policy in the 1990s. In one version, "competitive liberalization" resulted from a belief that trade liberalization at three levels—multilateral, regional, and bilateral—would be necessary for developing countries to implement economic reforms. In another version, "competitive liberalization" meant that bilateral PTAs with a hub-and-spoke architecture concluded by the EC, on one hand, and United States, on the other, would pressure excluded third countries (by operation of trade and investment diversion) to also demand PTAs with Washington and Brussels; the idea was that eventually the terms of these PTAs could be multilateralized at the WTO.[20] By mid-2006, the EC had concluded nearly forty PTAs, with additional negotiations under way to convert the Lome Agreement into a set of reciprocal free trade agreements covering an additional seventy-three African, Caribbean, and Pacific countries. By the same time, the United States had concluded PTAs covering trade with fifteen countries, covering nearly one-third of total American trade, and was negotiating to conclude more.

As far as we can tell, neither Washington nor Brussels fully appreciated the ways in which the strategy of competitive liberalization could backfire on multilateralism and make progress at the WTO more difficult. It is one thing to conclude a bilateral deal between Washington (or Brussels) and a smaller country; it is quite another to multilateralize its terms with a third country like China. Moreover, the PTA strategy accompanied a new intransigence on the part of the EC and United States in the Doha Round, in part a function of the availability of an alternative to WTO liberalization. Most important, however, the conclusion of these PTAs has diminished EC and U.S. bargaining power at the WTO by providing bilateral MFN guarantees to PTA partners. Legally, the proliferation of EC- and U.S.-centered PTAs has fatally constrained the ability of Europe and the United States to behave as hegemonic duopolists. Since each of the PTAs contains a MFN provision, neither Brussels nor Washington can replay the "power play" they used to conclude the Uruguay Round: the third countries with which they have concluded PTAs may rely on the MFN provisions in those PTAs to ensure continued market access to Europe and the United States without regard to whether they continue to enjoy an MFN guarantee through WTO agreements. Proliferation of PTAs therefore poses a significant legal-political constraint on European-U.S. hegemony, a constraint that did not exist a decade ago.

Because of these shifts—the end of non-reciprocity toward the South, sustained developing-country coalitions, and U.S.- and EC-centered PTA

[20] C. Fred Bergsten, "Globalizing Free Trade," *Foreign Affairs* 75 (May/June 1996), 105–120; Robert B. Zoellick, "Campaign 2000: A Republican Foreign Policy," *Foreign Affairs* 79 (January/February 2000), 63–78; Raj Bhala, "Competitive Liberalization, Competitive Imperialism, and Intellectual Property," *Liverpool Law Review* 28 (April 2007), 77–105.

proliferation—decision making has become increasingly difficult in the WTO. Nothing symbolizes and illustrates this power shift[21] better than the new "Quad." In Geneva, "the Quad" no longer refers—as it did for decades—to the EC, Japan, Canada, and the United States, a group that effectively governed the GATT and shared fundamentally convergent views on the desirability and content of liberalization. Now "the Quad" refers to Brazil, India, the EC, and the United States, a group that has been routinely convened to advance the Doha Round but holds comparatively divergent views about what should be liberalized and who should do it.

The South, now being asked to deliver their markets to international commerce, has become an important demandeur in trade negotiations. What they want, however, is not easily squared with domestic interests in the North. The agriculture and steel industries in Europe and the United States remain well organized, well financed, and opposed to liberalization. These long-standing protectionist sectors, which have long captured government in the North, have become a key obstacle to a successful multilateral negotiation.

At the same time, the South may be unable to deliver in negotiations on key issues. If there were a deal to be struck at the WTO, it would entail a commitment by the South to address new behind-the-border measures. Credibly committing to such reforms, however, is difficult, given the inefficiencies in state structures in most of the developing world. In Europe and the United States, constituencies now demand that trade negotiations focus on issues such as services, investment, competition policy, labor, environment, and culture. Yet, such demands fly in the face of fundamental principles of sovereignty in the state system. Unlike border measures that invoke a political problem because they lead to factor reallocation, many of these issues implicate fundamental features of these nations such as changes in the regulatory structure and capacity of the state, the political structure of society (for example, the power of organized labor), or the industrial structure of the economy. Rules addressing these areas are hard to establish in developing countries, where state capacity and authority structures are simply too poorly developed.

---

[21] These changes in Geneva and the ensuing stalemate do not reflect a fundamental shift in *market* power of WTO members. Some have claimed that the expanded number of developing countries in the WTO, combined with the spectacular economic growth of China and India, are shifting material bargaining power to the South. The data does not support this claim. China and India are growing, and the number of developing-country members is increasing, but their markets are still comparatively small. Still, we can assume that over the next thirty years, material power at the WTO is likely to shift as figure 7.1 illustrates. While predicted GDP from 2005 to 2035 is highly speculative, figure 7.1 suggests some interesting developments: material power at the WTO will diffuse, moving toward a five- or six-power system over the next thirty years, with the United States and EC still important, but in decline, and China and India clearly rising in prominence.

In summary, as a result of increased developing-country bargaining power at the WTO, a changed agenda, and a growing divide between North-South interests and their respective state capacities, multilateral liberalization through trade negotiations has become increasingly difficult. This explains the slow pace of negotiations during the Doha Round. The Cancun Ministerial ended in deadlock in 2003. In December 2005, the Hong Kong Ministerial ended with a fig leaf of proclaimed success but with no deep substantive progress on key issues. By the summer of 2006, negotiations had collapsed. Although they were revived, they have remained deadlocked. The South will not accede to northern demands that it reduce industrial tariffs and agricultural trade barriers; much of the South lacks the state capacity necessary to address behind-the-border issues that are of increasing interest to the North; and the North—due largely to domestic political capture—will not accede to southern demands to unilaterally reduce industrial and agricultural protection and subsidization.

Any outcome for the Doha Round will be minimalist. Compared to the ambitions of European and U.S. trade policymakers and policy wonks before the Round was launched—for a Round that would zero industrial tariffs, eliminate agricultural subsidies, and address environmental, labor, competition, investment, and transparency issues—the Round has been a failure. But while the ministers of the member nations have been unable to agree on the trade agenda, the judicial branch of the WTO has slowly begun to address contested policies.

THE RISE OF JUDICIAL LIBERALIZATION

While liberalization through negotiation has become more difficult in the last decade, liberalization (of a different quality, to be sure) has gotten easier through the litigation path. We contend that there is more litigation now than in the GATT years, that the contemporary dispute settlement system engages in more lawmaking than in the GATT years, and that WTO judicial lawmaking has a liberalizing bias.

The Institutional Context for Change

The rise of judicial liberalization in the GATT/WTO system, and the WTO's dispute settlement rules and processes, are best understood in the context of the GATT's dispute settlement rules and processes. The GATT was created to facilitate bargaining among participants over the regulation and liberalization of trade policy. Although concerned that nations live up to their promises, the mechanism for oversight depended upon a nation, in the name of a producer, complaining about a violation. The secretariat had neither oversight nor judicial power. Although the secretariat compiled data on trade practices starting in 1989 through the Trade Policy Review Mechanism (TPRM), the data in these reports constituted neither formal grounds for a dispute nor legal evidence of a country's trade practices. Monitoring occurred through oversight by individual contracting parties; when a complaint was filed, the Secretariat assisted in the formation of a panel. If the panel found in favor of the complainant, and no contracting party blocked a consensus to adopt the panel report, then the contravening party was legally required to change its behavior. In the absence of a change in practice, little could be done other than sanctioning retaliation—though that too required a consensus.

The weakness of the GATT dispute settlement procedure became increasingly apparent in the 1980s. In the early years of GATT, 1948–1959, contracting parties brought relatively few (53) legal complaints against each other. The panel procedure mentioned above was developed in these years and it was used in over half of these cases.[22] As the number of contracting parties grew, the number of conflicts increased. Perhaps reflecting dissatisfaction with the settlement procedures, the number of formal complaints did not rise and, in fact, fell after 1963. While almost sixty cases were dealt with by the dispute settlement process through 1962, only one new case was brought forward through 1970. Hudec argued the issue was legitimacy—the process was viewed as unfair.[23] Legitimate or not, the caseload increased in the 1970s to a total of thirty-two; in the 1980s the panel process began to be regularly invoked.[24] Of the 115 complaints filed in the 1980s, 47 led to panel reports. However, only about two-fifths of rulings for the complainant resulted in full compliance by the respondent.[25] Nonetheless, the increased caseload forced the Secretariat to create a separate legal division, which had the effect of encouraging even more legal complaints. As the number, visibility, and importance of cases increased, so too did the number of cases in which consensus was blocked.

During the 1970s and 1980s, in response to frustration with the GATT dispute system and in the face of a growing trade deficit and the perceptions of unfair trade practices abroad, the United States turned to domestic law to deal with its trade problems. Specifically, a "unilateral" ap-

[22] Robert E. Hudec, "The New WTO Dispute Settlement Procedure: An Overview of the First Three Years," *Minnesota Journal of Global Trade* 8 (Winter 1999), 1–53.

[23] Ibid.

[24] Ibid.

[25] Marc L. Busch and Eric Reinhardt, "Testing International Trade Law: Empirical Studies of GATT/WTO Dispute Settlement," in Daniel L. Kennedy and James D. Southwick, eds., *The Political Economy of International Trade Law: Essays in Honor of Robert E. Hudec* (Cambridge: Cambridge University Press, 2002), 473.

proach to addressing trade disputes was enacted by the U.S. Congress in the form of Section 301 of the Trade Act of 1974. Section 301 permits (and in some cases, requires) the president to impose retaliatory trade sanctions on countries engaging in practices that are "unjustifiable, discriminatory, or unfair"—as determined by the USTR. Thus, when a foreign government blocked the GATT dispute settlement process, the U.S. government often found itself in a position of threatening unilateral trade retaliation against that government unless it agreed to change its trade practices in accordance with Washington's demands. This American approach to the settlement of trade disputes was not viewed favorably by the rest of the world.

As part of an attempt to credibly commit to the regime in the post–Cold War days and because of a belief that the United States was in compliance with GATT rules, the United States championed a toughening of the dispute settlement procedures.[26] In 1989, the United States had supported a new dispute settlement understanding adopted in the Midterm Review of the Uruguay Round; in the next year, the United States heralded an even more radical change in the rules. The underlying theme was that it was time for member nations to agree to give up their right to block a consensus in the establishment of panels, the adoption of panel reports, and retaliation. Initially aligned closely with Canada but not the other Quad members, the U.S. proposal not only included the automatic adoption of panel reports, but also created a right to appeal to a new Appellate Body whose purpose was to oversee the work of panels on questions of law. The time limits established in this process would be modeled on its own Section 301 statute. For the United States, this seemingly radical position was contingent on a crucial proviso—that the substantive rules adopted in the Uruguay Round had to be adequately specific and reflect U.S. policy objectives.[27]

At home, increased delegation under these terms was argued to be consistent with American interests: the United States would remain more often in compliance with WTO rules that reflected its interests and policy objectives than would its trading partners. If the WTO's substantive rules were to its liking, and the dispute settlement procedures were consistent with the timeline for action under Section 301 and could ultimately authorize retaliation for noncompliance, then a more legalized WTO dispute

[26] For more details on this argument see Judith Goldstein and Joanne Gowa, "US National Power and the Post-War Trading Regime," *World Trade Review* 1 (July 2002), 153–170.

[27] This description of the U.S. position in 1990 is documented in "Dispute Settlement, U.S. Objectives for Brussels," in *The U.S. Delegation Briefing Book for the Brussels Ministerial* (United States Trade Representative, December 1990) (on file with the authors).

settlement system would legitimize U.S. use of its market power to pressure other countries to comply with U.S. trade policy objectives. Tellingly, the United States shifted to this position on dispute settlement reform at the end of 1990, at the same time that it reached agreement with the EC to impose the results of the Uruguay Round on developing countries via the "single undertaking." Few nations agreed with the U.S. analysis of who would end up in front of panels. But curbing U.S. unilateralism was one of the most salient elements in both Japan's and the EC's publicly stated interest in the Round, and both endorsed the reforms.

In the end, the new procedures occupied thirty-five pages of text and an elaborate accompanying description. The process is far more complex and precise than in the past and covers all areas of WTO agreements, including Section 301 actions by the United States. The DSU is far more obligatory, automatic, and apolitical than the GATT rules. The effect of the change—a vast increase in use of the DSU—was far broader than was anticipated by most. While 535 dispute settlement complaints were filed in the 46-year period of the GATT system, 269 complaints were filed in the first eight years alone of the WTO system.[28]

THE IMPACT OF REGULATORY CHANGE

The dispute settlement change meant that two substantive shifts occurred in the WTO judicial system. First, judicial action became more automatic. A consensus is now required to *block* the formation of a panel, adoption of a report, or an authorization of retaliation for continued noncompliance—a reversal of the former rule that required a consensus to move through each of these stages. Of course, petitioners would not agree to block establishment of a panel they are demanding, and prevailing parties would not block the adoption of favorable panel reports.

Second, the reform led to the creation of a judicial body to which nations could appeal panel reports. The Appellate Body's mandate is formally limited to the review of legal findings made by panels, given the facts established by the panel. The Appellate Body has seven members, chosen by the Members at large, and appeals are heard by a subset of three members.

[28] Data for the 1995–2003 period is from Kara Leitner and Simon Lester, "WTO Dispute Settlement 1995–2003: A Statistical Analysis," *Journal of International Economic Law* 7 (November 2004), 169–181. Data from the 1948–1995 period are from Busch and Reinhardt, "Testing International Trade Law: Empirical Studies of GATT/WTO Dispute Settlement," in Kennedy and Southwick, 473. These include complaints that ended prior to a panel decision and those that went on to be decided by a panel and adopted by the members.

The automaticity of the new system, and the promise that it has held for aggrieved members, has led to an increased caseload for the WTO dispute settlement system, compared to the GATT dispute settlement system. Moreover, because of automaticity, there were more dispositive reports (that is, adopted panel reports in cases where there was no appeal; adopted Appellate Body reports in all other cases) issued in the first six years of the WTO system than in the last twenty years of the GATT system.[29] And there are far more parties to WTO disputes than to GATT disputes. In the GATT era, it was rare for a case to feature more than one complainant. In contrast, in the WTO era, in nearly half of all cases there are multiple complainants or interested third parties. Not only have caseloads increased; so has the number of parties involved in each dispute.

The Emergence of Judicial Lawmaking

Many scholars have suggested that judges may behave strategically and favor increasing their authority,[30] yet few Uruguay Round negotiators anticipated or intended the Appellate Body to engage in lawmaking.[31] The switch to automatic, binding dispute resolution, and the establishment of the Appellate Body, were seen by the United States as an opportunity to foster implementation of and compliance with the deals struck in the legislative process—even if those deals were not optimally efficient and

[29] Marc L. Busch and Eric Reinhardt, "Developing Countries and General Agreement on Tariffs and Trade/World Trade Organization Dispute Settlement, *Journal of World Trade* 37 (August 2003), 719–735, 724; Richard H. Steinberg, "Judicial Lawmaking at the WTO: Discursive, Constitutional, and Political Constraints," *American Journal of International Law* 98 (April 2004), 247–275.

[30] Anne-Marie Burley and Walter Mattli, "Europe Before the Court: A Political Theory of Legal Integration," *International Organization* 47 (Winter 1993), 41–76; John Ferejohn and Barry Weingast, "The Limitation of Statutes: Strategic Statutory Interpretation," *Georgetown Law Journal* 80 (February 1992), 565–582; Erik Voeten, "The Politics of International Judicial Appointments: Evidence from the European Court of Human Rights," *International Organization* 61 (Fall 2007), 669–701.

[31] Richard H. Steinberg interview with A. Jane Bradley, former chief U.S. dispute settlement negotiator and Assistant USTR for Enforcement, Washington, DC, March 2007; and Richard H. Steinberg interview with Kenneth Freiberg, USTR Deputy General Counsel, Washington, DC, March 2007, support this conclusion. A handful of lawyers in the USTR's General Counsel's office were concerned about judicial lawmaking, but those at the political level in both Washington and Brussels were persuaded by the clarity of the WTO agreements and the WTO DSU Articles 3.2 and 19.2 mandates that neither panels nor the Appellate Body could "add to nor diminish the rights and obligations provided in the covered agreements." U.S. Senator Bob Dole was concerned enough about judicial lawmaking that he proposed establishment of a commission to review the decisions and behavior of the Appellate Body, but only twelve co-sponsors joined him in support of the proposal and it never passed the Senate.

even if they were not considered equitable. The dispute settlement process was to fulfill that purpose by offering a neutral judicial process to enforce WTO agreements the substance of which was largely favored by the United States. Most U.S. policymakers at the time expected WTO dispute settlement to enforce the WTO "contract"; they did not expect or accurately anticipate that the Appellate Body would make law.

As in domestic legal systems, rules and principles guiding the interpretation of public international law permitted the Appellate Body to take a range of interpretive stances: at one extreme, a restrained interpretive stance that is highly deferential to the express consent of states; at the other extreme, an expansive interpretive stance that is less deferential to state consent, favors dynamic interpretation of treaty provisions, and expands upon terms and gaps. Largely in the interests of completeness, coherence, and internal consistency of WTO law, the Appellate Body chose a more expansive stance both on questions of whether to interpret and on the method used for interpretation. The resulting judicial decisions have created an expansive body of new law.

WTO judicial lawmaking has two dimensions: filling gaps and clarifying ambiguities. Gap-filling refers to judicial lawmaking on a question for which there is no legal text directly on point, whereas ambiguity clarification refers to judicial lawmaking on a question for which there is legal text but that text needs clarification.[32]

First, the DSU's silence on many procedural questions has been seen by some as an invitation to the Appellate Body to make procedural rules. In some cases, the Appellate Body has created law that fills procedural gaps in WTO agreements, even though the existence of the gap has resulted from sharp disagreement among Members about how to fill it. For example, in *United States v. Import Prohibition of Certain Shrimp and Shrimp Products (Shrimp-Turtle 2000)*, the Appellate Body decided—without clear guidance from WTO agreements—that dispute settlement panels could consider *amicus curiae* briefs submitted by non-state actors. In so ruling, the Appellate Body relied on general language in DSU Article 13, which provides that panels have a right to seek information and technical advice from any individual or body that it deems appropriate. Regardless of the merits on the question, the Appellate Body's interpretation of Article 13 was made in the context of several years of North-South deadlock on the question of whether to permit *amicus* briefs: few developing countries would have consented to an agreement with that outcome, yet the Appellate Body chose to interpret the DSU as supporting it.

---

[32] Ultimately, the distinction between gap-filling and ambiguity clarification may be fragile, but the distinction is respected here out of convention. See generally H.L.A. Hart, *The Concept of Law* (Oxford: Clarendon Press, 1961).

Similarly, in *European Communities v. Regime for the Importation, Sale and Distribution of Bananas* (*EC v. Bananas 1997*), the Appellate Body established that private lawyers may represent Members in its oral proceedings, despite EC and U.S. opposition on grounds that the practice from the earliest years of the GATT was to permit presentations in dispute settlement proceedings exclusively by government lawyers or government trade experts. The Appellate Body acted at odds with nearly fifty years of GATT practice, reasoning that nothing in WTO agreements, customary international law, or the "prevailing practice of international tribunals . . . prevents a WTO Member from determining the composition of its delegation in Appellate Body proceedings." At the panel stage, this practice of permitting participation by nongovernment lawyers was subsequently adopted in *Indonesia v. Certain Measures Affecting the Automobile Industry* (*Indonesia v. Autos 1998*).

Second, the WTO Appellate Body has engaged repeatedly in a form of lawmaking by which it has given specific meaning to ambiguous treaty language. Such clarifications may cause a negative political reaction by Members or nongovernmental stakeholders that engaged in behavior that was within a range of possible meanings, given the ambiguity. For example, in *Shrimp-Turtle 2000*, the Appellate Body decided whether the United States could rely on GATT Article XX(g) to ban the importation of certain shrimp and shrimp products from Members that did not maintain laws that guaranteed particular methods of protecting endangered sea turtles in the process of shrimp fishing. GATT Article XX(g) excepts certain measures from the GATT's affirmative obligations if they are necessary for the "conservation of exhaustible natural resources," but the provision is ambiguous through silence on the question of whether such exhaustible natural resources must be located within the jurisdiction of the country invoking the exception. Earlier decisions suggesting that they must catalyzed enormous debate by the members. The Appellate Body offered a dynamic interpretation of the conditions under which the GATT Article XX(g) exception for conservation of exhaustible natural resources could be invoked, stating that it must be read "in light of contemporary concerns of the community of nations about the protection and conservation of the environment." After concluding that the measures in question fell within the meaning of Article XX(g), the Appellate Body interpreted the chapeau to Article XX and established at least five specific factors that would apply in considering whether a measure contravenes the terms of the chapeau. Some of the factors had no textual lineage (for example, whether the respondent's actions have an "intended and coercive effect on the specific policy decisions of other members"). In short, the Appellate Body ruling provided an approach to balancing trade-environment issues, despite WTO Members having been deadlocked for a decade about how to achieve balance on the question.

Third, in a number of instances, the Appellate Body has given precise and narrow meaning to language that was intentionally left vague by negotiators, either because they could not agree on more specific language, or in order to permit a range of alternative behaviors or national practices. For example, in three decisions, *United States v. Safeguard Measures on Imports of Fresh, Chilled or Frozen Lamb Meat from New Zealand and Australia (2001)*, *United States v. Definitive Safeguard Measures on Imports of Wheat Gluten from the European Communities (2000)*, and *United States v. Definitive Safeguard Measures on Imports of Circular Welded Carbon Quality Line Pipe from Korea (2002)*, the Appellate Body fleshed out the causation analysis to be used in safeguards cases, which Uruguay Round negotiators intentionally left ambiguous.[33] In the *Lamb Meat* case, for example, based on the obligation not to attribute injury from other causes to imports that were the subject of a safeguards investigation, the Appellate Body established an affirmative requirement that national authorities analyze not only the nature but also the "extent" of other causes. A similar approach was taken in the anti-dumping context in *United States v. Antidumping Measures on Certain Hot-Rolled Steel Products from Japan* (*U.S. v. Japan Hot-Rolled Steel 2001*). The U.S. government and commentators have identified several other cases in which the Appellate Body or dispute settlement panels have given a specific and narrow interpretation of language in WTO agreements that was intended by at least some of its negotiators to be ambiguous and to permit a range of national practices.[34] Decisions like these might enhance efficiency,[35] but they are certain to engender negative political reactions in countries that intended to consent to broader interpretations.

[33] In the Uruguay Round negotiations, U.S. negotiators had refused to agree to a test that would require national authorities to quantify the relative effects of imports and other factors on domestic industry. In so refusing, the U.S. negotiators intended to enable the ITC to continue using its qualitative approach to analysis of the "substantial cause" question in safeguards cases. Richard H. Steinberg interview with Tim Reif, Democratic Chief Trade Counsel, U.S. House Committee on Ways and Means, in Washington, DC, April 2002.

[34] United States Secretary of Commerce, *Executive Branch Strategy Regarding WTO Dispute Settlement Panels and the Appellate Body, Report to the Congress Transmitted by the Secretary of Commerce*, December 30, 2002, available at http://www.ita.doc.gov/Final Dec31ReportCorrected.pdf, 8–10; Daniel K. Tarullo, "The Hidden Costs of International Dispute Settlement: WTO Review of Domestic Anti-Dumping Decisions," *Law and Policy in International Business* 34 (Fall 2002), 109–181; Claude E. Barfield, *Free Trade, Sovereignty, Democracy: The Future of the World Trade Organization* (Washington, DC: AEI Press, 2001).

[35] Alan O. Sykes, "Trade Remedy Laws," in Andrew T. Guzman and Alan O. Sykes, eds., *Research Handbook in International Economic Law* (Cheltenham, UK: Edward Elgar Press, 2007).

Finally, a conflict between GATT/WTO texts (or between text and GATT practice) may create an ambiguity and in a handful of cases, the Appellate Body has read language across GATT/WTO agreements cumulatively in a way that has generated an expansive set of legal obligations. Perhaps most controversially, in *U.S. v. Lambmeat* and *Argentina v. Safeguard Measures on Imports of Footwear (1999)*, the Appellate Body ruled that national authorities imposing a safeguards measure must demonstrate the existence of "unforeseen developments." In the 1952 *U.S. v. Hatters' Fur* case, a GATT Working Party had agreed that the application of Article XIX safeguards measures could be based on an argument that an unexpected degree of change in consumer tastes that increased imports constituted demonstration of "unforeseen developments." Given that implicitly broad interpretation of the phrase, which would seem to allow almost any increase in imports to constitute "unforeseen developments," subsequent GATT panels did not require national authorities to demonstrate "unforeseen developments" prior to imposing safeguards measures. Moreover, the WTO Safeguards Agreement makes no reference to a requirement to demonstrate "unforeseen developments," and the negotiators expressly considered and rejected inclusion of any such requirement. The cumulation of GATT practice, relevant texts, and negotiating history created an ambiguity over whether "unforeseen developments" must be demonstrated in safeguards cases. Focusing on GATT Article XIX:1(a), the Appellate Body read all of the relevant GATT/WTO law and practice cumulatively in a way that led to the conclusion that a demonstration of "unforeseen developments" must be shown if a safeguards measure is to be applied.

While there is no doubt that the WTO Appellate Body is making law, we do not claim that it has, on balance, been irresponsibly "activist."[36] All courts make law to varying degrees. The Appellate Body has not shied

---

[36] "Activism" is a term subject to alternative definitions and normative assessments. For example, compare textualist with dynamic approaches to activist statutory interpretation. For example, Frank H. Easterbrook, "Statutes' Domains," *University of Chicago Law Review* 50 (Spring 1983), 533–552, 547; William N. Eskridge, Jr., "Politics Without Romance: Implications of Public Choice Theory for Statutory Interpretation," *Virginia Law Review* 74 (March 1988), 275–338; Karen M. Gebbia-Pinetti, "Statutory Interpretation, Democratic Legitimacy and Legal System Values," *Seton Hall Legislative Journal* 21, no. 2 (1997), 233–345, 281; John F. Manning, "Textualism as a Nondelegation Doctrine," *Columbia Law Review* 97 (April 1997), 673–739, 685; Nicholas S. Zeppos, "The Use of Authority in Statutory Interpretation: An Empirical Analysis," *Texas Law Review* 70 (April 1992), 1073–1144 , 1078–1079. Debates over WTO activism usually consider Appellate Body holdings that domestic measures contravene WTO obligations, or whether the Appellate Body has remained true to some posited, deduced, or constructed intent of those who negotiated a substantive provision of a WTO agreement. Most of those characterizing WTO dispute settlement as "activist" do so pejoratively.

away from lawmaking, but it has at times restrained itself, demonstrating some sensitivity to politics. For example, it has sometimes invoked the doctrine of "judicial economy" to limit the extent to which it interprets WTO agreements in any particular case.[37] This measure of self-restraint begs the question: How expansive is WTO judicial lawmaking and to what degree does it operate in the shadow of domestic regulatory law?

The Expansiveness of Judicial Lawmaking: The GATT and WTO Compared

Is WTO lawmaking more expansive than lawmaking in the GATT era? Some commentators have attempted to quantify the extent of judicial lawmaking (often referred to as "activism") in municipal or comparative contexts.[38] Virtually every such effort measures the rate at which constitutional courts strike down laws. Empirically, analysis of GATT and WTO dispute settlement reports reveals no statistically significant difference between the two systems in the per-case likelihood that national laws will be deemed inconsistent with GATT/WTO obligations.[39] However, these data imply that the annual volume of such lawmaking may have increased, since there are many more dispositive WTO reports per year than adopted panel reports per year in the GATT era.

Comparing the extent of lawmaking in the WTO and GATT eras by using such a measure is of limited value in explaining how the GATT/WTO legal system has changed. Conceptually, the nature of judicial action may change across several dimensions—not just the dimension measured by lawmaking—as political or constitutional context changes.

Evaluating the expansiveness of judicial lawmaking demands a multidimensional analysis that focuses on the rate and scope of judicial gapfilling and ambiguity clarification, factored by the volume of dispositive dispute settlement reports.[40] The rate of judicial lawmaking refers to the

---

[37] See, for example, World Trade Organization Appellate Body, *European Communities—Measures Affecting the Importation of Certain Poultry Products*, WTO Doc. WT/DS69/AB/R, ¶ 135, July 23, 1998; *United States–Measure Affecting Imports of Woven Shirts and Blouses from India*, WTO Doc. WT/DS33/AB/R, § VI, April 25, 1997.

[38] Bradley C. Cannon, "A Framework for the Analysis of Judicial Activism," in Stephen C. Halpern and Charles M. Lamb, eds., *Supreme Court Activism and Restraint* (Lexington: Lexington Books, 1982); Arend Lijphart, *Patterns of Democracy: Government Forms and Performance in Thirty-Six Countries* (New Haven, CT: Yale University Press, 1999).

[39] Steinberg, "Judicial Lawmaking at the WTO: Discursive, Constitutional, and Political Constraints," 247.

[40] See Robert Keohane, Andrew Moravcsik, and Anne-Marie Slaughter, "Legalized Dispute Resolution: Interstate and Transnational," *International Organization* 54 (Summer 2000), 457–488.

proportion of dispute settlement reports in which ambiguity is clarified or gaps are filled. The scope of judicial lawmaking refers to the extent to which ambiguity is clarified or a gap is filled. The volume of dispute settlement reports refers to the number of dispositive reports adopted annually by the Dispute Settlement Body (DSB).

Rigorous quantitative comparison of the expansiveness of GATT and WTO judicial lawmaking is difficult, because measuring the rate and scope of ambiguity clarification or gap-filling by a particular court entails highly qualitative judgments. Nonetheless, there are good reasons to believe that judicial lawmaking is more expansive in the WTO than in the GATT era. As discussed above, GATT panel reports were aimed at the diplomatic settlement of disputes, whereas WTO dispute settlement serves an essentially adjudicative function. GATT panel reports had no legal effect unless they were adopted by consensus; in effect, no law could be made without the consent of the Contracting Parties, whereas WTO dispute settlement reports are adopted by negative consensus. As a result, GATT judicial lawmaking could not be expected to have been as bold and far-reaching in scope as judicial lawmaking in the WTO. Moreover, even if no change had occurred in the rate of scope of judicial lawmaking since the GATT era, judicial lawmaking would still be more expansive in the WTO system because of the increased dispute settlement caseload described above.

Given the highly qualitative nature of any comparative assessment of the expansiveness of judicial lawmaking, the consequent contestability of any individual effort to make such an assessment, the potential selection bias inherent in the body of cases concluded by each of the two dispute settlement systems, and variance in the form of GATT dispute settlement over time (i.e., its increasing legalization), it is more useful to consider a few indicators of change in the expansiveness of judicial lawmaking than to offer any single commentator's reportedly quantitative or qualitative assessment of change.

Several indicators suggest that judicial lawmaking is more expansive in the WTO than in the GATT. Compare, for example, discussions about judicial lawmaking by DSU negotiators in the GATT Uruguay Round to discussions by DSU negotiators in the Doha Round. Analysis of publicly available notes by the secretariat concerning the Uruguay Round Negotiating Group on Dispute Settlement indicates no instance in which a negotiator suggested that GATT dispute settlement panels were activist or engaged in expansive lawmaking.[41] While the Uruguay Round preparatory

---

[41] Judicial lawmaking was raised several times in the Uruguay Round dispute settlement negotiations, but in all those instances participants were expressing a preference that prospective changes in the dispute settlement system should not create, by constructive interpre-

materials are incomplete, the leading secondary history of the Uruguay Round DSU negotiations nowhere mentioned any discussion of activism or lawmaking by GATT panels.[42] Finally, lawyers from the Office of the United States Trade Representative (USTR) identified only four GATT panel reports that were criticized by contracting parties as instances of overly broad lawmaking or inappropriate interpretation.[43]

In contrast, analysis of publicly available official documents of the Doha Round Negotiating Group on Dispute Settlement, which has convened in special sessions of the DSB, indicates that in just the first eighteen months of negotiations—by June 2003—concern about instances of or proposed solutions to judicial lawmaking by WTO panels or the Appellate Body were raised seventy-seven times by representatives of fifty-five members (including the EC and the United States), focusing on at least ten dispositive WTO dispute settlement reports adopted in the WTO's first eight years. Moreover, confidential notes on meetings of the DSU Reform Group, in which ambassadors representing approximately ten members have met regularly for informal discussions of concerns about the operation of the DSU, reveal that judicial lawmaking was considered at almost every meeting during the period for which the notes are available.

Consider also journal articles on the subject. Of 110 selected U.S. and Canadian law journal articles on GATT dispute settlement published from 1982 to 1994 (the last year of the GATT system), only two mention cases in which controversial, expansive, or activist judicial lawmaking might have taken place. In contrast, at least fifty-one articles published in similarly selected U.S. and Canadian law journals in the first eight years of the WTO discuss controversial, expansive, or activist judicial lawmaking for cases in the WTO period.[44]

More broadly, we note the emergence of a public policy debate over judicial activism in the WTO, a debate that simply did not exist in the

---

tation, obligations that were not established in the texts of GATT/WTO agreements. GATT Secretariat, *Meeting of 25 June 1987, Note by the Secretariat, Negotiating Group on Dispute Settlement*, GATT Doc. MTN.GNG/NG13/2, July 15, 1987; GATT Secretariat, *Summary and Comparative Analysis of Proposals for Negotiations, Note by the Secretariat, Negotiating Group on Dispute Settlement*, GATT Doc. MTN.GNG/NG13/W/14/Rev.2, June 22, 1988.

[42] John Croome, *Reshaping the World Trading System: A History of the Uruguay Round* (World Trade Organization, 1995).

[43] Telephone interviews by Richard H. Steinberg with A. Jane Bradley and Kenneth Freiberg, January 2003, described in Steinberg, "Judicial Lawmaking at the WTO: Discursive, Constitutional, and Political Constraints," 256, note 68.

[44] Steinberg, "Judicial Lawmaking at the WTO: Discursive, Constitutional, and Political Constraints," 247.

GATT years. Several prominent commentators,[45] lawyers,[46] leaders of nongovernmental organizations,[47] and politicians from the United States[48] and abroad[49] have suggested that the WTO Appellate Body is engaging in judicial activism.

Liberalization through WTO Dispute Settlement?

In most cases, Appellate Body interpretations have favored more trade openness. In all cases, complainants advance interpretations of WTO agreements that challenge a respondent's trade barrier, and respondents argue for interpretations that would permit maintenance of the barrier. For WTO cases initiated before 2001, 89 percent of the 152 dispositive reports held that at least one of the national measures at issue was WTO-inconsistent.[50] Qualitative assessments of Appellate Body decisions, such as those by Dan Tarullo, have also shown a liberalizing bias.[51]

Some might hypothesize that the Appellate Body nonetheless favors protectionist interpretations in cases involving measures putatively adopted for reasons related to consumer or environmental protection. But several decisions run contrary to that claim: for example, in the *EC v. Beef Hormones* case, and in the more recent *EC v. GMO* case, the WTO Appellate Body has shown little tolerance for interpretations favoring closure, even though those cases raised politically sensitive social concerns. Even in cases where the Appellate Body has ultimately permitted social measures to serve as a barrier to trade, it has made law that restricts the

---

[45] See, for example, Claude E. Barfield, *Free Trade, Sovereignty, Democracy: The Future of the World Trade Organization* (Washington, DC: AEI Press, 2001); Kal Raustiala, "Sovereignty and Multilateralism," *Chicago Journal of International Law* 1 (Fall 2000), 401–419; Tarullo, "The Hidden Costs of International Dispute Settlement: WTO Review of Domestic Anti-Dumping Decisions," 109.

[46] See, for example, John Ragosta, Navin Joneja, and Mikhail Zeldovich, "WTO Dispute Settlement: The System is Flawed and Must be Fixed," *The International Lawyer* 37 (Fall 2003), 697–752, 748–750.

[47] See, for example, Lori Wallach, "The FP Interview: Lori's War," *Foreign Policy* 118 (Spring 2000), 37–55.

[48] Senator Max Baucus stated that WTO panels are "making up rules that the U.S. never negotiated, that Congress never approved, and I suspect, that Congress would never approve." "US DSU Proposal Receives Mixed Reactions," *Bridges Weekly Trade News Digest*, December 20, 2002, at http://www.ictsd.org/weekly/02-12-20/wtoinbrief.htm (accessed April, 10, 2008).

[49] *Negotiations on the Dispute Settlement Understanding, Proposal of the Africa Group in the WTO* ¶ 2, October 2002 (on file with author).

[50] Busch and Reinhardt, "Developing Countries and General Agreement on Tariffs and Trade/World Trade Organization Dispute Settlement," 724.

[51] Tarullo, "The Hidden Costs of International Dispute Settlement: WTO Review of Domestic Anti-Dumping Decisions," 109.

conditions under which such measures may be maintained or applied, as in the *U.S. v. Shrimp-Turtle* case analyzed above. We do not argue that the Appellate Body always favors liberalization, but its decisions do seem biased toward liberalization and its opinions tend to suggest a view of the WTO more as an instrument of liberalization than a reflection of a contractual balance between liberalization and protection captured by the concept of embedded liberalism.[52]

Away from Capture: Why Judicial Liberalization Works

WTO judicial liberalization may be as, or even more, efficient at reaching the stated goal of the WTO to liberalize trade than the traditional trade rounds. In this sense, the WTO is a good example of the internationalization of regulatory regimes, as described by Mattli and Woods. Here, judicial decision making freed states from capture by entrenched import-competing interests in a way that negotiated liberalization was not able to accomplish. This regulatory shift explains the strikingly high rate of compliance with judicial lawmaking.

Since its creation, in only one out of over twenty dispositive WTO cases has a losing party been held to have failed to comply within a "reasonable period." This 95 percent rate of compliance with judicial decisions would be respectable in most national legal systems. That it persists in an international legal context, which many describe as "anarchic," may be surprising. This compliance rate is particularly impressive, given that compliance with WTO dispute settlement decisions typically involves political defeat for historically powerful and intransigent protectionist sectors that for decades have captured domestic trade policymaking. Why does the WTO dispute settlement system enjoy such a high compliance rate?

As a matter of international law, there is a legal obligation to comply with adopted WTO Appellate Body decisions.[53] But as a matter of domestic law, few if any national legal systems give direct effect to Appellate Body decisions. As a matter of domestic law, sovereignty has not been "delegated" to the WTO Appellate Body. Therefore, behaviorally, compliance is a domestic political decision.

The essence of the mechanics by which the dispute settlement system enjoys such a high compliance rate is rooted in decentralized enforce-

---

[52] Ernst B. Haas, "Words Can Hurt You; Or, Who Said What to Whom About Regimes," *International Organization* 36 (Spring 1982), 207–243.

[53] John H. Jackson, "The WTO Dispute Settlement Understanding—Misunderstandings on the Nature of Legal Obligation," *American Journal of International Law* 91 (January 1997), 60–64.

ment—a legitimized retaliatory threat that reconfigures domestic politics in the contravening country. At the interstate level of analysis, when ruled against, a Member is expected to comply within a "reasonable period of time" (which is determined by a WTO panel). If not, the adversely affected complainant can retaliate. Retaliation takes the form of raising tariffs on goods originating in the territory of the contravening country to a level that is intended to have the effect of eliminating demand for the imports in proportion to the adverse effect of the contravening measures.

At the domestic politics level, the potency of this mechanism becomes clear. The dispute settlement system provides national leaders with a way to get around domestic pressures to keep the market closed. The potential of retaliation is an important means to motivate exporters who will be hurt by the sanction. Since countries publish a list of products that will be affected by the sanction (in the U.S. case, the government publishes a proposed retaliation list in the Federal Register thirty days prior to the effective date of retaliation), this has the effect of pitting those politically powerful export-oriented producers against the industry that champions the contravening measures. If targeted smartly, the proposed retaliation list mobilizes sufficient political muscle within the contravening country to result in WTO-consistent reform. In this way, the DSU works in conjunction with domestic laws, regulations, and politics to foster compliance with the legislative outcomes that are codified in the WTO agreements.[54]

The use of judicial action to open markets and the acquiescence of the United States to appellate decisions does not imply that the United States favors the extent of judicial liberalization currently taking place at the WTO. As we argued above, there is little evidence in the negotiating history of the DSU to suggest that the move to legalization of GATT/WTO dispute resolution was intended or expected to lead to expansive judicial liberalization. Then why hasn't judicial liberalization been checked?

In effect, the expansive interpretive stance by the Appellate Body *has* faced *some* limits. For example, powerful members, particularly the EC and the United States, have had a de facto veto over the appointment of Appellate Body members: in the WTO's early years, these powerful members engaged in a comparatively cursory review of Appellate Body nominees; in more recent years, as the Appellate Body's capacity to make law became apparent, the United States began engaging in a thorough review and interview of Appellate Body nominees, blocking the appointment of some nominees who were seen as too activist. Similarly, members have not been shy about complaining when the Appellate Body engages

[54] Judith Goldstein and Lisa Martin, "Legalization, Trade Liberalization, and Domestic Politics: A Cautionary Note," *International Organization* 54 (Summer 2000), 603–632.

in lawmaking they dislike, and proposals by powerful members to rewrite parts of the DSU in the Doha Round may have had a sobering effect on the Appellate Body. To some extent, agent slack has been limited.

Nonetheless, developing countries have not joined efforts to curb judicial liberalization at the WTO. While many developing-country representatives have complained about judicial "activism" by the Appellate Body, their bigger complaint appears to focus on the relative incapacity of developing countries to fully avail themselves of the dispute settlement system. As a formal matter, developing countries have as much access to the WTO dispute settlement system as developed countries do. Yet in practice, there is emerging evidence that developing countries may use dispute settlement procedures significantly less often than developed countries. The explanations for this difference are a topic of contemporary debate, but they include the lack of resources in developing countries to spend on WTO litigation (that is, large bills from lawyers and econometricians); the structure of interest organization in developing countries, where collective-action problems may have not been overcome; pressure from Brussels and Washington to refrain from bringing cases; and the lack of legal and economic expertise and sophistication in developing countries.[55] Despite these problems, some developing countries, such as Brazil and India, have not been shy about taking developed countries, such as the EC and the United States, to dispute settlement. Insofar as more sophisticated developing countries that may be on the edge of development choose to litigate, they may act as proxies for the developing world, knocking down protectionism in the North.

Perhaps that is why the developing countries have blocked U.S. efforts to rein in WTO judicial lawmaking. In the Doha Round, the United States has proposed several judicial reforms that are intended to curb Appellate Body lawmaking. The central U.S. proposal in this regard would permit the parties to a dispute to agree to excise from draft Appellate Body decisions language they find objectionable. Such a rule would (and is intended to) enable the parties to a dispute to have greater control over the content of Appellate Body opinions. It is also obvious that under that rule a powerful respondent (such as the United States) could offer a petitioner a side payment (or compliant behavior) in order to eliminate disagreeable acts of Appellate Body lawmaking. Despite their own complaints about Appellate Body activism, the developing countries have blocked progress on

---

[55] Chad P. Bown and Bernard M. Hoekman, "WTO Dispute Settlement and the Missing Developing Country Cases: Engaging the Private Sector," *Journal of International Economic Law* 8 (December 2005), 861–890; Andrew T. Guzman and Beth A. Simmons, "Power Plays and Capacity Constraints: The Selection of Defendants in World Trade Organization Disputes," *Journal of Legal Studies* 34 (June 2005), 557–598.

this proposal and others on the ground that they would diminish the Appellate Body's independence.

More broadly, a lack of consensus on all aspects of ministerial decision making helps explain the lack of oversight of the judiciary. Legislative deadlock in the WTO has diminished the ability to check the Appellate Body.

CONCLUSION: CONSEQUENCES OF JUDICIAL LAWMAKING AS THE LOCUS OF WTO LIBERALIZATION

No one at the time of the signing of the WTO agreement predicted that the organization would suffer from legislative gridlock. Similarly, there was scant indication that the Appellate Body would be a force for economic liberalization. Both were unintended byproducts of the change in regulatory focus in the WTO. In fact, the EC and the United States had considered and rejected alternative legislative decision-making rules, such as trade-weighted voting, because in the early 1990s they saw no challenge to their joint management of the regime. And as suggested above, when U.S. negotiators supported a shift from the GATT to the WTO dispute settlement rules, they expected the new dispute settlement system to neutrally enforce rules that were favored by the United States and Europe—not judicial liberalization. The rise of a developing nation coalition bloc, like the rise of judicial liberalization at the WTO, was the result of fundamentally unanticipated institutional and political developments. And the lack of consensus among the ministers has led to an absence of oversight of their judicial agent. In short, legislative deadlock led to a shift in regulatory authority of the judicial branch of the WTO.

Though unanticipated, legislative stalemate and judicial lawmaking may solve a dilemma facing free trade–oriented leaders in the advanced economies. Trade liberalization today is more difficult than in any earlier period. With more information in hand, groups that will suffer from a change in trade policy are more knowledgeable and better organized than ever before, making it difficult for elected leaders to support WTO market-opening efforts. More than ever, negotiated liberalization is difficult and export interests do not necessarily hold sway over powerful private groups unwilling to face international competition. The WTO dispute settlement system offers an alternative to negotiated liberalization with a potential for liberalizing subsectors that could not be opened through traditional trade negotiations. While big bundled deals gained majority support in the United States and elsewhere during the GATT years, judicial action has come to be a more salient and effective means of defeating recalcitrant protectionism. In trade negotiations, U.S. steel, sugar, cotton, apparel, and other inefficient producers have succeeded for a half century in assuring their continued protection: facing certain devastating losses from liberalization, they have remained united in successfully keeping themselves off the bargaining table, capturing U.S. trade policy. Negotiated liberalization of these sectors has been stuck in the mud.

The WTO dispute settlement process turns that politics on its head. By making decisions individually, the courts undermine the ability of groups to bundle their interests with that of other groups. At the end of the dispute settlement process, the threat of retaliation pits one of the offending protectionist subsectors against a large number of export-oriented interests. If retaliation occurs, certain loss will now befall the exporters, motivating them to support ending the protection under challenge. In the dispute settlement context, the export-oriented producers who in the legislative context merely had a possible gain are now threatened with a clear and credible loss, motivating them to act decisively against protection. This asymmetry—many exporters against a single import-competing group—creates the political space that pushes liberalization forward. And over the longer term, those sectors that are liberalized by judicial action will adjust and often die, eliminating them from a potential coalition that might otherwise emerge to oppose judicial liberalization.[56] Judicial liberalization is currently a crucial piece of the contemporary WTO liberalization story. And as detailed by Mattli and Woods in their framework chapter, the WTO's regulatory structure appears to have moved unintentionally from "capture" to "common interest."

This important role for the WTO dispute settlement system is reminiscent of the crucial liberalizing role played by the ECJ in the 1960s through the late 1980s—until the Single European Act. In that period, the Council was paralyzed by the Luxemburg Compromise, which effectively required unanimity for any important action. The ECJ's exercise in "negative liberalization," striking down national protectionist measures in such famous cases as the *Rheinheitsgebot* and *Cassis de Dijon* cases, is credited with being the main engine of internal market liberalization in the period.[57] Of course, the ECJ's role is distinguishable from that of the WTO Appellate Body in the contemporary period: perhaps most significantly, the ECJ established direct effects and unqualified supremacy of its decisions in

---

[56] Oona A. Hathaway, "Positive Feedback: The Impact of Trade Liberalization on Industry Demands for Protection," *International Organization* 52 (Summer 1998), 575–612.

[57] Anne-Marie Burley and Walter Mattli, "Europe Before the Court: A Political Theory of Legal Integration," *International Organization* 47 (Winter 1993), 41–76; Geoffrey Garrett, R. Daniel Kelemen, and Heiner Schulz, "The European Court of Justice, National Governments, and Legal Integration in the European Union," *International Organization* 52 (Winter 1998), 149–176; Karen J. Alter, "The European Union's Legal System and Domestic Policy: Spillover or Backlash?" *International Organization* 54 (Summer 2000), 489–518.

member-state legal systems, whereas the Appellate Body has to rely on the political mechanisms described above for compliance. Yet, as with the ECJ, the effect of judicial action has been to undermine the regulatory structures that deter trade. In this sense, and akin to the ECJ, the Appellate Body has exercised negative liberalization.[58]

None of this suggests that judicial liberalization is a perfect substitute for negotiated liberalization. Judicial liberalization is limited in its pace; it liberalizes one product or subsector at a time. It is limited in its depth; for example, litigation usually cannot reduce tariffs. And it is limited in its breadth; it is hard to see how the Appellate Body could comprehensively address the newer issues of integration—environment, labor, competition law, and investment—that many from the United States and Europe would like to see on the WTO's legislative agenda. Legal language in WTO instruments offers some discursive constraint on the Appellate Body's establishment of new, comprehensive rules on these topics.

And we are not predicting a permanent demise of negotiated liberalization at the WTO. As countries develop, some of their interests are likely to change and may converge with those of the EC and United States. Moreover, as judicial liberalization peels off and defeats protectionist sectors, it may be easier to agree to negotiate liberalization. In this way, judicial liberalization may feed back onto negotiated liberalization.

Nonetheless, there is strong evidence that the dispute settlement process will remain a key feature of WTO liberalization for years to come. Ultimately, agent slack for a judiciary is inversely related to the possibility that the legislature can correct it. In the WTO, the capacity to legislate is diminishing. The Doha Round collapsed, and although it has been formally revived, little progress has been achieved. Trade policy interests among the members have diverged and the GATT/WTO system has evolved from a hegemonic structure, to a hegemonic duopoly, to tripolarity (the United States, EC, and developing countries) today—and over the next few decades it seems headed for multipolarity with a divergence of interests of key members. In the foreseeable future, legislating trade policy will be difficult and this lack of consensus will mean less oversight of the WTO organization itself. This would suggest increasing agent slack for the WTO's judicial system and the persistence of judicial liberalization.

---

[58] On negative integration in world markets, see Fritz Scharpf, "Negative Integrations: State and the Loss of Boundary Control," in Christopher Pierson and Francis G. Castles, eds., *The Welfare State Reader*, 2d ed. (Cambridge: Polity Press, 2006), where he looks at the tension between domestic regulation of market activities and the pull of international forces.

CHAPTER EIGHT

Economic Integration and Global Governance: Why So Little Supranationalism?

Miles Kahler and David A. Lake

ECONOMIC MODELS of international governance predict that greater levels of global economic integration are likely to produce changes on two institutional dimensions. The site of governance should shift from the national to the regional and global levels as states pool their decision-making powers. At the same time, delegation to supranational institutions should be favored for managing the governance requirements of a more integrated economic order. Not only should states coordinate their responses to global challenges, the gains from specialized governance and the need for enhanced credibility and dispute resolution should also lead states to transfer authority to supranational agents.

Yet, the record of international economic governance over the past quarter-century of globalization does not support these predictions. Outside the European Union, the functions and delegated authority of global and regional economic institutions have not uniformly increased. Regulatory policies in particular have not generally migrated from national governments to new or expanded supranational institutions. Given the rapid increase in global economic integration— whether measured by policy liberalization, by trade, capital, and migration flows, or by price convergence—why is there so little supranationalism?

After describing the puzzling (for economic models) variation in supranationalism across issue-areas, we present a two-step explanation for this "missing" supranationalism. We describe two additional modes of international governance: hierarchy, in which states transfer regulatory authority to dominant states for certain limited purposes, and networks, in which states, private actors, or both share regulatory authority through coordinated and repeated interaction. Hierarchies and networks serve as functional substitutes for supranational delegation to international institutions.

In a second stage of our explanation, political models of international governance are deployed as substitutes for or supplements to economic models of governance. Economic models predict too much supranationalism and cannot explain variation among the three modes of governance. Efficiency is often overwhelmed as a driver in the presence of distributional and institutional conflict, which often characterizes regulatory policies. Drawing on earlier work, political explanations for the apparent "missing" supranationalism are provided, and preliminary conjectures on the politics of choice among alternative governance models are presented.[1] Political models and the conjectures that they inspire also offer explanations for the relative frequency of regulatory capture among these alternative forms of international governance. The likelihood of regulatory capture is determined by both international and national variables. None of the governance modes—supranationalism, hierarchy, or networks—are inherently immune from capture.

GLOBALIZATION AND SUPRANATIONALISM: UNEXPLAINED VARIATION

In contrast to the first era of globalization (before 1914) and the interwar decades of economic turbulence and closure, planning for international economic governance after World War II awarded a far more central role to intergovernmental organizations (IGOs) than had been the case under the League of Nations. The turn toward formal IGOs, however, was not a result of increased economic integration: those institutions, whatever their liberalizing goals, were designed during World War II and its aftermath, a low point in international economic integration. As global economic integration increased, particularly after 1980, its effects on these institutions of supranational delegation were far from uniform. One favored prediction had been that such integration, if it did not induce a nationalist backlash, would require substantial increases in the authority of supranational institutions. Although economic integration proceeded at a different pace according to region and issue-area, its advance in key areas of trade, finance, and foreign direct investment could not be questioned. Yet institutional outcomes at the global level were hardly uniform. Globalization produced a marked increase in supranational delegation in the trade regime, a decline in supranationalism in the monetary and financial regimes, and a complete failure to delegate in the rules governing foreign direct investment.

The trade regime has most closely followed the predicted path of increasing authority delegated to global and regional IGOs. The scope of the World Trade Organization (WTO), founded in 1995, was larger than

[1] See Miles Kahler and David A. Lake, "Globalization and Governance" and "Globalization and Changing Patterns of Political Authority," in Miles Kahler and David A. Lake, eds., *Governance in a Global Economy* (Princeton, NJ: Princeton University Press, 2003).

its predecessor, the GATT, encompassing trade in services, as well as behind-the-border policies that had previously been considered outside the scrutiny of intergovernmental institutions. In particular, regulatory domains, such as intellectual property, health and safety regulations, and technical standards were all brought under the purview of the new organization. For the first time, regulatory policies were brought within the trade regime in their own right and not "as an adjunct to a larger concern about border trade issues."[2]

Competition policy, rules on foreign investment, and labor and environmental standards were promoted as new (and traditionally domestic) spheres for future negotiation; they were already included in regional trade agreements. In each of these cases, new domestic actors were mobilized, distinct from the old exporter and import-competing constituencies, and the trade regime integrated new principles and norms to govern these issues.[3] The new authority of the WTO was reflected in a more efficient Dispute Settlement Understanding that reduced the power of national governments to deflect and delay panel reports and in an Appellate Body that could engage in judicial lawmaking.[4]

In the oversight of national financial, monetary, and exchange rate policies—where global economic integration has progressed further than it has in trade in goods and services—supranationalism has retreated since 1945. The International Monetary Fund (IMF), created with substantial (at least on paper) powers for the oversight of exchanges rates and exchange restrictions on current account transactions, lost much of that formal authority after the breakdown of the fixed parity exchange rate regime in 1971–73 and the Second Amendment to the Articles of Agreement of the IMF that confirmed the new regime. The IMF has been peripheral to exercises in macroeconomic policy coordination among the G-7. Although the IMF and the World Bank have assumed a greater role in surveillance of national financial regulations, particularly among emerging market economies, the Bretton Woods organizations are part of a network of regulatory oversight agencies, and they have not been delegated any substantial new powers in the regulatory domain. Recent debate over the IMF's medium-term strategy has revealed support for some increases in delegation to the IMF, particularly in the realm of surveillance.[5] Despite pressure from the United States, members appear to have

---

[2] John Barton, Judith L. Goldstein, Timothy E. Josling, and Richard H. Steinberg, *The Evolution of the Trade Regime: Politics, Law, and Economics of the GATT and the WTO* (Princeton, NJ: Princeton University Press, 2006), 209.

[3] Ibid., 94–98, 125–151.

[4] Ibid., 75–87.

[5] The International Monetary and Financial Committee (IMFC) has emphasized greater independence in the surveillance function, greater transparency, and a larger reliance on the Independent Evaluation Office (*IMF Survey*, May 1, 2006, 118–119).

little enthusiasm for a restoration of an independent IMF role in the oversight of exchange rate adjustment among the major economies.

If supranational delegation has increased in the trade regime and declined in the monetary and financial domains, the international rules governing foreign direct investment, a major driver of globalization, reflect yet another distinct pattern. The old regime of investment protection, maintained through imperial rule and then through sanctions administered by the major powers, began to crumble in the 1970s. In response, the United States and other industrialized countries began to negotiate bilateral investment treaties (BITs), some 153 in the decade from 1977 to 1986. A second inflection upward in BITs occurred in the 1990s, as former socialist economies used these agreements to signal their embrace of capitalism.[6]

This web of bilateral treaties, now totaling more than seventeen hundred, was a less efficient means to the end of investment protection and liberalization than a multilateral investment regime. Negotiations to produce a Multilateral Agreement on Investment (MAI) at the OECD failed in 1998, however, in the face of a concerted campaign by NGOs and weak support from the corporate sector. The Doha round of trade negotiations at the WTO included the relationship between trade and investment as part of its original agenda, but it was dropped in the July 2004 package agreement. The OECD Code of Liberalization of Capital Movements remains the "only multilateral framework in force on international capital flows, including FDI."[7] The WTO oversees several investment-related codes, in particular, the agreement on Trade-Related Investment Measures (TRIMS) and the General Agreement on Trade in Services (GATS). The degree to which regulatory authority over foreign direct investment has migrated to the global level and has been delegated to IGOs is minimal, however. This leaves the network of BITs as the primary governance structure in this issue-area.

Alternative Modes of Global Governance

This marked variation in supranational governance—variation that could be demonstrated in regulatory regimes as well—is explained in part by the existence of alternative modes of global governance. In the realm of international economic governance, including regulatory regimes, na-

[6] Kenneth J. Vandevelde, "The Political Economy of a Bilateral Investment Treaty," *American Journal of International Law* 92, no. 4 (1998), 628.

[7] Stephen S. Golub, "Measures of Restrictions on Inward Foreign Direct Investment for OECD Countries," OECD *Economic Studies* 36, no. 1 (2003), 89.

tional governance within the boundaries of the territorial state remains dominant. Under anarchy, states act unilaterally in pursuit of their interests and rely upon ad hoc forms of cooperation buttressed by voluntary but self-enforcing international regimes when interacting with others. This is the classic model of international relations portrayed in neorealism or neoliberal institutionalism.[8] When national governance is insufficient, many have expected supranationalism to replace it. Two alternative modes of governance at the international level—hierarchies and networks—can substitute for both national governance and supranationalism, however.

Supranationalism shifts political authority from individual states to states acting as a collective body along two independent dimensions. States pool or share sovereignty at the regional or global level by creating a collective unit that can make binding or authoritative decisions for its members. The authority assigned to the collective can vary in extent, covering more or fewer policy domains, and in centralization, especially whether the collective power is subject to checks and balances by other institutions and, importantly, by its member-states (the equivalent of different federal arrangements). States can also delegate authority to a supranational agent or IGO. Delegation entails a conditional grant of authority from a state or collective of states to an actor for some specified purpose. Most commonly, states delegate to supranational agents in the forms of investigatory agents (e.g., IAEA) or dispute resolution bodies (e.g., in the WTO), although other forms are possible.[9] These two dimensions should be kept analytically separate. A decision to form a collective decision-making unit is not a decision to delegate authority to an agent, or vice versa.[10]

Hierarchy shifts political authority from one or more subordinate states to a dominant state that is empowered to issue authoritative decisions. The degree of hierarchy varies by the number of policy issues over which a dominant state can legitimately regulate the behavior of its subordinates. Also important are the residual rights of control, or the ability to decide which party has authority over what when they disagree. If the

---

[8] See Kenneth Waltz, *Theory of International Politics* (Reading, MA: Addison-Wesley, 1979); and Robert O. Keohane, *After Hegemony: Cooperation and Discord in the World Political Economy* (Princeton, NJ: Princeton University Press, 1984), respectively.

[9] On delegation to IOs, see Darren Hawkins, David A. Lake, Daniel Nielson, and Michael J. Tierney, "States, International Organizations, and Principal-Agent Theory," in Darren Hawkins, David A. Lake, Daniel Nielson, and Michael J. Tierney, eds., *Delegation and Agency in International Organizations* (New York: Cambridge University Press, 2006).

[10] David A. Lake and Mathew D. McCubbins, "The Logic of Delegation to International Organizations," in Hawkins, Lake, Nielson, and Tierney, eds., *Delegation and Agency in International Organizations*.

subordinate retains these residual rights of control, the relationship between dominant and subordinate state is more anarchic, and if the dominant state acquires these rights, the relationship is more hierarchic.[11]

In international relations, authority and, in turn, hierarchy rest not on a formal-legal foundation but on an exchange relationship in which the dominant state provides a social order or public goods of value to the subordinates, and subordinates in turn recognize an obligation to comply with rules or resource claims that are necessary for the production of that social order or public goods. In this way, hierarchy forms an equilibrium that is regarded by both sides to the exchange as legitimate or appropriate. For this equilibrium to endure, both the dominant and subordinate states must hold to their sides of the implicit contract—the dominant state must provide the social order or public goods, the subordinates must comply with its legitimate commands. The key contracting difficulty under hierarchy is restraining opportunistic behavior by the dominant state. Having yielded authority, subordinates correctly fear that the dominant state will exploit them or seek to renegotiate the contract in its favor at some future date.[12]

Perhaps the best illustration of hierarchy in the contemporary international economy is dollarization, the hardest of exchange rate pegs, in which one country adopts the currency of another as its own.[13] In such cases, the dollarized economy accepts the monetary authority of the country with the dominant currency. It does not participate in decision making regarding monetary policy in the dominant currency country, and it exercises no influence on that policy. Authority runs in one direction, at least in this domain. The authority relationship, even in this extreme example of monetary hierarchy, is not a permanent transfer. The dollarized country can unwind its adoption of the dominant currency—at considerable cost—and such relationships have ended with some frequency, particularly when political hierarchies have been disrupted.[14] But within that relationship, the subordinate country imports the dominant country's monetary policy as its own.

Networks are enduring or repeated interactions among multiple actors that are typically characterized by reciprocity. Distinguishing networks from alternative forms of governance requires a narrowing of recent de-

[11] David A. Lake, *Entangling Relations: American Foreign Policy in Its Century* (Princeton, NJ: Princeton University Press, 1999); David A. Lake, *Hierarchy in International Relations* (Ithaca, NY: Cornell University Press, forthcoming).

[12] Lake, *Hierarchy in International Relations*.

[13] Despite the name, dollarization applies to any such adoption, such as the use of the euro as a national currency by Montenegro or Kosovo.

[14] On the costs and benefits of dollarization and near-dollarization, Benjamin J. Cohen, *The Future of Money* (Princeton, NJ: Princeton University Press, 2004), 123–139.

scriptions, which define networks as "a pattern of regular and purposive relations among like government units working across the border that divide countries from one another and that demarcate the 'domestic' from the 'international' sphere."[15] Joel M. Podolny and Karen L. Page distinguish a network from either hierarchy or market, defining it as "any collection of actors (N_2) that pursue repeated, enduring exchange relations with one another and, at the same time, lack a legitimate organizational authority to arbitrate and resolve disputes that may arise during the exchange." In contrast to markets or, in our case, national level governance without international collaboration, relations between states in a network are enduring, not ad hoc. Networks are sometimes defined as interactions in the absence of any authority, although it is more accurate to think of them as sharing authority between the nodes or constituting authority from the interactions themselves. If supranationalism implies delegation of authority to an IGO, networked governance entails migration of authority to the policy network, but no formal delegation. In contrast to hierarchies, recognized dispute settlement authority and residual rights of control do not reside with any member of the network.[16] If hierarchy in international regulatory governance implies one-way transmission of templates with authority residing in one national government, a networked structure implies reciprocity (even if one member of the network has a more central position or more influence over outcomes than others).[17] Networked international governance, then, is based on shared or pooled authority and on repeated, enduring, and reciprocal relationships among actors in different national jurisdictions.

Public-private and private networks were a familiar part of international governance in the decades before 1945. In certain respects, the IGO-dominated institutions after 1945 were created as substitutes for a form of networked governance that was viewed as a bastion of unaccountable power and uncertain membership. Transgovernmental networks did not disappear, however, and increasing economic interdependence produced both renewed reliance on networked governance and a scholarly rediscovery of those networks. Among transgovernmental networks, regulatory networks of executive branch officials have received

[15] Anne-Marie Slaughter, *A New World Order* (Princeton, NJ: Princeton University Press, 2004), 14.

[16] Joel M. Podolny and Karen L. Page, "Network Forms of Organization," *Annual Review of Sociology* 24 (1998), 59.

[17] Walter Powell and others also add a distinctive ethic or norm that governs network relations, particularly the norm of reciprocity and the consequent accretion of trust among its members. See Walter W. Powell, "Neither Market Nor Hierarchy: Network Forms of Organization," *Research in Organizational Behavior* 12 (1990), 304–305. See also Miles Kahler, ed., *Networked Politics: Agency, Power, and Governance* (Ithaca, NY: Cornell University Press, forthcoming).

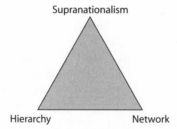

Supranationalism

Hierarchy   Network

Figure 8.1. Modes of global governance

particular attention.[18] Networked regulatory governance often includes public-private networks or purely private networks with substantial regulatory authority. Layna Mosley has described three functions that private actors may play in financial governance: sole developers and enforcers of rules, joint developers of rules with public authorities, and enforcers of standards developed by others.[19] Networks of nongovernmental organizations have also participated in thwarting regulatory initiatives by other actors (the MAI described above) and in serving as enforcers and developers of regulations in other instances. Of course, not every involvement by government bureaucracies, private organizations, or NGOs is networked governance as defined above. Involvement may concentrate on political action within national jurisdictions, or activities may be ad hoc and limited in time. Rather than engaging in reciprocal, long-term relations, actors may be in a competitive, arms-length relationship with one another. Nor does every network possess supranational authority: many purely informational networks do not exercise authority because national governments resist sharing that authority (and adjusting their regulatory regimes).

These three stylized modes of global governance permit many hybrid forms. International governance structures map on to a triangle with supranationalism, hierarchy, or networks in pure form at each apex (see figure 8.1). Observed modes of governance are likely to exist in the interior of the triangle, combining elements of each form but in different proportions. Few actual examples of global governance will lie at the ideal-typical apexes of this triangle. For example, even a formal IGO, such as the International Monetary Fund, may be embedded in a network of transgovernmental ties among national finance ministries. The density and importance of those network ties are likely to vary among groups

[18] Slaughter, *A New World Order*, 36–64; Kal Raustiala, "The Architecture of International Cooperation: Transgovernmental Networks and the Future of International Law," *Virginia Journal of International Law* 43, no. 1 (2002), 2–92.

[19] Layna Mosley, "Private Governance for the Public Good? Exploring Private Sector Participation in Global Financial Regulation." Paper prepared for a Festschrift in Honor of Robert O. Keohane, Conference at Princeton University, February 2005, 17.

of states within the IMF, with the major industrialized countries (G-5, G-10) more networked than the developing countries. The degree of hierarchy within IGOs is a more controversial issue. Many observers claim that the United States exercises much more influence within the IMF and international monetary affairs than indicated by formal voting rules. Even so, the fact of multilateral organization implies little true hierarchy, in which policy choice is simply delegated to more influential states and accepted by others.

This triangle bears some resemblance to the governance triangles constructed by Kenneth Abbott and Duncan Snidal.[20] In contrast to Abbott and Snidal, however, our analysis of alternative modes of governance focuses on national governments and their collaboration. Although other actors, such as the NGOs and firms of central concern to Abbott and Snidal, could be examined with regard to their governance structures, that question is left aside in this chapter. Our division of governance modalities does suggest an alternative formulation of competencies to that provided by Abbott and Snidal, however: supranationalism, networks, and hierarchies have strengths and weaknesses as modes of collaboration, apart from the exclusion or inclusion of non-state actors in regulatory standard-setting.

EXPLAINING GLOBAL GOVERNANCE

Identifying possible alternatives to supranationalism does not explain why these alternatives are sometimes selected. The existence of alternatives is a necessary condition for unraveling the mystery of the missing supranationalism, but it alone is not sufficient. The expectation that supranational governance would replace national governance follows from a reliance on economic models of global governance. These models, we argue, need to be replaced by political models that focus on the preferences of actors and the institutions that condition their behavior and choice of governance structures.

Economic Models of Global Governance

Economic explanations of global governance largely focus on the migration of authority from the national to the supranational level and are essentially functionalist, explaining the choice of institution on efficiency grounds. Economic explanations hinge on three variables: externalities or

[20] Kenneth Abbott and Duncal Snidal, "The Governance Triangle: Regulatory Standards Institutions and the Shadow of the State," this volume.

spillovers, economies of scale in the production of public goods, and the heterogeneity or homogeneity of national preferences.[21]

Externalities are key to the shift of governance upward in regulatory regimes, as the increased mobility of economic agents threatens to undermine national regulatory policies. The responses of national authorities in turn produce regulatory changes that have their own spillovers in other national jurisdictions. Although it is certainly reasonable to assume that national regulatory policies produce more externalities than they did under conditions of lower economic integration, the scope of externalities must be examined in each sector.

Economies of scale in the production of public goods may also create demand for greater supranational authority. Economic models assume a drive for more efficient outcomes over time: public goods production will take place at its most efficient site. The evidence for such a bias is thin, however, at both the international and national levels. (Consider the production of different public goods in a federal system such as the United States.) More significant in considering the migration of regulatory authority from the national to supranational level is possible conflict between externalities and efficient scale in producing the public good of regulation. In many regulatory domains, globalization produces growing cross-border externalities, but the most efficient site for regulation remains national jurisdictions. Supranational regulatory cooperation must then center on the effective coordination and mobilization of national regulatory authorities for cooperative ends rather than the creation of a new supranational regulatory authority.

Tugging against the pressures of externalities and economies of scale in economic models are heterogeneous national preferences over the public goods that might be produced cooperatively at a supranational level. The intuition here is that smaller units of governance (national rather than supranational) will be more likely to produce policies that are closer to the preferences of their citizens.[22] In the case of regulatory policies, greater diversity of preferences within and among national electorates is likely to arrest the movement of authority to higher (regional or global) levels. Such preferences are not exogenous to globalization itself, however, and a key issue, one that pervades the debate over "national capitalisms" and

[21] These models are reviewed in Lisa L. Martin, "The Leverage of Economic Theories: Explaining Governance in an Internationalized Industry," Michael J. Hiscox, "Political Integration and Disintegration in the Global Economy," Kahler and Lake, "Globalization and Governance," and Kahler and Lake, "Globalization and Changing Patterns of Political Authority," in Miles Kahler and David Lake, eds., *Governance in a Global Economy: Political Authority in Transition* (Princeton, NJ: Princeton University Press, 2003).

[22] Charles M. Tiebout, "A Pure Theory of Local Expenditures," *Journal of Political Economy* 64 no. 5 (1956), 416–424; Alberto Alesina and Enrico Spolaore, *The Size of Nations* (Cambridge, MA: MIT Press, 2003).

their persistence, is whether economic integration produces more heterogeneity in preferences (particularly between the winners and losers from economic integration) or greater homogeneity through processes of diffusion and competition.[23] Economic models of global governance have relatively little to say about regulatory capture, as defined by Mattli and Woods in the framework chapter of this volume.

Economic explanations of international hierarchy or network forms of governance are less well developed. Indeed, supranationalism has been the focus of research in this area, with the European Union being the motivating example, and other governance structures have been largely ignored. As predominantly functionalist or efficiency-based explanations of governance change, in turn, economic models are not well adapted to explain choices across alternative forms of international governance. Nonetheless, economic explanations of hierarchy would include, in addition to the variables explaining supranationalism above, a focus on levels of asset specificity. Drawing on relational contracting theories of the firm, economic theories would predict that hierarchy is most likely to emerge when there are large gains from successful cooperation but states are asymmetrically dependent on assets specific to particular dyadic relationships.[24] Economic explanations of networks emphasize personal, cultural, or institutional ties between actors that facilitate through reciprocity the making of credible commitments over time and space.[25] Neither of these augmented economic explanations, however, seek to explain the choice of governance structure from among the array of alternatives.

Political Models of Global Governance: Conflict, Preferences, and Institutions

Economic models offer some leverage over trends in the site of international economic and regulatory governance over time. A generalized political model is more promising as an explanation for both the migration of governance sites and the choice among alternative modes of governance.

---

[23] In their description of a key frontier of regulatory oversight, corporate governance, Gourevitch and Shinn, for example, argue that national divergence persists in the face of increased capital and corporate mobility. See Peter A. Gourevitch and James Shinn, *Political Power and Corporate Control* (Princeton, NJ: Princeton University Press, 2005).

[24] Jeffry A. Frieden, "International Investment and Colonial Control: A New Interpretation," *International Organization* 48, no. 4 (1994), 559–593; Lake, *Entangling Relations*; and Beth V. Yarbrough and Robert M. Yarbrough, *Cooperation and Governance in International Trade: The Strategic Organizational Approach* (Princeton, NJ: Princeton University Press, 1992). In cases of symmetrical dependence or "mutual hostages," no formal governance structure may be needed (states revert to the default structure of national sovereignty).

[25] Avner Greif, *Institutions and the Path to the Modern Economy: Lessons from Medieval Trade* (New York: Cambridge University Press, 2006); James E. Rauch and Alessandra Casella, eds., *Networks and Markets* (New York: Russell Sage Foundation, 2001).

Such political explanations begin with the premise that the choice of governance structure is the pursuit of politics by other means. That is, actors have no intrinsic preference for one or another governance structure, but struggle to influence the choice of structure so as to maximize their political aims. Since different governance structures favor different policies and political outcomes, actors—including states—with stakes in these alternatives will attempt to influence the selection. The conflict over governance is largely a conflict over policy, once removed. Regulatory capture, in turn, is endogenous to the choice of governance structure. Actors seek to influence the design of governance institutions—including their permeation by narrow, rent-seeking interests or their responsiveness to broader, "public interest" rationales—so that the institutions produce the policies desired.

Political explanations focus on two sets of variables—preferences and institutions—to explain which governance structure is ultimately selected. Elsewhere, we have developed a set of insights based on a political model for the choice of supranationalism.[26] In this section, we pose a set of conjectures using variations in preferences and institutions to explain the choice between supranational, hierarchic, and network forms of governance. These conjectures are quite tentative and are intended only to structure and stimulate further discussion and research. All are based, however, on the assumption that governance institutions reflect the interests of politically powerful actors as mediated through existing political institutions. Regulatory capture, in this view, is a function of the political equilibrium between competing forces within an issue area.

PREFERENCES AND INTERNATIONAL GOVERNANCE

Nearly all policies, and especially regulatory policies, favor some groups or countries over others. There are few "neutral" policies that make everyone better off while making no one worse off. Free trade raises national welfare, but favors exporters over import-competing industries and abundant over scarce factors of production.[27] Industry regulation that limits competition creates rents for producers at the expense of consumers,[28]

---

[26] Kahler and Lake, "Globalization and Governance," 19–28. In addition to supranationalism, we also considered the devolution of political authority to substate units and private transnational actors.

[27] Jeffry A. Frieden and Ronald Rogowski, "The Impact of the International Economy on National Policies: An Analytical Overview," in Robert O. Keohane and Helen V. Milner, eds., *Internationalization and Domestic Politics* (New York: Cambridge University Press, 1996).

[28] George J. Stigler, "The Theory of Economic Regulation." *Bell Journal of Economic and Management Science* 2 (1971), 3–21; Samuel Peltzman, "Towards a More General Theory of Regulation," *Journal of Law and Economics* 19 (1976), 211–240; and John Richards, "Towards a Positive Theory of International Institutions: Regulating International Aviation," *International Organization* 53, no. 1 (1999), 1–37.

while environmental regulations raise costs to producers and possibly current consumers (through higher prices) but benefit future generations. Industry standards are among those issues with the fewest distributional implications, yet even here any standard is likely to favor the producers and countries that use that standard and harm those who must convert to it.[29]

Our first conjecture is that *the greater the distributional consequences within or between countries, the more likely states are to favor supranational or hierarchical over network forms of governance.* Our intuition is that divisive issues must be decided by an authoritative actor capable of imposing a solution, whether as a collective body or a single state. Networked governance relies on cooperative interactions between equal members and reciprocity as the mechanism of enforcement. They are, therefore, often ill-suited to resolve disputes between members.[30] Conversely, the smaller the distributional consequences, or the more similar the preferences of the actors, the more likely states will favor networks. When the issue is more about coordination than collaboration, members may need only focal points or rules of the road that, once established, are largely self-enforcing.[31] In this case, supranational or hierarchic forms of governance are likely to be unnecessary, more costly to set up and maintain, and to carry a higher risk that a collective entity or dominant state will act opportunistically by expanding its authority to additional issues over time. A corollary of these conjectures suggests that *networked governance is most likely when regulatory capture—and its distributional consequences—are relatively unchallenged at the national level.* As the hold of particular interests is challenged in a given sector, one may expect a shift to either supranational or hierarchical modes of governance. This conjecture and its corollaries appear to be supported by the growth of regulation by networks in the European Union.[32]

In turn, *the greater the authority of the dominant state or the greater the legitimacy attached to its leadership in a particular issue-area, the more likely a hierarchic governance structure will emerge.* In such cases, subordinate states accept the right of the dominant state to set rules in an issue-area either because of the value assigned to its leadership, its special position or unique needs with regard to the issue, or its normative status.

[29] Walter Mattli, "Public and Private Governance in Setting International Standards," in Kahler and Lake, *Governance in a Global Economy: Political Authority in Transition.*

[30] On the role of power within networks, see Kahler, *Networked Politics.*

[31] Arthur Stein, *Why Nations Cooperate: Circumstance and Choice in International Relations* (Ithaca, NY: Cornell University Press, 1990).

[32] Renaud Dehousse, "Regulation by Networks in the European Community," *Journal of European Public Policy* 4, no. 2 (1997), 246–261.

Similarly, *the greater the divergence between the dominant state's preferred policy and the median of a supranational collectivity, to a limit, the more likely hierarchy will emerge.* Here, the dominant state is a preference outlier and will benefit more from its preferred rules rather than those selected by the median state in a supranational collective. It will therefore invest more in actively legitimating and building a coalition in favor of its special role. Nonetheless, even if successful, hierarchy will be fragile precisely because the majority of states prefer an alternative outcome and mistaken estimates by the dominant state of its support are likely to erode its legitimacy in setting the rules for all. Beyond some degree of preference divergence, however, no global governance mechanism will be possible. If preferences vary excessively, cooperation will simply fail. National regulatory regimes will remain the default outcome.

The greater the number of those disadvantaged by a policy relative to those that benefit from the policy, or the more diffuse the costs relative to the gains, the more states will favor network forms of governance composed only of winners. Larger numbers of losers, and especially those for whom the costs of the policy are widely dispersed, will suffer from more acute collective-action problems. A smaller number of winners who enjoy more concentrated benefits will have greater incentives to organize and lobby states for preferred policies—and especially the ability to set those policies themselves.[33] Concentrated interests with similar preferences can coordinate effectively through networks. Although they may still require the power of states to impose those policies on the broader group of losers, the winners will seek to maximize their autonomy and control within networks they dominate. This implies that networks are particularly prone to regulatory capture by relatively narrow interest groups that receive concentrated benefits.

NATIONAL INSTITUTIONS AND INTERNATIONAL GOVERNANCE

Existing national institutions condition the choice between national governance and new international modes of governance in at least three ways. First, all institutions contain some policy bias.[34] *The greater the policy bias of a national institution, the more biased will be any new form of global governance created by that institution.* For example, national regulatory agencies that exhibit "capture" by their regulated clients will create international governance that replicates or reinforces that bias. Un-

---

[33] Stigler, "The Theory of Economic Regulation"; Peltzman, "Towards a More General Theory of Regulation."

[34] Ronald Rogowski, "Institutions as Constraints on Strategic Choice," in David A. Lake and Robert Powell, eds., *Strategic Choice and International Relations* (Princeton, NJ: Princeton University Press, 1999).

less existing rules are modified to engineer a different result or new interests are mobilized, institutional bias will be reproduced. Indeed, the losers from this institutional bias may eventually be purged as their resources and influence steadily diminish.[35] This effect may explain the resilience of national governance, particularly in regulatory regimes. If institutions of international governance are created, domestic policy bias does not appear to favor the choice of a particular mode of governance (networks, hierarchy, or supranationalism). Rather, it suggests that patterns of regulatory capture at the domestic level are likely to be reproduced at the global level, with the privileged actors selecting that form of global governance that locks in their control over policy.

Second, national institutions vary in the number of veto players they possess. Veto players are institutionally defined actors who can block a proposal from being enacted.[36] The greater the number of veto players, the less likely is a move away from the status quo. *The more veto players there are, the more likely national governance and ad hoc cooperation remain as the prevailing modes of governance.* Depending on who the veto players are in any institution, certain modes of governance will be more or less likely. If a shift from sovereignty to a form of global governance impedes a veto player's interests, that player will block the change or demand a side payment from groups favoring the change. Nonetheless, it does not appear that the presence of more veto players at the national level systematically biases the choice for supranationalism, hierarchy, or networks.[37]

Finally, national institutions vary in the ability they grant actors to set the agenda or act unilaterally to change the status quo. For instance, executives can sometimes issue orders or enter into agreements without the approval of other branches of government. Even when others can override these actions or fail to implement them, the executive has altered the status quo, presumably in a direction that he favors. Other political actors

[35] Oona Hathaway, "Positive Feedback: The Impact of Trade Liberalization on Industry Demands for Protection," *International Organization* 52, no. 3 (1998), 575–612.

[36] George Tsebelis, *Veto Players: How Political Institutions Work* (Princeton, NJ: Princeton University Press, 2002).

[37] The decision rules of international organizations also make states less likely to delegate to an IGO by enhancing the autonomy of the international agent and therefore making state principals wary of delegating greater authority. Change in the decision rules—such as the European Union's shift from consensus voting to qualified majority voting on a widening range of issues—may accelerate delegation. Since many global international organizations still abide by consensus decision rules, a slower pace of delegation to these IGOs should not be surprising. Multilaterals with weighted voting, in which larger shares are awarded to larger shareholders, may be more likely to delegate as a result.

can also possess agenda-setting power. This is, in essence, Karen Alter's explanation of the role of the European Court of Justice in propelling supranationalism forward in Europe.[38] *The greater the agenda-setting power of any actor, the more likely we are to observe a shift away from national governance.* Yet, like the other institutional attributes discussed here, agenda-setting power alone does not appear to favor any particular alternative governance structure. Only with information about the preferences of the agenda-setter can we make predictions about the likelihood of a move toward supranationalism, hierarchy, or networks.

INSTITUTIONAL CHARACTERISTICS AND INTERNATIONAL GOVERNANCE

Modes of international governance—supranationalism, networks, and hierarchies—display certain institutional characteristics that may be favored or opposed by particular interests. In this regard, modes of governance differ in at least two ways: the credibility that they add to policies and their policymaking decisiveness.

When faced with a time-inconsistency problem or the threat of an exogenous shift in preferences, groups may attempt to lock in or pre-commit to a particular policy. *Countries that lack domestic institutions to make commitments credible will borrow credibility by transferring authority to another state or to a supranational organization.* In the monetary arena, for example, states can gain credibility by fixing their exchange rates or "dollarizing," both of which create a measure of hierarchy by transferring effective control over monetary policy to the target state. States may also seek credibility by creating a regional monetary system, such as the European Economic and Monetary Union (EMU). Perhaps because policies are emergent properties produced by the actions of the parties themselves, networks appear to confer little credibility.

Although both hierarchies and supranational institutions can confer credibility, the choice between the two modes is conditioned by a second credibility dilemma. Dominant countries in hierarchical relationships face a key problem: How do they commit to a particular policy and, as noted above, how do they commit not to exploit the authority they acquire over subordinate states? Countries will only fix their exchange rates to the dollar or use it as their primary medium of exchange if they are confident that the dollar is stable in value and can be exchanged for goods and services elsewhere. In turn, they must also be confident that, having fixed to the dollar or dollarized, the United States will not use the leverage it acquires over them to demand additional policy changes or concessions.

---

[38] Karen J. Alter, "'Who Are the 'Masters of the Treaty?' European Governments and the European Court of Justice," *International Organization* 52, no. 1 (1998), 121–147.

This is the classic problem of tying the sovereign's hands.[39] Since domestic institutions can provide some check on the capriciousness of even dominant states, *dominant states that lack domestic institutions to make credible commitments or those that have a greater need to establish credibility will favor supranational over hierarchical governance structures.* This suggests, paradoxically, that a large and powerful state may be a strong advocate of supranationalism in order to legitimate its leadership position, much as Germany was a primary advocate of creating the euro and an autonomous European Central Bank. At the very least, the need for credibility creates a trade-off for potentially dominant states between the ability to enact their own preferred policies and the credibility that comes from tying their hands in a supranational institution.[40]

Modes of governance also differ in their policy decisiveness. *Hierarchy allows the most decisive action, so long as subordinates regard the proposed action as legitimate.* The dominant state decides, and subordinates fall into line behind its preferred policies. Such hegemonic leadership may appear in crises, whether military (the first Gulf War), humanitarian (Somalia), or economic (the Latin American debt crisis of the 1980s), when the United States intervened first and coalition partners followed. Hierarchy is dependent, however, on the policy preferences of dominant and subordinate states; a dominant state can lead only where its followers want to go. Decisive and arbitrary behavior could well lead to pressure on a relationship founded on a high demand for policy credibility and stability.[41]

Networks may also display decisiveness when new issues arise requiring prompt resolution. If those issues have no established institutional home, networks may be an attractive alternative. Eilstrup-Sangiovanni points to the low start-up costs of networked governance, when compared to the IGO alternative, which may require lengthy negotiations.[42] An *existing* IGO with substantial delegated powers, however, may also be able to provide ready solutions to new problems with speed comparable to a transgovernmental network or hierarchy. In such cases, coordinated action in a network may provide a temporary stopgap until an IGO solution can be advanced. The dependability of IGO decisiveness rests on their decision rules: cycling by alternative majorities or veto players able to block action can produce policy stalemate.

[39] Douglass C. North and Barry R. Weingast, "Constitutions and Credible Commitments: The Evolution of the Institutions of Public Choice in 17th Century England," *Journal of Economic History* 49 (1989), 803–832.

[40] Chad Rector, *Federations* (Ithaca, NY: Cornell University Press, forthcoming).

[41] European discontent with its hierarchical security relationship with the United States has usually increased in line with greater U.S. global activism and policy volatility.

[42] Eilstrup-Sangiovanni, "Varieties of Cooperation."

POWER DISTRIBUTION AND MODE OF GOVERNANCE

Asymmetries in power would appear to predict hierarchical governance, and certainly most hierarchies are to be found in such circumstances. A more refined political analysis, foreshadowed above, suggests that powerful states might well choose any of these governance alternatives, depending on the context. Hegemonic stability theory and the use of constitutional orders by dominant states center on the circumstances under which dominant states choose hierarchy or supranationalism.[43] Hierarchy serves to curb opportunistic behavior, but only with increased governance costs (the dominant power bears all of those costs in contrast to more distributed costs of supranationalism or networked cooperation). Supranationalism presents potential agency costs, but those may be offset by a major power's independent sources of information (curbing one potential advantage of an IGO agent) and by decision rules that award a dominant role in decision making to the major power. Finally, networked organization may appear the least attractive to a major power, but the powerful may exercise disproportionate influence in the network, depending on its structure, and national power may be more easily and usefully disguised in a networked structure.

These conjectures suggest implications for regulatory capture, the focus of the framework chapter by Mattli and Woods in this volume. Secure, concentrated interests—those that enjoy regulatory capture at the national level—are most likely to prefer that regulation remain national or that informal, networked governance emerge at the international level. Networks will tend to arise when the cross-national distributional implications of alternative regulatory policies are not large (international agreement is relatively easy), but when networks do emerge they are most likely to be composed of and captured by actors reflecting narrower interests. If their position at the national level is challenged (if distributional conflict in the regulatory arena grows), they may choose to defend their position with a sturdier form of international governance—supranationalism or hierarchy. Each of these entails risks, however, as outlined above.

Supranationalism is typically more transparent and open to political scrutiny than networked governance. Although supranational institutions may be created or adapted to serve the purposes of narrow, rent-seeking interests, supranational institutions appear to be an empty vessel, equally subject to claims by competing interests over time. For example, private financial interests in the United States, who preferred a return to the gold

---

[43] G. John Ikenberry, *After Victory: Institutions, Strategic Restraint, and the Rebuilding of Order after Major Wars* (Princeton, NJ: Princeton University Press, 2001).

standard or a binational monetary accord with the United Kingdom, initially viewed the IMF with skepticism or hostility. By the 1980s, however, the IMF was routinely viewed as serving the interests of large, international financial firms in the major industrialized countries. There does not appear to be any inherent bias for or against regulatory capture in supranationalism relative to hierarchy or networks, although any particular set of supranational institutions may favor one group over another.

If the choice is hierarchy, the preferences reflected in the policies of the dominant power may not perpetually match those of the beleaguered interests. Outcomes under hierarchy will reflect politically powerful interests in the dominant state. The preferences of groups that have captured regulatory policies in the dominant country may coincide or compete with concentrated interests in other countries. If interests in the dominant country are competitors or if that country has regulatory institutions that favor the public interest, then its policy will be biased against interests in the subordinate countries. Setting international policies through hierarchy may be unwise in such cases. The preferences of follower states also matter. The need for followers limits the agenda-setting power of the dominant power. If followers are more extreme in either direction—favoring or opposing narrow interests—the policy of the leader will be tempered in ways necessary to satisfy the interests of its subordinates.

These conjectures, based on a generalized political model of governance, require systematic investigation across regulatory regimes. Their embedded hypotheses regarding capture go some distance toward explaining the regulatory puzzle described earlier: the institutional variation among the trade, financial, and direct investment issue-areas. Trade has long been a site for intense distributional conflict among competing and concentrated interests. The international arena in the 1930s and 1940s became a means for export interests and economic liberalizers to introduce a policy bias toward trade liberalization. The level of distributional conflict within and between countries, however, prevented a networked solution. A weak form of supranationalism, the GATT, was the default solution after the failure of the International Trade Organization to win congressional approval. In both the GATT and WTO, however, protectionist interests were accommodated; neither organization could be described as captured by export interests or liberalizers, despite their policy bias toward liberalization.

The international governance of foreign direct investment displayed a different pattern. To the degree that national governments chose to coordinate their regulation of foreign direct investment, that coordination took place among the industrialized countries in an organization with little supranational authority that served as the locus of networked cooperation: the Organization for Economic Cooperation and Development

(OECD). When the international agenda shifted to more robust constraints on national policy in the interests of international investment, conflict increased, and complaints of capture by multinational corporations forced a retreat to the previous networked forum.

Finally, financial regulation and monetary policy demonstrate the most complex historical variation. The Great Depression unleashed political forces that disrupted the transnational network of central banks and private banks that governed international finance before 1914 and during the 1920s. The domestic political power of finance was in retreat throughout the industrialized world, as central banks were nationalized, capital flows were circumscribed, and national governments claimed new regulatory authority. The banker to the central banks—the Bank for International Settlements—was nearly abolished at the time of the Bretton Woods conference. Nevertheless, the networked alternative persisted, and, as distributional conflict over financial regulation subsided and the industrial world moved toward liberalization of capital flows, networked organization at the BIS reclaimed its central role. It was not the only governance choice in international monetary and financial policy, however. The variety of governance modes that can be found in contemporary international financial regulation makes that issue-area an ideal site for a further survey of governance choices and their effects on regulatory capture.

FINANCIAL REGULATION AND THE VARIETIES OF GLOBAL GOVERNANCE

International finance has been the leading edge of globalization in recent decades. Since the early 1980s, when capital markets were liberalized in most OECD countries, international financial transactions of all kinds have exploded in magnitude. Foreign exchange transactions, international lending, cross-border mergers and acquisitions, and other forms of finance have all grown at unprecedented rates over the last two decades. Although there are still large border effects in international trade, indicating the absence of fully integrated goods markets, and international migration remains tightly controlled by national policies, international capital markets increasingly approximate the "law of one price" that prevails in a single, efficient, and integrated market.[44]

Economic models predict that international financial regulation should take a largely supranational form. Outside Europe, this has not been the case. With capital market liberalization, national governments—and collective action by those governments through supranational institutions—

[44] International Monetary Fund, *World Economic Outlook: Globalization and External Imbalances* (Washington, DC: International Monetary Fund, April 2005), 110–123.

have largely retreated from the active regulation of capital flows. Although new supranational institutions endowed with stronger regulatory authority have been suggested in the wake of recurrent financial crises, none of those initiatives have succeeded.[45] The international financial realm is not "ungoverned," however; global governance has taken hierarchic and networked forms.

Regulatory Hierarchies: Extraterritoriality and "Emulation or Else"

Examples of true hierarchy between units in financial regulation are difficult to discern in the contemporary international system: few countries, even small, open economies, are willing to accept openly the authority of another sovereign in the politically sensitive domain of regulation. Regulatory hierarchies are often subtle and are almost always hidden from public view. At least two variants of hierarchy have been significant in international regulatory policy, however. The first, extraterritoriality, extends back to the era of imperialism, when dominant powers asserted authority over their nationals within the territorial jurisdiction of another state. Extraterritoriality in that era was imposed on societies outside the group of "civilized" nations as a type of informal empire. The most notable example was China, where extraterritorial concessions imposed during the nineteenth century were not ended until 1943. Such wholesale imposition is no longer part of international practice, but the growth of modern regulatory states in the twentieth century provided a new incentive for asserting extraterritorial authority outside their boundaries.[46]

Extraterritoriality in the contemporary era is deployed by dominant states as a means of reasserting regulatory control over actors who are escaping from or undermining their national regulatory regimes. Extending the reach of the state into other jurisdictions is a primary means of defending the regulatory state; Tonya Putnam argues that U.S. courts have used extraterritoriality primarily as a defensive weapon to deal with threats to the domestic regulatory order.[47] Modern regulatory assertions of extraterritoriality are not claims of authority over another polity;

[45] Barry Eichengreen, "Governing Global Financial Markets: International Responses to Hedge-Fund Problem," in Kahler and Lake, *Governing a Global Economy: Political Authority in Transition.*

[46] On extraterritoriality and the U.S. constitutional order during the first era of globalization and the contemporary era, see Kal Raustiala, "The Evolution of Territoriality: International Relations and American Law," in Miles Kahler and Barbara Walter, eds., *Territoriality and Conflict in an Era of Globalization* (New York: Cambridge University Press, 2006).

[47] Tonya Putnam, "Back to the Future with Sovereignty: Extraterritorial Regulation as a Source of Rules in Global Governance." Paper prepared for presentation at the American Political Science Association Annual Meeting, September 1–4, 2005, Washington, DC.

rather, they are claims of authority over individuals (or other agents, such as corporations) who reside in other sovereign jurisdictions. In effect, the state making the claims is inserting its domestic hierarchy (its regulatory rules) into the domain of another state. In one recent instance, for example, the Trail Smelter case (*Pakootas v. Tech Cominco*), U.S. plaintiffs for the first time have attempted to apply American environmental law against a Canadian firm operating solely in Canada for environmental externalities in the United States. As Austen L. Parrish notes, many in Canada see this as "environmental imperialism," an effort to force foreign companies to follow U.S. environmental regulations in order to avoid legal liability.[48] The targeted state has three possible responses: to resist those claims, often through "blocking legislation"; to accommodate to the existence of conflicting rules within its jurisdiction; or to harmonize its regulations with the other jurisdiction.[49] The last response indicates that extraterritorial assertions can be used as levers to obtain more permanent regulatory hierarchy (harmonization).

For much of the past half-century, "corporate and government lawyers around the world have often thought of extraterritorial jurisdiction in terms not only of limiting the reach of the regulatory state, but specifically in terms of cabining and limiting U.S. power."[50] The United States is no longer the sole actor in asserting extraterritorial regulatory claims, however, as the European Union and other industrialized countries have become more active. As can be observed in financial regulation, the industrialized countries as a group may construct regulatory hierarchies with those outside their club. Although it is by no means clear that creditor and debtor countries would have identical interests in any event, this imposition of a regulatory apparatus fashioned in the developed countries most likely reflects a degree of capture within the more powerful states. Barry Eichengreen's examination of the debate over hedge fund regulation demonstrates that the preferences of the industrialized countries dominated the ultimate regulatory outcome. Those preferences—for market-based, national regulation—were also very close to the preferences of the hedge fund industry and its investors, concentrated in those same countries.[51]

[48] Austen L. Parrish, "Trail Smelter Déjà vu: Extraterritoriality, International Environmental Law, and the Search for Solutions to Canadian-U.S. Transboundary Water Pollution Disputes," *Boston University Law Review* 363 (2005).

[49] Putnam, "Back to the Future with Sovereignty," 32.

[50] Anne-Marie Slaughter and David T. Zaring, "Extraterritoriality in a Globalized World," in Teo Keang Sood et al., eds., *Current Issues in International Commercial Litigation* 72 (1997).

[51] Eichengreen, "Governing Global Financial Markets."

Regulatory harmonization also takes place by means of emulation, simple imitation by one state of another's regulatory practices. Although emulation may result from processes of learning or diffusion, such imitation may also disguise hierarchical relations in which a dominant power imposes its regulatory policies through the use of incentives or sanctions, what we call "emulation or else." Most often, the incentives and sanctions are centered on market access. In the well-known Tuna-Dolphin panel decision at the GATT, the United States attempted to use market access to extend the reach of its environmental regulations.[52] The United States is not alone in wielding market access for regulatory ends. Regulatory hierarchy achieved through implicit or explicit sanctions or incentives has been part of the European Union's expansion to the south and east. In negotiations with prospective member states, the *acquis communautaire*, the entire body of legislation of the European Communities and Union, must be accepted before new members can join the European Union. Judith Kelley has described the use of membership conditionality to influence politically sensitive legislation affecting the treatment of ethnic minorities.[53]

How can regulatory hierarchy be distinguished from emulation based on diffusion, learning, or competition? First, the emulation is consistently in one direction: regulatory adoption is not a process of consensus-building by both parties. There may be little evidence of genuine consultation or negotiation (apart from the timing of the regulatory changes). Second, an implicit or explicit threat of sanctions exists if regulatory harmonization does not take place; positive incentives and technical assistance may also be part of the hierarchical relationship. Finally, one-way emulation is sustained over time: if regulatory rules change in the dominant party, they are highly likely to change in the emulating state as well. In the case of collective membership organizations, of course, hierarchy ends when membership occurs: the new member will have some role, however small, in shaping new decisions on regulatory changes from within the organization.

Regulatory hierarchy is not always contrary to the interests of the party that adopts the regulations in question. The costs to national autonomy may seem high, but, as in the case of dollarization, the adoption of an external regulatory standard may serve long-run economic interests or create a more credible regulatory regime. On the other hand, in addition to autonomy costs, unnecessary harmonization may be imposed

---

[52] A GATT panel found against the United States, in this instance.

[53] Judith Kelley, "International Actors on the Domestic Scene: Membership Conditionality and Socialization by International Institutions," *International Organization* 58, no. 3 (2004), 425–457.

in the interests of economic actors resident in the dominant countries. A careful examination of each alternative and the counterfactual outcome (in the absence of hierarchy) is required to assess the effects of regulatory hierarchy.

The United States has used "emulation or else" and extraterritoriality in recent efforts to extend its financial regulatory reach across national borders. Efforts to control money laundering in other financial jurisdictions were an early and important feature of the U.S. war on drugs. Using the Kerry Amendment to the 1988 Anti-Drug Abuse Act, the U.S. government wielded access to U.S. financial markets, including the all-important clearing systems, as a threat to enforce its regulatory preferences. This initial use of hierarchy later led to a club-like and networked arrangement among those regulators who came to share U.S. preferences.[54]

In a more recent instance, the United States was able to use a similar threat to reduce financial transfers to the newly elected Hamas government, after its electoral success in the Palestinian Authority (PA). The United States and the EU had announced in April 2006 that they would halt official payments to the PA, while at the same time permitting aid to the Palestinians to flow through the United Nations and independent organizations.[55] This joint action does not suggest the presence of hierarchy. However, the United States also invoked a federal law that makes it a crime to provide funds to terrorist groups. Even though the U.S.-EU action permitted aid to flow through other channels, most international banks stopped handling wire transfers to the West Bank or Gaza for fear of legal entanglements with the United States, hindering the delivery of aid by sympathetic Arab and Muslim countries. As in the case of money laundering, the U.S. Treasury did not impose the threatened sanction of prosecution, but the threat against those viewed as assisting Hamas was sufficient to embargo most financial transfers into the PA. With the split between Fatah in the West Bank and Hamas in Gaza, funds have once again started to flow to the PA, but are still embargoed against Gaza. In both of these cases, the United States exploits its pivotal—and hierarchi-

---

[54] Eric Helleiner, "The Politics of Global Financial Regulation: Lessons from the Fight Against Money Laundering," in John Eatwell and Lance Taylor, eds., *International Capital Markets: Systems in Transition* (New York: Oxford University Press, 2002). See also Beth Simmons, "The International Politics of Harmonization: The Case of Capital Market Regulation," *International Organization* 55, no. 3 (2001), 589–620; and Renee Marlin-Bennett, "Dirty (Money) Laundry: Regulating Surveillance of Suspicious Money Transactions: Or How the Governor of New York Became a Casualty of the Wars on Drugs and Terrorism." Presented at the annual convention of the International Studies Association, San Francisco, CA, March 6, 2008.

[55] Steven R. Weisman and Craig S. Smith, "U.S. and Europe Halt Aid to Palestinian Government," *New York Times*, April 8, 2006, Late Edition-Final, A6.

cal—position in the international financial system to extend its regulatory reach into countries that do not share its policy preferences.

In another instance of the exterritorial reach of American anti-terrorist policies, the U.S. government was able to use its subpoena power to gain access to the financial records of the Society for Worldwide Interbank Financial Telecommunications (SWIFT), itself a network of member banks, sited in Belgium, that processes approximately 80 percent of all financial transfers worldwide. Although SWIFT maintains that its response was not voluntary but occurred only in response to a valid subpoena, since 9/11 it has provided broad access to U.S. agencies to examine transactions that have occurred not only between individuals in the United States and abroad, but also those that have occurred entirely on foreign soil. Immediately after the terrorist attacks in 2001, in fact, the United States gained access to the entire SWIFT database, although this access was later modified.[56] The revelation of SWIFT's accommodation to U.S. legal demands in 2006 brought a sharp response from Belgium's privacy commission, which accused SWIFT of flouting European data protection rules. The European Central Bank disclaimed SWIFT's actions as beyond its regulatory competence.[57] SWIFT was caught between two regulatory regimes—one American, emphasizing counter-terrorism, and one European, focused on individual privacy. In the end, the United States largely won, reaching an accord with the European Union that gave it full access to the data under the proviso that it be retained for only five years.[58]

In a final case, that of the "NatWest three," three British bankers were extradited to the United States for financial fraud as part of the Enron scandal. Although the suspects are British and the "crime," if there was one, occurred entirely in Britain, the three were to be tried in the United States because the main evidence was in Houston and the alleged fraud, it was maintained, could not have occurred without the complicity of Enron executives. The three executives were seized under a treaty of expedited extradition that Britain but not the United States has ratified. If the circumstances were reversed, Britain would not have had the same rights to extradite American executives. Moreover, under the treaty, the national court systems are not treated equally. American courts decide whether there is sufficient evidence before requesting extradition from Britain,

---

[56] Eric Lichtblau and James Risen, "Bank Data Sifted in Secret by U.S. to Block Terror," *New York Times*, June 23, 2006, Late Edition—Final, A1.

[57] Dan Bilefsky, "Europeans Berate Bank Group and Overseer for U.S. Access to Data," *New York Times*, October 5, 2006, A11.

[58] James Risen, "U.S. Reaches Tentative Deal with Europe on Bank Data," *New York Times*, June 2, 2007. http://www.nytimes.com/2007/06/29/washington/29swift.html?ex=1340769600&en=14a25a856f41710d&ei=5090&partner=rssuserland&emc=rss, accessed July 16, 2007.

after which the expedited process comes automatically into play, while American courts also decide whether the evidence submitted by Britain in support of a request of extradition is sufficient. In a form of one-way authority, the United States benefits from the ability to prosecute British citizens in ways that Britain does not possess in return. Despite significant protest about this asymmetry within Britain, the three suspects were extradited to the United States in July 2006. They eventually pled guilty to a single count of wire fraud in November 2007, each receiving a 37-month jail sentence.[59]

These cases highlight several of the conjectures developed above. First, in all three instances, the distributional consequences of the issue are large but not so large as to scuttle agreement completely. In each instance, the United States benefits from the exercise of its authority and its ability to impose its preferred outcome on other states. But at the same time, this authority is wielded in pursuit of larger public goods, specifically anti-drug trafficking, counterterrorism, and deterring corporate fraud. Certainly in the cases of the PA and SWIFT, the United States had especially strong preferences, but its disproportionate gains from imposing its preferred policies on others were tempered by broader benefits. U.S. leadership appears to be more palatable when it is not captured by private interests but is exercised in the broader public interest, defined in some of these cases as the interest of national security.

Second, the United States benefited from its traditional position as the country responsible for managing the international financial system, a role that other countries have accepted and, indeed, consented to through decades of past practice. The United States possesses a measure of legitimacy in regulating international financial transactions that it does not enjoy in other issue-areas. This authority, in turn, rests on the crucial role of American capital markets in the global economy and a perception of reliable American stewardship of international financial markets.

Third, in the PA and SWIFT cases, at least, the United States possessed a measure of extraordinary legitimacy generated by 9/11 and the salience of counterterrorism. Even though the war in Iraq has generated considerable opposition and undermined American authority, the United States still benefits from considerable sympathy from other countries because of the attacks on 9/11. Since it was able to connect the opposition to Hamas

---

[59] "Unintended Consequences" and "America's Long Shadow," *The Economist*, July 15, 2006, 12 and 56–57. Andrew Clark, "NatWest Three Express Remorse as They Are Jailed for 37 Months," *The Guardian*, February, 22, 2008, http://www.guardian.co.uk/business/2008/feb/22/banking.enron, accessed March 29, 2008.

and the extraordinary access to the SWIFT records to counterterrorism, it benefited from the acquiescence if not active support of other countries.

Finally, in each case, as expected, the key controversy is how to ensure that the United States does not abuse its position of authority by destroying the PA, by extending its monitoring of international financial transactions to the selective control of those transactions, or by the unjust extradition of foreign citizens. The credibility problem is how to constrain the United States. The difficulty of solving this problem has rendered these cases visible, public contests. In truly hierarchic relations with settled conceptions of authority, the rights exercised by the dominant state would not be contested and probably would not generate much press attention. That these cases came to light and generated controversy, even if direct opposition from other countries is relatively muted, suggests that in each case the United States is testing the limits of what other states will accept.

Regulatory Networks: Harmonization behind Closed Doors

Network regulation is also difficult to identify within the contemporary international economy. Network regulation is defined by frequent reciprocal interactions between connected parties and the absence of a third-party arbiter for dispute resolution. By its nature, network regulation may be observationally equivalent to multiple unilateral actions by concerned states. There is no central authority to command the individual nodes, and each may simply adopt current "best practice" in any given issue area. What characterizes networked governance is not so much the outcome but the process by which shared policies are adopted. States are not driven to a common policy by competitive constraints or some hegemonic set of ideas. Rather, network nodes develop a pattern of cooperation embedded within deep reciprocal ties.[60] In international finance, the pattern of cooperation among central bank and related monetary authorities exemplifies a regulatory network "at work."

Central bank cooperation and the public-private network that sustained it date to the first era of globalization before 1914 and deepened during the 1920s.[61] Central banks during this era were quasi-public or

---

[60] Networked governance is similar to but distinct from models of diffusion. See Beth Simmons, Frank Dobbin, and Geoffrey Garrett, eds., *The Global Diffusion of Markets and Democracy* (New York: Cambridge University Press, 2008).

[61] Controversy continues over the degree of central bank cooperation before World War I. Although the idea of a central bankers' "club" originated in the 1920s, domestic political constraints prevented its creation. Claudio Borio and Gianni Toniolo, "One Hundred and Thirty Years of Central Bank Cooperation: A BIS Perspective." Monetary and Economic Department, Bank for International Settlements, BIS Working Papers No. 197, February 2006, 6–7.

private entities in their internal governance structures. The creation of national systems of banking regulation and supervision during the Great Depression and the postwar decades—another facet of the new regulatory state—did not produce a need for central bank cooperation on regulatory issues, given the low level of cross-border financial flows and banking activity. The shock that stirred the central bankers to greater collaboration was a clear example of new cross-border externalities: a series of banking failures in the early 1970s—Franklin National Bank and Herstatt Bank—that stemmed from involvement in the rapidly growing Euromarkets. Banks were slipping away from national regulatory regimes into a new, virtually unregulated financial market, at great peril to themselves and to national financial systems.

The initial response of the central bank regulators was to construct a forum for coordination of international banking supervision, the Basel Committee on Banking Supervision (BCBS) at the Bank for International Settlements (BIS). The BIS had been created in 1930 to assist with the interwar problem of German reparations; its initial institutional form was supranational, aimed at contract enforcement (future payments by Germany) and facilitating collective action by creditors in case of default.[62] With the speedy demise of its reparations role during the Great Depression, the BIS might have become moribund. Instead, during an era of economic nationalism, it reinvented itself (for the first time) as a convenient site for central bankers to maintain their cooperative dialogues. It also developed a research capacity that was highly valued by its central bank clients and a wider economic policy community.[63] It developed into a classic network organization, facilitating policy collaboration among central banks after World War II, first in the liberalization of the postwar European payments system and later, in the 1960s, in defense of the Bretton Woods exchange rate regime. Throughout, the monthly meetings of central bank governors were key, contributing to networked cooperation through the "creation of institutional ties, the provision and dissemination of high-value information, and actual decision making."[64] In its networking role, the BIS was sustained by its peculiar organizational structure. Not only was there very little delegation of formal supranational powers, it was guaranteed a high degree of independence from national governments by its additional role as a bank, incorporated under Swiss law. Fees for its banking activities on behalf of central bank clients awarded it budgetary autonomy.

[62] Ibid., 9.

[63] Gianni Toniolo, *Central Bank Cooperation at the Bank for International Settlements, 1930–1973* (New York: Cambridge University Press, 2005), 178–179.

[64] Ibid., 474–475.

At first glance, the BCBS might seem to be a predictable response of supranational delegation in the face of unwanted externalities. However, the BIS did not receive any substantial delegated powers as a result of this new cooperation in banking supervision and regulation. The initial understandings in the BCBS were designed to extend *national* banking supervision in an agreed fashion to offshore and international financial markets. The BIS is best characterized as a central node in a structure of networked governance in financial regulation. Its networked structure meant that formal membership was seldom an issue; the network could be expanded when needed. The U.S. Federal Reserve, for example, did not become a member of the BIS Board of Directors until 1994, but it was a full member of the network before that time. As financial institutions have become more complex and the boundaries between banks and other institutions have blurred, the network has expanded gradually to include additional central banks, as well as new national financial regulators responsible for banking regulation and supervision.[65] The most recent step in network expansion was the creation of the Financial Stability Forum (FSF), based at the BIS, as a "network of networks" with representation from finance ministries, international financial institutions, and regulatory agencies, as well as central banks.[66]

The activities of the central bank network centered on the BIS were typical of networked governance. The game, as Michele Fratianni and John Pattison describe, was "repetitive": "Repeated face-to-face contacts and loss of reputation are strong deterrents to cheating and actually provide an incentive to respect agreements."[67] Regulatory cooperation was accomplished through "soft law": "Setting standards through non-binding agreements reached by national authorities, implemented largely through peer-group pressure within national jurisdictions, possibly after adjustments to the local law, and with the support of market forces, has become the norm for most of the standards."[68] The wider network, beyond the BIS, is attracted to the service provision of the BIS (as secretariat

[65] Geographical expansion on the part of the BIS included an increase in shareholding central banks (from 32 in the early 1990s to 55 by 2005) and the opening of representative offices in Latin America and Asia. Borio and Toniolo, "One Hundred and Thirty Years of Central Bank Cooperation," 24.

[66] On the evolution of the BIS and the central banking network, ibid.; Michele Fratianni and John Pattison, "The Bank for International Settlements: An Assessment of Its Role in International Monetary and Financial Policy," *Open Economies Review* 12 (2001), 197–222.

[67] Fratianni and Pattison, "The Bank for International Settlements," 213.

[68] Borio and Toniolo, "One Hundred and Thirty Years of Central Bank Cooperation," 22–23.

and research unit) and its reputation for useful and constantly updated expertise. The networked form and vague criteria for membership permitted the BIS to incorporate new participants without diluting the leadership of its decision-making core. At the same time, international authority did reside in key parts of the network. The BCBS became "a rule-making body, whose standards and recommendations are recognized and implemented in legislation on a global scale."[69]

Despite their network characteristics, the BIS and central bank cooperation also contain elements of hierarchy. The initiation and implementation of the Basel Capital Accord of 1988, an unusual instance of regulatory harmonization enacted through the BCBS, provides evidence for both networked and hierarchical governance. The impetus for an agreement on capital adequacy for internationally active banks in the G-10 countries and Luxembourg came originally from the U.S. Congress, intent on protecting the U.S. financial system from undercapitalized banks in the wake of the Latin American debt crisis. With political pressure to increase capital requirements on American banks, the competitiveness concerns of those banks induced the Federal Reserve to propose an international accord that would level the playing field with other international banks. In the face of resistance from other central banks and their banking sectors to the Federal Reserve's initiative, the Federal Reserve forged a bilateral agreement with the Bank of England—linking the two dominant financial centers in the world economy—and eventually won approval in Basel for a version of the U.S.-U.K. definition of bank capital.

Two interpretations of this outcome are possible. Beth Simmons claims that market-based incentives to emulate the United States and the United Kingdom moved the eventual bargain forward and also induced countries outside the G-10 to adopt the capital adequacy standards in some form. Reluctance to be seen by financial markets as under-regulated coupled with network influence in the form of dissemination of the new standards and technical assistance to developing-country regulators produced eventual harmonization on the standards preferred by the top financial powers.[70] Ethan Kapstein presents a different picture that includes less networked emulation and more hierarchy: the U.S.-U.K. proposal was accompanied by an implicit threat that international banks failing to meet the new standards would be denied banking applications to operate in the world's largest financial markets. Within the G-10, this "emulation

---

[69] De Swaan, cited in Fratianni and Pattison, "The Bank for International Settlements," 206.

[70] Simmons, Dobbin, and Garrett, eds., *The Global Diffusion of Markets and Democracy.*

or else" strategy was not purely hierarchical: the Federal Reserve and the Bank of England accepted changes that would ensure adequate implementation of the agreed standards.[71] If the shadow of hierarchy was this apparent within the major industrialized countries, however, one may well ask whether the extension of the capital adequacy standards to banking systems outside the G-10 was not also owed to hierarchical regulatory governance as well as the threat of market sanctions. In this view, the extension of capital adequacy standards more closely resembled the anti-money laundering case described above.[72]

Both the more hierarchical and the less hierarchical explanations for harmonization of capital adequacy standards fit with considerable influence—if not outright capture—by large financial institutions in the United States and the United Kingdom. Their competitive interests were served by this break with the past model of financial collaboration, introducing both more hierarchy and more supranationalism (in the form of agreed international standards) into what had been governance by network.

Despite these changes, the BIS governance structure, particularly among the industrialized countries, continues to approximate a networked form of global governance. This network provides support for the conjectures above. First, banking supervision and capital adequacy requirements produce relatively small distributional consequences. Central banks and related monetary authorities have similar preferences for coordinating monetary policies and pursuing financial stability. As Eric Helleiner describes, these are "tight transnational networks of officials who share similar world views."[73] Private banks, the objects of supervision and capital requirements, are concerned less with the level of capital they must maintain and more with leveling the playing field on which they must compete. Although each state (and its associated banking interests) might prefer looser regulations for itself to gain a competitive advantage, the G-10 countries at the heart of the BIS system all have large domestic financial markets and appropriate concerns over stability. Together, these states also recognize the potentially disastrous consequences of a race to the bottom in banking regulation. Private markets in many cases reinforce the upward regulatory pressure: major banks wish to be seen as regulated

---

[71] Ethan B. Kapstein, *Supervising International Banks: Origins and Implications of the Basel Accord*. Essays in International Finance, No. 185. Department of Economics, Princeton University. December 1991, p. 21, Ethan B. Kapstein, *Governing the Global Economy: International Finance and the State* (Cambridge, MA: Harvard University Press, 1994), 103–128.

[72] Helleiner, "The Politics of Global Financial Regulation," makes this comparison.

[73] Ibid., 188.

by market participants. More a problem of coordination than collaboration, the actors within the network primarily need to establish a focal point on bank capitalization, a mechanism for periodic monitoring of national practice, and a network that is sufficient for these purposes.

Second, given the relative autonomy already granted to central banks and other monetary authorities by national governments, a network of like-minded financial actors could be created to exclude other, larger groups (e.g., debtors who favor a higher rate of inflation, financial services institutions that would like to expand into private banking) that suffer from collective-action problems and are already prevented by domestic institutions from being veto players in the issue area. Within the restricted group of financial authorities, frequent and collegial interactions could arise that bolster cooperation. Indeed, although central bank cooperation has received attention as a networked governance structure,[74] it may well approximate a "best case" for the emergence of this particular form not because of any inherent agreement on monetary and financial policies but because opposing interests are either unable to organize effectively or are excluded institutionally from exercising power and influence in this area.[75] The regulatory network centered on the BIS is clearly composed of a narrow set of actors—central banks and other monetary authorities—that might represent capture of regulatory policy at the expense of other groups in their societies. Distributional conflict is not so intense within those societies, however, so as to motivate pressure by competing groups outside the financial sector for a different mode of international governance. If coordination of international financial regulation represents capture, it is relatively uncontested.

Given the relative autonomy of central bankers in the G-10 and their existing statutory power to set capital adequacy requirements for banks in their jurisdictions, financial and monetary authorities within the network do not need to import policy credibility by shifting national authority to a supranational or hierarchical governance structure. Since their hands were already untied to create monetary and financial credibility at the domestic level (and to tie the hands of domestic politicians who might otherwise undermine confidence in the financial system), no higher authority was necessary, and networked governance was reinforced at the international level.

---

[74] Slaughter, A New World Order.

[75] See Joanne Gowa, "Public Goods and Political Institutions: Trade and Monetary Policy Processes in the United States," in G. John Ikenberry, David A. Lake, and Michael Mastanduno, The State and American Foreign Economic Policy (Ithaca, NY: Cornell University Press, 1988).

CONCLUSION

Attention in the media to successive "crises" in global IGOs—the United Nations, the WTO, and the IMF—may suggest that the fate of global governance hinges on their success. Supranationalism is not the only form of global governance, however, even within a single issue-area like international financial regulation. Throughout the global economy, supranationalism plays a less central role than many believe or expect. In the governance of international finance, including financial regulation, supranationalism did not play a central role after 1945: national governance retained its dominance until the opening of financial markets after the 1970s. Even today, it is principally the international coordination of national policies that occurs at the global level. Hierarchies and networks are often effective alternatives to supranationalism in this case and, we suspect, others. Any explanation of supranationalism, therefore, must also explain why not hierarchy or networks (or hybrid forms).

Our perspective on regulatory governance both reinforces the findings of Abbott and Snidal in their contribution to this volume, and suggests additional lines of research. As they note, the role of governments in regulatory standard-setting may be greater than suggested by the limited competency of national governments and the apparently shrinking role of intergovernmental organizations. Our addition of the modalities of networks and hierarchies suggests that the influence of governments may remain even greater than Abbott and Snidal estimate. At the same time, considering the modes of governance among the actors discussed by Abbott and Snidal, which we have not undertaken here, may suggest additional reasons for conflict in setting new regulatory standards. For example, negotiations between corporate and public hierarchies on the one hand, and networked NGO coalitions on the other, may create obstacles to bargaining and stable agreements in addition to the barriers outlined by Abbott and Snidal.

Do any one of these forms—supranationalism, hierarchy, or networks—guarantee international governance that is more representative of a global public interest and less likely to be captured by narrow economic interests? As we have argued, networked governance, despite its many benefits and its recent fashionable status, is the likeliest to incorporate capture by narrower economic interests. Its very strengths, such as informality, fluid membership, and flexibility, can easily be transformed into barriers to wider participation, legal accountability, and public scrutiny. Of course, supranationalism and hierarchy are not absolute barriers to capture, either. Captured national regulatory bureaucracies can transpose their pattern of regulation to a supranational venue: witness the European Union's Common Agricultural Policy. The national policy preferences of a dominant power may also represent domestic regulatory capture, although the narrower the interests represented, the less likely that followers will accept the leader's interpretation of global interests. Finally, contention, scrutiny, and accountability are most likely to move global governance toward representation of a broader set of interests, breaking the hold that old patterns of interest may wield, even at the global level. Instilling each of these institutional alternatives with such avenues toward openness can move them toward a representation of the global public interest.

Contributors

Kenneth W. Abbott is Professor of Law and Global Studies and Willard H. Pedrick Distinguished Research Scholar at Arizona State University.

Samuel Barrows is a doctoral student in the Department of Government at Harvard University.

Judith L. Goldstein is Professor of Political Science and the Janet M. Peck Professor of International Communication at Stanford University.

Eric Helleiner is CIGI Chair in International Governance and Professor at the University of Waterloo.

Miles Kahler is Rohr Professor of Pacific International Relations at the University of California, San Diego.

David A. Lake is Professor of Political Science at the University of California, San Diego.

Walter Mattli is Professor of International Political Economy and a Fellow of St. John's College at Oxford University.

Kathryn Sikkink is Distinguished McKnight University Professor at the University of Minnesota.

Duncan Snidal is Associate Professor of Political Science at the University of Chicago.

Richard H. Steinberg is Professor of Law at UCLA and Senior Scholar at Stanford University.

David Vogel is Solomon P. Lee Distinguished Professorship in Business Ethics at the University of California, Berkeley.

Ngaire Woods is Director of the Global Economic Governance Programme and Professor of International Political Economy at Oxford University.

Index

Page numbers in italics refer to figures in the text